ROBERT CONQUEST

Stalin BREAKER OF NATIONS

WEIDENFELD · LONDON

First published in Weidenfeld paperback in 1993
by Weidenfeld & Nicolson,
a division of the Orion Publishing Group,
Orion House, 5 Upper St Martin's Lane,
London WC2H 9EA

A catalogue record for this book is
available from the British Library.

ISBN 0 297 81388 9

Printed in Great Britain by
Butler & Tanner Ltd,
Frome and London

Contents

Illustrations

Svetlana Stalin with Lavrenty Beria (Topham)
Nadezhda Alliluyeva, 1932 (Topham)
Nadezhda Alliluyeva's grave (Topham)
Lenin's Politburo, 1917 (Weidenfeld & Nicolson Archives)
Stalin with Poskrebyshev (Weidenfeld & Nicolson Archives)
Stalin with Yezhov, Molotov and Voroshilov at the opening of the
    White Sea–Baltic canal (Weidenfeld & Nicolson Archives)
Stalin and Ribbentrop at the signing of the Nazi–Soviet Pact
    (Weidenfeld & Nicolson Archives)
Stalin's mother in old age (Weidenfeld & Nicolson Archives)
Vasily and Svetlana in wartime (Topham)
Stalin's son Yakov as a German prisoner of war (Hulton Deutsch
    Collection)
Stalin kissing the sword of Stalingrad (Weidenfeld & Nicolson
    Archives)
Roosevelt, Churchill and Stalin, Teheran, 1943 (Central Press Photos)
Celebrating Stalin's seventieth birthday (David King Collection)
Stalin lies next to Lenin in the Red Square mausoleum (Weidenfeld &
    Nicolson Archives)

REPORTER: Does the date 21 December mean anything to you?

WOMAN: No.

REPORTER: On this day was born I. V. Stalin.

WOMAN: Better if he hadn't been born.

(Moscow street interview on Radio Rossiya,
2 pm, 21 December 1990)

For Ronald and Charmian Hartley

Prefatory Note

For this portrait of a man who perhaps more than any other determined the course of the twentieth century, I have relied on the insights of many writers (which I discuss in the Chapter Notes at the end of this book), but in particular on the great flow of new information and comment from the Soviet Union itself, which has helped decisively in flushing out the image of the strange being with whom we deal.

Acknowledgements are due to the John Olin Program for the Study of the Soviet Union at the Hoover Institution, Stanford University; to the editorial boards and editors of *Neva, Novy Mir, Druzhba Narodov, Knizhnoye Obozrenie, Voprosi Istorii, Rodina* and *Izvestiya* for fruitful discussion; to my editor Allegra Huston for much improvement in structure, style and accuracy; to Christine Pevitt; to Dr Mikhail Bernstam; to Delano DuGarm and Semion Lyandres for invaluable research assistance; to Amy Desai, for her admirable secretarial support, as also to Farah Desai; and, as ever, to my wife.

Some of the material in this book first appeared in *Izvestiya* and *National Review*.

Robert Conquest
Stanford 1991

Introduction

'Stalin died yesterday' was the title of a recent Soviet article.[1] Another tells us that 'Stalin's ghost still stalks the land'.[2]

Few men in history have had such long and devastating effects – and not only on their own countries but on the world as a whole. For two generations Stalin's heritage has lain heavy on the chests of a dozen nations, and the threat of it has loomed over all the others, in the fearful possibility of nuclear war. Stalin, to whom the aura of death clings so strongly, is himself only now ceasing to live on in the system he created. When he died in 1953 he left a monster whose own death throes are not yet over, more than a generation later.

The continued weight of Stalin and Stalinism on the life of the countries of the Soviet bloc was not so apparent even a few years ago, and some Western writers treated him and it as no longer significant. But it has since become clear that this was an error. As soon as glasnost liberated the Soviet intellect the issue of Stalinism, and of Stalin himself, became one of the most urgent and vital issues on the public agenda. In this context the present writer can claim a certain status in Stalinology, if only because his books on the period have lately been published, with warm acclaim, in the Soviet Union. Meanwhile Soviet writers have begun to come to grips with, to exorcise Stalin. A good deal of fresh material about him, not available to previous biographers, has been published in the USSR, which strongly contributes to a fuller portrait.

[1] *Rabochi klass i Sovremennyi Mir*, no. 1, 1988.
[2] *Moscow News*, 14 July 1988.

2

There could hardly be a better description of Soviet history than Joseph Conrad's remark, 'Hopes grotesquely betrayed, ideals caricatured – that is the definition of revolutionary success.' Stalin is to be seen today in the light of the political, intellectual, moral, social and ecological collapse of the system he created.

We are bound in any case to view him outlined against a background of turbulent public events. One of the adulatory Soviet biographies of the 1930s says that writing about Stalin 'means describing all the peripeteias of the party's struggle'. But the purpose of the present book is not to record every event in Stalin's life, let alone in the politics of the party. I have tried to give, not an exhaustive chronicle, nor yet anything like a formal psychological analysis, but rather a portrait. Of course, it is, or includes, a political and historical portrait. Still, I have not tried to record, indeed have often deleted, the intricate details of his political struggles, or of his conduct of the war. I have sought, rather, to thread around the unavoidable central column of this history the details which seem most to illuminate Stalin's nature. I have often developed these not for their 'significance' in any profound sense, but as adding, in however minor fashion, some illumination to the whole. What strikes the present writer as a piece of highly illustrative behaviour on Stalin's part is often recorded in none, or sometimes just one, of the various available biographies. Yet, as Plutarch wrote, 'The evidence of vice and virtue is not confined to famous accomplishments. Often some trivial event, a word, a joke, will serve better than great campaigns as a revelation of character.'

This book originally looked as if it would run to the six or seven hundred pages customary in modern biographies and similar works. On reflection, a large effort has gone into removing material which added to its length more than to its weight. The details are of interest to those of us who have had to study the special circumstances. But in a general work like this biography, it seems sensible to rely on Gibbon's procedure with the 'tedious' and 'diffuse' documentation of the aftermath of the Synod of Ephesus: 'The most patient reader will thank me for compressing so much nonsense and falsehood into a few lines.' Yet if exhaustive presentation of these politically intricate manœuvres would overload the story, we cannot avoid consideration of Stalin's whole system of beliefs – that is, Marxism in its Leninist version, together with amendments added by Stalin himself. There is no doubt that these doctrinal convictions remained the justification, and self-justification, of his whole career, and that the definition and extirpation of heresy, or the attribution of heresy to enemies or rivals, was a major element in his life.

3

We see a vast, dark figure, looming over the century, and we know much of the devious and brutal manœuvres by which he achieved and maintained despotic power. But above all, perhaps no other system has ever been so completely based on falsehood and delusion. This falsification also extended, and massively so, to Stalin's own career. When it comes to feelings and motives Stalin, who throughout his life played his cards very close to his chest, is not so easy to grasp. One of his outstanding characteristics was an ability to give the impression of calm and even benignity, while in fact harbouring plans of massive vengefulness. But, even at the level of ordinary observation, this calm was often interrupted by demonic flashes of rage or hate or suspicion. He resembled one of those large black clouds which are sometimes seen, vaguely ominous, but at first sight floating quietly across the sky: then, as the cloud gets closer, you notice the flickers which are signs of lightning deep inside it, the hidden churning of its central material.

He himself did his best to retreat into a sort of impersonality, most often referring to himself simply as 'Comrade Stalin'. Perhaps we cannot penetrate – certainly we cannot fully penetrate – the glooms of his nature. But we can develop new detail, new chiaroscuro, the highlights of his public persona, the accumulation of long unpublishable anecdotes, the reminiscences and private letters of friends, and enemies.

As with the life of anyone, we are thus bound to be working inward from externals, and in Stalin's case more than most. Much of this external evidence available in the 1930s was consciously or unconsciously (mostly consciously) designed to deceive. Not only in Russia: for a number of Western progressives the vast territory of the Soviet Union had ceased to lie in the sphere of geographical reality. Like the interior of Africa two centuries ago it was an area of legend, populated by mythical beasts – socialism, revolution, five-year-plan ... Stalin's career, and his character, were falsified in that context. Still, there were leaks, there were cracks in the carapace. And even the deceptions often betrayed a pattern of realities below the surface, behind the inadequately impenetrable screen. Not merely did he inflict death on a titanic scale; he also showed something in his character best thought of as an absence of life in its fullest sense. But his most striking attribute remains his ability to deceive others, often experienced politicians or intellectuals, about his own motives and aims. Beyond that there was massive deception about not only his own nature but the mere realities of the society he had constructed.

4

In his life of Somerset Maugham Ted Morgan writes, 'The biographer becomes attached to his subject in a way that cannot be duplicated in other relationships.' It is probably impossible to have that sort of sympathetic relationship when Stalin is the subject.

He combined patience with outbursts of capricious rage. He combined a certain heavy ordinariness with the ability to force through quite extraordinary social and political changes. And his inner drives, or demons, never rested.

His latest Soviet biographer calls his character contradictory and complex. It was certainly contradictory, in the sense that it combined what would ordinarily be regarded as very disparate elements into a single strange conglomerate. But I don't know that it was particularly complex.

Trotsky said that Stalin was a mediocrity but not a nonentity. Another of Stalin's rivals, Lev Kamenev, spoke of him as 'just a small-town politician'. Yet another, Nikolai Bukharin, took 'laziness' to be one of his major characteristics. In the sense that he neglected the issues Bukharin thought of as important, this is true. But, in Stalin's own words, he never neglected 'the little things' – in particular everything connected with personnel, seen as the human material of the power struggle. Bukharin also called him 'a small-minded, malicious man', and Lenin saw that he was often driven by 'spite', which (Lenin said) plays the worst role in politics. But these pettinesses and meannesses were served by a massive strength of character, an unappeasable drive for power – to the degree that Hitler could comment in the summer of 1942, while engaged in a ruthless war against Stalin, that 'he is a beast, but he's a beast on the grand scale', and 'Stalin, too, must command our unconditional respect. In his own way, he is a hell of a fellow!'

The nineteenth-century Russian liberal writer Herzen said that what he most feared for the future was 'Genghis Khan with the telegraph'. Stalin has often been typified, in the USSR itself as well as elsewhere, as an Oriental despot. In some ways, clearly, the description is apt. But Stalin appears at a cruder level than many Oriental despots of the past, some of whom, like Babur or Kublai, were outstanding characters by any standards, not merely ordinary men with a hypertrophied will.

Moreover, Stalin was a rootless, or uprooted man, to whom his origins meant little, who was neither an intellectual nor a worker, whose record did not satisfy his wishes and had to be heavily rewritten. For he was also afflicted with a marked insecurity. It is perhaps in this context that we should look at the way he tried, not only for effect but clearly as a real desire, to become among his intimates something like a backslapping man of the people, at home in an atmosphere of coarse jollity. Yet he was also always highly sensitive to affronts to his dignity, and concerned to project the image of one far above ordinary humanity. The two attitudes conflict; but both carry a feeling of uncertainty, even unreality.

Overall Stalin thus gives the impression of a large and crude clay-like figure, a golem, into which a demonic spark has been instilled. It is in this sense that we might broadly sum him up, in Churchill's phrase, as 'an unnatural man'.

How unnatural, or natural, will appear in these pages.

Chapter 1

Gori

W hen Stalin was long established in Moscow as the ruler of a vast, largely Russian empire, his young son told his even younger daughter, 'You know, Papa used to be a Georgian once.' The comment is true. Stalin was indeed a Georgian, but one who had to a large degree broken his links with his homeland. He himself once referred to the country in a speech as 'a little piece of Soviet territory called Georgia'.

Stalin's native tongue was Georgian and we are told that he spoke it with exceptional purity. He only started learning Russian when he was eight or nine years old, and he never lost his strong Georgian accent. According to some accounts, he occasionally mumbled the case endings, unsure if he had them right – a feeling with which many foreign speakers of Russian might sympathize. As late as 1939, in his speech to the Eighteenth Party Congress, he mispronounced the name of the People's Commissariat of Agriculture, as 'Narkomzyom' instead of 'Narkomzem' (with the result that speakers who followed all used Stalin's form, Molotov explaining much later that otherwise Stalin would have taken offence). And, in public at least, he almost always spoke Russian slowly, in measured and carefully developed phrasing.

He was to assimilate himself in the first place to the internationalist ideas and organization of the largely Russian Bolshevik revolutionaries, and only later, or as part of a gradual and doubtfully conscious process, to Russian supremacy as such.

His temperament was, by all usual standards, very unGeorgian. His Bolshevik colleague Ordzhonikidze later said of him that though he was a Georgian he could not take a joke. Georgians are always described as cheerful, nimble, hospitable, generous, loyal, chivalrous, pleasure-loving, lazy, independent, prodigal, changeable – all adjectives taken

1

from various travellers' descriptions over recent centuries. They are typically seen as drinking their light wines hour after hour, without the brutish drunkenness of the north; dancing, making witty and magniloquent speeches. Stalin is certainly hard to fit into such a stereotype – though their other characteristic, common in any mountain people, of readiness for revenge, is closer to the mark.

But Georgia is a land of fair size (about the area of Scotland without the islands) and temperaments can vary widely among the different communities of such a country. The people of Upper Kartli, Stalin's region, have a reputation for dourness among their easier-going neighbours.

Stalin was to find his native Georgia a hostile and troublesome area. His daughter saw him as 'completely Russified'. His younger children were brought up ignorant of Georgian, but taught first German and later English. His second wife, Russian but with a Caucasian background, would 'once in a long, long while' dance a Georgian *lezghinka*, the only attention to anything Georgian his daughter ever noted in their household.

We are told that he was always irritated by Georgians. On one Soviet view he resented the Georgians because 'they saw themselves as a European island in an Asiatic sea'. In fact, Georgia was a country without an unsocial Russian-style peasant *narod* which would reverence a distant despot. Its people were not separated from its intellectuals like different castes.

He told his daughter later in life that he had largely forgotten Georgian. But in fact he continued to relish using it with Georgian colleagues and thus excluding others from the conversation at will; and one account tells us that towards the end it was his Russian which started to deteriorate.

But however we look at it, the fact that he was in a sense neither fully Georgian nor fully Russian must be of great significance to his character as it finally developed.

2

Iosif Vissarionovich Dzhugashvili, later to be called Stalin, was born on 21 December 1879 (9 December Old Style) in Gori, Georgia, the third but only surviving son of a Georgian couple, Vissarion and Yekaterina Dzhugashvili.

This simple sentence has been queried on five different counts!

Most are, indeed, trivial. His mother once gave his birthdate as January 1880, perhaps confusing it with the date of his baptism, one tsarist police document has 1881, and on one occasion he is himself reported as giving a different date. His mother, again, once said that there were *three* previous sons who had died in infancy. Then, tsarist police records gave his birthplace as not Gori but nearby Didi Lilo, his father's home village. An American visitor in Didi Lilo in 1932 was told by the inhabitants that this was where Stalin was born; she was even showed the alleged site. There is no real reason to give these points any credit.

One of the other two queries is of some significance, the other possibly of greater.

It was common for Georgians anxious for the reputation of their country to maintain that Vissarion's grandfather was not a Georgian at all, but an Ossetian immigrant who changed his name from Dzhugaev. There is nothing inherently improbable about this. The present South Ossetian Autonomous Soviet Socialist Republic is only twenty miles or so from Gori. There was a normal and continuous drift of individuals, assimilated in a generation or so.

Georgians in any case found the idea of an Ossetian Stalin convincing. Ossetians had a reputation in tsarist times for providing the toughest police cadres. And Stalin's temperament seemed too dour for a Georgian. At any rate, the story is widespread. Stalin was referred to as an Ossetian in the satirical poem which led to the downfall, and later the death in labour camp, of the great Russian poet Osip Mandelstam. Stalin's rival, Zinoviev, also used to refer to him as a 'bloodthirsty Ossetian'. Still, though Vissarion may well have been of Ossetian origin, he was now completely Georgian. Stalin was in any case of a physical type not too rare in the area. I have seen boys in and around Gori who looked un-cannily like Stalin as he appears in his school photograph at the age of ten.

The final query about the details of Stalin's birth is more striking. Was Vissarion really his father?

As is common among the humbly born who eventually rise to fame, there are various legends of Stalin's real father being a prince or a count. This is not impossible. Georgia probably had the world's highest concentration of princes per square mile in the world. A listing of 1851 gives 47 Georgian princely families (and only about 200 other families of gentry). But there is no reason to believe the story, and no evidence for it whatever.

The most picturesque rumour (lately mentioned in several Moscow papers) is that Stalin's real father was the celebrated traveller General Nikolai Przhevalsky, after whom the last true wild horse – the Przhevalsky horse – is named. Przhevalsky was one of the great scientific explorers of the nineteenth century, with his long and impeccably recorded voyages through Mongolia, Tibet, Turkestan and the inner Far East. He was back in Russia in 1877–9, and perhaps available in Gori. There is a resemblance between his pictures and those of Stalin, even apart from similar moustaches; and perhaps that is the basis of the legend.

We now come to the least romantic, but most plausible, of these possible fathers.

Yekaterina, or Keke, eked out her husband's erratic income by working as a domestic servant in richer households. One of them was that of Egnatashvili, merchant of the second guild (that is, prosperous by small-town standards). Egnatashvili reportedly had relations with the handsome young servant girl – which is not in any way implausible or even rare: after all Karl Marx, still alive at the time, had a child by the family maid.

The point of this story, such as it is, is twofold. First, that Egnatashvili is said to have paid the necessary money towards Stalin's education. It is true that Stalin gained a 'stipend', and that his mother is said to have saved from her meagre income to help. But it is also true that very few boys as poor as he was could go to his schools.

Stalin was said to have known the story, but still to have believed he was really Dzhugashvili's son. But there is some reason to believe that, taunted with her conduct by others, he became cynical about his mother. There are a number of stories of his referring to her in very coarse terms in later life. This is one of those matters in which the truth is no longer available and the evidence is in itself uncompelling. A leading Soviet researcher tells me that the clinching fact, in his view, is that Stalin did not attend his mother's funeral – which, he says, is quite unheard of in a Georgian family.

But even if Egnatashvili thought he was or might be the father, this does not prove that he really was. As we have noted, Stalin always believed that Vissarion, whom he is said to have closely resembled, was indeed his true father.

Stalin's career was to be subject to an unprecedented amount of retrospective falsification. This is not so true of his earlier years, but, as we see, there is already much that is obscure or dubious.

4

3

Vissarion Dzhugashvili and Yekaterina Geladze had been married in 1874; they were both born serfs, though Emancipation came (later than in Russia proper) while they were still children. Vissarion had worked as a peasant before coming to Gori to set up as a cobbler. Stalin's class is given as 'peasant' in early tsarist police records, no doubt a reference to his father's original status. In later police files Stalin's status is either left blank or given as 'clerk'. When he was in control, his biographical entry in the *Large Soviet Encyclopedia* spoke of Vissarion as an 'artisan-cobbler, later worker in a shoe factory': in the post-Stalin edition he is deproletarianized to merely 'artisan-cobbler'. And in Stalin's own registration form as delegate to the Party Congress in 1922, he did not answer the question about his social category.

Just as, in adulthood, Stalin had no clearly established national consciousness, so his class background was uncertain and indeterminate. Similarly again (to anticipate further) he was to be educated to a level which left him, as was rare among the Bolsheviks, neither a worker nor an intellectual, a member neither of the masses nor of the intelligentsia. Thus he was, or became, up to a point, a man of no nation, no class and no status – except what he created for himself.

4

Stalin was undoubtedly born a Georgian and as a child was a complete Georgian by any usual standard. His parents spoke no other language, and as we have said he himself knew no Russian until he started to learn it at school at the age of eight or nine.

When Stalin was born Georgia had only been under Russian rule for two to three generations. We see the maps, and the political fact of the incorporation of Georgia into Moscow's empire. But the Georgian and Russian nations arose far apart, from totally different ethnic stocks, and with not even any serious political contact until two or three centuries ago. Ethnic Georgia even now has no common border with ethnic Russia, or Slavdom.

Georgian is not even an Indo-European language. Like some other languages of the Caucasus, it represents an older stock which was not submerged by the dominant Turkic and Indo-European, which overcame almost all opposition over a great part of Eurasia from Cadiz to Calcutta, from Killarney to Kashgar. With neither of these does it have any connection whatever.

Georgian is often linked to Basque. The resemblances are very slight, but this connection is doubtless true in the sense that, though too long apart and too far apart for identifiable surviving traces, they both represent an earlier stratum of speech – which also included the mysterious Pictish, known only from a few incomprehensible inscriptions.

Perhaps the simpler languages to some extent spread more easily for their very simplicity. At least, so one may feel when faced with the accumulation of Georgian consonants. 'Khrdsna' (to corrupt) or 'me vbrdsgomav' (I shine) are extreme examples. But quite ordinary Georgian personal or place names are full of 'Mtskh' and 'Tskhr': not untypical is the name of the organ of the Georgian Social Democrats in exile in the 1920s – *Brdzolis Khma*.

Nor is the grammatical structure easily mastered, as when one is told that 'according to the tense involved, the grammatical subject of a transitive verb may be in the nominative, the dative-accusative or the ergative case, while the object will be in the dative-accusative or the nominative'.

And all this is written in the (to us) alien Georgian alphabet, all loops and curlicues.

The connection between Georgia and Russia is nevertheless stronger than such considerations might make it appear. Both are seats of Orthodox Christianity. Georgia, indeed, received Christianity soon after its triumph in the Roman Empire, more than six hundred years before the conversion of Russia. The Georgian Church had its own Patriarch until 1811 (and has again in modern times). Even today, or again today, one may see priests leading pilgrimages beside the highways and walking respected through the cities.

Still, the link with Russia was not so much religious fellow-feeling as a more negative motive. Georgia throughout its existence had been the subject of devastating invasions and occupations by powerful neighbours to the south. By the time Russia began to appear over the northern horizon in the role of a possible ally, in the seventeenth century, Georgia's enemies were Turkey and Persia, both seeking the imposition of Muslim imperial rule. (Even today I have heard Georgians in Tbilisi demanding total independence, but at the same time insisting on Russian protection from the 'Musulmans'.)

Georgia more than once appealed for Russian support. At a moment of desperation in 1783, King Irakli put eastern Georgia under Russian suzerainty, and in 1801, the Russians annexed his kingdom. The rest of Georgia was reduced over the following decades.

The Russian Empire was up to a point successfully assimilative. Even before the annexation a prince of the Georgian ruling house, Prince Peter Bagration, had entered the Russian service, and become one of Alexander I's most successful generals before being killed at Borodino. (One of Stalin's major offensives in World War II was called Operation Bagration, perhaps nostalgically.)

The Georgian nobility were recognized with higher titles than their true level required. When it came to Georgia as a whole, the Russians were less successful. Russification failed, and the great majority of Georgians continued to speak only their own language. Even the religious link turned sour, not only with the suppression of the Georgian Patriarchate, but more particularly later in the century with a Russianization of the whole Georgian church system – including the schools – in both language and personnel.

In the nineteenth century, in Georgia as elsewhere, national feeling entered its modern phase. As in other national movements – though this was to be more common in the twentieth century – a socialist and moderate Marxist trend entered, and later dominated, Georgian politics.

5

Not only in its climate, but in the ways of humanity, Georgia has much of the feel of a Mediterranean country. One example relative to our theme, at least around the end of the last century, is the figure of the *kinto* – the sly, sharp and self-confident petty crook, comparable to the *lazzarone* of Naples, and (again as in southern Italy) incorporating the old tradition of mountain bandits. Georgian comrades were often to refer to Stalin as a *kinto*.

As a recent Soviet article notes, the rules and customs of a provincial town in Georgia were then full of 'remnants of the past, of the Middle Ages', and even by Marxist standards the population suffered 'less from capitalism than from the lack of it'. Gori in 1879 was a small town in a semi-Asiatic corner of a vast semi-European empire. Though thoroughly Georgian, the town had a foreign element – Armenians, Russians, Ossetians. The language barrier may appear insurmountable to those brought up within a monoglot culture where alien tongues are almost never heard. Nowadays, with recent immigration in many British,

French, German or American cities, some sort of mutual understanding may be beginning. In the smaller countries of Eastern and Central Europe, where it is a matter less of immigrants than, as it were, of overlap, this multilingualism was long-established in the towns, at least among those in contact with a general public. In Bratislava/Pozsony/Pressburg, or in Kolozsvar/Klausenburg/Cluj, every waiter could manage three languages. Gori was not as cosmopolitan. All the same, it was not, linguistically, the equivalent of Helena or Hereford.

We do not know if Stalin developed in Gori any of the racial prejudices he showed in later life. Anti-Semitism does not seem to have arisen: but one of the leading NKVD figures of the Beria period had changed his name from Mamulian to Mamulov and said privately that he had done so because Stalin 'did not like Armenian names'. It is true that Stalin had Armenian associates like Mikoyan; but then he had Jewish associates like Kaganovich and Mekhlis, while promoting anti-Semitism. So perhaps there is something in it.

6

It was in this small and pullulating semi-Oriental town that Stalin was born, in what was then 10 Sobornaya (Cathedral) Street.

It lost that name in the 1920s. Later the whole street, and several acres around it, were torn down. Instead there is now a park, with the Stalin birthplace at its focus. The house is protected by a high marble structure built over it on Beria's instructions. It is part red brick and part wood, fronted by a veranda with a wooden paling and carved pillars. These do not appear in a photograph taken about 1930, but whether they represent the original state of the house or are an invention of Beria's restorers is unknown.

Dzhugashvili and his wife shared it with his employer or partner. Their own section was a room upstairs, plus a well-lit basement room below. The amount of space in the main room, at a rough check, is about fifteen feet square: more than many families have in Moscow today. A Russian middle-peasant house of the period in the 'wooden museum' outside Suzdal is considerably larger (though built for a family of five or six, and containing the large Russian stove).

A contemporary says that in winter the walls were damp. There was no drainage except for a ditch along the street. Nor is it possible any longer to get the feel of the neighbourhood. In the photograph taken before the restoration it looks ramshackle: but that was nearly fifty years after Stalin was born and wooden or part-wooden structures can deteriorate quickly.

At any rate, just as American presidents have long been able to claim origins in log-cabins, Stalin's birthplace was a humble one.

A taller, two-storey building is to be seen in the park area behind the birthplace, though directly hidden by trees so that it does not overlook it. This is the Stalin Museum. It has been closed a good deal in recent years: a decade ago for 'repairs', then for short periods to set up material on his daughter Svetlana when she returned to the Soviet Union, and to remove it again when she left for the second time. In 1989 it was closed for 'rearrangement'.

Stalin and his parents only lived in the birthplace from 1879 to 1883. By the time he went to school they were elsewhere. This second home has never been celebrated, but it seems that for ten years it was in the house of a priest, Father Charkviani, which may retrospectively have been thought unsuitable.

There were two Charkvianis at the Gori school which Stalin attended. It has been suggested that one of the family was the father of the N.K. Charkviani who was First Secretary of the Georgian Communist Party from 1938 to 1952. There is no known warrant for this, but it is worth remembering that family links in a small country may indeed be commoner than elsewhere. On another more generally accepted account the two sons of Egnatashvili were the two men of that name who held lesser positions under the Soviet regime, one in the Secretariat of the Supreme Soviet, the other as one of Beria's Lieutenant Generals of State Security.

7

We do not really know for certain a great deal about Stalin's childhood and youth. In part this is due to a shortage of information, in part to the fact that informants often contradict one another, or at least give views which are hard to harmonize. Much of it was remembered forty or fifty or sixty years later, and by people who had reasons, conscious or unconscious, to distort the picture.

But this is no more than a rather extreme case of our usual predicament about the childhood of famous men. Where there are scores or hundreds of witnesses, giving their testimony in circumstances where their political or similar feelings can be discounted, and where there is massive contemporary documentation, this matters little. Or rather, it matters, but it can be sorted out without too much difficulty into a balanced account.

But even with the more exiguous material of a childhood or youth like Stalin's, we are not in too bad a position. Almost the whole of history and biography is based on the interpretation of inadequate testimony; and perfect reconstruction is a dream. In Stalin's case, the main thing seems to be not to accept as facts what are only probabilities and, where accounts are incompatible, to leave them to speak for themselves, or take a view of them and explain why.

The usual account of Stalin's childhood is quite a simple one. His father, a ne'er-do-well cobbler, drank and beat him. His mother defended him and got him an education. He hated the one and loved the other.

This story may be true, or partly true. There is good evidence that his father beat him. But fathers beat their children in peasant and semi-peasant households the world over without necessarily forfeiting their loyalty. It does indeed seem to have been a primitive, violent household. The mother would sometimes hit her drunken husband. On one occasion Stalin is reported to have thrown a knife at his father, and to have had to hide with friends for a day or two.

Stalin himself said in an interview that he had had a happy childhood. But this violence is well attested. Our earliest informant, Iosif Iremashvili, implies that the beatings were particularly cruel: on the other hand, like most of Stalin's schoolmates he came from a less crude social stratum, and may have been extra-sensitive to what would have been regarded as more or less usual in Gori's slums or semi-slums.

Moreover, in Stalin's case (as he later told his daughter), his mother beat him too.

Not that the circumstances were much alike, but as I write I chance upon an article by the dancer Mikhail Baryshnikov where he says of his father, in passing, 'Once in a while, he'd smack me in the face, but this happens in every family.' 'Violent' in any case, does not imply 'violent all the time', or 'merely violent', nor the absence of other more pleasant memories.

Stalin's second wife, Nadezhda Alliluyeva, could not touch alcohol without feeling sick. He used to annoy her by dipping his fingers in wine and letting the babies suck them. This surely dates back to his Georgian days, and was perhaps one of the customs his father shared with others. It was clearly a pleasant memory.

Stalin himself never said anything against his father. Indeed a recent Soviet account holds, contrary to most commentators, that Stalin had warm feelings towards his father, and that he resented his mother's treatment of Vissarion. It speaks of him going out for the day with his father to the village of Ateni, a few miles from Gori, where there were customers for new shoes and a day or two of shoe-repairing, and greatly liking the life, in contrast to the gloom of serious schooling.

One reflection on Stalin's attitude comes up in the early 1930s. It concerns the case of the notorious Pavlik Morozov. Then aged fourteen, he denounced his father to the authorities for 'hoarding' grain. The father was shot, and in revenge the villagers killed young Morozov. He became a leading Pioneer hero. With other young denouncers of their parents, he was inscribed in the Pioneer 'Book of Heroism'. Statues were put up to him, edifying books written about him. The Palace of Culture of Young Pioneers in Moscow was named after him. However, a recent Soviet article describes Stalin's private reaction: 'What a little swine, denouncing his own father', he said, adding that his example must nevertheless be used politically, as a weapon against the recalcitrant peasantry.

Thus Stalin either loved or hated his mother, and either admired or hated his father! If we have to leave the question of his family ties in this unsatisfactory state, it is mainly a psychoanalytical type of approach that will suffer. On the more general question, it is clear that the young Stalin lived, like the majority of the urban population, in poverty and uncertainty, and that this was made more glaring by his association with richer schoolmates.

The characters of Lenin and Stalin were in many ways dissimilar. They both came to hate the established order, they both saw themselves as the destined leaders of Russia, they both accepted the same supposedly infallible doctrine: yet Lenin was brought up in culture and comfort, amid a happy family life.

8

Whatever the effects, or indeed the facts, of his home life, in September 1888 Stalin started to attend the Gori Church School, and we begin to know him as an individual. Always at this time called 'Soso', the

Georgian abbreviation of Joseph, he was a good pupil. But in spite of excellent marks, he took six years to cover the four-year course.

Around the time Stalin and his mother had moved to Father Charkviani's, Vissarion had given up his private business and moved to Tbilisi to a job in the Adelkhanov shoe factory, though he frequently visited his Gori home. At one point he came back and took Stalin, old enough at ten, to work with him, apparently for about a year: Stalin's only experience of manual labour. Stalin later told a parable about an unnamed shoe worker who became proletarianized in this way, but never lost his petty-bourgeois habits of mind, and looked forward to setting up on his own again. The truth seems to be that Vissarion did not think in such categories, and simply wanted to be a cobbler, independent when possible, employed when not.

Egnatashvili was among those who tried to persuade Vissarion to let the boy continue his education. And Stalin's mother eventually managed to get him back to school. Henceforth Vissarion fades away: he is given various death dates (and is credibly reported as being stabbed in a tavern brawl in Tiflis in 1909, though this may be a confusion of names).

Stalin may have lost another year from illness. At some point he had smallpox, which left his face badly pitted for life. He got blood poisoning, perhaps as a result of an accident he had when he was knocked down by a carriage, leaving his left arm permanently shortened and stiffened.

Stalin grew to a height of five feet four inches. In addition to his smallpox-pitted face and his crippled arm, the second and third toes of his left foot were joined (as a police record tells us). The height, at least, seems always to have been a regret. Bukharin later said 'it makes him miserable that he cannot convince everyone, including himself, that he is a taller man than anybody else. That is his misfortune: it may be his most human trait and perhaps his only human trait; his reaction to his "misfortune" is not human – it is almost devilish; he cannot help taking revenge for it on others, but especially on others who are in some way better or more gifted than he is . . .' In the 1930s Stalin got the head of his NKVD guards, K. V. Pauker, to find him 'platform' shoes; and at parades he usually stood on a slightly raised wooden slab.

One striking educational event took place when he had been at school for two years. In 1890, Russian became the language of instruction. This was part of the intensive Russification campaign of the period, for which the Orthodox Church's educational institutions became important instruments. It caused bitter resentment, though more particularly in the secondary schools. Georgian teachers seem to have been replaced by Russians. Soso is reported among the boys who made trouble and incurred some punishment in connection with this change. If so, it did not affect his school career.

A school photograph, with five teachers and twenty-one boys, shows Stalin in the middle of the back row, a good three inches smaller than those around him. He is described as swarthy and yellow-eyed. His eyes seem to have been among his most striking characteristics. The Bolshevik leader Krestinsky was to speak of his 'tigerish eyes', and the writer Sholokhov, too, was to comment, 'He smiles, but his eyes are like a tiger's' – the supreme beast of prey, which yet has the capacity to lie patiently in wait for its victim.

In spite of poverty, he was always well dressed, with good jackets and boots. He is said to have had a good voice and to have sung in the choir. His daughter, years later, mentions that his singing voice was pleasant, unlike the harshness of his speaking.

His friend at school and later, Iremashvili, tells us – and the story is now a familiar one – of a wrestling match between Stalin and himself. When Iremashvili turned away, thinking it was over, Stalin sprang on him and triumphantly threw him to the ground. The two boys then shook hands and embraced. (In adult life too, he would sometimes wrestle with Bukharin, to amuse their families and guests, but he usually lost.)

Stalin is described as physically fit, in spite of his smallness and his awkward arm. His mother later said that, at the age of fifteen, 'he was one of the strongest boys you ever saw'. (Bruce Lockhart, meeting him in 1918, speaks of him as 'strongly built'.) A story of 1934 vintage has him winning a swimming contest against a skilled adult when still a boy at Gori: his daughter, on the other hand, tells us he never learned to swim ... Another tale (also from 1934) is of himself and his group going in 1892 to see the public hanging of some bandits. In its first version Stalin calmly tells his friends that, punished sufficiently here and now, they will not suffer in the afterlife. If the story was concocted to please Stalin, it does not seem to have worked; a later (1940) version has him and his friends forced to attend and being much agitated. There may be some basis for the story, but of course no reliance can be placed on anything written in 1930–40: alleged memories of fifty years previously, touched up by editors for homiletic reasons, do not carry much weight. The one valid implication of the first version is that the young Stalin was noted for his piety.

13

Apart from piety, and love of nature, and so on, the boy's great love was reading. He frequented a Gori bookshop, and read the Georgian classics – and the non-classics too, such as a wild novel in the Walter Scott tradition, Kazbegi's *The Patricide*. The hero, a daring Georgian outlaw called Koba, leads mountaineers against the tsar, is betrayed and kills the betrayer. Koba (Iremashvili tells us) became the boy's 'dream figure and idea'. Later, long before he took the name Stalin, 'Koba' was his chosen underground alias: and many Bolsheviks who knew him well, like Bukharin, called him 'Koba' to the end. (One biographer has suggested that taking the hero of *The Patricide* as his model means Stalin identified with the killer of a father. But it is not Koba who is the patricide in the story.)

Stalin's schoolmate also describes another aspect of the boy's character. He greatly liked climbing cliffs, going into the wild countryside, and to the strange 'cave city' of Uplis Tsikhe, founded in the pre-Christian era and long since sacked and abandoned. His love of nature, as often with small boys, included an addiction to throwing stones at birds.

Georgia's mountains and valleys are quite unlike the steppes and forests of Russia. When Suvorov – the last Generalissimus in Russian history before Stalin himself – led his army into the Alps in his incredible and almost successful attempt to destroy the French revolutionary forces, his Russian troops were almost superstitiously horrified at the monstrous landscapes of mountains and glaciers. So were the first Russian troops in the Caucasus, which is even higher than the Alps: Kazbek is higher than Mont Blanc. On the other hand, Pushkin, Lermontov, Gorki and others loved the wild Caucasian scenery (and Pushkin complains of the 'dull Moldavian steppe').

Stalin's daughter tells us that, though it sometimes depressed him, on the whole he loved the Siberian scenery of his exile – not a perverse taste, but a strange one for a mountaineer. In any case, this did not mean a total rejection of the Georgian landscape. He seldom went back to Georgia after the Revolution, and particularly after a stunning rebuff he received there in 1921. But when he did (especially in later life), he would stay at such secluded spots as the Likani Palace in the mountain spa of Borzhomi, on a gorge of the upper Kura – never going to nearby Gori, or even to Tiflis (though at one point he did set off for Gori, but was so disgusted by the uproarious welcome of villages in between that he turned back).

Among all his mental and physical attributes, Iremashvili noted more centrally that Soso's love of nature was not matched by a love of human beings. He 'was incapable of feeling pity for man or beast. Even as a child he greeted the joys and tribulations of his fellow schoolboys with a sarcastic smile. I never saw him cry.' When he had an aim in view, he was 'unbalanced, unrestrained and passionate'.

Meanwhile, he did well in school, especially in the ecclesiastical subjects and in history, geography, Georgian and handwriting – though less well in Greek and arithmetic. He was also learning Russian, and not as people learn foreign languages in many Western schools, but very effectively. The boys were required, in principle at least, to speak Russian even in ordinary lessons. However reluctantly, Soso became proficient. Napoleon, indeed, spoke very little French till he went to Autun at the age of nine (and for years afterwards sympathized with the Corsican cause, until persuaded that the island people's liberty was mergeable into the more general principles of French republicanism ...). Of course the two men differ in many ways. Yet it is not hard to see that an ambitious man from a small nation may gain an advantage over his circumstances of birth by throwing in his lot with a major power, and a major language.

Stalin left the Gori school at or near the top of his class, in July 1894.

Chapter 2

Seminary

Stalin had won a stipend to the Tiflis Theological Seminary: not enough to support him, though clothes were also provided. But once more either his mother scrimped and saved, as is usually said, or her protector helped, or both, and he remained a student for five years. His mother much wanted him to become a priest (and during his ascendancy, she repeated this in an interview – which pleased him greatly). On one report, this was because she felt that with his physical makeup he would not do well in the other professions open to a child of his background.

We have so far largely dealt – even if in an unavoidably inconclusive way – with what might be called the passive, outward pressures or constraints in the production of Stalin. We can now increasingly watch his character manifesting its own autonomous behaviour.

The Theological Seminary in Tiflis was very much Georgia's leading academic institution. There was no university in the country, and those who could afford it sent their sons to the Russian or German universities. After a course at the Tiflis Seminary, it was sometimes possible to go on to higher things. It attracted, or produced, much of the country's new intelligentsia.

The Seminary, now a Museum of Arts, is a handsome classical building, set between two streets which radiate from the tree-lined Pushkin Square. Inside, the fourteen or fifteen rooms include the old chapel and the dormitories where the boys slept. Conditions were as good, or better, than in English public schools of the time. Indeed Harrow, where Churchill (five years older) was educated at the same period, was in many ways more unpleasant.

The students had long been fractious against authority. In 1885, after the Russian rector Chudetsky made a remark offensive to Georgia, the student Sylvester Dzhibladze had struck him in the face. He was sentenced to three years' imprisonment, and later became a leading Georgian Marxist – though one always hostile to Stalin.

In June 1886 the rector was shot and killed by a recently expelled student, who was executed. The Seminary was closed for a year. After it re-opened, increasing Russification caused further trouble. In 1890 there seems to have been some sort of strike; and in 1893, students demanded teaching in Georgian, a Georgian literature course, and the dismissal of the most objectionable of the staff. This was refused, and they again went on strike. Over eighty were expelled, including 'Lado' Ketskhoveli, who was to be one of Stalin's first mentors, and Mikha Tskhakaya, a future colleague of Lenin's. In fact, Stalin's own period at the Seminary, starting in September 1894, was, comparatively, a quiet one.

Education at the Seminary was thorough. There was a heavy concentration on Liturgy, Scripture, Church Slavonic, Greek, Latin and Russian. Stalin not only never objected to its methods but restored them in the Soviet schools after the disastrous experimentalist period which preceded his coming to power.

It has often been suggested in both friendly and hostile biographies that Stalin was greatly influenced, if not by the beliefs, at least by the forms of ecclesiastical education (just as Christopher Isherwood writes of W. H. Auden that at one point his high Anglicanism had evaporated 'leaving only the height'). Stalin's way of expressing himself throughout his life was very much in the tradition of the catechism. A recent Soviet article notes his use of 'What does correct selection of cadres mean? – Correct selection of cadres means...' as one of his typical turns of phrase, and gives other examples of 'the catechetical form, with endless repetitions with one and the same phrase used as a question and then as an answer, and once again with a negative participle'. This modern Soviet critique speaks of 'the grandeur of an ostentatiously slow shaman, the rhetoric and devices of a semi-educated seminarist, bureaucratic jargon' ... the last adjective at least unattributable to his youthful education.

Another recent Soviet article speaks of his always demonstrating his 'meagreness of expression in a language foreign to him'.

2

It was at about this time that Stalin wrote poetry. As well as his addiction to Koba, he was by now reading much other Georgian literature: the national epic of the twelfth or thirteenth century, Shohta Rustaveli's *The Knight in the Tiger Skin* and more recent works devoted to the ideals of Georgian freedom, like Prince Ilya Chavchavadze's *The Hermit*.

Chavchavadze edited the magazine *Iveriya*. When Stalin was fifteen to sixteen it published six poems of his, or at any rate poems attributed to him by a Soviet paper in 1939. Doubt has been cast on this, as the period was full of creative invention about Stalin's entire life story. The verses were signed 'I. Dzh ... shvili' or (in one instance) 'Soselo', and sceptics have noted that a Georgian poet Ivan Dzhavakishvili was writing at the time and may have used the first 'pseudonym', misleading the eager mythologists nearly fifty years later. But 'Soselo' can hardly be so explained. The 'Soselo' poem is the only one of which some lines later appeared in Russian translation. These run:

> Know that he who fell like ash to the earth
> Who long ago became enslaved
> Will rise again, winged with bright hope
> Above the great mountains

The *Iveriya* original, entitled 'To the Moon', has 'holy' instead of 'great', and other verses contain the line 'great is the providence of the Almighty'. The 'Dzh ... shvili' poems are apostrophes to Georgia, its countryside, its history, its oppressed peasants. They sometimes descend (at least in translation) into soggy bathos. With all Stalin's love of nature, as Ronald Hingley says, it must be odd to find him even when young writing:

> The rose opens her petals,
> And embraces the violet.
> The lily too has awakened.
> They bare their heads to the zephyrs

It may seem odd to find Stalin writing poetry at all – though Mao Tse-Tung and Castro and Ho Chi Minh also practised the art at one time or another. Apart from anything else, this might in Stalin's case have been designed to provide an entry to the Georgian literary intelligentsia, though we have no record of this happening. It is a typically obscure, though possibly revealing episode.

The Seminary had two outstanding negative characteristics. First, and increasingly so, it represented the Russian Church in its much resented Russifying role. Second, the methods of supervision were sneaky in the worst ecclesiastical tradition – reminding one of the ways of the nastier teacher-priests in Gabriel Chevalier's splendid *Sainte Colline*.

In his first year at the Seminary, Stalin had high marks for conduct and for work, and his fellows noted his piety. But in his second year, this matured into a bitterly rebellious attitude – that is in 1895–6, when he was about sixteen.

Among the more idiotic of the school's rules was the banning not only of suspect Western literature, but even of Dostoevsky, Turgenev and Tolstoy. Since the students were free to go out into the city for two hours in the afternoon, this sort of rule combined being infuriating with being unenforceable. Thus, to augment the narrow range of seminary education, Stalin now worked as an autodidact. He and his friends would get books from the local 'Cheap Library'. And they often took them back into the seminary to read illicitly.

The Russian rector Hermogen, his Russian assistants Murakhovsky and Rzhavensky, and his Georgian 'Inspector' Abashidze conducted a continual campaign against suspect students. There are first-hand accounts of Stalin's locker being broken into and erring books confiscated. And later, when Stalin was older (in December 1898), he intervened in a search of students and attacked the procedure as nonexistent in other seminaries. The supervisor's report adds that Dzhugashvili was generally disrespectful, and in particular refused to bow to Murakhovsky, as was customary. He was sent to the cell for five hours.

As Stalin himself said later, this atmosphere of constant petty espionage, or as he put it 'the outrageous regime and jesuitical methods prevalent at the Seminary' left him ready to become a revolutionary.

It is hard to imagine a system less likely to produce loyalty to authority, and devotion to the idea of the priesthood for which the school was supposed to be training its pupils, let alone to bring out the best in an already difficult character. Some commentators have derived from his seminary experiences much of Stalin's gloomy and suspicious personality in later life. In a broad sense this seems reasonable. All the same, his methods were to be different. The monks were at least seeking, in their squalid way, for real evidence on which to bring charges of a breach of the rules. Stalin, in his prime, had quite a different system: he had people arrested and then invented the evidence. And though incarceration for hours in the Seminary's punishment cell must have rankled, it scarcely matched Stalin's own extension of the death penalty to children as young as twelve.

3

In the Seminary, as at Gori, Stalin was the acknowledged leader of his group, but had bad relations with all who could not accept his dominance. He refused to follow the convention of embracing fellow-students on return after the summer break: 'I don't want to be a Pharisee,' he said, 'and kiss those that don't love me.'

He was constantly expounding his opinions to his fellows. Whenever another student tried to lead the discussion, Stalin is always reported becoming angry and shouting him down. Iremashvili, still a fellow student (and named in a Soviet article as a member of one of Stalin's 'discussion groups'), adds that Stalin saw in everything 'the negative, the bad side'.

If, away from his own circle, he was bested in argument, he would smile sardonically and walk away.

Stalin was put on report on 19 September 1898 for gathering a group of students and reading to them from 'books not sanctioned by the seminary authorities'. A full list of this unsanctioned educative material is illuminating.

Churchill remarked of Hitler that he was 'loosely educated'. In a sense this is also true of Stalin. His formal teaching, indeed, was rigorous, but it was very narrow. What he learned outside was Georgian literature, some of the Russian classics such as the satirical Shchedrin and Gogol, some Western books (in Russian translation) such as *Vanity Fair* and Victor Hugo's *Ninety-Three* and *Toilers of the Sea*. Hugo's work in particular came into the sphere of revolutionary romanticism. But in addition, there were books carrying broader Western ideas, though we need not believe one later Soviet claim that he read Darwin's *The Origin of Species* at the age of thirteen while still at Gori, and told a fellow pupil that it proved the nonexistence of God. This story fails on several obvious counts, including Stalin's remaining religious, even pious, for some years longer.

The books we know he read while at the Seminary are simply the ones he was caught with. He was detected thirteen times, though only the Hugo books and finally Letourneau's *Literary Evolution of the*

Nations, which he was caught reading on the chapel stairs, are actually recorded.

This book seems reasonably typical of the radical students' reading. Dr Charles Jean Marie Letourneau (1831–1902) was the author of a whole series of books on the 'evolution' of property, marriage, politics, religion and so on. In the tradition, as one of his books has it, of 'scientific materialism', they amount to a vast and immensely tedious encyclopedia of all knowledge from the point of view of a French radical of the period. Letourneau, a typical all-purpose sage at the level of popular portentousness, evidently saw himself as a successor to the encyclopedists of the previous century. He is not now to be found even in the indexes of French or English encyclopedias. *Evolution littéraire dans les diverses races humaines* is (in the French edition) 574 pages long. It says much for Stalin's urge to self-education, and for the tedium of seminary life, that he took it up. Other books more generally reported as in circulation among the students indicate that he indeed now read Darwin's *Descent of Man*, and also Charles Lyell's *Antiquity of Man*, the two books which revolutionized the world's view of the human situation in life and time.

In addition, apart from the Russian and Western fiction we have mentioned, he had access to Feuerbach, Buckle and Spinoza, to lives of Copernicus and Galileo, and to Mendeleyev's *Chemistry*. It is not clear how much he made of any particular book. In 1932, on the tercentenary of Spinoza's birth, *Pravda* ran a celebratory article with quotations from Stalin, but these had little to do with Spinoza.

4

Stalin's unofficial reading was thus of works more or less sharply opposed to established ideas. In a general sense both 'revolution' and concepts described as socialism or anarchism had long pervaded intellectual circles. As early as the 1820s Pavel Pestel, the most theoretical of the Decembrists, proposed what amounted to a Utopia enforced by terror. The leading pre-Leninist revolutionaries used the same tone. P. N. Tkachev, in the 1860s, urged the rule of the intellectual minority, as of 'higher mental and moral development', and feared that industrialization and Westernization would bring bourgeois values to the Empire. Peter Zaichnevsky in 1862 spoke of 'the revolutionary party', on coming to rule, preserving its centralization and 'seizing dictatorial powers'. Above all, Nikolai Chernyshevsky, from whom Lenin first learned revolutionary ideas (which he acknowledged through his life), was insisting on elite rule and hatred of liberalism.

Tkachev was right. Aside from the traditions of imperial and of revolutionary despotism, the reforms of the 1860s were indeed beginning to produce, in Pasternak's words, first 'aristocrats ... deeply stirred by Western ideas' and later 'the birth of an enlightened and affluent middle class, open to Occidental influences, progressive, intelligent, artistic'. It is remarkable that none of the great writers of the Russian enlightenment supported the revolutionary intelligentsia, with the partial exception of Herzen: and even he had written 'Communism is the Russian autocracy turned upside down!' – a formulation to be repeated, specifically of Lenin's Bolsheviks, by Rosa Luxemburg half a century later.

But Tolstoy and Dostoevsky, Turgenev and Chekhov, could not qualify for inclusion in the 'intelligentsia', while Chernyshevsky (whose immensely influential *What is to Be Done?* has been described as the worst novel ever written), was a member in good standing. To be an 'intelligent' one needed no qualifications except devotion to 'the Idea'. The Idea, or a variant of it, was ready to hand.

5

Stalin's extra-curricular reading, and his own comments, show clearly enough that with him rebellious or revolutionary feeling preceded Marxism. We know it did with Lenin, who became a Chernyshevskyite revolutionary at the age of eighteen, long before he became a Marxist. There seem to be few, if any, cases in which an apathetic or reactionary mind read Marx and became a Marxist. It was almost always a matter of a suitable mind-set welcoming a complete and apparently sophisticated system of certainties.

The gradualness, the stages, by which this took place in Stalin's case are indicated in an answer he gave in 1926 to an American admirer who had asked him how he became a revolutionary: 'It is difficult to describe the process. First one becomes convinced that existing conditions are wrong and unjust. Then one resolves to do the best one can to remedy them...'

Stalin's original non-scholastic education had made him ready for Marxism. It was, of course, to be supplemented later by a reasonably full reading of the Marxist classics. These provided new dogmas to replace the religious ones he had repudiated. Stalin's mind, then, in the sense of its intellectual furnishings, was a venue of the linguistic, historical and theological lore of his school, the Georgian and Russian classics, some of the Western scientific and literary tradition, and this all-purpose doctrine.

6

Marxism had made its first Russian converts in the early 1880s when G. V. Plekhanov and others formed a group for 'the Liberation of Labour' in exile in Geneva. Russian revolutionaries had hitherto mostly been of the Narodnik, Populist, persuasion, believing that socialism could be based on the ancient peasant commune without capitalism being allowed to develop. Unfortunately, Marx himself had agreed that, in the special circumstances of Russia, this might be possible. More orthodox Russian Marxists coped with this either by implying somewhat sacrilegiously that Marx had been misled, or by saying that though such an evolution might have been possible, it was being, or had been, overtaken by the increasing industrialization of Russia, forcing the country into the ordinary style of Marxist development with capitalists, workers and all.

A century later, the way in which Marxism quickly triumphed among a large section of the politically active intelligentsia may astonish us. Nowadays, of course, Marxism proper only holds the allegiance of a backward intellectual stratum in the USSR and a few other socialist countries, of a handful of Western academics and others, and of the leaderships of a few Third World regimes or guerrilla movements. Its teachings on the nature, and the future, of both 'capitalism' and 'socialism' have proved fallacious.

It is true that even at the time of its greatest political successes, few historians accepted its historical theory, few economists accepted its economic theory, and few philosophers accepted its philosophical theory. Its strength lay elsewhere. In the nineteenth century the world seemed everywhere to be breaking out of the old moulds. Industrialization, railways, steamers, the telegraph were the physical counterparts of an equally striking breakthrough in the world of thought. The new geology and the new astronomy had vastly extended the physical world in time and space. Faraday and Clark Maxwell and a dozen others had discovered new physical laws. And Darwin had put humanity and its whole origins into a new, and, as it seemed, iconoclastic framework.

Now the Darwin of society had appeared. A German Doktor had discovered the 'iron laws' of history, and, indeed, of the universe in general. In Russia Marxism had a special appeal. As a young revolutionary of the time, later a colleague of Lenin's (and later still an opponent), N. F. Valentinov, explained:

'We seized on Marxism because we were attracted by its sociological and economic optimism, its strong belief, buttressed by facts and figures, that the development of the economy, the development of capitalism (this was why we were so interested in it), by demoralizing and eroding the foundations of the old society, was creating new social forces (including us) which would certainly sweep away the autocratic regime together with all its abominations. With the optimism of youth we had been searching for a formula that offered hope, and we found it in Marxism. We were also attracted by its European nature. Marxism came from Europe. It did not smell and taste of home-grown mould and provincialism, but was new, and fresh and exciting.'

Moreover, as the Russian philosopher Berdyaev later wrote:

'Scientific positivism, and everything else Western, was accepted in its most extreme form and converted not only into a primitive metaphysic, but even into a special religion supplanting all previous religions.'

In Russian circumstances there was a special point. The Populists of earlier decades had 'gone to the people' in a disastrous campaign in which the peasants rejected these city intellectuals with obstinate contempt. But the individual terrorism to which they turned instead was also a failure. Marxism, on the other hand, promised new forces in the form of the 'proletariat' to destroy not only tsarism but also the newer 'exploiting classes'.

In Georgia the Marxist movement had been started by Noe Zhordania, future President of independent Georgia, while he was a student at the Seminary. It took the name Mesame Dasi, 'The Third Group' – the first having been the liberals around Prince Chavchavadze, and the second a more radical and more ephemeral circle.

Zhordania's group was, at first, mainly concerned with studying and propagating the Marxist view. It produced *Kvali* ('The Furrow') weekly, and *Moambeh* ('The Herald') monthly. Marxian work was legally publishable in the Empire at this time – indeed the police long regarded the non-terrorist Marxist socialists as less of a menace than the old People's Will and the newly developing Socialist Revolutionary Party, for whom bomb and revolver were normal political weapons.

Stalin is reported reading *Kvali*, and in 1896 or 1897 he began to consider himself a Marxist. His discussion circle, which he increasingly dominated, devoted itself to Marxist ideas. He and other seminary students now seem to have made some contact with a few workers in Tiflis, mainly in informal railwaymen's discussion groups.

When we think of Gori and Tiflis in those days, we need, as I have said, to get out of our minds the vague idea of a 'small town' or a 'provincial capital' in the American or West European sense. They were more in the nature of Eastern or Mediterranean towns. And this was all a century ago. The social order in Tiflis, as in Gori, was semi-medieval, comparable in some ways to Paris in François Villon's time, with its urban population in which clergy and officials, merchants and students, criminals and journeymen overlapped in a curiously intimate potpourri. This sort of ambience contained, like all early cities, a 'proletariat' in the old Roman sense – that is, not the industrial working class to which the term was transferred by Marx, but the broad class of urban poor without property except themselves.

In Tiflis, it is true, modernization was starting. Railway yards had their employees; and there were a number of small factories, some still in the workshop stage, some larger. The railwaymen, in particular, were a small but genuine proletariat in the Marxist sense.

In late 1898 Stalin went to Zhordania and said that he had decided to leave the Seminary and take up full-time propaganda among the workers. Zhordania asked him some questions and found that his knowledge of history, sociology and political economy was superficial, and had come from articles in *Kvali* and the Programme of the German Social Democratic Party. He advised him to stay another year in the Seminary and improve his political education.

Stalin said he would think about it. He seems to have taken some offence at this rebuff, and was heard making a heated attack on Zhordania to a group of students.

He remained in the Seminary until May 1899 when he was notified that he would be expelled for failing to sit his examinations, being given two days' grace to explain this lapse. He failed to do so, and his formal expulsion took place on 29 May 1899.

Stalin himself later said that he had been expelled for 'propagating Marxism' (though his mother claimed that she had taken him home on account of illness). Stalin's assertion is obviously untrue as it stands. But it is reasonable to think that he may have chosen a simple method of getting clear of the Seminary and into the full revolutionary life. He was not alone in dropping out. Only fifty of the three hundred students who had matriculated up to 1900 completed the full course.

Stalin had been broadening his contacts with Marxist circles through one of his roommates, 'Vano' Ketskhoveli, brother of the 'Lado' Ketskhoveli who had led the student strike in 1893. It was at this point that he first came across writings by Lenin, under the pseudonym 'Tulin'.

It was now, too, that Stalin took his first political pseudonym, 'Koba' – the heroic brigand and avenger he had identified with when a few years younger. And, whatever Zhordania's earlier scruples, Stalin was soon fully admitted into the Marxist ranks. Over the next few years they rallied for two main campaigns: action to influence the new industrial working class, and internecine strife among the Marxists themselves.

In March 1898, the so-called 'First Congress' of the Russian Social Democratic Labour Party had been held in Minsk. In, so far, a rather shaky way, a political organization proper to which the Marxists could turn now existed.

Chapter 3

Underground

We do not know what Stalin did between his expulsion from the Seminary and the end of 1899. If his mother, as she later put it, in fact took him away because he 'was so run down that the doctors said he would catch tuberculosis', then he presumably went home to Gori to recuperate.

By the winter he was back in Tiflis, and on 28 December 1899 he got his first and only regular employment, as an accountant at the Tiflis Observatory. His duties were a little broader than this description implies. There were six such junior employees, who did night shifts in rotation, and kept the meteorological records up. Some temperature readings in his handwriting, dated January 1900, are in the Stalin Museum at Gori.

Stalin had got the job through his fellow-student Vano Ketskhoveli, who already worked there. It was an ideal situation for the young revolutionaries, who were able to store forbidden literature in various nooks on and near the premises.

On 23 April 1900 a Tiflis May Day celebration was held – not in public but outside town, in secret. Such a meeting had been organized by Lado Ketskhoveli the previous year, when about seventy workers and others are said to have attended. This time the number given is two hundred, and Stalin was one of the speakers. By now Stalin was in official charge of Marxist propaganda among the circles of the railway workers with whom he had made contact while still at the Seminary.

On the night of 21 March 1901, however, the police raided the observatory and other hideouts of the Social Democrats and arrested a number of them. Stalin was not caught, and though his room was searched, no illegal literature was found there. But of course the job was no longer available, and from now on he lived the life of a professional revolutionary.

The 1901 May Day demonstration was held publicly, and illegally, in Tiflis. 'Nearly two thousand' are reported participating. There were clashes with the police and Cossacks; fourteen workers were injured (not killed, as one biography wrongly states) and over fifty were arrested. This demonstration was greeted by Lenin, in Switzerland: 'This day marks the beginning of an open revolutionary movement in the Caucasus.' In fact there was little trouble in Tiflis for several years thereafter.

Stalin was credited in later legend with having been the leader and organizer of the demonstration. Pictures were painted showing the young revolutionary, surrounded by red banners, facing with his fellow-workers the police attacks. He does seem to have played some minor part, but he was neither hurt nor arrested. Nor was he arrested afterwards, though a number of Social Democrats, including Noe Zhordania, were briefly imprisoned.

Stalin was beginning to write articles, and when on Lado Ketskhoveli's initiative the first illegal Georgian radical newspaper, *Brdzola* ('The Struggle'), appeared in the autumn of 1901, at least part of one of the anonymous contributions was Stalin's work.

Meanwhile, the Tiflis Social Democrats were becoming increasingly annoyed by Stalin's tactics: 'We appointed him to conduct propaganda against the government and the capitalists, but as it turned out he was conducting propaganda against us.' This had by now alienated not only comparative moderates like Zhordania, but even radicals like Sylvester Dzhibladze, earlier famous as the seminarian who had struck the rector.

At the end of the year a party 'court' expelled Stalin from the Tiflis branch. By December he was in the Georgian Black Sea port of Batum, where the local Social Democratic organization was headed by Chkheidze, another moderate of the Zhordania outlook. Chkheidze was to be a prominent figure in the democratic regime of 1917, as Chairman of the Petrograd Soviet – the 'old eagle', as John Reed was to call him.

It seems odd to historians more used to the tight discipline of later party life that Stalin, expelled by his Tiflis colleagues, could simply move on to Batum. But in 1901 there was little in the way of formal party organization. And while Stalin's Tiflis circle had virtually collapsed, Batum was in many ways a far more fruitful field for revolutionary activists' work. The seaport was more cosmopolitan, with many Russian workers in the Rothschild and other plants. A strike in late February led to the arrest of some workers; at a demonstration against this three hundred more were arrested. On 9 March 1902, a demonstration of two thousand workers, demanding the release of their fellows, attacked the detention barracks. The police fired on them. Fifteen were killed and fifty-four wounded, and over five hundred were arrested. This became a cause célèbre, and a governmental court of inquiry made an exhaustive investigation. Stalin is described in later literature as having organized and led the demonstration; but his name is not mentioned in the inquiry. However, there seems no doubt that he had played an important role in the agitation and discussion which galvanized the movement – though we are also told that the Batum workers were disgruntled at having been led into a situation where their mates had been killed and wounded to no apparent purpose.

At any rate, he was arrested a month later, on 5 April 1902, with other Social Democrats. He was held for eighteen months first in Baku jail, and then in that of Kutaisi, the main inland city of western Georgia. We have a description of him from a cell-mate who noted his stealthy gait and inability to laugh heartily; unusually for him, he also showed much self-control, and did not shout or curse. Perhaps this, his first imprisonment, was part of a maturing process, or rather of the development of control external to, and never fully harmonized with, his character.

On 9 July 1903, he was sentenced to three years' exile in Siberia, arriving at his allotted destination, the village of Novaya Uda in Irkutsk province, on 27 November 1903. Here he lived in a peasant household and, according to biographers, did much reading by candlelight. But he escaped on 5 January 1904, and was soon back in the Caucasus.

This was the first of his many escapes from exile. These escapes, it should be said, were by no means the desperate and daring moves we might associate with the word. By later standards, tsarist exile was astonishingly easy and lax. Later, under Stalin's rule, it was a matter of barbed wire, guard turrets and total regimentation. But the politicals of the pre-revolutionary period were merely under not very effective 'supervision' by a few police officials. Moreover, after an escape attempt the penalty was sometimes no more than returning the culprit to finish his term, or at most sending him to more distant and difficult areas. A large proportion of the leading Bolsheviks and Mensheviks and others sentenced to exile escaped fairly frequently. Escapes in the strict sense, from jail, were rarer though not unknown. Stalin did not get out of the Kutaisi, Baku or St Petersburg prisons, but nor was there any good reason for him to do so, even after a year or more, as exile was the next step and provided an easier target. Even in exile, it was sometimes preferable to serve out the sentence. (Stalin made this point when later serving out a full sentence, arguing that there were advantages in returning with legal status.)

This time he was back in Tiflis in February 1904.

2

In Stalin's absence from the Social Democratic scene, the movement had been going through what were to prove climactic events.

The 'First Congress' of the Russian Social Democratic Labour Party in 1898 had not amounted to much, and most of the nine delegates had been promptly arrested, joining prisoners or exiles from the earlier groups like Martov's and Lenin's League of Struggle for the Emancipation of the Working Class.

Though the 'Congress' was illegal, it included the so-called 'Legal Marxists' who wished to operate publicly. They were soon to be sloughed off by the main body, and to become constitutional liberals. But it is worth repeating, first, that the tsarist secret police were always, not unnaturally, rather more urgently concerned with the assassination-prone Populists and Socialist Revolutionaries than with the Marxists. And secondly, much of the Marxist literature, including *Das Kapital*, was legal, if not from the point of view of the Tiflis Seminary, at least as far as the public were concerned. This was even true of Lenin's first book, *The Development of Capitalism in Russia,* published in 1899.

Lenin's early view of the party and its relationship with the working class had been:

'The task of the party does not consist in thinking up out of its head any kind of modern methods of helping the workers, but in linking itself with the labour movement ... The workers acquire an understanding of all this [class consciousness] by constantly drawing it from the very struggle which they are beginning to wage against the factory owners. ... The struggle of the workers against the factory owners for their daily needs of itself and inevitably forces the workers to think about state, about political questions.'

This view – obviously quite unlike later Leninism – pervaded the Social Democratic Party. But soon Lenin and most of the leadership, including future Bolsheviks and Mensheviks alike, were confronting a fatal flaw which had become apparent in the Marxist scheme.

In the first place, as a practical matter, the newly emerging Workers' Unions – even in Russia – far from being radicalized by their economic struggle, concerned themselves increasingly with immediate interests and had little use for theory. And this was a reflection, or a confirmation, of a profounder ideological crisis.

Marx had predicted the polarization of society into an ever-decreasing owner class and an ever-increasing proletariat; and the progressive pauperization of that proletariat. This was not some offhand guess. It was a rigorous deduction from the central thesis of Marxist economics – that capitalist profit was surplus value obtained by denying the proletariat its full earnings. But this meant that as capital accumulated, the *proportion* of labour costs in the total turnover regularly decreased. So the capitalist would be forced to squeeze more and more out of the wage fund to maintain the level of profit. This would produce Marx's 'increasing misery', and also meant that the poor would less and less provide a market for the capitalist to sell goods to, thus producing the 'crisis of capitalism'.

Even Marx, before his death, had seen that something had gone wrong; but he put it aside for further study. But now the young Marxist Eduard Bernstein produced his *Evolutionary Socialism,* which in principle 'revised' Marx on this point. Bernstein noted that the rate of profit had not fallen; that capitalism had not ceased to expand production; that revolutionary situations had not arisen in the industrialized countries. In effect, he refuted and abandoned Marx. Marxists, in both the West and Russia, bitterly attacked him. The German and other Western Social Democratic Marxists retained the old doctrine in principle – but gave it up in practice. But the Russians, by and large, denied both in practice and in theory that it had ever been refuted. Or so it appeared. Looked at more closely, the reaction of the exiled Russian Social Democratic leaders was to devise a counter to the unadmitted truth. In 1900 they founded *Iskra,* specifically to combat the 'Economists' who still maintained that the party's job was to develop the natural proletarian movement in its supposedly inevitable path to revolution. In 1902 Lenin published *What is To Be Done?* It asserted that the proletariat would after all not develop in that direction on its own. For:

'The working class exclusively by its own efforts is able to develop only trade-union consciousness ... Modern socialist consciousness can only be brought to them from without ... can arise only on

31

the basis of profound scientific knowledge. The bearers of science are not the proletariat but the bourgeois intelligentsia. It is out of the heads of members of this stratum that modern socialism originated ... Pure and simple trade unionism means the ideological subordination of the workers to the bourgeoisie ... Our task is to bring the labour movement under the wing of revolutionary Social Democracy.'

Or, to put it in another way, the theory had proved wrong, and society would have to be dragged by force into what Marxism had supposed to be its natural evolution: rather as if that other Victorian pseudo-science, phrenology, had failed to fit real human beings, and it had become necessary to clout them on the head to produce the theoretically correct bumps. As Czeslaw Milosz has written, they 'learn to predict a fire with unerring precision, then burn the house down to fulfil the prediction'.

Thus, in effect, though no one admitted it, Marxism as a set of scientific laws of the development of history and society had gone. What was left?

First, the aim of a society without conflict was maintained, if as a subjective desire rather than an objective prediction. That is, the old pre-Marxist revolutionary utopianism lost its temporary scientific veneer, and reverted to what it had been, in one guise or another, for millennia.

Second, the inevitability of capitalist crisis was maintained in theory, even though its empirical basis had collapsed.

Third, the 'class' analysis of society remained central; together with the notion that the industrial proletariat would eventually in some sense become the governing class and produce socialism (this, too, was not a specifically Marxist view, being shared by many anarchists, Syndicalists and non-Marxian socialists).

Fourth, the sacredness even of the refuted Marxist predictions was maintained. The prestigious idea of 'scientific socialism' remained. And the whole apparatus of dialectical materialism continued to satisfy the philosophical needs of the faithful.

In 1903, the 'Second', but in effect the first real, Congress of the RSDLP was held in Brussels and London. Its original aim was to crush the 'Economists'. They had majorities in St Petersburg and among important sections elsewhere. But, as Lenin explained, 'the composition of the Party Congress was settled in advance by the Organization

Committee' – not the last time the movement was to experience such methods.

As a result the 'Economists' had only three voting delegates out of fifty-one. There were a number of uncommitted delegates, but the anti-'Economist' vote was a solid thirty-three – that is two-thirds.

But now a new split started to emerge among the victors, which resulted in the famous Bolshevik–Menshevik schism. The main issue was whether the party was to be radically centralized and become an organization of professional revolutionaries. The key vote was between the Menshevik leader Martov's definition of a party member: 'one who accepts the party's programme and supports it by material means and by regular personal assistance under the direction of one of the party's organizations'; and Lenin's: 'one who accepts the party's programme and supports it by material means and by personal participation in one of the party's organizations'. On the face of it the difference is minimal; but, as Lenin said, 'My formula restricts the conception of party worker while Martov's broadens it.' As Martov pointed out, Lenin wanted a party of professional revolutionaries. Indeed, he had already urged in *What is To Be Done?* that the party should consist 'first and foremost of people whose profession is that of revolutionist' and, in some ways even more strikingly, 'As this is the common feature of the members of such an organization, all distinction as between workers and intellectuals must be dropped.'

Thus, he was proposing a party which would be full-time, professional and not definable in class terms – extraneous to society and working on it from outside ...

Lenin lost the vote on this issue by twenty-eight votes to twenty-two. Even the young Leon Trotsky argued that while the party should not follow behind the working class, it was unMarxist for it to separate itself from the working class and 'undertake its obligations'. The famous vote on which Lenin obtained a majority (twenty-two to twenty with two abstentions), from which he henceforth called his faction Bolshevik (Majoritarian) as against Martov's Mensheviks (Minoritarians), was who should control the party organ *Iskra*.

One myth should be laid to rest straight away. The Mensheviks and other 'moderates' were not prudent respectable bourgeois types, reluctant to struggle against tsardom and capitalism. Quite the contrary: some of the boldest of the revolutionaries were Mensheviks, and they suffered as much imprisonment and persecution as any Bolsheviks. The distinction was quite different.

First, the Mensheviks did not believe in violent confrontation for its own sake – indeed this tactic was regarded in post-1917 Communist Parties too as a 'left' deviation or even an anarchist error (not an unreasonable description of Stalin's early activities). Second, the Mensheviks believed in the revolutionary overthrow of tsardom, and the eventual revolutionary overthrow of a capitalist successor regime, but they did not believe in a Social Democratic seizure of power by an armed putsch when the vast majority of the population was against them.

Meanwhile, we see the open creation of a separate Leninist group: but such factions within broader parties have occurred in political organizations, in the West as elsewhere, without implying break-up. In fact, this Bolshevik–Menshevik split, later to figure so portentously, did not have that appearance at the time. Various votes had been taken, groups had committed themselves to different views, people had changed sides on particular issues. In fact, even given that the arguments were fierce, they were assumed to have taken place within a party broad enough to handle them. At the branch level in Russia, overwhelmingly engaged in practical resistance, they did not yet mean much. It was not clear to most Social Democrats there that the voting and factions at the Second Congress were of any particular significance.

When Stalin returned to the Caucasus from Siberia late in 1904, he was, insofar as he was anything, a 'Menshevik' – at least a later police record describes him as a Bolshevik, former Menshevik. But this Menshevism must have been in a brief period of disorientation. In fact, it will be apparent that Stalin was a natural Bolshevik: as Robert C. Tucker puts it, Stalin's 'militant' circles might already be regarded as 'proto-Bolsheviks'. He was now a 'professional revolutionary', he had always favoured the more extreme positions, and he was soon an active Bolshevik, while the veteran Georgian Social Democrats now identified themselves with the Mensheviks.

Within each of these groupings there was also to be a further differentiation. Some moved to the centre of Russian politics – such as the Mensheviks Tseretelli and Chkheidze, who became prominent in the 1917 government and soviets, and the Bolsheviks Stalin and Ordzhonikidze. Some stayed on in their own country, like Zhordania himself and his Menshevik followers who succeeded in winning a great majority in Georgia in a free election (something the Bolsheviks could never boast even in Russia); and Filip Makharadze and others among the Bolsheviks, who remained a tiny minority until supported by Moscow's armies.

On his arrival back in Tiflis in 1904 Stalin went first to the house of

Lev Kamenev, who was to appear at various points in Stalin's life in a number of different capacities. Kamenev, the son of a railwayman, younger than Stalin, had graduated from the Tiflis gymnasium in 1901, gone on to the Moscow University of Jurisprudence, and been arrested as an active Social Democrat. He had gone to Paris, met Lenin and became an Iskraite (and also married Trotsky's sister). Lenin himself had sent him back to Tiflis in 1903. At this stage, he was a fully-fledged, ranking Bolshevik while Stalin, his senior in age, was still laboriously working his way up from a lower level.

3

Kamenev was arrested soon afterwards, and Stalin was immediately involved in factional dispute with those remaining. Rivalries developed in the Caucasus even within the miniscule Bolshevik sect. First, Stalin and Filip Makharadze (later President of Soviet Georgia) came to blows. Then there was a more serious conflict with Stepan Shaumyan, who later came to believe that Stalin had betrayed him to the police.

A comrade describes Stalin at a meeting as having 'a lively and shrewd gaze, animated, free and easy, self-sufficient'. But this favourable impression faded when 'with his first words' he began attacking the local party's leaflets as 'insufficiently militant'. He seems to have put his own line direct to activists among the ordinary workers, but to have been rebuffed so firmly that he walked out. At one meeting, he 'insulted everyone in the room as "petty-bourgeois"', and left with a few adherents. Stalin was by this time well-known among the Georgian Social Democrats, and very much so in the small militant wing. But even they were slow to give him full confidence. It was above all his extraordinary rudeness, and coarseness, in debate which put people off.

Lenin, and the Leninists in general, were free with their abuse of comrades they disagreed with, as deviationists, traitors and so on. Lenin himself was to admit, when called before a party court for such conduct, that his controversial tactics were 'calculated to evoke hatred, aversion and contempt ... calculated not to convince, but to break the ranks of the opponent ... to evoke the worst thoughts, the worst suspicions about the opponent'. But this violent and slanderous sectarianism was only one of the components in Stalin's conduct. He is constantly described as breaking up meetings by crude heckling in language both coarse and vituperative. He would say, in defence, that this was how the 'people' talked, unlike prissy intellectuals (though in fact Georgian working men seem to have behaved very correctly at meetings). Once he denied that he was behaving indecently, on the grounds that he hadn't taken his trousers off. Once he spoke of Martov and Dan as 'circumcised yids'. He referred to the veteran Vera Zasulich as 'an old bitch'. And so on. 'He's a real Koba' became a normal phrase among Transcaucasian Social Democrats ...

Meanwhile, the thin ranks of the militants had been thinned yet further. Lado Ketskhoveli, incarcerated in Tiflis's Metekh prison, had shouted revolutionary songs and speeches from his cell window and (though warned by a cell-mate, Stalin's future father-in-law Sergei Alliluyev, to keep quiet and leave the window) was shot by a guard.

Even so, and with all his apparent prowess, Stalin was not an automatic choice of the Georgian Bolsheviks. He was not among the delegates who met in Tiflis for the first Conference of Transcaucasian Bolsheviks in November 1904. Nor was he one of the four Transcaucasian delegates to the (all-Bolshevik) Third Party Congress in London in April 1905 – they were headed by Kamenev, his later colleague and victim, who had amongst other things recently organized Stalin's hideout in Tiflis. Even this Congress, admitted by Lenin to be 'formally illegal', refused to expel the Mensheviks, and the Social Democrats remained a single party in principle until 1912 – with the factions fighting for control of the newspapers, the committees and the purse.

1905, the year of the first Russian Revolution, is an odd year in Stalin's biography. He was now, according to one Menshevik, 'a fully-fledged, orthodox, committed Leninist, repeating the arguments of his Master like a gramophone'. But he seems to have played little part in the great events of the year.

It is true that the movement was largely spontaneous, and took all the Social Democrats by surprise. As late as March there were only a few hundred Social Democratic workers. But as the events moved on, some Social Democratic involvement and leadership materialized – in particular when Trotsky, Stalin's coeval, won world fame as Chairman of the newly emerged Petersburg Soviet, while other Mensheviks eventually played a leading part in Sevastopol, the most violent focus of revolution.

In the chronology attached to Stalin's official biography, the year's events are meagre. He addressed some mass meetings and wrote twelve articles and pamphlets. But the main actions are such things as his speaking 'against the Menshevik leaders' at a discussion meeting in

April, and 'against the Anarchists, Federalists and Socialist Revolutionaries' at another one in July.

In December 1905, after a Constitution had been granted and the
revolutionary wave had died down, Stalin was at last a delegate to an
important party meeting. This was a (purely Bolshevik) conference at
Tammerfors in Finland – as far as we know the first time, apart from
his Siberian exile, that he had been outside the Caucasus. This was also
the first time he met Lenin. He much later described his feelings:

> 'I was expecting to see the mountain eagle of our party, a great
> man, not only politically, but if you will, physically, for I had
> formed for myself an image of Lenin as a giant, stately and
> imposing. What was my disappointment when I saw the most
> ordinary-looking man, below middle height, distinguished from
> ordinary mortals by nothing, literally nothing.
>
> It is the accepted custom for a great man to arrive late at meetings
> so that the assembly may await his appearance with bated breath,
> and then just before he appears come the warning whispers: "Hush-
> silence-he is coming!" This ceremony seemed to me to have its uses,
> for it inspires respect. What was my disappointment to learn that
> Lenin had arrived before the other delegates, had sat down some-
> where in a corner, and was unassumingly carrying on a most
> ordinary conversation with the most ordinary delegates at the
> conference. I will not conceal from you that I thought his behaviour
> to be a violation of certain essential rules.'

At this time, Georgian Social Democrats tell us, Stalin himself
was accustomed to arrive late at party or faction meetings, in order to
secure at least a limited effect. But, whether or not because he was impressed by Lenin's unostentatiousness, in later life he himself dressed
modestly (at least until the war) and did not throw his weight about
in public. Ronald Hingley, indeed, compares him to the dreaded Count
Arakcheyev, who had ruled Russia so ruthlessly in Alexander I's time,
but 'wore a simple, threadbare cloak when appearing before dazzling
assemblages ... therefore striking universal terror as the one man who
didn't have to bother'.

It is also true that, though Stalin's public polemics remained fierce all
his life, and his language in private and limited circles was always coarse,
he was soon eschewing the crudest vulgarities in public or semi-public.
Over the next few years, if mainly in polemics *within* the Bolshevik
faction, Stalin is reported as 'taciturn, placid, serious, not raising his

voice; it was impossible to guess his real thoughts – he did not reply to offensive attacks at the time, but patiently waited for an opportune moment to have his revenge'.

The Bolsheviks were as ever a tiny clique in the Transcaucasus, against about five thousand Mensheviks. In Batum only ten or fifteen of about a thousand Social Democrats were Bolsheviks, and there were only a few dozen in Tiflis. The Mensheviks had, in fact, come out as the leading political movement in Georgia, in part by using the electoral campaign under the new Constitution to win five of the eight Georgian seats in the First Duma (and all the Georgian delegates to the Second Duma).

When, on 10–25 April 1906, a full-scale Fourth Party Congress met in Stockholm, Stalin was the single Bolshevik delegate from Tiflis, with ten Mensheviks. Overall, the Mensheviks had a full majority in the Congress. And the rank-and-file membership had impressed even on many of the Bolshevik delegates its impatience at all the recent factiousness and disunity.

4

It was in April 1906 that there came one of the most obscure of all the events in the Transcaucasian underground. A secret printing press, concealed off a sunken well in an unpretentious building specially constructed for the purpose, had operated in the Tiflis suburb of Avalbar since 1903. The whole operation was, of course, controlled by the Social Democrats, and their Caucasian Union Committee.

Here, with presses in Russian, Georgian and Armenian typeface, thousands of leaflets and pamphlets were produced – over a quarter of a million in 1905. In 1906, after the 'reunification' of Mensheviks and Bolsheviks, a new Tiflis Committee was formed, with a few Bolsheviks. Early in the spring of 1906, the printers and their equipment seem to have been transferred to St Petersburg, and the premises turned (by the still predominantly Menshevik Committee) into an arms cache and bomb laboratory. The Tiflis Okhrana, which had long searched in vain for the press, had by now been given a tip-off, from a source never yet identified. The Avalbar installation was watched from the beginning of April, and raided on 15 April. As a result, a large number of leading Social Democrats were arrested in the area or in Tiflis proper. But Stalin, who had been in Tiflis when supervision started, was by this time in Stockholm attending the Party Congress.

This has led to much speculation that Stalin might somehow be implicated in the betrayal or, more plausibly, that an associate, arrested but soon released, might have been involved – though not necessarily with Stalin's knowledge, or perhaps over-fulfilling Stalin's instructions or suggestions. The evidence is extremely skimpy, and the only reason for not dismissing it at once is the extraordinarily touchy and incoherent way in which the affair was later treated in the Soviet press – until, indeed, a new Stalinist version emerged in the 1930s, which gave a perfectly clear account, with Stalin the founder and organizer of the underground press and its chief hero (which is, of course, a complete invention).

The Avalbar affair, taken with other peculiar events, has long since led to the suspicion that Stalin acted as an agent of the Okhrana. There are documents which show, or might show, that he was indeed such an agent: but on the evidence at present available, they seem to be forgeries. The revolutionary movement was indeed full of Okhrana agents and provocateurs as senior as the full member of the Central Committee Roman Malinovsky. Mistrust and suspicion were endemic, and often justified.

Nevertheless, on the evidence we have (including recent Soviet research), the charge that Stalin acted for the Okhrana must be dismissed. But there is a milder version, as it were, in which Stalin is charged with betraying rival Social Democrats, including Bolsheviks, to the police, no doubt by anonymous tip-offs. At any rate, there were several occasions when Stalin seemed to be the logical suspect. Again, however cumulative the stories, proof is lacking. It would hardly be out of character, certainly not as we now know it. Even at the time, the charge seemed plausible to many.

5

The Stockholm Congress was, under rank-and-file pressure, intended to register and impose party reunification. As Zinoviev, by now Lenin's close aide, put it, 'Under the pressure of the masses, the general staff of the Bolsheviks and the Mensheviks were forced to unite ... there was nothing for the Bolsheviks but to submit.'

Nor was there for a time anything like 'party discipline' within the factions. The father of Russian Marxism, Plekhanov, voted first with one group, then with another. (Lenin himself, at a party conference in 1907, was to vote with the Mensheviks against an otherwise unanimous Bolshevik stance.)

Stalin was not yet the loyal Leninist of later myth. He spoke against a proposal of Lenin's on peasant land tenure – an important issue. After Lenin had (changing his earlier view) come out against boycotting the State Duma, Stalin repeated the boycott line – having attacked the Menshevik claim that their electoral 'participation' constituted 'action', by saying that merely throwing shards in a box did not amount to what he would call 'action'. And when Lenin issued a faction manifesto reserving the right of the Bolsheviks to some measure of independence within the party, twenty-six of the Bolshevik delegates signed it, but Stalin was one of the fourteen who did not.

The most crucial decision of the Stockholm Congress was a strong condemnation of robbery as a means of financing Social Democracy. The upheavals of 1905 had seen a fair amount of politically-motivated crime, hold-ups, extortion, and so on. The Congress, without open opposition from Lenin, argued that 'Criminals and the scum of the urban population have always used revolutionary upheavals for their anti-social aims', and insisted that revolutionaries should not descend to such tactics. Many Bolsheviks supported this view.

This was good disciplined Marxism, and contrary to an old tradition of overlap between the revolutionary and criminal worlds. The anarchist Mikhail Bakunin had written:

'In Russia, the robber is the only revolutionary ... the robber in the woods, in the cities and in the villages, robbers all over Russia and robbers imprisoned in innumerable jails throughout the country make up one, indivisible, closely linked world – the world of the Russian revolution ... He who wishes to plot revolution in earnest in Russia, he who desires a popular revolution, must enter this world.'

Indeed, all Russian revolutionaries knew this world, but 'scientific socialists', progressives who rejected the dark and medieval past, repudiated it as the Congress did.

Lenin, however, had a problem. If a party is made up of 'professional revolutionaries', the corollary is that they have to be paid. Lenin had no compunction about the methods. Some cash came from rich donors, but the faction-fighting had put many of them off. Various shifts such as the seduction and marriage of heiresses to suitable Bolsheviks helped. But 'expropriations' remained an attractive source of funds. As soon as the Congress finished Lenin set up several committees, illicit from the party's point of view, which included a secret centre for military and financial affairs. Its main role was bank robbery.

It was on Stalin's return that he wrote his 'Notes of a Delegate', published in the Russian language *Proletarii* in Baku. It was a forthright anti-Menshevik polemic, and won Lenin's approval, the first sign we find of interest in Stalin by the older man. It is also notable for the well-known remark that one of the Bolsheviks 'had observed in jest that the Mensheviks constituted a Jewish group while the Bolsheviks constitute a true Russian group, and, therefore, it would not be a bad idea for us Bolsheviks to organize a pogrom in the party' – a passage retained in Stalin's *Collected Works,* which appeared in 1946, at the beginning of his main anti-Semitic actions.

6

With his new financial resources and by various other means, Lenin was able to win a majority at the Fifth Congress held in London in May 1907. Stalin was present, though the Transcaucasian Social Democrats had this time denied him any accreditation at all and denounced as fake one he had brought. Lenin was with difficulty able to count him in as a consultative delegate without a vote – as in the cases of a few others. Though this gave him speaking rights, Stalin is this time not quoted in the record as having said a word. The only incident reported of his London experience is of being attacked by angry dockers and saved by another delegate in the form of his future Foreign Commissar Litvinov.

When the Bolsheviks returned to Russia, the expropriations started on a big scale. In the Caucasus an old protégé of Stalin's, the half-crazed 'Kamo' (Ter-Petrosian) – also from Gori – organized the most famous and dramatic coup. On 13 June 1907, in Yerevan Square in Tiflis (later Lenin Square) he led a group of gunmen and bomb-throwers in a violent and spectacular seizure of funds.

The plotters had learned that a very large sum was being sent from St Petersburg to Tiflis. As the specie of the State Bank, escorted by a detachment of Cossacks, was leaving Yerevan Square in a carriage, seven bombs were thrown. A final bomb thrown under the panicking horses, which had started to gallop off, brought them down; and the sacks of cash and bonds were successfully seized by the conspirators. In the attack several people were killed, and some fifty, mainly onlookers – it was a busy time of day – were wounded.

There is no doubt but that Kamo and his band were operating under instructions personally issued by Lenin and his 'committee'. There is no direct evidence of any involvement by Stalin. But the numbers in the plot are given as between fifty and sixty, and fifteen names of actual participants are listed, all but one of them Georgians. It would be strange if a leading, and militant, operative in the area had not at least been kept informed, if only for the security arrangements of his own group in the inevitable police reaction. As with much else among these obscure phenomena, nothing can be said for certain, but there is more definite evidence of Stalin's involvement in later expropriations.

Such acts of violence were common enough in Russia at the time. Lenin's group cooperated with Socialist Revolutionaries and 'Maximalists', uninhibited advocates of terror and expropriation. Even the Mensheviks countenanced or organized particular assassinations, such as that of a Tiflis police chief.

It is not surprising, then, that the Bolsheviks were suspects in the (still obscure) murder of Prince Chavchavadze, father of the Georgian cultural renaissance, on 28 August 1907: he had spoken out strongly against the revolutionary left. They were also suspects in that of Archbishop Nikon, Exarch of Georgia, on 28 May 1908. When the latter assassination took place, the Mensheviks suggested that anyone with information should tell the police. Stalin, then in jail, wrote that of course Social Democrats opposed such murders, but equally opposed 'betraying' the perpetrators.

The Yerevan Square robbery and killings caused a sensation throughout Europe. Socialists were aghast at what they saw as a crude and ruthless act of banditry. In the event, the notes were traced when attempts were made to use them in Western Europe, and the Bolshevik intermediaries were arrested. Almost all the money was recovered, and Lenin was left only with the resulting obloquy.

Eventually, as a result also of Lenin's diversion of funds earmarked for the Social Democratic Party as a whole, a confidential committee of the Second International ordered him to hand over the money. A 'Court of Honour' of the Russian Social Democrats ordered a clean-up. In 1911, when Lenin failed to honour its decision, Martov published the evidence.

As for Stalin, he too was under censure. In fact, in 1907, he was expelled from his party organization for expropriation activity. This

42

was mentioned by Martov in an article in 1918, after the Revolution. Stalin denied it (in the careful phraseology that he was never 'expelled from my party') and had Martov tried by a Bolshevik court, for 'slander of the Soviet government'. Martov offered to produce witnesses, both Menshevik and Bolshevik. It is perfectly clear from a recent full account of the proceedings that Stalin, and to a lesser degree the court itself, was concerned to suppress the evidence, and no witnesses were allowed. As a diversion Martov was mildly censured for other statements in the article.

In fact, (though Stalin's denial has sometimes been taken as casting doubt on the story), it is clear that in 1907 the local party indeed found him guilty of involvement in the hold-ups, and the involvement is indirectly confirmed in both Bolshevik and Menshevik memoirs. The most remarkable aspect of the affair is that Stalin took Martov to court, and at least succeeded in confusing the issue. The German writer Emil Ludwig tells of Stalin's replies when he interviewed him in 1931:

'Since this story has been suppressed in Stalin's official biography, though it is definitely established that he had the directing hand in the robbery, I asked him about it, expecting that he would deny it in so many words, but that I would be able to get the truth from the expression on his face. "In Europe," I said to him, "you are described either as a bloody Tsar or as a Georgian bandit . . ."

Stalin began to laugh in that heavy way of his, blinked several times and stood up, for the first time in our three-hour interview. He walked over, with his somewhat dragging footsteps, to the biography in Russian; but, of course, there was nothing in it about my question.

"You will find all the necessary information here," he said – laughing slyly to himself because he had "put one over" on me. The question of the bank robbery was the only one he would not answer – except to the extent that he answered it by passing it over. His manner of evasion gave me a new insight into his character. He could have denied it; he could have confessed it; or he could simply have described the whole thing as a legend. But he acted instead like a perfect Asiatic . . .'

After his expulsion, Stalin moved to Baku in Azerbaijan, the great oil centre on the Caspian Sea. Here, since the Baku Party Committee was controlled by the Mensheviks, Stalin and his fellow Bolsheviks formed a breakaway committee. In the summer of 1907, he attempted to organize a refinery workers' strike, being opposed (as Ordzhonikidze tells us) by both Mensheviks and Bolsheviks, and he was overruled.

As a Bolshevik memoir published in the 1920s put it, Stalin was a 'Left' Bolshevik, and the others mostly 'Right'; and he was 'the last to adjust to the new possibilities for legal activities by the workers'.

7

In (apparently) 1905 Stalin had married Yekaterina Svanidze. We know little about their brief life together, though acquaintances say that while she prayed for his redemption from his dangerous career she was, in the Georgian tradition, obedient to his wishes; on his side, the official Social Democratic notion of the equality of the sexes played no part. Nonetheless, though occasionally brutal, he is reported to have been very fond of her. In 1907 a son, Yakov, was born. Her brother and other relations were also to figure in Stalin's later life, but Yekaterina herself died in 1907. An old friend – though by now, as a Menshevik, a political opponent – accompanied Stalin to the funeral. Afterwards Stalin said: 'This creature softened my stony heart. She is dead and with her have died my last warm feelings for all human beings.'

The son, Yakov, was left to be brought up by his uncle and aunt. When he eventually came to Moscow he knew little Russian. His later fate will emerge as we go on.

8

On 25 March 1908, Stalin was once more arrested, and sent to Baku's Bailov Prison until early November.

We have interesting accounts of Stalin in this prison, in particular from the Socialist Revolutionary Semyon Vereshchak. (He published his reminiscences abroad in 1928; but much from them was soon reprinted in *Pravda*.) Vereshchak was to know Stalin later, in exile in Siberia; in 1917, as representative from the Tiflis Soviet, he met him again at the First Congress of Soviets.

In this 'open jail' the political prisoners, including Socialist Revolutionaries and both factions of the Social Democrats, were organized for debate and action under a committee of which Vereshchak was a member.

Stalin struck him as the epitome of 'mistrust', in whom 'reason, slyness, truth and falsehood were interwoven'. He incited other prisoners to riot, but never took part himself. In a 'game' in which prisoners harassed one of their number with insults, false allegations and general provocation, they could never upset Stalin. When executions were taking place, and all the others were much shaken, he 'slept soundly, or quietly studied Esperanto . . .'

On one occasion, after a major riot, the politicals were made to run the gauntlet of soldiers' rifle butts. Stalin walked through the ordeal calmly and bravely, reading a book.

Contrary to the accepted rule, he associated freely, and by preference, with the common criminals, 'cutthroats, robbers, gunmen'. However, he organized regular discussion groups. His own contributions, rude though not notably coarse, dry and humourless, depended for their effect on clinching climaxes from the Marxist texts, on which he was by now very well briefed. The disputations were heated, but he remained cool – unlike his fellow Bolshevik, Sergo Ordzhonikidze who, during a discussion on agrarian policy, hit a Socialist Revolutionary in the face, and was then beaten by his victim's comrades – not the last time this more typically 'fiery' Georgian would get into trouble in this way. There were bizarre incidents. Once Stalin started a rumour that an innocent inmate was an informer, and the man was then beaten up. Another, perhaps not innocent, was knifed.

On 29 September 1908 Stalin was given a sentence of two years' exile, and deported to Solvychegodsk, in Vologda Province. Solvychegodsk is in the middle of what was later to be one of the largest of the Stalinist labour camp areas, around Kotlas. Here again, he associated by preference with the common criminals, as he later told Khrushchev, who says:

'I've never forgotten how he described his exile. The tale helped explain why he drank so much. He was sent somewhere in Vologda Province. Many political and criminal convicts were sent there. Stalin used to say: "There were some nice fellows among the criminals during my exile. I hung around mostly with the criminals. I remember we used to stop at the saloons in town. We'd see who among us had a rouble or two, then we'd hold our money up to the window, order something, and drink every kopeck we had. One day I would pay, the next someone else would pay and so on, in turn. These criminals were nice, salt-of-the-earth fellows. But there were lots of rats among the political convicts. They once organized a comrades' court and put me on trial for drinking with the criminal convicts, which they charged was an offence.'

He was ill for a time, but escaped again at the end of June 1909. He went to St Petersburg, where he was in contact with Sergei Alliluyev, his former colleague in Tiflis and future father-in-law. By mid-July he was back in Baku.

He was re-arrested on 23 March 1910, spent another six months in Bailov Prison and was returned to Solvychegodsk. There, billeted in local homes with a government allowance sufficient for board and lodging, he spent much of the time reading and writing. He had already somewhat impressed Lenin with his rough and aggressive 'Notes of a Delegate', about the London Congress, and with other articles. By now, Stalin had a record of a decade of underground work, arrests, exile, escapes and militant opposition to Mensheviks and all other heretics. If he had disagreed with Lenin, it was on minor issues and was expressed in a bluff worker sort of way. Now, at the end of December 1910, he wrote a letter to a contact of Lenin's in Paris.

He sends 'hearty greetings to Lenin, Kamenev and the others', and agrees with the Lenin line on the current party struggle. He adds, 'The plan for a bloc reveals the hand of Lenin – he is a shrewd fellow and knows where the crayfish hide in winter.' But he concludes that these manœuvres are, even so, less important than 'organizing the work in Russia' where, he argues, the Mensheviks are more effective; and he urges that, 'The most important thing is to organize the work in Russia ... In my opinion, our immediate task, the one that brooks no delay, is to organize a central group (in Russia), to coordinate the illegal, semi-legal and legal work at first in the main centres (St Petersburg, Moscow, the Urals, the south). Call it what you like – the "Russian section of the Central Committee" or auxiliary group of the Central Committee – it makes no difference, but such a group is as essential as air, as bread.'

This seems to have secured Lenin's attention. And the idea of a series of operative centres inside Russia was to be accepted. But in a few weeks Stalin was writing to the Moscow Bolsheviks about 'the storm in a teacup abroad', with Lenin and Plekhanov opposing Trotsky, Martov and Bogdanov. The bluff practicality had now got out of hand, with Stalin saying that the workers seemed to support the former group, 'but in general the workers are beginning to look contemptuously on "abroad", saying "Let them crawl on the wall to their hearts' desire, but the way we feel about it, he who has the interests of the movement at heart should keep busy; as for the rest it will take care of itself." ' As a way of impressing Lenin, this was wildly misconceived, and it is hard to imagine what Stalin thought he was doing when he wrote.

When Lenin got to hear of the letter, he was incensed. He told Ordzhonikidze, in Paris with him for six or seven months from November 1910, that though Stalin had done useful work, these jokes about storms in a teacup 'betray the immaturity of Koba as a Marxist'.

These letters had been intercepted and copied by the Okhrana, and supervision of the exile became stricter. However, he was released on the expiry of his sentence in June 1911, though he was required to live outside St Petersburg, Moscow and the Caucasus. He chose Vologda, but went to St Petersburg in September, where he again saw Sergei Alliluyev, but was almost at once re-arrested, and began a new three-year exile term in Vologda in December 1911.

In January 1912, Lenin organized, with only his own men present, the Prague Conference, at which the Bolsheviks finally split off from the Mensheviks and founded their own party. A Central Committee was elected with seven members (including the police agent Malinovsky) and four candidate members. Lenin was given the power to co-opt others, and soon after the end of the Conference he nominated Stalin, and the metal worker Belostotsky, to the Committee.

9

By now almost all Lenin's earlier aides had proved wanting. His allies against the soft tendencies in Social Democratic politics, in particular Bogdanov, had disagreed with him on philosophical issues. Lenin, very much against his will, had felt obliged to play down these (presumably basic) doctrinal disputes in view of immediate political action. But then Bogdanov and his allies had proved independent-minded on political matters too. Who was left?

When the Bolsheviks came to power many observers noted the lack of real talent among their leaders. Much of the revolutionary elan and attack came from the more militant of the former Mensheviks and others who had only joined the Bolsheviks months before the seizure of power – Trotsky, above all, but also figures like Antonov-Ovseyenko, who led the storming of the Winter Palace.

The Bolsheviks in fact were in bad shape. As Stalin himself wrote later, 'During the period 1909–11 the party went through a period of complete disintegration, with wholesale desertions, not only on the part of intellectuals, but also on the part of working men.' Or, as Molotov later told Djilas, 'Our party was in a very weak state, its organization not connected but scattered, and with a small membership.' In five years this small and disintegrating sect was to rule Russia.

It has been argued that Lenin's Central Committee selections were somewhat capricious and represented the feelings of the moment and that he was only really concerned to make sure of nominees who would follow his lead at all times. It is certainly true that the members of the 1912 Central Committee did not, for the most part, figure among the leading figures of the Revolution. Apart from Lenin and Zinoviev, only Stalin was re-elected to the Central Committee in April 1917. Kalinin was to become prominent later. Ordzhonikidze, of course, rose to the post-Lenin Politburo. Bubnov was to have high appointments of the second rank. Stasova, Lenin's secretary, remained a crucial minor figure. But Sverdlov, Kamenev, Rykov, Bukharin, Tomsky, Krestinsky, Rudzutak and Kuibyshev, Old Bolsheviks not in the 1912 Committee, had a far weightier future in the Soviet regime.

The 1912 elected members already included one Georgian, Ordzhonikidze, who had been one of the young Bolsheviks Lenin had brought to his party school at Longjumeau, near Paris. Lenin had met him at the Third Congress, in London, and found him promising. It seems plausible that Lenin had heard, and not only from Ordzhonikidze, of Stalin's tireless organizational intrigues against powerfully entrenched non-Bolshevik elements in the Caucasus – resembling, at a cruder level, Lenin's own. In any case, Lenin was long to value him above all as a ruthless and dependable enforcer of the Bolsheviks' will.

That Lenin nominated him to the Central Committee immediately after the Prague Conference, rather than putting his name forward for the delegates to vote on, is usually treated as an afterthought on Lenin's part. But Lenin, the great political pragmatist, was seldom subject to such sudden vagaries. And his conduct has another explanation: that the delegates had a fair idea of the other, or negative, side of Stalin's character, and might have voted him down. As we shall see, even in 1917 before Lenin's return, Stalin was refused a position because of 'certain personal characteristics'.

In any case, this was, in principle, the highest operational party body. Stalin's promotion meant that he was now in a position of weight and seniority.

Without this move of Lenin's, Stalin would have remained a minor figure, or at least would have needed more time to fight his way up. Lenin may have acted on inadequate information; nevertheless, when he came to Petrograd after the February 1917 Revolution, he did not go back on the decision.

Chapter 4

Rising Revolutionary

In Vologda, Ordzhonikidze brought Stalin the news of his election to the Central Committee, about which (Ordzhonikidze wrote to Lenin) 'He is very pleased ... the news made a splendid impression on him.'

Stalin got away from Vologda in March 1912. He went first to Tiflis and Baku – where he had a comparatively amicable discussion of party business with the (non-Georgian) Menshevik Boris Nicolaevsky, an even more famous escaper. Stalin then went to St Petersburg and entered serious politics, on the basis of his newly-won Central Committee membership. Here he found a new situation. The famous massacre of strikers in the Lena goldfields had just taken place, and a wave of protest strikes had followed all around the country. It appeared for a time, and was so taken by the Bolsheviks, that a fresh revolutionary upsurge was beginning. In the capital, Stalin wrote a number of articles.

One of these, published on 2 April 1912, consisted of a long indictment listing what the 'nation needed' and in each case the negative reaction of the regime. It is an interesting example of the more emotional strain in his rhetorical style, often described as 'liturgical', with its listings and repetitions. A more interesting comparison might be with the complaints of the American Declaration of Independence. The difference is largely in the specific character of the latter, and the inflated rhetoric of Stalin's article: 'tens of millions of peasants are starving' – a statement which had almost no basis in fact (though it would be applicable ten years, and again twenty years, later).

After the Prague Conference, Lenin had had a secret meeting in Leipzig with Bolshevik members of the Duma, and planned the Bolshevik newspaper *Pravda*. Stalin had arrived in St Petersburg when all the arrangements for its publication were well advanced. It would later be claimed that the whole enterprise was his, but in fact it was largely managed by the Okhrana agent Malinovsky, and the first editor was another Okhrana agent. An anonymous article from the first issue was later claimed to be by Stalin, though apparently it was really written by another.

There is a story of Stalin at this time, briefly alone with the nine-year-old son of a Bolshevik family, striking him on the cheek and saying that the boy would now remember him. There is said to be a Georgian peasant custom in which, on the visit of a prince to a peasant hut, the peasant strikes his little son so that he will not forget the occasion: a mnemonic method also found in the English 'beating the bounds'.

At any rate, Stalin was now for a few weeks at the centre of party activity in Russia and for a short time took part in various important discussions. He was re-arrested on 5 May 1912. He spent a few weeks in the Shpalerny Prison, later to have such a fearful reputation under Stalinism. He was then sentenced to three years' exile at Narym, in Siberia. In Vologda, en route, he again met Nicolaevsky, who was being sent to a well-populated exile town and therefore let Stalin have a kettle, which might be harder to come by in Narym.

This Siberian area, three hundred miles up the Riber Ob from Tomsk, was at that time a leading centre for political deportees. (Later, in 1930–31, nearly 200,000 peasants were deported into its swamplands on Stalin's orders and most of them perished. In Stalin's time of exile, however, food and housing were provided even for the political enemies of the regime.) Here he spent a couple of months. His colleagues in this special exile area included Vereshchak and the Bolshevik Yakov Sverdlov. But apart from a fairly jocose admission by Stalin that he duped Sverdlov into doing most of the household chores, there is little to be told of this brief exile. Stalin escaped again later in the summer.

2

At much the same time that he entered the central organs of the Bolshevik machine, he began to be known, though not yet exclusively, as Stalin.

Stalin, as we have called him throughout, had not yet claimed that name. 'Soso' at school, he was 'Koba' to his comrades in the revolutionary movement right through the first decade of the twentieth century – and he was still using it as late as 1911 in signing a letter to Lenin.

But this was not a permanent, or official, revolutionary pseudonym like Lenin or Trotsky. Stalin had many writing pseudonyms over the period. Sometimes he was 'Vasily'. He was 'Ivanovich' at the London Congress, and Lenin used that name of him as late as 1912. At this time his articles have various signatures: 'Salin'; 'K. Solin'; 'Koba Ivanovich'; 'K. Stefin'; 'K. Kato'. One article in 1912 used 'Stalin' and it was in 1913 that this became his regular pseudonym.

Stalin – the steel one – is on the same lines as 'Kamenev' (stone), or 'Molotov' (hammer). Its import is obvious. But this may not be the explanation, or the only explanation: 'Dzhuga' is said to mean 'iron' in one of the Caucasian dialects, and he was possibly drawing on his original name.

It had certainly been difficult for the party to keep 'Dzhugashvili' in mind. Even Lenin, writing three years after co-opting him on to the Central Committee, asks a comrade, 'I have a great favour to ask of you. Find out the name of Koba – Iosif D . . . . . We have forgotten it.' In exile in 1915 Sverdlov was still referring to him as 'Dzhugashvili' in his letters. The name Stalin had not yet stuck, perhaps had not yet been thought of even by its owner as more than a newspaper pseudonym.

By 1917, it had become 'official'.

3

In the winter of 1912 Stalin twice illegally crossed the Austrian border and saw Lenin. Their previous encounters, such as they were, had been among crowds of congress delegates in London and Stockholm. Now they met alone, or almost alone. The 'Old Man' was living in Cracow. They discussed the national problem, now much on Lenin's mind. From Lenin's point of view, as from Marx's, international proletarian interests were the central issue, and nationality was a temporary distraction. But recent years had shown something of the power of national feeling. Lenin required a formula by which minority nations within a future socialist Russia would have these primitive aspirations gratified without allowing them to undermine revolutionary unity.

Stalin himself had previously shown no signs of interest in pleasing or placating the national feelings of the Georgians or any other national- ity. It was Lenin who concluded that in a multinational empire, the national problem needed attention, that it could either be exploited by the Bolsheviks or become a hindrance to their struggle for power.

The orthodox Marxist view was, of course, that 'the proletarian has no country'. And this remained the principle of Rosa Luxemburg and other representatives of left-wing Marxism. Lenin's view was that the 'nation' was a category marking the epoch of capitalism; that socialism would overcome this and, eventually, 'merge' the nations; that 'the interests of socialism are above the right of nations to self-determination' – but that, since Russia was going through a period when nations counted, 'we require an item on our programme on the right of nations to self-determination'. As he was later to say, every serious belligerent in 1914 sought to use the minorities in the enemy alliance against their rivals, and so the Bolsheviks should use nationality as far as possible against their rivals in Russia.

When Lenin decided this, he determined on a brief theoretical work on the subject.

Stalin agreed with all that Lenin said, and was entrusted with putting their joint ideas into written form. He made an excellent impression. Lenin wrote to Gorki of a 'wonderful Georgian here, who has settled down to write a major piece for *Proveshchenye* [a 'legal' Bolshevik theoretical journal], for which he has gathered all the Austrian and other material. We are working on it.'

The result was *Marxism and the National and Colonial Question*, making, at some length, the points gone into above.

On the question of how far the work was indeed Stalin's, we are assisted by the fact that on his own he wrote (in 1915) an essay on the subject. This takes the basic Leninist view, but it is a far cruder – indeed shoddier – piece of work, as are two articles published in *Pravda* in March 1916. These contain some astonishing errors about American federalism – and noted, incidentally, that there was no basis for 'national oppression' in the USA. But this was not only a 'hopelessly provincial analysis', as Trotsky put it, but (as he also put it) showed that Stalin 'seemed to have entirely forgotten his own work on the national question, written early in 1913 under Lenin's guidance'.

The conclusion seems to be that *Marxism and the National and Colonial Question*, Stalin's chief theoretical work, was almost entirely the product of Lenin's instructions and editing. From Lenin's point of view, which he was later to regret, here was a minority spokesman who would be his agent in rallying the party to a rationally justified and strategically pragmatic treatment of the problem.

But even if Stalin wrote *Marxism and the National and Colonial Question* fairly strictly to Lenin's brief, Lenin valued the work, and wrote of it that it 'stands out in first place' among current Marxist writing on the matter. Robert C. Tucker suggests that Lenin's thoughts, at any rate a year or two later in his own 'The Right of Nations to Self-Determination', inclined to greater stress on national independence or autonomy and that this adumbrated the later discord on the issue between the two men. But if so, it was not then apparent to Lenin.

Stalin went to Vienna for some weeks in January 1913 to work on the draft and get help from Bolsheviks who could read German properly, including his future rival Nikolai Bukharin. He also met another future enemy, Leon Trotsky, again. Trotsky recalls his 'dim but not commonplace' air, and the enmity in his 'yellow eyes'. (In Vienna in 1948 the Soviet authorities set up a marble plaque to celebrate Stalin's working place of a generation earlier.)

This was Stalin's final experience abroad (apart from the few days of the Teheran and Potsdam conferences in 1943–5 in rather different circumstances). On his return, at the beginning of March 1913, he was arrested for the last time. He was sentenced to four years' exile at a place even more distant than Narym – the Turukhansk area over a thousand miles down the great Yenisei river in Siberia.

From there he wrote a highly characteristic letter to Lenin:

'My greetings to you dear Ilyich, warm, warm greetings. Greetings to Zinoviev, greetings to Nadezhda Konstantinovna. How are you? How is your health? I live as before, chew my bread, completing half my term. It is rather dull, but can't be helped. How are things with you? It must be much livelier where you are. I recently read Kropotkin's articles – he's an old fool, completely out of his mind. I also read a short article by Plekhanov in *Ryech* – an incorrigible old gossip! *Ekh-mah*! And the Liquidators with their deputies – agents of the Free Economic Society! There's no one to give them a drubbing, devil take me! Are they to be allowed to get off scot-free? Rejoice our hearts by telling us there will soon appear a newspaper which will smite them across the jaw, and lay it on heartily, too, with a vengeance.

In case you should want to write to me, the address is Turukhansk Territory, Yeniseisk Province, Monastyrskoye Village, for Suren Spandaryan.

Yours,
Koba

P.S. Timofey [Spandaryan] asks that his most bitter regards be sent to Guesde, Sembat and Vandervelde in their glorious (ho! ho!) ministerial posts.'

This letter merits our attention. We can be sure that, with little else to do, Stalin drafted it with care. Its most obvious characteristic is its appearance of bluff common sense suitable to a solid worker type. But this does not seem quite to come off: wrong notes are struck here and there. At any rate, this was the persona Stalin wished to convey. There is no reason to think that Lenin cared particularly one way or another, but at least it seems to have done Stalin no harm.

At first Stalin was with a whole group of Bolsheviks including Kamenev and Sverdlov. After various minor unpleasantnesses, the authorities learned (through Malinovsky) of an escape plan and moved Stalin and Sverdlov to the little settlement of Kureika, north of the Arctic Circle. Stalin took with him some books belonging to a prisoner who had just died, although they were supposed to have become common property. A Bolshevik sent to Kureika to complain was sent off with a flea in his ear.

In Kureika, Sverdlov found sharing a billet with Stalin something of a strain. At first he merely complained: 'He's a good fellow, but wants his own way too much in day-to-day life. I happen to like a certain amount of tidiness, and there are times when I get nervy.' But a couple of months later he wrote: 'We know each other too well. The saddest thing about exile or prison is the way a man's character comes out and reveals the petty side ... My comrade and I live in separate quarters now, and seldom meet.'

Stalin's secretary of a later period writes that this ill-feeling had arisen in Monastyrskoye a little earlier, with rivalry over a Bolshevik woman exile who preferred Sverdlov. At any rate it was probably during this period that Stalin, as his sister-in-law recounts in her memoirs, had an illegitimate child by a local woman.

4

After the few weeks of friction with Sverdlov, Stalin settled down to reading, writing, shooting, fishing. It was now, his daughter tells us, that he was really penetrated by the feel of Russia. The provincial towns of the Vologda Province, the dull marshes of Narym, even – apparently – life in the capital, had not more slightly eroded his Caucasian background. But now he settled down to several years in the special ambience of the Russia north of the taiga and the great rivers, of the long-lit summers and the deep snows of winter. Escape prevented, he had no responsibilities but to think and write and relax. He fished and hunted, and seems to have, in some sense, been more at home than he ever had been in the past.

The great spaces seem to have pleased him, in some moods, more than, or as much as, the gorges and mountains of his childhood. In his years of power he was always to live outside the city whenever possible, and to be much interested in his garden or estate. All the same, he last visited an actual Russian village twenty-five years before his death. (His holidays were to be taken, understandably, not in Siberia but on or near the Black Sea coast.)

The area near Igarka, in which he served his exile, was to become one of the harshest, and most heavily populated, of the Stalinist labour camp areas a quarter of a century later. In 1947–8 prisoners erected a marble structure round the little house where he had lived. Steamers going up or down the Yenisei were required to stop for two hours while their passengers paid their respects at the shrine. In 1961, word reached Igarka that this was obsolete. During the night the statue set up near the house was, without announcement, pitched into the Yenisei, and the building gradually became dilapidated.

Stalin went to Monastyrskoye in July 1915 for one troublesome intra-party case. Kamenev (as editor of *Pravda*) had been tried for treason along with the Bolshevik deputies to the Duma, on the grounds that Lenin had publicly committed the Bolsheviks to the defeat of Russia, under his slogan 'Turn the Imperialist War into a Civil War'. Social Democrats were required to work for the defeat of their own countries, but especially in the case of Russia. Kamenev had defended himself and his fellow accused by the claim (quite true in his own case) that they had not in fact supported Lenin's extreme position. Kamenev had already been censured by party circles. Now Sverdlov and others drew up a formal condemnation of this error; but Stalin, in what was thought of as a typical evasion, took a noncommittal line. As a result there was no majority against Kamenev and the case was dropped. This made a fairly bad impression on Sverdlov and others. But in fact the doctrinal dispute does not seem to have much engaged Stalin's attention, as with his previous apathy on émigré disputes which had so annoyed Lenin. In any case, his noncommittal attitude was, as often in such disputes, to leave Stalin at least relatively undamaged.

There is a photograph of Stalin with Kamenev and the others. In the years of high Stalinism it continued to appear, but with a small tree in the place where Kamenev had stood.

Stalin was soon back at Kureika. But in 1916, the tsarist government decided to call exiles to the colours. En route Stalin was brought back to Monastyrskoye, but remained aloof from most of the other Bolsheviks, causing ill-feeling.

They were all taken up-river to Krasnoyarsk and, in December 1916, Stalin was rejected for military service on medical grounds – namely his left arm. His sentence was nearly up, and he was not sent back to Kureika, but joined Kamenev and others at the small town of Achinsk. There, another exile recalls, he failed to shine, and remained 'taciturn and morose, quietly smoking his pipe', while Kamenev spoke brilliantly. The smoke irritated Kamenev's wife Olga (Trotsky's sister), and she tried to stop his smoking, without result.

For two and a half years Russia had fought an unsuccessful but not catastrophic war. No doubt there was war-weariness among the troops. But Russian losses were proportionately lower than those of France or Britain, and generally speaking the Russian armies had put up a sturdy defence. The besetting problems of supply and production had been largely overcome. There was little overt sign of any impending collapse of the regime. Even Lenin, as late as January 1917, ended a lecture to Swiss students, 'We of the older generation may not see the decisive battles of this coming revolution.' He was forty-six years old.

The weaknesses hidden from, or not grasped by, Lenin were not among the masses, but at the centre. 'The fish begins to stink at the head.' It was above all in the circles close to the ruling camarilla, among the establishment liberals, that it had come to be felt that the situation was intolerable. The Tsar and many of his current ministers were of narrow intelligence and shallow understanding. The Tsaritsa, suspected of sympathy with her native Germany and (until his murder in the winter of 1916) under the influence of the sinister Rasputin, was widely hated in patriotic circles. The political feeling was not against the war: on the contrary, it was for a more efficient prosecution of the war than the Tsar and government could be trusted to undertake. The regime's authority had become a hollow shell, ripe for collapse.

When the unexpected news of the Tsar's overthrow reached Achinsk in February 1917, Stalin, with Kamenev and Muranov (a Bolshevik Deputy to the Duma), at once set off for Petrograd.

Chapter 5

Revolution

The first few weeks after the February Revolution are among the most bizarre in the internal story of Bolshevism.

The train carrying the exiles took some time. On the way speeches were made, information obtained. At one stop Kamenev telegraphed congratulations to the Grand Duke Michael, in whose favour the Tsar had abdicated (but who had rejected the offer) – a telegram which was to cause a certain amount of trouble later.

But more remarkable was what followed the arrival of Stalin, Kamenev and Muranov in Petrograd.

A few days of food riots had brought down the three-hundred-year-old dynasty. Hundreds of thousands of people had demonstrated in the streets. The troops had refused to fire on them. Nicholas II had abdicated on 2 March. And within days suddenly there was a vacuum where power was supposed to be.

A Petrograd Soviet of Workers' Deputies had been established on 27 February, in the midst of the revolutionary events. This was done on the initiative of Mensheviks and Socialist Revolutionaries, though a few Bolsheviks were allowed on to its Executive Committee. The Soviet, in fact, had been created from above by the Executive Committee. Unlike the soviets of 1905, which were spontaneous workers' strike committees, this soviet was thus from the start run by the intellectuals and professional revolutionaries of the socialist parties.

At the same time, an exiguously validated constitutional body had come to the fore in the form of a Provisional Committee of the Fourth Duma, which declared itself the Provisional Government and had at least some claim to rule the country as a whole. The two bodies existed in a state of 'dual power', the Government exercising what authority it possessed under more or less constructive 'Soviet' criticism.

The dissolution of the old order was manifest in the unwonted luxury of the new Bolshevik headquarters. They had taken over the palace of the ballerina Matilda Kshekinskaya, the Tsar's mistress before his marriage, later to become in exile the wife of the Grand Duke Andrei and to outlive Stalin by many years.

Here the remnants of the Bolsheviks' Russian Bureau, which had been set up earlier by Lenin, assumed the acting leadership of the party. They were headed by Lenin's chief direct agent in Russia, the worker Aleksandr Shlyapnikov. He was to give trouble in the earlier period of Lenin's rule as leader of the Workers' Opposition, and be first degraded, then shot by Stalin. The same fate awaited the second figure, Peter Zalutsky. The third was Vyacheslav Molotov.

On 6 March they produced a legal *Pravda*. They called for a revolutionary government and opposition to the new regime.

When Stalin, Muranov and Kamenev arrived a few days later, there was a remarkable struggle. On 12 March, the Russian Bureau, by now already enlarged to a dozen or so members, voted to co-opt Muranov. Stalin, they noted, was on the Central Committee, 'and therefore it could be advisable to have him as a member ... However, in view of certain personal characteristics, the Bureau decided to give him only a consultative vote.'

Once again, and not for the last time, knowledge or experience of Stalin's behaviour resulted in a notable rebuff. The extent of this personal distrust and hostility is quite astonishing when we consider that it was taken to outweigh his high official standing. Moreover, it was a matter not just of keeping him out of the Bureau but of preventing him from having any power: power in Stalin's hands, the members seemed to be saying, is always misused. If, even in the course of revolution, a body of his party comrades could take such a stand, it indicates, to put it mildly, very strong reservations among the Bolsheviks about him and his attitudes, methods and intentions.

Kamenev too was ill-received, though in his case evidently on policy grounds associated with the moderate position he had taken on the war. It was decided to let him work on *Pravda*, though not to sign articles.

However, on 13 March, Stalin was after all admitted as a full member, and named to the *Pravda* board. On 15 March, a new 'presidium' of the Bureau was set up with Stalin, Muranov, Shlyapnikov and Zalutsky plus the self-effacing veteran Yelena Stasova. The same day Stalin,

Muranov and Kamenev were named Bolshevik delegates to the Executive Committee of the Petrograd Soviet.

This amounted to the defeat of Shlyapnikov. It is to be seen largely as a repudiation of the Leninist line on war and revolution. Shlyapnikov had been in the closest contact with Lenin while Stalin and Kamenev had been out of touch in Siberia. Lenin had co-opted him on to the Central Committee in 1915, and he was the true representative of Lenin's line.

But Shlyapnikov had no specific instructions from Lenin. Cut off in Switzerland behind the German lines, Lenin had not yet been able to send the party his evaluation of the totally new situation produced by the February Revolution. Meanwhile, Shlyapnikov's view was unpopular not only with the newly returned exiles, but also among many of the Petrograd Bolsheviks. Stalin and his fellows had general support when they took the view that they, the senior leaders on the spot, must handle the situation according to their lights – and that this meant abandoning extreme concepts as no longer applicable.

Over the next weeks, Stalin and Kamenev pursued a policy of rapprochement with the Mensheviks, of toleration of the Provisional Government, and of opposition to the slogan 'Down with the War'.

When Stalin took his seat on the Executive Committee of the Soviet, he seems to have been given a reasonably warm welcome by his old Georgian opponents Nikolai Chkheidze (now the Soviet's Chairman) and Irakli Tseretelli. Stalin made no remembered contribution to debate and seems to have spent his time mainly in sounding out and establishing relations with the other socialist delegates.

One of Stalin's colleagues on the Executive Committee was the Menshevik Sukhanov, who thus had a fairly good opportunity to observe him and register the effect he now made in circles outside the Bolshevik milieu. Sukhanov's *Notes on the Revolution*, based on his diaries of 1917, were published in Moscow in 1922 and praised by Lenin. Of course, his famous description of Stalin is in its own way subjective enough, but Sukhanov is recognized as an honest observer. He wrote of the impression made by Stalin:

'In those days, besides Kamenev, Stalin also represented the Bolsheviks in the Ex.Com. He was one of the central figures of the Bolshevik Party and perhaps one of the few individuals who held (and hold to this day) the fate of the Revolution and of the state in their hands. Why this is so I shall not undertake to say, since "influence" in these exalted and irresponsible spheres, remote from the people and alien to publicity, is so capricious. In any event it is impossible not to be perplexed by the role of Stalin. The Bolshevik Party, in spite of the low level of its "officers" corps, the overwhelmingly ignorant and casual rank and file, includes a whole series of great figures and able leaders in its general staff. Stalin, however, during the course of his modest activity in the Ex.Com., gave me the impression – and I was not alone in this view – of a grey blur which flickered obscurely and left no trace. There is really nothing more to be said about him.'

Sukhanov was, indeed, describing activity, or remarked presence, in the foreground of the Revolution, among the orators and agitators. In the background, at his desk, Stalin was more active. He continued to argue the 'moderate' line.

In the six articles and one editorial Stalin published in *Pravda* over the next two weeks, he argued that 'the stark slogan "Down with the War" is absolutely unsuitable,' and that the policy to be pursued should be 'pressure on the Provisional Government to make it declare its consent to start peace negotiations immediately' – just the line taken by Mensheviks and Socialist Revolutionaries.

It is fairly clear that most of the Bolsheviks now felt that the underground phase was over, and that a reunited, less doctrinaire Social Democratic Party would be the vehicle for the next phase of 'proletarian' political development. As far as they personally were concerned, they had already gained positions within the system, and perhaps looked forward to serious political careers. The alternative possibility, of a purely Bolshevik Soviet Government in which they would rise higher and quicker, must have appeared a chimera. At the time, it did not look as though a small party, with a small minority even in the soviets, could condemn all other political movements, remain in sectarian isolation and yet take over the state. Even in hindsight, it has every appearance of improbability. The younger Petrograd Bolsheviks who had advanced such a line may appear, and may have appeared to Stalin and Kamenev, to be naive sectarians. The whole situation was chaotic, novel, disorientating. And while, in the event, Lenin bet everything on the attempt to seize power, he only got his opportunity owing to a series of unpredictable events and unforeseeable blunders on the part of his opponents. Even then, final success was a near thing.

2

On 19 March, Lenin's first 'Letter from Afar' arrived in the *Pravda* office. The party's leader, in his exile in Zurich, had taken a quite different line from that of Stalin and Kamenev. Far from conditional support for the Provisional Government and pressure on it to make peace, Lenin urged an all-out revolutionary struggle and asserted that only socialism could bring peace.

Stalin and Kamenev printed the Letter, but cut it considerably – omitting, in particular, its strongest attacks on the Provisional Government and the Mensheviks. A second 'Letter from Afar' may not have been delivered; the question is obscure. If it arrived, as seems probable, Stalin and Kamenev simply suppressed it. It is clear that, as before, Stalin thought that he, on the spot, had a clearer view of the political situation than Lenin far off in Switzerland.

At an All-Russian Conference of the Bolsheviks starting on 27 March, Stalin reported on the Provisional Government. Perhaps to some degree influenced by Lenin's remarks, he was a little sharper than in his previous analysis, but he still urged support for the Government to the extent that it pursued a revolutionary programme – as Robert Slusser points out, this means that he took it as a matter of political tactics, whereas Lenin condemned the Government lock, stock and barrel as bourgeois and hence incorrigible.

The Conference accepted Stalin's line, and passed on to other issues. Lenin had sent a telegram, which reached the Russian Bureau on 13 March, demanding that there should be 'no rapprochement whatever with the other parties'. A proposal had emerged for the unification of the Bolsheviks with the left-wing Mensheviks. Stalin, who had been in contact with Tseretelli, favoured this, and argued for unification of all Social Democrats who had opposed the war. This would be on the basis of the 1915 and 1916 Zimmerwald and Kienthal conferences of various left-wing anti-war groups. But Lenin, though he attended these conferences, had condemned their decisions as inadequate.

There were voices against Stalin's proposal, in particular Molotov's, but he was empowered with three others to start conversations with the Mensheviks, with the responsibility of reporting on the matter to a joint meeting of representatives of the two parties.

The striking thing is that Stalin had persisted with these policies in the face of disapproval from Lenin. Perhaps he thought that when Lenin returned he would be persuaded that Stalin was right, or at least feel obliged to compromise with his lieutenants. If so, Stalin had totally miscalculated. He had misunderstood Lenin's certainty about the complete correctness of his own views – one of his most central characteristics. And he had underestimated Lenin's ability to dominate the Bolsheviks.

On 3 April Lenin and his group from Switzerland arrived in Petrograd. Kamenev and others had boarded the train out of Belo Ostrov, and Lenin's first remark was: 'What's this you're writing in *Pravda*? We've seen a few issues and we cursed you roundly!'

In history as rewritten under high Stalinism, Stalin's own meeting with Lenin was represented as one of total accord and support. 'It was with great joy,' ran one later account, 'that the two leaders of the Revolution, the two leaders of Bolshevism, met after their long separation.' There are paintings of the imaginary scene.

Shlyapnikov was in fact chief of the Petrograd Bolshevik reception of the returning leader at the Finland Station, while Chkheidze, for the Soviet, gave him a more formal welcome. Stalin's absence appears to have been due to his attending the talks on a possible Bolshevik–Menshevik merger.

The evening of his arrival Lenin told an audience of Bolsheviks and others (in what came to be called 'The April Theses') that peace would only be possible after the 'overthrow of capitalism', and that the army should be encouraged to fraternize with the Germans. A full revolutionary programme, including a fantasy of immediate 'communal' agriculture, was proposed. There should be no unity with the Mensheviks.

At a meeting of the Russian Bureau on 6 April Stalin still made some criticisms of Lenin's 'Theses', though Kamenev offered the strongest opposition. When the Theses were published in *Pravda* next day, an editorial note pointed out that they represented only Lenin's personal view; Stalin was, of course, co-editor. Kamenev continued to argue against Lenin in *Pravda*, but Stalin soon switched, and by 11 April he was supporting Lenin.

By now – for the three weeks before the Party Congress – he was sharing an office with Lenin, and over the next few months was to be a devoted executant and propagandist of the new line.

3

On 24 April the Seventh Party Conference opened. As rapporteur Lenin put his militant views. Dzerzhinsky, the future police chief, then said that clearly many delegates disagreed, and suggested a second report putting the other view. Kamenev delivered this, in the name of the Moscow delegation. At present, he said, the correct line for the Soviet, which the Bolsheviks too would have to follow, was to exercise 'control' over the Provisional Government.

After a prolonged and confused debate, it was decided to allow two final speakers for each proposition. Stalin led for Lenin, effectively as far as vigour was concerned, though quite misrepresenting Kamenev's position. Zinoviev supported him, less effectively. After Nogin and Rykov had spoken for the moderates, Lenin and Kamenev made final speeches.

A resolution was finally drafted, more on Lenin's lines than Kamenev's – Kamenev himself having to some extent come round to Lenin's way of thinking. The interesting point is something else – that Stalin had been nominated by Lenin as his chief supporter. He was bound to carry weight as a former leading advocate of Kamenev's line. And judging by the continued fractiousness of many delegates, his contribution may have been decisive to Lenin's victory.

On 27 April the Conference elected a new Central Committee. Lenin spoke in support of two candidates – Kamenev, of whom Lenin said that his conduct in 1915, in not opposing the war, had been purged, and that his 'wavering' in the early post-revolutionary months should be forgotten. Kamenev had a good record, and could not be expected to agree with the new policies without argument. As for Stalin, 'Comrade Koba has been known to us for a great many years. We saw him in Cracow where our bureau was located. His activity in the Caucasus was important. A good worker in all responsible jobs.'

Then, for the first time, Stalin was *elected* to the Central Committee. The voting was Lenin 104, Zinoviev 101, Stalin 97, Kamenev 95.

Stalin was also selected, naturally enough, to present Lenin's resolution on the national question. The main argument was about its guarantee to all nations in Russia of the 'right to secede freely'. Many delegates saw this as a concession to bourgeois nationalism, but Stalin and Lenin, in an adumbration of future Soviet policy, argued that the party must retain its unitary organization, and its branches in those nations given the *right* to secede would work against secession. Stalin pronounced himself as personally opposed to secessionist nationalism in the Caucasus, 'bearing in mind the common development in Trans-caucasia and Russia, certain conditions of the struggle of the proletariat and so on'. The whole issue was to fester over the first seven years of Soviet rule, and later.

Over the next month or so, the party's work was chiefly organization, agitation and propaganda. Stalin's old rival Sverdlov, back at the centre, was proving an organizational genius. The other leaders, especially Zinoviev, spoke with various degrees of effectiveness to factory meetings and so forth, in which Stalin hardly took part. He did not even write very much – an article or so a week.

When the First All-Russian Congress of Soviets met on 1 June, he was one of the Bolshevik delegates. Lenin, Zinoviev and Kamenev were the party's main spokesmen, while Sverdlov and Stalin acted as party whips. Here Stalin was tough and effective: his old fellow prisoner, the Socialist Revolutionary Vereshchak, was much impressed.

Meanwhile Lenin needed as much political talent in the militant line as he could get. From early May, in spite of the reluctance of his colleagues, he approached Trotsky, with whom he and the Bolsheviks had long been on bad terms, with an offer of leadership positions for him and some of his followers. Trotsky had just arrived back (from the United States) and had at once pronounced himself in favour of Lenin's revolutionary line. His first speech to the Soviet had a powerful effect. (After weeks of negotiation, Trotsky and his group were to merge with the Bolsheviks in late July, though Trotsky was soon under arrest, and unable to contribute much until his release early in September.)

While the Congress of Soviets was in session, the Bolsheviks, by now well financed and reasonably well organized, started to discuss mass action against the Government. Stalin threw himself with great vigour into a plan for a demonstration of workers and soldiers for 10 June.

The Congress of Soviets overwhelmingly condemned the planned demonstration and the Bolshevik Central Committee finally cancelled it. Stalin then resigned: but his resignation was not accepted.

Though another demonstration sponsored by the Soviet on 18 June was largely taken over by the Bolsheviks, the popular mood soon changed, and Lenin said that if power were now seized it could not be kept.

On 3–4 July, however, some of the newly Bolshevized soldiers, under the influence of radical Bolsheviks who ignored the Central Committee's orders, forced a demonstration, and this was to be an armed demonstration. The 'July Days' have aroused much controversy, but it seems that the Bolsheviks at one point hoped the demonstration would after all lead to the overthrow of the government. But Lenin, with Stalin's eventual support, retreated.

Of much interest from the point of view of Stalin's character is the story of Stalin's advice to the Kronstadt sailors on their conduct in the demonstration. The representative of the sailors asked Stalin, then on duty at *Pravda*, whether they should come with or without weapons. Stalin's reply was, or may have been, 'We scribblers always carry our weapons – our pens – with us wherever we go. As to your weapons, you can be best judges of that.' This story was only published in December 1929, when Stalin had just triumphed over the last of his political opponents. It was then recounted for the Soviet audience as an example of Stalin's 'cunning'. He had avoided telling the sailors to come armed, so that if things went wrong he could not be blamed, but at the same time he had hinted that they should indeed carry their weapons.

Historians have debated at length whether the story is true. Either way, Stalin's recounting it to an interviewer more than a decade later shows that he regarded the reply as much to his credit as a leader, and thus it certainly contributes to our idea of the way he thought about politics and of himself.

4

The July Days had one major result for Stalin. The Provisional Government ordered the arrest of the Bolshevik leaders. Trotsky and Kamenev went to jail. Lenin and Zinoviev went into hiding. The lesser figures (at least as the Government saw it) of Sverdlov and Stalin were the senior Bolsheviks left in charge Sverdlov again managed the machine, and Stalin was the leading figure on the political side proper.

Stalin had to handle part of the retreat of the Bolsheviks. He had a conversation with Tseretelli to negotiate the surrender of the Kshekinskaya palace, which the Government now took over.

Lenin hid out at the Alliluyevs', Stalin's current home, for several days before moving out of Petrograd to a safer asylum, and the two men had a further opportunity to deepen their understanding, and misunderstanding, of each other.

The Provisional Government now launched its most effective propaganda counter-attack. It had obtained some information about the German funds with which Lenin was financing the Bolsheviks, and invented more. On this basis, they alleged that Lenin was a German agent.

Lenin was not, of course, a German agent. But he had certainly received German funds (the whole matter was publicly aired in the Soviet press in the 1920s). At this point the Germans and Lenin had a common interest – the defeat of Russia. From the German point of view it was the same calculation which had allowed the 'sealed train' with Lenin and his colleagues to pass through Germany on the way to Petrograd in April.

But if Lenin was not in fact a German agent, the story of the German funds certainly made him appear one. Stalin was sent to the Soviet headquarters to deny the story and ask that it be suppressed. He spoke to Chkheidze, appealing for socialist solidarity. And Chkheidze, with the more reluctant acquiescence of the other Georgian Menshevik Tseretelli, agreed to block the story. However, it did appear in the newspapers. The result was a great falling off of Bolshevik influence, especially in the army units.

Stalin now received Lenin's latest theses. These argued that it was no longer appropriate to demand power for the soviets, since they were under Menshevik–Socialist Revolutionary control, and the Mensheviks and SRs had gone over to the side of counter-revolution. Lenin now relied on the Bolsheviks alone, and called for the mobilization of forces for an 'armed uprising'.

Stalin seems to have redrafted the theses, changing 'armed uprising' to 'determined struggle', and so it eventually appeared in the Kronstadt Bolshevik organ. But at a Central Committee meeting on 13–14 July, and at a Conference of Petrograd Bolsheviks on 16 July, the mood was still against militant action. At the Conference, Stalin was the leading speaker. His report was in principle a defence of Lenin's new line and he repeated the view that the soviets were at present unworthy of power. But he did not produce Lenin's theses, and as a result, a large group of delegates abstained from supporting them on the grounds that Stalin had neither presented them nor defended them. Stalin had certainly appeared as a leading figure. But he had made a dubious impression.

Lenin seems to have met Stalin shortly afterwards, and Stalin was soon, once again, more effectively Leninist. On 28 July, the Bolshevik Sixth Congress opened – a small, semi-legal affair, interrupted by a lack of quorums. Stalin, absent at first, in the end delivered the main report.

He again argued for Lenin's theses, though again in a rather less militant tone than Lenin's. From the point of view of the future, we may note the emergence of yet another rival – Nikolai Bukharin gave the report on the international situation.

In his peroration Stalin made this significant statement: 'The possibility is not excluded that Russia will be the country which paves the way to socialism ... we reject the out-of-date view that only Europe can show us the way. There is dogmatic Marxism and creative Marxism. I stand on the ground of the latter.'

A new Central Committee was elected. This time the four with the highest votes were Lenin, Zinoviev, Kamenev and Trotsky. The vote for the others, including Stalin, is not recorded.

There was now another lull. But at the end of August, in a blaze of incompetence and misunderstanding, came an open breach between Kerensky, the Head of the Provisional Government, and the Army Command under General Kornilov. Kornilov marched on Petrograd, and was defeated with the help of Bolshevized units. As Lenin saw, the power of the Government was now an empty formality.

Lenin, still in hiding, urged an early seizure of power. The Central Committee, with Kamenev leading the moderates, rejected this. Stalin seems to have vacillated. Trotsky was now in the ascendant – and was chosen on 24 September as Bolshevik candidate for chairmanship of the Petrograd Soviet. Sverdlov too, became even more prominent as a 100-per-cent Leninist. On 10 and 16 October Lenin attended, and dominated, meetings of the Central Committee. Only Zinoviev and Kamenev now voted against insurrection, and on 18 October published their well-known letter in Maxim Gorki's *Novaya Zhizn'*, saying so.

Lenin's fury was intense, and he demanded their expulsion from the party as 'strike-breakers'. Zinoviev wrote to the party paper *Rabochii Put'*, edited by Stalin (which had temporarily replaced the now illegal *Pravda*), denying Lenin's charges and saying that the matter could be discussed later. Stalin published this, and even added an editorial comment expressing the hope that the matter might 'be considered closed' as, in spite of Lenin's 'sharp tone', the Bolsheviks were 'fundamentally' in agreement. When the Central Committee met again on 20 October, Stalin opposed the expulsion of Zinoviev and Kamenev. When criticized, he offered his resignation as editor.

On 21 October, however, Stalin was sent as one of the Central Committee's ten representatives to the Executive Committee of the Soviet. At the same time Sverdlov and Milyutin managed the agenda for the forthcoming meeting of the Second All-Russian Congress of Soviets in which the Bolsheviks would control a majority and which they would thus be able to declare the formal basis of their power.

The crisis was now approaching. Stalin wrote on 24 October an editorial for *Rabochii Put'* calling for a soviet government. He stopped short of urging an armed rising, arguing that the workers should 'lay their demands before the Congress of Soviets', and form a government which would exercise power until 'the timely convocation of a Constitutent Assembly'.

Post-Stalinist historians in the USSR point out that this was scarcely a call for urgent armed insurrection. On the other hand, it has been argued that such a call could not have been publicly printed in quite those terms. But it may be that Stalin had not fully grasped Lenin's intentions. And, while Lenin had continued to value him in spite of their disagreements, and was to value him in future, he does not seem to have found in him the drive and daring that Trotsky, Sverdlov and others channelled into the seizure of power.

For we now come to a strange phenomenon. Power was seized on 25 October. But Stalin plays no apparent role. One prominent scholar, Adam Ulam, feels that this may have been due to a decision to keep him in the background, as an uninvolved Bolshevik, in case of failure – the role, in fact, that roughly speaking he had assumed after the July Days. There is no evidence for such a decision, and most writers treat his inactivity as (in Isaac Deutscher's words) a 'queer and undeniable fact'. The probable truth, it has been argued by others, is that in the urgency of organizing the coup, those chiefly concerned (and in particular Trotsky and Sverdlov) called in only those felt immediately necessary, and Stalin's name did not occur to them.

In fact, when we look at Stalin's conduct over the period March–October 1917, what stands out is his slowness to adapt to crises and changes. His instinct at every key moment was to temporize, think things over, and only then adjust to the new situation. Even when it was Lenin who took a sharp view, Stalin at first disagreed, and apparently really saw himself as an independent braking force, though sooner or later he gave in. His was not the temperament for the uncertainties of revolution. Or, at least, it might be said of his whole career that sudden crises other than those he himself had planned and initiated left him disorientated – as he was to be, indeed, on 22 June 1941.

Meanwhile with however little aid from Stalin himself, his party had seized the Winter Palace and arrested the Provisional Government. The

Bolsheviks were now in possession of state power. Early next year they broke up by force the Constituent Assembly, newly elected by popular vote, which Stalin had so recently described as the legitimate source of Russia's future government.

5

When Lenin proclaimed the Soviet Government, Stalin was listed (fifteenth and last) as People's Commissar for Nationalities. He was apparently reluctant to take the job, preferring, like Sverdlov, to return to his party responsibilities. Moreover, the post was not, like those of other Commissars, a former ministry still more or less in operational order. It had no staff, no premises and no evident state function. That is to say, it was partly a propaganda agency for the party, partly a channel for negotiations with secessionist governments. In any case, its workload was small, and Stalin had time for other activity. The Commissariat was got off the ground by the volunteer S. Pestkovsky, a graduate of the London School of Economics, who had at first tried for jobs in the Commissariats of Foreign Affairs and of Finance, before finding Stalin at a table in a single room, and being taken on.

Before the first meeting of the new Council of People's Commissars, Stalin had a peculiar and revealing encounter with Trotsky. The two men were in a committee room where, behind a partition, the Bolshevik sailor Pavel Dybenko (at this point Commissar of the Navy) was having an amorous conversation with his mistress, the aristocratic free-love advocate Alexandra Kollontai (whose views on sex Lenin deplored). Stalin gesticulated towards the partition and smirked in a vulgar manner.

Trotsky drew himself up and rebuffed this hail-fellow crudity: 'Stalin sensed that he had made a mistake. His face changed and in his yellow eyes appeared the same glint of animosity that I had noticed in Vienna. From then on he never attempted to engage me in conversation on personal matters.'

Trotsky certainly seems to have shown excessive prissiness, not rare in the puritanical intelligentsia, but perhaps requiring a modicum of adjustment to broader circles. Stalin was, no doubt, projecting his persona of an earthy representative of the masses. He too had misjudged the occasion. At any rate, we may see in this strange vignette some indication of the personal as well as political animosities of the future.

6

On 15 November, Stalin signed, and Lenin countersigned below him, the Decree on Nationality (officially 'on the Rights of the Peoples of Russia to Self-Determination'). This granted:

(1) The equality and sovereignty of the peoples of Russia.
(2) The right of free self-determination of the peoples of Russia, including the right to secede.
(3) Abolition of all privileges and disabilities based on nationality or religion.
(4) Free development of national minorities and ethnic groups inhabiting Russian territory.

The decree was, of course, primarily a strategic one, designed to rally the minority nations to the regime. But it also had a more general aim – to register Bolshevik good intentions and principles for the future, in case their still fragile power collapsed.

Stalin went to Helsinki on 27 November to address a Congress of the Finnish Social Democrats. He promised independence from Russia, and simultaneously urged that only workers' revolutionary power could be trusted. And he offered them help, should they need it. Independence was granted on 1 March, though in the ensuing Finnish Civil War the Bolsheviks were unable to give adequate help, and were eventually faced with a non-Communist Finland. Finland had always been a special case, not ruled by the tsars in their imperial capacity, but as a separate Grand Duchy with broad constitutional liberties. It was to remain a special case throughout Stalin's life.

Meanwhile, Stalin had been appointed to an informal foursome with Lenin, Sverdlov and Trotsky to deal with urgent problems – though any other Central Committee member who happened to be available was to participate. Sverdlov was busy with organizational matters, and Trotsky and Stalin were Lenin's usual confidants.

Stalin had offices near Lenin's in the Smolny Institute, the former aristocratic girls' school which was now revolutionary headquarters, and was often summoned for discussion, acting (as Trotsky put it) as 'chief of staff' over the next two or three months. It is almost certainly at this point that Stalin gained, for the time being, Lenin's full trust as an effective and devoted Bolshevik operator – a trust which was to stand the strain of Stalin's refractory conduct over the next couple of years.

Chapter 6

Civil War

When, in March 1918, it looked as though the Germans might capture Petrograd, the capital was transferred, after a two-hundred-year break, to Moscow.

Stalin took with him his sixteen-year-old secretary Nadezhda Alliluyeva, whom he was to marry the following year. The witnesses are reported as being Avel Yenukidze, the Georgian Bolshevik whom Stalin had known in his Tiflis underground days, now a close friend, and Stanislav Redens, the Polish Communist who had married Nadezhda's sister Anna. Or such is the usual version, though one recent Western account has the marriage taking place rather earlier.

There are several stories of Stalin forcing himself on Nadezhda in a sleeping car on the train. We have no means of knowing if this is true, and if so, to what degree. A certain roughness in seduction, if that is what happened, is very commonly reported of a whole series of Bolsheviks – though not, usually, of the intellectuals among them. Such things are difficult to assess, but if the story has any truth, it is clear that, given Nadezhda's character, she would never have married a man who had subjected her to mere rape in the usual sense.

Stalin had known the Alliluyevs for some time. Nadezhda's father, Sergei, had come to Tiflis at the end of the last century, married a Georgian, and been prominent in the Social Democratic movement. He later praised Stalin's role in the demonstrations of that time, but they do not seem to have met until 1904, when Stalin was back in Tiflis after his first exile. Nadezhda was then three years old. One story is that Stalin saved the child, and her eight-year-old sister Anna, from some risk of drowning, presumably in the Kura river.

In 1908 Stalin had again visited the family, now living in St Petersburg, and once more, briefly, in 1911. In 1912, back again in the capital, he had seen a lot of them, and occasionally slept at their place. His future sister-in-law writes of him as 'usually uncommunicative and reserved' but also capable of jokes and amusing stories: in particular he could give hilarious imitations of others. She describes one merry sleigh ride.

In his final exile, he corresponded with the Alliluyevs. They sent him letters and clothes, and he sent thanks. One letter was later published in Anna Alliluyeva's memoirs – printed in 1946, and suppressed almost at once. A view taken by Alex de Jonge is that, apart from other objections to the book, this particular letter may have shown Stalin in a light which he would have preferred to have left unpublicized – 'deferential, obsequious even, and a little sorry for himself'.

The letter runs:

'I am more than grateful to you, dear Olga Yevgenievna, for your kind and good sentiments toward me. I shall never forget the concern which you have shown me. I await the time when my period of banishment is over and I can come to Petersburg to thank you and Sergei personally, for everything. I still have two years to complete in all.

'I received the parcel. Thank you. I ask only one thing: Do not spend money on me; you need money yourselves. I should be happy if you would send me from time to time postcards with views of nature and so forth. In this forsaken spot nature is reduced to stark ugliness, in summer the river and in winter the snow, that is all there is of nature here, and I am driven by a stupid longing for the sight of some view, even if it is only on paper.

'My greetings to the boys and girls. Wish them all the very best from me. I live much as before. I feel all right. My health is good as I have grown accustomed to conditions here. But nature is pretty fierce: three weeks ago we had 45 degrees of frost.

'Until I write again.

Respectfully yours,
Iosif'

The letter does indeed convey a – perhaps temporary – mood not entirely suited to revolutionary heroism. But it is hardly anything to be ashamed of. And it does, at least, give a view into what Stalin was feeling, or at least saying.

On the day of his arrival in Petrograd in 1917 he had gone straight to the Alliluyevs, who were living inconveniently far out of town, though looking for a more central apartment. He told them of his exile, and amused them by imitating the revolutionary orators who had met the train at the stations on the way back: 'Holy revolution, long-awaited, dear revolution, has finally arrived ...' He asked the Alliluyevs to set aside a room for him when they found their new quarters. He moved in that summer.

Lenin, as he was to show later, valued the Alliluyevs' loyalty. They, including their growing daughters, were a family of devoted revolutionaries of the old type. The father was a skilled worker – earning enough to pay for an apartment which, as his granddaughter was to point out, was larger than a well-paid Soviet professor could afford in the 1960s. His children were brought up in the tradition of the cultured revolutionary intelligentsia. Stalin, though still to some degree projecting his rough 'people' persona, had adapted himself to their ways, and gave no offence. His personal modesty extended to his clothes, which were few and tattered. Olga Alliluyeva, the mother, mended and replaced them, and knitted him a scarf. He entertained and impressed the girls with stories of his revolutionary past. He told tales of his adventures in exile – of his prowess in fishing, how the local peasants admired him, his cunning in various situations.

Once Nadezhda was clattering around clearing the apartment, and Stalin put his head out of his room and said, 'What's all the noise ... oh, it's you! A real housewife has settled down to work.' Nadezhda bridled and asked, 'What's wrong with that?'

This homey badinage was perhaps suitable to the family surroundings. As Auden writes in another context:

> 'It's pleasant as it's easy to secure
> The hero worship of the immature'

There seems no doubt that Nadezhda was much taken with this experienced and important revolutionary. He used none of the crudity or coarseness with which he was later to treat her. Whatever the circumstances of his later wooing, it is clear that she thought of the marriage as a fine and noble enterprise.

2

In Moscow, Stalin and Pestkovsky sought premises for their National-ities Commissariat. They tried to take over the Great Siberia Hotel, tearing down notices claiming it for the Supreme Council of National Economy and substituting their own, but failed. Pestkovsky noted this as one of the rare occasions on which Stalin was defeated. However, they obtained other premises. Pestkovsky found his chief gloomy to work with and lacking in small talk. But Stalin gradually recruited a personal machine (notably I. P. Tovstukha, who would be his political secretary for nearly a decade).

Lenin's first priority was peace at any price with the Germans. He saw that for practical purposes no military resistance could be offered by the disintegrating remnants of the old armed forces nor yet by the newly constituted Red Army, founded in principle in February 1918. But many Bolsheviks still either expected help from the German pro-letariat to prevent a German attack or, even more illusorily, thought in terms of a 'revolutionary war' such as that which the French had waged in the 1790s.

At first Lenin could not win over the Central Committee, which accepted (by nine votes to seven) Trotsky's formulation: 'end of the war, non-signature of peace, and demobilization of the army'. At the next meeting, Stalin said that this 'intermediate position' at least pro-vided a way out. Then he suggested that 'it is possible not to sign, but to begin negotiations'. Lenin answered, 'Stalin is wrong,' and demanded acceptance of the German terms.

Over the next weeks, and at the Seventh Party Congress which followed in March, many resignations were offered – Trotsky, Bukharin, Pyatakov, Bubnov, Uritsky. Finally Lenin got his policy accepted. Stalin had once again, in Lenin's view, wavered, but was nevertheless sounder than Trotsky and the others.

The Treaty of Brest-Litovsk was signed on 3 March 1918. Now for a brief period the regime, though stripped of the Ukraine, the Baltic states and the Caucasus, seemed to be in control of the bulk of Russia.

3

This comparatively idyllic period ended in the early summer of 1918, when the Bolsheviks moved into a 'socialist phase', with nationalization, food requisitioning and all the other dictatorial measures later described as 'War Communism' – though at the time clearly presented as the fulfilment of the party's long-term aims.

Those opposed to the new regime had long assembled in the southeast, and civil war was about to begin in earnest.

We have to envisage a country precariously in the grasp of a determined minority. As Lenin said, if 200,000 landlords and so on could rule Russia, why not 200,000 Communists? He employed, it is true, the mechanism and much of the personnel of the old state. He used 'bourgeois specialists' not only in military affairs. But his policies after the spring of 1918 led to worker unrest on a massive scale and, since his method of obtaining food was armed requisitioning, to even greater peasant rebelliousness. Millions were soon starving, and the economy was in a state of collapse.

World War I had seen millions of Russian troops at the front. The old army had now been broken down, by the Bolsheviks themselves. And the Civil War was fought against White armies numbering only tens of thousands while (though there was now large-scale conscription into the Red Army) the Reds were only able to deploy in battle a few scores of thousands. In this war of 'little courage and less mercy' both sides were highly unpopular.

It was only by extreme measures that the Bolsheviks prevailed – even though, as Adam Ulam says, their terror methods alienated many possible allies.

The minor and ill-conceived insurrection of a few thousand Left Socialist Revolutionaries in July 1918 nearly overthrew the Bolsheviks. More than once the regime seemed to hang by a thread. A Czechoslovak force of 75,000 advanced without adequate opposition, and had it not been evacuated could easily have ruined the regime. When it was inaccurately reported that *two* British divisions had landed at Archangel, the leaders in Moscow took it for granted that the end had come. Time and again military and other crises shook Lenin's rule. Only interior lines, the use of the telegraph and the railways, and above all the utmost decisiveness, saved the new state.

For Stalin, the new period had three major episodes.

4

First, in June 1918, he was sent on a major mission to cope with the first result of the new Bolshevik moves – a catastrophic food shortage. As Director General of Food Supplies in the South of Russia, he was invested with extraordinary powers: 'Local and provincial councils of people's commissars, soviet departments, revolutionary committees, staffs and commanders of units, railroad organizations and stationmasters, organizations concerned with commercial shipping by sea and river, posts and telegraphs, provisioning organizations, all commissars and emissaries are required to carry out the orders of Comrade Stalin.'

And so Stalin, for the first time in his life, had plenipotentiary power. His extraordinary conduct in such conditions tells us an enormous amount about his personality and its potentialities.

Stalin arrived in Tsaritsyn, the future Stalingrad (and even more recently Volgograd), with an armoured train, a bodyguard of four hundred men, and Nadezhda in her secretarial capacity, on 6 June 1918. With the Ukraine in German hands, this was the best supply point for the food resources of the lower Volga and the North Caucasus. At first Stalin worked at this task. He fixed food prices and improved rationing. He succeeded in discovering and seizing significant quantities of meat and fish. He constantly asked Moscow for more money, railway repair gangs, equipment, control of the Volga and Caspian flotillas. On their part, the Moscow authorities kept complaining that food was not arriving, while Stalin told them to hold out until communications were restored. There was already sporadic White resistance, and on one occasion Stalin's train was attacked – believed to be the only occasion in his life when he actually came under fire.

In addition to his food supply duties he reorganized the local branches of the Cheka, Lenin's new secret police, and put down a number of plots, or supposed plots, executing the participants and all their known associates.

But at the beginning of July a new phase begins, and between then and the beginning of October comes Stalin's first military experience – later to be transformed in Stalinist myth into the crucial operation of the Civil War. The White and Cossack forces to the south were beginning to approach Tsaritsyn. On 7 July Stalin wrote to Lenin:

'Comrade Lenin!

I am hurrying to the front. I am writing only on business.

The line south of Tsaritsyn has not yet been restored. I am driving and scolding everyone who deserves it, and I hope it will soon be restored. You may rest assured we shall spare no one, neither ourselves nor others, and we shall get you the grain in spite of everything. If our military "specialists" (the dolts!) had not been sleeping and wasting time, the line would not have been broken, and if the line is restored it will not be thanks to the military, but in spite of them. South of Tsaritsyn large quantities of grain have accumulated on the rails. As soon as the line is cleared we shall send you grain on the through trains.

Have received your communication. Everything will be done to forestall possible surprises. You may rest assured that our hand will not flinch . . .'

And more reasonably, he demanded: 'Give somebody (or me), special authority in military matters to take urgent measures in South Russia before it is too late.'

Of course, there was already an official chain of command starting with Trotsky as People's Commissar for War. But on 10 July Stalin appointed Kliment Voroshilov to active command of the armies on the Tsaritsyn front, signing the order as 'Member of the Council of People's Commissars and Commissar for Nationalities', which of course was no authority at all.

Stalin had come to know Voroshilov as leader of an oil workers' strike in Baku, and when they were both delegates to the Stockholm Congress in 1906 they are said to have shared a room. Voroshilov had more recently been in the Cheka, and then raised and commanded an irregular Bolshevik force on the lower Volga.

Voroshilov was now in practice, and even to a large degree in theory, supporting a hoary revolutionary theory about the superiority of a people's militia over regular troops – in spite of definite decisions to the contrary in Moscow. His appointment was more or less overtly presented by Stalin as a rebuff to Trotsky's method (fully approved by Lenin) of staffing the Red Army with 'experts' – that is to say trained former officers of the tsarist Army. They were supervised and generally spied on by political commissars, but as was clear to all but a section of the more ignorant or high-minded Bolsheviks, without them the army could not have survived the Civil War. They amounted to some three-quarters of the Red officer corps. Many were kept in line by threat, or had families as hostages in Red territory. But others really supported the Bolsheviks, often seeing them as devoted to a centralized Russia and, as socialists, no worse than the Socialist Revolutionary–Menshevik regimes now arising beyond the Caspian as representative of the Constituent Assembly.

Stalin, however, seems to have thought that any competent Bolshevik, including himself, could be retrained in days as a strategist or tactician – an attitude which was to persist, in slightly less extreme form, right through his career. The mere drive of the struggle for power – in this case against Trotsky – was also a powerful motive. On the day Voroshilov was appointed Stalin sent another extraordinary letter to Lenin:

'Knock it into Trotsky's head that he must make no appointments without the knowledge of the local people, otherwise it will become a scandal for the Soviet power.

Unless you can give us airplanes and airmen, armoured cars, and six-inch guns, the Tsaritsyn Front won't be able to hold out and the railroad will be lost for a long time.

There is a great deal of grain in the south, but to get it we need a well-organized apparatus, which does not have to face obstacles from provisioning agents. The food question is definitely connected with the military question. For my work I need military powers. I have already written about this, but there has been no reply. Very well. In that case I shall myself, without any formalities, throw out the army commanders and commissars who are ruining the work. The interests of the work dictate this, and of course not having a bit of paper from Trotsky is not going to stand in my way.'

Stalin meanwhile was writing on orders from Trotsky to Voroshilov, 'To be ignored'. As for the 'military specialists', he arrested many of them in connection with the plots which he was continually discovering. Some were held on a barge on the Volga which was eventually sunk, in obscure circumstances, with all remaining prisoners apparently still aboard. Others were executed; on one occasion, described in recent Soviet publications, Stalin ignored an order from Moscow insisting on further investigation, and went on with the shootings regardless. When a subordinate suggested to him that this might cause problems, he is quoted as answering that it would not, on the grounds that 'death solves all problems: no man, no problem'. He was proved right; no more was said about the matter.

As to military issues proper, Trotsky thought at first that Voroshilov rather than Stalin was to blame for the total insubordination of the Tsaritsyn force. He later noted that at this point Stalin's support for Voroshilov was done 'in such a way that he could beat a retreat at any moment'.

This did not last. At the end of August a former tsarist officer, P. P. Sytin, was sent from Moscow as supreme commander of the Southern Front. When he arrived in Tsaritsyn, Stalin and Voroshilov declared that he did not have, as he claimed, 'full authority in the conduct of operations'.

On 2 October, Stalin and his Revolutionary Military Soviet of the Southern Front ordered the removal of Sytin and his replacement by Voroshilov. Sverdlov immediately telegraphed from Moscow. The Central Committee had just met, and

> 'examined the question of subordination of all party comrades to decisions from the centre. One does not need to prove the necessity of unconditional subordination. The proposal of the Revolutionary Military Soviet was accepted by the Central Executive Committee. All decisions of the Revolutionary Military Soviet are compulsory for the Military Soviets of Fronts. Without subordination there is no single army. Failure to fulfil decisions may be appealed to the highest organs – the Council of People's Commissars, or the Central Executive Committee, or in extreme cases the Central Committee. It is compulsory to put into effect the decisions of the Revolutionary Military Soviet. If you consider them harmful, or incorrect, we propose that you come here, to discuss together, to take the proper decisions. There should be no conflicts.'

So we find Sverdlov sending Stalin instructions on the whole principle of Bolshevik 'democratic centralism' which should have been known to the rawest recruit to the party – even in peacetime. When one adds that it is also an undisputed rule in any army in the field, one sees how far Stalin had gone in defying and departing from both Bolshevik and military essentials.

Trotsky finally wrote, on 4 October: 'I insist categorically on Stalin's recall. Things are going badly in the Tsaritsyn section despite superior forces. Voroshilov is capable of handling a regiment, but not an army of 50,000 men. However, I will leave him in command of the 10th Army if he reports to the Front Commander.' Trotsky added that he himself had ordered reports to be sent twice daily, but it had not been done. If this were not corrected immediately he would have Voroshilov court-martialled.

For a time Trotsky actually considered sending normal Red Army units to put down Voroshilov's semi-mutiny.

Stalin was summoned back, in an attempt to settle the problem. Trotsky insisted on the removal of Stalin's military clique.

'Do you really want me to dismiss them all?' Stalin asked. 'They're fine boys.'

Trotsky replied, 'These fine boys will ruin the Revolution, which can't wait for them to grow up. All I want to do is to draw Tsaritsyn back into Soviet Russia.'

Stalin returned to Tsaritsyn, but further action was still needed.

Lenin finally sent Sverdlov to Tsaritsyn, and after examining the matter he took Stalin back to Moscow. Another effort was made to reconcile the dispute with Trotsky and 'put aside former differences and arrange to work together as Stalin so much desires'. This seems to have been Stalin's attempt to extricate himself from the troubles which had arisen entirely because of his wilful behaviour. He was appeased by appointment to the Revolutionary Military Soviet of the Republic (though he never attended its meetings). Lenin appears to have appreci-ated his energy, and approved of his less controversial measures, though commenting that while it was permissible to sacrifice 60,000 men if necessary, in this case the Tsaritsyn losses were unnecessary. 'Had there been specialists ... one would not have had to throw away 60,000 men,' Lenin added. As Trotsky said, the Bolsheviks had always had great numerical superiority in the area, and the threat was easily containable given normal military action.

This whole episode was the first time Stalin had exercised a measure of power which was, for a while, almost untrammelled. He had acted with an almost unbelievable lack of discretion. He had grossly exceeded his powers. He had disobeyed orders, and refused to implement the Soviet policy on military experts.

The operations round Tsaritsyn were later represented as crucial to the whole Communist war effort. Holding the city was the key, it was argued, to preventing the Whites in the south and east uniting. The defence was a heroic and decisive enterprise against all the odds. None of this was true. The fighting was desultory. Tsaritsyn, though import-ant, was not strategically decisive – the Whites captured it later and held it for a year without much affecting the Red position as a whole.

What were the main results?

First, Stalin had shown himself capable of decisive action when outside the immediate control of the centre. It was this that Lenin valued – most of Lenin's colleagues were incapable of such leadership. Lenin's summing-up seems to be based on the principle, accepted in military thinking in all armies, that a faulty plan energetically pursued is better than indecisiveness. Lenin finally saw Stalin's disqualifications only in the last year or so of his life. We may ask why it took so long, when Stalin had given a variety of causes for complaint over the period. Even the obvious answer, that there were few Old Bolsheviks with qualities of decision and leadership, does not seem quite adequate. Nor is the fact that other able men, including Trotsky, Kamenev, Bukharin and Pyatakov, had also proved unsatisfactory at various times.

It is fair to say that Lenin was in many ways a poor judge of character, and unwilling to give up misconceptions about people. The Okhrana agent Malinovsky had been his favourite just at the time Stalin first entered the Central Committee. Malinovsky was a worker, for one thing, and in his way a capable executor of Lenin's will. But Lenin defended him long after the bulk of the Social Democrats viewed him as a traitor.

As to Tsaritsyn, Stalin evidently thought he could get away with it. And, in spite of losing the dispute, he was not seriously disciplined, so in a sense he was right about the latitude Lenin would allow him. The more interesting point is why he undertook these provocative, ill-considered decisions. Politically he was, no doubt, continuing a feud with Trotsky, and was to do so in similar situations over the next couple of years, if never again so recklessly. But beyond that he was revealed as determined to enforce his will as far as possible, almost regardless of the consequences. Given power, Stalin had shown the traits power brought out in him, and was to bring out in the future.

He had shown he could scarcely brook orders from others. His character emerges as demonic, egotistical, capable of cunning but not yet of the considered undermining of options suggested by others. Moreover, he had concluded that he possessed military skill, and in spite of everything he was never to abandon this notion. And he had accumulated a clique in the newly burgeoning army, as he had been doing in the new bureaucratic apparatus. It was not a matter merely of Voroshilov, but of others under him. Stalin was further to consolidate this foothold in the military on his return to the south in 1920. His clients were to include Voroshilov's protégé, Semyon Budenny, who headed a band of partisan cavalry. (Budenny himself was later to mention Trotsky's view of him and his men: they were a 'horde' under 'an Ataman ringleader ... where he leads his gang, there they will go; for the Reds today, tomorrow for the Whites'. Later, one of his commanders actually shot a commissar who complained about their sack of Rostov.)

On Trotsky's suggestion Voroshilov was transferred to the Ukraine. But he continued to pursue the same disruptive policies, apparently relying on Stalin's support. Trotsky again complained, and by now had a full report on the Tsaritsyn affair. A meeting of the Politburo condemned Voroshilov, and Lenin ordered him to desist, later telling Trotsky to intervene in the resulting crisis of materiel.

The whole Tsaritsyn episode is a truly astonishing exhibition of Stalin in action, disposing of real power for the first time and unable or unwilling to use it except in the service of his own characteristic desires and drives.

5

Soon after Stalin's arrival back in Moscow, he wrote a celebrated article in the issue of *Pravda* of 6 November 1918 celebrating the first anniversary of the seizure of power, in which he warmly praised Trotsky! It contains such phrases as:

'All the practical work of organizing the insurrection was done under the immediate direction of Trotsky, the Chairman of the Petrograd Soviet. It can be safely asserted that for the rapid desertion of the garrison to the side of the Soviet and for the clever organization of the Military Revolutionary Committee, the party is above all, and primarily, indebted to Comrade Trotsky.'

It seems that, as with his approach for a reconciliation a little earlier, Stalin was now, whatever his motives, really trying to effect a détente with Trotsky. Plainly, in the years that followed, an alliance with Trotsky might have been a possible manœuvre, one of the available political configurations. Trotsky was never to be won over; but for the moment he seems to have been somewhat appeased. He does not appear to have opposed Stalin's nomination to the Revolutionary Military Soviet.

More striking was Trotsky's attitude following the rise of the first great White Army under Admiral Kolchak, who took power in Omsk on 18 November 1918. The Red forces facing his advance were in considerable disarray. On 31 December Lenin telegraphed Trotsky concerning reports from Perm,

'about the catastrophic state of the army, and about drunkenness. I am forwarding them to you. They ask that you go there. I thought of sending Stalin. I am afraid Smilga will be too soft with Lashevich, who is said to drink and is unable to restore order. Telegraph your opinion.'

Trotsky replied at once that he was in favour of sending Stalin with full powers to restore order. Here we see the view of a man certainly not prejudiced in Stalin's favour, who nevertheless found him the most ruthlessly effective Bolshevik available. This implied encomium from such a source greatly reinforces the accuracy of Lenin's estimate.

Lenin and Trotsky faced the sort of problem that affects all political leaderships. Every member of a Politburo or a Cabinet, together with his positive qualities, has glaring deficiencies, and is involved in bitter rivalries. The Chairman or President or Prime Minister has to make continual judgements, achieve what appears to be the best available solution, or compromise, consistent with success. It is sufficient to read the memoirs of British Cabinet ministers of the 1960s to get some feel for the problem. Lenin's was different in intensity but not in substance.

Stalin was capable of producing order out of chaos, of crushing faction and hesitation. What he did with order when he had achieved it, especially in areas like the military of which he knew nothing, was another matter.

Stalin now set out, accompanied by the Cheka chief Dzerzhinsky, and arrived at the front at Viatka on 5 January 1919. The same day he sent Lenin a report (written by him but signed also by Dzerzhinsky), saying the situation was critical, and that 'the units sent by the Commander-in-Chief are unreliable, some are even hostile, and they need to be seriously purged.' 'Sent by the Commander-in-Chief', is, of course, a clear criticism of Trotsky – not himself 'Commander-in-Chief' but appointer and defender of that ex-tsarist officer, I. I. Vatsetis. Lenin telegraphed demanding more concrete answers to the military problem, but got little satisfaction. Stalin was back within the month, with a long report blaming the Revolutionary Military Soviet. Lenin then appointed him head of a new Control and Inspection Commission under the Defence Council, with powers of organization behind the front, but not at the fronts.

Lenin still valued Stalin's abilities, but may have hoped to detach them from the direct strategic and tactical problem. At any rate, when Stalin was decorated for his war services no mention was made of the Eastern Front episode (nor of the Tsaritsyn affair), but his next exploit, Petrograd, was lavishly praised.

This, again, has its odd points. It appeared in May 1919 that a joint White Russian–Finnish–British offensive against Petrograd was in the offing. In May, Lenin sent Stalin to cope. In fact the military threat was negligible, but Zinoviev had panicked. Two minor forts went over to the Whites on 13 June and Stalin organized their recapture, overriding professional advice; by 16 June they were again in Red hands. Two days later Stalin reported a 'vast conspiracy' among the officers at Kronstadt and elsewhere (apparently just men who had disagreed with him) and executed sixty-seven of them. It would be wrong to give the impression that Stalin was alone in seeking to improve morale by mass execution: Trotsky too was active in this way. But the main interest in this episode lies in the letter Stalin wrote to Lenin on the recapture of the forts, which ended:

> 'The naval specialists assert that the recapture of Krasnaya Gorka from the sea runs counter to naval science. I only deplore this so-called science. The swift capture of Krasnaya Gorka came about as a result of the crudest intervention by me and other civilians in operational matters, even to the point of countermanding orders on land and sea and imposing our own.
>
> I consider it my duty to announce that I shall continue to act in this way in future in spite of all my reverence for science.'

Trotsky says that Lenin was annoyed by this telegram and its 'provocative braggadocio', as well he might be. Apart from anything else, it was an open attack on Lenin's and Trotsky's ideas about using military specialists. Psychologically, it is astonishing. Once again Stalin is shown as – openly – exhibiting a manic, even on the face of it self-defeating, egotism. His conviction that he could judge a situation better than the professionals was to be with him all his life – not only as to military science, but in physics, biology and other fields, and always to the detriment of his own plans.

Stalin was back in Moscow on 3 July. After a tour of the Western Front, where nothing much was happening, he was sent to the Southern Front on 3 October. The White General Denikin was mounting a major offensive against Moscow, which ground to a halt about three weeks later. Stalin now wrote another of his astonishing letters. Here he argues

85

at length against one of the Red high command's alternative plans for a counter-offensive – in fact one briefly considered and already abandoned. Stalin argues that the plan he favours 'must be adopted without delay' and adds, 'without this my work on the Southern Front will be meaningless, criminal and futile and this will give me the right, or rather compel me, to go anywhere, even to the devil himself, rather than to remain on the Southern Front'.

In the days of his power, Stalin's analysis was put forward as an example of his supreme military skill. At the time, he was censured by the Politburo for supporting arguments with the threat of resignation (though Trotsky had only recently put in his resignation and been asked to remain by a large majority, including Stalin ...). But of course the most striking thing, once again, is the extraordinary and characteristic tone. The letter was, as Lenin saw, an immediate political manœuvre. But it was also in a profounder sense a declaration of a personal right to power; indeed, up to a point, it was yet another gamble of Stalin's actual political value against a further extension of his influence and power.

Stalin at one point refused to add his signature to that of the front commander, Yegorov, on the Commander-in-Chief's order to transfer forces. A political commissar's signature was necessary to validate the order, and eventually that of Central Committee member R. I. Berzin, the other political commissar, was obtained. But the troops were even then not transferred. Lenin, Trotsky tells us, said in somewhat embarrassed fashion, 'What can we do about it? Stalin again caught in the act.'

On the other side of the coin, Trotsky recalls that at this time he asked the Old Bolshevik Serebryakov, then working with Stalin on the Southern Front, if he could not manage things without Stalin, to economize on staff. He answered, 'No, I cannot exert pressure like Stalin. It is not my speciality.'

On 20 November 1919, the Central Executive Committee awarded the first Orders of the Red Banner. Trotsky was the obvious recipient, but then it was learned that Stalin too was to be honoured. Kalinin asked in surprise, 'For what?' Bukharin took him aside afterwards and explained, 'Can't you understand? This is Lenin's idea. Stalin can't live unless he has what someone else has. He will never forgive it.'

In early 1920, Stalin was again arguing with Moscow. Lenin complained of his 'carping', and wrote to tell him to cooperate and 'not pick a quarrel about departmental fields of competence'.

Back in Moscow in April 1920, he was sent late in the following month to the fifth and last of his military-connected assignments. The Poles had invaded and captured Kiev. An attempt to cut them off failed, in part (apparently) because Stalin and his military henchman Yegorov mismanaged Budenny's new 1st Cavalry Army. The Poles retreated in reasonably good order and the Red counter-invasion followed in July. The main attack was on the northern flank, where Tukhachevsky struck north of Warsaw, and was eventually defeated. The Red dispositions were in any case risky, but Stalin and his associates attacked Lwow in the south, disobeying orders to transfer troops to assist Tukhachevsky. They are usually blamed, at least in part, for depriving the invasion of whatever chances it had. Lenin, at least, took this view: 'Who on earth would want to go to Warsaw by way of Lwow?'

Post- and pre-Stalinist analyses published in the USSR regard Stalin's actions as at least (as Robert Tucker sums it up) 'an extremely significant contributing factor' to the defeat. The question was debated in closed session at the Tenth Party Congress in 1921, when Stalin laid the blame on Smilga, as political representative at Tukhachevsky's headquarters. But this was unconvincing. 'In silent hostility the congress listened to the sullen orator with that yellow glint in his eyes,' is how the naturally unfriendly Trotsky describes the scene. He adds that the speech hurt Stalin, and he received no support. The general feeling was that Stalin and his military clique were trying to gain prestige on their own by an independent victory, and simply ignored the bigger picture.

When Stalin was in power, it was asserted that the Lwow operation was correct and that Trotsky and Tukhachevsky had acted as traitors. The incident thus greatly rankled in later years (and the whole Soviet army suffered as a result: but that was seventeen years later).

Stalin had complained on 20 February 1920, when Lenin had asked him to speed up the transfer of troops to the Caucasus, that this was the job of the High Command, 'not that of Stalin, who is overburdened with work as it is'. Lenin reproached him for arguing about jurisdiction instead of doing all he could to help. And just before the Polish debacle, Stalin had written Lenin that he was exhausted and could only manage another two weeks' work before he took a rest. He seems to have been fairly ill at various times during these years. Lenin was concerned, and advised specialists and even surgery which, as McNeal points out, suggests the possibility of ulcers. On 17 April 1920, the day of Tukhachevsky's defeat, Stalin was in Moscow for the Ninth Party Conference. He asked for two weeks' leave, which was granted, but during the leave he applied to the Politburo for permanent relief from military duties.

The military side of this portion of Stalin's career was over.

Stalin's exploits were less striking than he claimed at the time, and as Stalinist historiography later insisted on. Moreover, they need also to be assessed from the broader Bolshevik perspective. As early as the spring of 1918, the Red Army had six fronts and nineteen armies. Over the Civil War, these figures increased. And every front had prominent Bolsheviks sent to oversee critical actions. At the end of hostilities, Stalin had not impressed the party membership as a whole with any specially outstanding reputation in military affairs.

As Trotsky points out, at least eleven senior Bolsheviks – including I. N. Smirnov, Smilga, Ordzhonikidze, Frunze and Antonov-Ovseyenko – spent the entire three years of the Civil War at the front, some of them with immeasurably more effect than Stalin, either as civilian members of the front command or as military commanders, like Sokolnikov and Lashevich. Stalin only spent about a third of this time in the field.

It was a peculiar career, and on the face of it marked in the main by factiousness, boastfulness, sulking and incompetence. And there is no doubt that these aspects of Stalin's character are strikingly illustrated time and time again. But there were compensatory points. The capture of the Petrograd forts had been a success, and though small in substance it was a great psychological relief to the regime after the panic preceding it. The Southern Front, whatever the clumsiness of Stalin's 'strategic' letter, had performed handsomely in the final victory over Denikin's White Army. If Stalin had erred in Poland, so had Lenin – who had ignored advice from Radek and others that the Poles would fight him to the last. And Stalin had, when not intervening in military affairs, managed the vast territories in the fighting areas with the maximum firmness and effectiveness.

And if over the whole Civil and Polish War period Stalin had thrown his weight about in a way that sometimes exasperated Lenin, this may be seen as a sign, even though exaggerated, of confidence in his own indispensability.

6

The history books, Stalinist, anti-Stalinist and non-Stalinist, write mainly about the military side of events when dealing with this period, but this only gives us a partial view. From 1918 to 1921 the desperate struggle to hold power was not only against organized White, Cossack and Polish formations. Even more critical, and more continuous, intense and prolonged, was the fight to impose the regime on the population as a whole.

'War Communism' entailed the seizure of food from the peasantry, and the suppression of peasant resistance, sometimes on the scale of single villages, sometimes against peasant armies as large as any fielded by the Whites. The ill-organized popular resistance was not everywhere handled as effectively as by Stalin. It culminated in March 1921 with the Kronstadt rebellion. This was the last straw which forced Lenin to abandon War Communism in favour of the New Economic Policy, restoring the market mechanism in the countryside.

The economic, or rather anti-economic, policies of the Bolsheviks were the main cause of the newest disaster to afflict Russia – the frightful famine of 1921, in which about 5 million people died, bringing the excess mortality of the post-revolutionary period up to some 14 million. Stalin, in the Kremlin, had sufficient food. He was a member of a Commission on Famine Relief, but his main work was in checking Herbert Hoover's American Relief Administration. Perhaps the most effective humanitarian effort ever launched, this programme saved millions of lives in the Volga and elsewhere. Stalin, like most of the Bolsheviks, regarded it with distaste and suspicion. But while most of them accepted it as an unfortunate necessity, Stalin became involved in various schemes against the Americans, starting with an absurd proposal to charge them for the transport of the food they brought. He was specifically given responsibility for the liquidation of the unofficial relief committee which provided the main backing of the American effort, but consisted largely of surviving Mensheviks. Lenin suspected them of working on this 'with counter-revolutionary aims'. When the Americans were leaving Stalin had these Russians arrested, and they would have been executed but for vigorous intervention by Hoover and others.

As to Stalin's record outside Moscow, even the military errors were evidently not enough to counterbalance Lenin's view that he could be relied on to act decisively and suddenly, as the situation required.

Moreover, by a stroke of good fortune for Stalin's ambitions, Sverdlov had died of Spanish flu on 16 March 1919, making Lenin's pool of effective administrators smaller than ever.

The political situation was by all usual standards extraordinary. If we judge it by the criteria we may feel, consciously or unconsciously, to be natural, we cannot grasp it. The huge territories of Russia were now ruled by a party which on the eve of revolution had numbered no more than about 250,000 and even in 1920 no more than 300,000. And of these, the majority were new and junior converts. As Lenin said '[The party's] policy is determined at present not by its rank-and-file, but by the immense and undivided authority of the tiny section which might be called the party's Old Guard.' It was from this narrow cadre alone that all the ruling elite were to be drawn for at least another decade.

But who were the Old Bolsheviks? They had been, only a few years earlier, a small millennarian sect. They were a very thin segment of the population. Their experience had been in sectarian organization and in doctrinal dispute, like some underground Gnostic brotherhood in ancient Alexandria.

It was a very strange and shallow reservoir from which to draw the leadership, at every level, of a large state. It included men of intelligence and men of practical ability (and these were not necessarily the same). Revolution and civil war had, by a process of natural selection, tended to bring these to the top. But there were not many of them. We should remember that in the struggles ahead, Stalin was not competing against the whole of a country's potential political talent; indeed, there was in any case little political experience available in Russia. Lenin won against Kerensky: it would have been vastly more difficult against even the German Social Democratic leaders Noske and Scheidemann. Stalin was to face a narrower field still.

Apart from his roving commitments, Stalin was often in Moscow, running his Commissariat of Nationalities – if not with any notable results. In March 1919, Lenin made him in addition People's Commissar of State Control, later merged into the Workers' and Peasants' Inspectorate, a body established in the hope of controlling a pullulating and inefficient bureaucracy by means of a fresh set of bureaucrats. It is clear that the number of effective Communists Stalin demanded were never made available – he asked for over a thousand of the very best, but got only 250 of dubious quality, most of them (according to Trotsky) dropouts from the main administration or scraped up from nowhere.

As always with such bodies in Soviet conditions, the Inspectorate had little effect.

At the founding of the Communist International on 4 March 1919, Stalin was present with Lenin, Trotsky, Zinoviev and Bukharin, as one of the Russian delegates.

On 18–23 May 1919 he attended the Eighth Congress of the party and was elected to the two new bodies – the Politburo (henceforth the central organ of power) and the Orgburo, which at this time was supposed to be a subcommittee of the Central Committee concerned with party organization. When it was suggested (at the Eleventh Party Congress in 1922) that no one could carry out all Stalin's party responsibilities and at the same time administer two People's Commissariats, Lenin replied that no one could name another suitable candidate for the high political responsibilities of the Nationalities Commissariat 'other than Comrade Stalin' and, 'the same applied to the Workers' and Peasants' Inspectorate. A gigantic job ... you have to have at the head of it a man with authority.' This shows how Lenin now judged Stalin, and the extent to which the latter's reputation had grown, regardless of particular errors and insubordinations.

7

Though the White armies had been finally defeated by November 1920, and peace had been made with Poland in October, one military task remained. In the Caucasus independent republics had come into existence in Azerbaijan, Armenia and Georgia. Azerbaijan had been taken over in April 1920 by Bolshevik forces under the control of Ordzhonikidze. And in early December Armenia succumbed.

But Menshevik Georgia had given Lenin pause, and for some time he had restrained Ordzhonikidze, who had been urging invasion since the moment he had seized Azerbaijan. Lenin had in fact signed a treaty in May 1920 formally recognizing Georgia's independence under Stalin's old patron Noe Zhordania, and explicitly renouncing sovereignty: 'Russia recognizes without reservation the independence and sovereignty of the Georgian State and renounces of its own will all sovereign rights which had appertained to Russia with regard to the people and territory of Georgia', and at the same time 'obliges itself to desist from all interference in the internal affairs of Georgia'. In November 1920 Stalin was sent on a tour of inspection of Ordzhonikidze's fief, and Lenin telegraphed for his opinion. Stalin seems to have agreed on temporary abstention from invasion, and (elsewhere) gave as his reason that he hoped the Menshevik regime would gradually crumble and become detached from its Western supporters under non-military pressure. Lenin himself feared that invasion might actually trigger 'a new war' with the Western powers, but he also saw that Georgia was particularly unassimilable to the Bolshevik order.

While in the Caucasus, Stalin made a triumphant return to Baku. In the Azerbaijan capital, Ordzhonikidze gave him a welcome which was excessively adulatory by the standards then prevailing, though much resembling what came to be accepted later during the period of the 'cult of personality'. No doubt Ordzhonikidze gauged his guest correctly. The local Central Committee announced that:

'Comrade Stalin, a worker leader of exceptional self-dedication, energy and stalwartness, the only tested and generally recognized authority on revolutionary tactics and leader of proletarian revolution in the Caucasus and the East, had come on a visit. Knowing Comrade Stalin's modesty and dislike of official pomp, the Central Committee of the Azerbaijan Communist Party (bolshevik) had to give up the idea of special meetings connected with his arrival. The Central Committee believes that the best greeting and reception which our party, the Baku proletarians, and working people of Azerbaijan could give our dear leader and teacher would be to bend every effort again and again to improve party and soviet work in every way. All out for harmonious militant work worthy of the seasoned proletarian fighter Comrade Stalin – the first organizer and leader of the Baku proletariat.'

In fact, Ordzhonikidze, contrary to the announcement, did organize a ceremonial meeting of the Baku Soviet. Stalin spoke, predicting revolution in the east. He also sneered at 'backward Tiflis among the Georgian social-innkeepers'.

When he got back to Moscow he gave an interview to *Pravda* (30 November 1920) saying that Menshevik Georgia 'is now living its last days'. In January 1921 he came out in full support of a further strong request from Ordzhonikidze to invade Georgia, and Lenin now finally came around to their view. On 15 February, supposedly in response to a feeble 'rising' by a few Georgian Communists, the Red Army attacked.

After ten days of fighting Georgia succumbed to a vastly superior force. Lenin still wanted to handle his new prize carefully, and suggested that some Mensheviks might join the new Georgian government. But Ordzhonikidze stood for a harsher line to his homeland.

So did Stalin. He was not directly involved in the operations. He seems to have had an appendectomy in December 1920 (Lenin checked daily with the doctors). And though he had recovered quickly, on 30 April 1921 he was ordered by the Politburo to take the cure at the watering place of Nalchik in the North Caucasus. During his time there, in June–July 1921, he went to Tiflis at Ordzhonikidze's invitation to attend a plenum of the Bolsheviks' Caucasian Bureau which had organized the re-annexation of the Transcaucasus. It was his first visit to the country for nine years.

It was not a success. During the plenum he spoke at a meeting of railway workers, his old power base. He was shouted down with cries of 'renegade' and 'traitor'. Two old Mensheviks in the audience received ovations. One, Alexander Dgebuadze, said, 'Why have you destroyed Georgia? What have you to offer by way of atonement?' The other, Isidor Ramishvili, was carried up to the platform, and spoke instead of the official guest. Stalin is reported to have grown pale, and he left the hall with his Cheka bodyguards.

At a meeting of the Tiflis party organization which followed this debacle, Stalin was at his most vengeful. He attacked the local Bolshevik leadership for softness, and ordered them to 'crush the hydra of nationalism', to cauterize 'with red-hot irons'. One passage is quoted:

'You hens! You sons of asses! [a common epithet among Georgians and others]. What is going on here? You must draw a white-hot iron over this Georgian land! ... It seems to me that you have already forgotten the principle of the dictatorship of the proletariat. You will have to break the wings of this Georgia! Let the blood of the petit bourgeoisie flow until they give up all their resistance! Impale them! Tear them apart! Make them remember the days of Shah-Abbas!' [the bloodthirsty Persian invader who had ravaged the country in the eighteenth century].'

Even so, a partial realization of the political feelings of the Georgian population led to comparatively mild treatment of some of the Mensheviks. Zhordania and others had escaped before the final subjugation. But over sixty Mensheviks were simply expelled to the West in 1922, among them Stalin's old schoolmate Iremashvili. He had been offered a post if he conformed to the new regime, but had refused and had been arrested. His sister is reported pleading with Stalin. At any rate the milder measure was taken – as indeed it was with leading Russian Mensheviks, including Martov himself.

Stalin now removed from the chairmanship of the local Council of People's Commissars his old rival Filip Makharadze, who had been following Lenin's comparatively conciliatory line, replacing him with Budu Mdivani (who was later to prove even more resistant to the harder policy).

One comment in Stalin's speech to the Tiflis Bolsheviks has not received as much attention as it deserves. He said that, on coming back to Tiflis after so many years, he was unpleasantly struck by the lack of the solidarity that had earlier existed between workers of different nationalities, and by the way nationalism had developed among the workers and peasants.

There seems no doubt, in fact, that he (with Ordzhonikidze and others) had thrown in their lot with and given their allegiance to what was then a broad internationalist or supranationalist movement, and that they were unable to come to terms with the fact that a powerful, and almost unanimous, nationhood had developed which rejected that line. In their youth the Georgian landowning class had largely accepted, and been incorporated into, the supranational tsarist order. The peasants were inactive. And the new workers' movements were of mixed nationality, with the Bolsheviks in particular having a multi-national membership.

Stalin was, apparently, surprised to find, half a generation later, that the feeling of nationality he felt the civilized world was growing out of, as he had himself grown out of it after the adolescent fervour of his early teens, had instead flourished and strengthened. His old rivals, the Georgian Mensheviks, had understood what he had failed to understand, and had won the support of the revived nation on a programme of real and total independence.

To some extent this rebirth of nations, and not only in Georgia, had taken all the Bolsheviks by surprise. Lenin himself had great difficulty in coming to terms with the resurgence of the Ukrainian nationality in the twentieth century, after a hundred years of suppression. It is true that Lenin had understood in a general way even before World War I that there was a 'national question' in Europe and especially in the Russian Empire. But his and Stalin's solution was inadequate, and admittedly tactical: and was anyhow largely concerned with the established nations.

By 1921, Lenin and Stalin remained in agreement on the central point of the necessity of Communist rule wherever it lay in their power to impose it. But by now Lenin had learnt more about the power of nationality, and urged the maximum possible concessions compatible with Communist rule – especially in Georgia. Stalin had not: he stood for derisory concessions and maximum force – especially in Georgia.

Over the period since 1917, Stalin had supported all Lenin's main policies, sometimes with temporary reservations, but he was always to be relied on at the critical moment. He had not followed Zinoviev and Kamenev in their opposition in November 1917, nor Bukharin the following year. He had recently stood by Lenin against a powerful effort by Trotsky to create labour armies, which had reached an acrimonious crisis at the Ninth Party Congress.

Only now do we see a real dispute with Lenin. On the Soviet nationality policy in general, a long controversy ensues. On the Georgian issue itself Stalin, opposed both by Lenin and by the Georgian Communists, and supported only by Ordzhonikidze (who had also made his career in Russia) and other déraciné Bolsheviks like the Pole Dzerzhinsky, stubbornly fought against Lenin, almost to the point of his own political ruin.

Meanwhile, we may look at his extreme anger in the following light. He had been rejected by his own people, and even by that section of it on whom he had a special claim. One more of his links to humanity had been cut.

Chapter 7

The Long Death of Lenin

From now on, Stalin remained almost all the time in Moscow. It was here he conducted his struggle first for survival, then for leadership.

Though he was still not widely known to the party membership as a whole, he had established himself among those in the know as a major and decisive figure. When Lenin, now exhausted, took a rest in January 1922, Stalin and Kamenev were named to supervise the party and state respectively.

Stalin had already impressed some outsiders – John Reed, just before his death in 1920, commented, 'He's not an intellectual like the other people you will meet. He's not even particularly well informed, but he knows what he wants. He's got will-power, and he's going to be on top of the pile some day.'

Over 1922 and 1923 even the politically naive representatives of the American Relief Administration spoke of him as 'closer to Lenin than anyone else' or at lowest 'second only to Trotsky'. A few Western journals published reports suggesting that he might be Lenin's successor. One American quoted Radek as telling him (on 14 March 1923) 'that should Lenin die, Stalin would become leader of the party', though Radek was an opponent of Stalin's.

In the upper echelons the opinion was that he had the strongest force of character, and some great abilities. The only reservation, that he had spilt more blood than was strictly necessary, was perceived as a minor blemish.

On 4 April 1922 he received what was to prove his key job. Following the Eleventh Party Congress, he was appointed, on Lenin's recommmendation, General Secretary of the Central Committee. He accepted the post on condition that he should be allowed to give up his Rabkrin

(Workers' and Peasants' Inspectorate) appointment.

One peculiar episode of the time has never been properly explained. Stalin's wife Nadezhda had been working since 1919 in Lenin's secretariat. Described by Lenin's chief secretary Lidia Fotieva as 'almost always beautiful, but sometimes uninteresting', she was expelled from the party in 1921 by a purge commission. How this could have happened without it being seen, or even intended, as a blow against Stalin is a mystery. And not Stalin, but Lenin, eventually interceded for her, on the grounds that her family had helped him in 1917 and were politically impeccable, while it was possible that 'in view of the youth of Nadezhda Sergeyevna Alliluyeva the commission has remained in ignorance of this circumstance'.

Nadezhda seems to have been restored, though at first only to candidate membership. The reason for her expulsion was only made clear in 1989 – it was 'passivity': that is to say lack of party activity. We are now told (on the authority of Fotieva) that in addition to her job with Lenin Stalin kept her so busy taking his own dictation, looking after his guests and so on, that she had no time for anything else. The commission seems not to have known her marital status.

Perhaps Nadezhda was sometimes 'uninteresting', as Lidia Fotieva puts it. Others saw her as 'an outstanding personality' and in particular as unassuming and honest, unlike many women of the new class now rising. She was not an intellectual – Stalin sneered at intellectual women as 'herrings with ideas', the very image of the stringy spinster suffragette caricature to be found, though scarcely in 'progressive' circles, in the capitalist West.

If Nadezhda had been less 'honest', her position in Lenin's secretariat might have been of great use to Stalin. No doubt he learned some things from her, but there is nothing to show that she behaved in any way disloyally to Lenin. And after Stalin was given charge of Lenin's arrangements her name no longer appears in the secretarial logs. Stalin no doubt reclaimed her for his own use.

2

On 25 May 1922, Lenin had his first stroke. A wholly new situation was created. Over the next year, until soon after his final incapacitating stroke of 10 March 1923 (followed by his death on 21 January 1924), the leadership of the country was in a peculiar state of provisional impermanence. Lenin was sometimes unable to influence events, but sometimes recovered enough to impose his will. During this difficult interval Stalin almost wrecked his promising career.

Lenin's first political dispute with his colleagues at this time was on the issue of the state monopoly of foreign trade; Lenin insisted on it but many of the leadership were hostile or, in Stalin's case, lukewarm. Lenin's view had been accepted by the Politburo on 22 May 1922, but over the year the Central Committee voted for a considerable relaxation of the monopoly. Lenin then worked for weeks to get the decision annulled. Stalin had noted on Lenin's first complaint that 'Comrade Lenin's letter has not made me change my mind on the correctness of the decisions of the plenum', but he and the others soon gave in. The main political result was that Lenin relied almost entirely on Trotsky as his ally and spokesman, who 'will uphold my views as well as I'.

This 'alliance' was to extend to other critical matters over the year. Its immediate result was to provoke the beginnings of the anti-Trotsky bloc of Zinoviev, Kamenev and Stalin, which becomes noticeable over this issue and others.

Stalin had not been the leading offender in the row over the foreign trade monopoly, but now a major policy dispute arose which involved him directly and unambiguously.

On 10 August 1922, the Politburo instructed the Orgburo to create a commission on the relations between the Russian Soviet Federal Socialist Republic and the Ukraine, Byelorussia and the three Caucasian republics. Stalin was its leading figure. It recommended that the other republics should enter the Russian federation as 'autonomous', and that the current Russian government should simply become the government of the expanded entity. The Georgians in particular objected strongly.

When the proposal was sent to Lenin, he answered with a memorandum suggesting instead a 'Union of Soviet Republics' on a constitutionally equal basis. Stalin told Kamenev, 'We must be firm with Lenin'; and he transmitted Lenin's memorandum to the Politburo, with a covering letter in which he objected to Lenin's suggestions, and accused him of 'national liberalism'. However, the Central Committee finally accepted Lenin's formulation, which is the basis of the present USSR. It will be seen that Stalin's proposal did not give even the appearance of sovereignty to the lesser republics, but quite overtly reduced them to being, once again, part of Russia. There was a total lack of the sensitivity towards minority nations on which Lenin was now insisting.

Nor did this disagreement remain merely a matter of differences on high policy. It rapidly became an urgent and bitter dispute, as Lenin found that Stalin and his circle were acting as 'Great Russian chauvinists' not merely in theory, but in crude (and unacceptable) practice.

Lenin had at first thought that the intransigence of the Georgian Communists on the issue was excessive, and even secessionist. When the Georgian Central Committee almost unanimously rejected the 'Russian' solution on 15 September 1922, Ordzhonikidze (as head of the Caucasian Bureau) ordered them to obey, and not to publicize their disagreement. Lenin did not at first take a Georgian protest against this seriously, and told the Georgians to use a 'more seemly and loyal tone' to Ordzhonikidze, adding that the dispute should be settled by the Secretariat – that is, Stalin. On 22 October the great majority of the Georgian Central Committee (nine out of eleven) resigned. Ordzhonikidze then appointed a new Central Committee, but when he went to Tiflis to install it he was met by much hostility. At one meeting he lost his temper and struck one of the Georgian Communists (not, in fact, on political grounds, but because his opponent had suggested that he had unethically accepted the present of a horse).

Before Lenin heard of this he had received a complaint that Ordzhonikidze was threatening Georgian Communists, and when a commission of enquiry was appointed by the Secretariat, he abstained on the vote for its membership. Consisting of Stalin's nominees, it cleared Ordzhonikidze and blamed the Georgians. And it insisted on the transfer from Georgia of the rebellious members of the local Central Committee.

Lenin's health improved in June, and he was again involved in the political issues by interviews and letters, though he did not return to the Kremlin from Gorki to work until the beginning of October. He spoke at the Comintern Congress on 13 November, and to the Moscow Soviet on 20 November. From 7 to 12 December he was again resting in Gorki. During this period he became aware of the truth about the Georgian affair. Two more strokes on 13 December slowed him up, but did not stop his political activity.

On 18 December the Central Committee made Stalin responsible for his medical supervision.

On 22 December Stalin learned that Lenin had just written to Trotsky congratulating him on their victory over the trade monopoly. Stalin telephoned Lenin's wife, Krupskaya, and abused her in terms both vulgar and violent for having let Lenin write in his state of health. Krupskaya kept this from Lenin for the moment, but wrote to Kamenev that 'Stalin subjected me to a storm of the coarsest abuse yesterday about a brief note Lenin dictated to me with the permission of the doctors. I didn't join the party yesterday. In the whole of the last thirty years I have never heard a coarse word from a comrade.' She added that she knew better than the doctors what could or could not be said to Lenin, 'and in any case I know this better than Stalin'. She asked to be protected from gross interference in her private life, and unworthy abuse and threats. Stalin had threatened to take her before the Party Control Commission, and she said she had no doubt that if it came to that she would be unanimously supported there, but she had no time for such a 'farce', and her nerves were 'at breaking point'. The 'coarse words' she had never heard in party circles are said to have included 'syphilitic whore'. Stalin's loss of self-control seems to have been total.

Lenin had another stroke that very day (22 December), but over the next two days recovered enough to refuse treatment unless he was allowed to dictate some notes. The Politburo granted this, and the next few days were spent in writing what came to be called his Testament.

In this well-known document, suppressed for thirty-three years, he started by saying that the most immediate danger of a split in the party arose from the relationship between Stalin and Trotsky – 'the two most able leaders of the present Central Committee'. His praise of Trotsky's ability – 'He is personally perhaps the most capable man in the present CC' was subject to the qualification that he showed 'excessive self-assurance' and was over-preoccupied with the 'purely administrative side of work'. Stalin, 'having become General Secretary, has unlimited authority concentrated in his hands, and I am not sure whether he will be capable of using that authority with sufficient caution'. Lenin then listed, with various comments, Zinoviev, Kamenev and (of the 'younger' forces) Bukharin and Pyatakov. The first two must have been piqued to see Stalin's ability thus demonstratively ranked higher than their own. And in fact one of the most striking points of the Testament is precisely Lenin's estimate of Stalin's talents.

Over the next few days Lenin elaborated his view of the qualities needed in a leader. He must be able to grasp 'the totality of a situation', have qualities of personal appeal, and be an efficient organizer and administrator – even though 'the combination of these two kinds of qualities in a given person will rarely be found, and it is hardly necessary'.

By this time Lenin had become fully informed about the Georgian question. On 30–31 December he dictated notes on the issue. He was particularly infuriated with Ordzhonikidze's loss of temper and urged his expulsion from the party for a period, with official reprimands to

Stalin and Dzerzhinsky. He accused them all of Great Russian chauvinism, adding that Russified non-Russians of their type were particularly prone to this vice.

It seems to have been as a result of this further consideration of the Georgian affair (for he had not yet learned of Stalin's conduct to Krupskaya) that, on 4 January 1923, he added a postscript to the Testament, proposing Stalin's dismissal:

> 'Stalin is too rude, and this defect, though quite tolerable in our midst and in dealings among us Communists, becomes intolerable in a General Secretary. This is why I suggest that the comrades think about a way to remove Stalin from that post and appoint another man who in all respects differs from Comrade Stalin in his superiority, that is, more loyal, more courteous, and more considerate of comrades, less capricious, etc.'

We should note, incidentally, that the word always translated as 'rude' – *grub* – has in Russian a far broader significance than mere discourtesy: it carries a stronger implication of crudity and of a gross and bullying lack of normal social decencies.

The Testament, or as Lenin himself called it, 'Letter to the Party Congress', including this postscript on Stalin, did not become known even to the leadership until after Lenin's death. His other documents of this time, including his notes on Georgia, were available to them, but the Testament itself was given to Krupskaya in a sealed envelope, to be opened and transmitted to the party in case of his death. He presumably feared that this was imminent, but that if he survived or recovered, he could put the case more effectively and at greater length in person.

Fotieva had been forbidden by the Politburo to let him know their 'day-to-day' decisions, and he extracted the information from her with difficulty. It was in such hard circumstances over the next few weeks that Lenin dictated a number of articles for *Pravda,* one of them attacking Stalin's old fief the Rabkrin as 'not enjoying the slightest authority. Everyone knows that no other institution is worse organized.' It needed immediate and fundamental restaffing and reorganization. Though written on 10 February, this did not appear until 4 March. A majority in the Politburo opposed its publication, and it was even suggested that only a single copy of *Pravda* should be printed, for Lenin's eyes alone. But finally Trotsky was able to persuade Zinoviev and Kamenev to let it appear. Trotsky was, in fact, approached by Lenin about this time, and asked to take up the struggle against bureaucracy. Trotsky answered that the task was impossible because every bureaucrat was under the protection of some 'important party leader'. Lenin then said that this implied that the struggle should include the 'fight' against bureaucracy in the Orgburo itself. Trotsky agreed and Lenin proposed they should act together on the matter.

At a Politburo meeting on February 1923, Stalin told those present (Trotsky, Zinoviev and Kamenev) that Lenin had asked for poison. Trotsky replied that Lenin's doctor, whom he shared, said that he might recover with very slight impairment. Stalin said that Lenin only wanted to have the poison to hand in case his sufferings become intolerable. Stalin got no support, and no more was heard of the idea. The oddest part of the whole affair is that it took place in February, when Lenin was in better health than he had been and also least likely to trust Stalin. Perhaps the request (which has lately been confirmed in Soviet published archives) had come in December, before the falling-out between them.

In February, too, Lenin went still more deeply into the Georgian affair. The Politburo had meanwhile, without his knowledge, again condemned the Georgian Communists and acquitted Ordzhonikidze and Stalin. Lenin's secretary Fotieva let Lenin know of this debate and he asked for the papers. Stalin said he could not have them without the Politburo's permission as this would be taxing Lenin with 'day-to-day details'. Lenin was angry and insisted on having them. Stalin thereupon asked without success to be relieved of the supervision of the invalid.

At about this time, as memoirs of hers printed for the first time in Moscow late in 1989 make clear, Stalin approached Lenin's sister Maria, herself an Old Bolshevik, who was helping to look after him. Stalin, who seemed very upset, said he had not been able to sleep all night, and that Lenin was obviously now against him – treating him 'like a traitor'. He himself loved Lenin, and asked that he be told this. Maria was sorry for Stalin and told Lenin that Stalin sent warm greetings, and said he loved him. Should she give him Lenin's regards?

'Give them,' Lenin replied coldly.

She then said, 'But Volodya, he's very intelligent.'

'He's not in the least intelligent,' Lenin answered – 'decisively' though 'without any irritation'. (Maria herself was, or was to become, a supporter of the Stalin–Bukharin group.)

Trotsky, himself speaking from a hostile point of view, is still probably not far off the mark when he says that Lenin valued Stalin for 'his firmness, and his direct mind', but in the end saw through 'his ignorance

... his very narrow political horizon, and his exceptional moral coarseness and unscrupulousness'.

Lenin set up a private commission of his secretaries with full instructions to report on the Georgian affair. On 5 March he charged Trotsky with the conduct of the whole matter, noting that Stalin's impartiality could not be trusted.

He now learned of Stalin's violent attack on Krupskaya, and he wrote Stalin as follows (with copies to Kamenev and Zinoviev):

'Very respectable comrade Stalin,
    You allowed yourself to be so ill-mannered as to call my wife on the telephone and to abuse her. She has agreed to forget what you said. Nevertheless she has told Zinoviev and Kamenev about the incident. I have no intention of forgetting what has been done against me, and it goes without saying what was done against my wife I also consider to have been directed against myself. Consequently, I must ask you to consider whether you would be inclined to withdraw what you said and to apologize, or whether you prefer to break off relations between us.

Respectfully yours,
Lenin'

One of Lenin's secretaries, Maria Volodicheva, gave Stalin the letter personally. He remained calm and said slowly, 'It is not Lenin speaking, it is his illness. I'm not a doctor. I'm a politician. I'm Stalin. If my wife, a member of the party, acted wrongly and they punished her, I would not assume the right to interfere in the matter. But Krupskaya is a party member. If Lenin insists I am ready to apologize to Krupskaya for rudeness.' Volodicheva returned with the oral apology.

Stalin immediately also wrote a reply (which, like some of the rest of the information about the episode, has only just been published in the Soviet Union). In effect, he brazened it out. He said he had spoken to Krupskaya 'approximately as follows, "The doctors forbid giving Lenin political information, believing this regime the best way of treating him, but you Nadezhda Konstantinovna, it seems, have broken this regime. Do not play with Ilyich's health," ' and so on. This could not, he said, be regarded as rude, impermissible, or directed 'against' Lenin. He had done his duty, though there seemed to have been a misunderstanding. If 'to preserve "relationships" I have to "withdraw" the words mentioned above, I can withdraw them, but I cannot understand in this business, where my "guilt" is, and what exactly is wanted of me.'

Stalin can hardly have thought that Lenin would believe him rather than Krupskaya on the facts of the case. The letter has very much the air of a document prepared for defence in future repercussions, if Lenin was able to raise the issue before the party and its leadership. As it was, the question did not arise. Lenin never saw Stalin's letter.

At the same time that he had written his letter to Stalin, Lenin wrote to the Georgian Communists:

> 'To Comrades Mdivani, Makharadze and others (copy to Comrades Trotsky and Kamenev)
>
> Esteemed Comrades, I follow your affairs with all my heart. I am outraged at the rudeness of Ordzhonikidze and the connivance of Stalin and Dzerzhinsky. I am preparing for you notes and a speech.
>
> With esteem
Lenin'

He had earlier told Trotsky to keep his notes on the Georgian affair from Kamenev, who would tell Stalin 'and Stalin would make a rotten compromise in order then to deceive'. But he now asked that Kamenev be told. He was in fact prepared for open hostilities. He told Krupskaya that Stalin 'is devoid of the most elementary honesty, the most simple human honesty'.

One of Lenin's secretaries told Trotsky that Lenin was now preparing 'a bomb' against Stalin; and Kamenev learned from another of his secretaries that Lenin had decided 'to crush Stalin politically'.

On the following day, 7 March 1923, Lenin had another stroke, his last. He was never to recover the power of speech, though he did not die until 21 January 1924. On 23 April he was operated on to remove a bullet three millimetres from his carotid artery, left from the assassination attempt of 1918, and now primarily blamed for the dangerous state of his circulation.

For Stalin it had been a very near thing. His hatred of Georgia and his loss of self-control had nearly destroyed him. There were always rumours that Lenin had been poisoned. That Lenin is indeed reported to have earlier asked Stalin to make poison available to him, in case of physical necessity, is a different thing; and there is no evidence, and little likelihood, that the last stroke was so caused. On the contrary, Lenin was working hard at his political plans until the last moment. Stalin was saved, in fact, by luck alone.

Chapter 8

The Fight for Power

The years between the Revolution and the end of Lenin's political life had seen the new regime in a desperate struggle to survive. Stalin himself had moved from one emergency to another, applying brute force and drive to cope with highly refractory situations.

In the next phase, things were different. The regime had been, however reluctantly, accepted by the population, and to secure that acceptance it had restored a large measure of at least economic freedom. It was within the party that the major struggles now took place, and Stalin, after a difficult start, was able to deploy his hitherto inadequately remarked powers of manœuvre.

The Twelfth Party Congress followed Lenin's final incapacitation by a few weeks. It started on 17 April 1923. On the face of it Trotsky was in a strong position. One of his supporters said to him that, having Lenin's explicit support, he was now sure to have a preponderant role. Trotsky answered that, on the contrary, it would unite all his rivals against him. He and Lenin together, had the latter recovered, would have been an overwhelming force, and they could no doubt have brought Stalin down, and purged his new bureaucratic elite. Even with Lenin ill, but still capable of intervention from his home, the combination would have been very strong and perhaps successful. But with Lenin totally incapacitated, Trotsky was exposed to every blast – and even more so, of course, when Lenin's death finally removed any question of even partial recovery.

Trotsky could still have made a fight of it. He had a number of distinguished supporters, his power base in the army, and a large following among the younger section of the party membership. But he seems to have felt that such a struggle would be harmful, and might lead to serious trouble. It is plain, moreover, that he had no clear idea of political tactics; the Bolshevik experience of intra-party intrigue and committee-fixing was alien to him. He was an outsider and distrusted by the veteran party members. If he had played his cards right he might, even so, have taken power. As it was he did not even carry out Lenin's last instructions.

Stalin suggested that Trotsky should present the main report at the Twelfth Congress but Trotsky sensibly refused, rightly believing that this would be taken as an assumption of Lenin's mantle. In the event, Zinoviev gave the report. What is more, Zinoviev clearly saw himself as the leading figure in the party, the inheritor of Lenin – threatened only by the interloper Trotsky. What came to be called the 'triumvirate', or 'troika', opposing Trotsky, had already begun to emerge, with Kamenev and Stalin standing behind Zinoviev. On the face of it (though these analyses are a little shaky), Zinoviev and Kamenev on their own had a fair majority on the Central Committee. Stalin was over the next year or so anyhow to appear both less powerful and more moderate than his allies. These three, moreover, had the general support of the rest of the Politburo, though Bukharin and others made sporadic attempts to encourage reconciliation.

The Congress brought little obvious change. Stalin presented the organizational report, among other things suggesting an increase in the number of Central Committee members. Lenin had recommended this, in the hope that it would in some way control fissiparous tendencies among the top leadership. In fact, it was to have two results. First, Stalin was able to bring in more of his own supporters without, at first, arousing acrimony by removing others. Second (as was to become very important over the rest of the decade), the larger the body, the easier it was to organize the harassment, or even shouting down, of opponents. The Central Committee was, in fact, expanded from twenty-seven to forty full members. Meanwhile, Stalin benignly suggested that the party's ten or fifteen most prominent leaders were now sufficiently experienced to make the right decisions nine times out of ten – an ostentatious plea for moderation, and for continuing Lenin's tolerant handling of occasional error.

Stalin also presented the report on the nationality problem. He took a fairly mild line, agreeing with all that had been said about Great Russian chauvinism, but adding that 'local chauvinism' was also an evil, as in Georgia when it led to the persecution of even smaller minorities like the Abkhaz (a valid point which was to re-emerge in the 1980s). In general, Stalin appeared in a moderate role. He, as it were, deflected Lenin's published criticisms by formal agreement, diversionary qualification and practical inaction – and not only in Georgia, but also over the organizational problem.

More generally the struggle died down in the summer, as always. The leaders were by this time taking holidays on the Black Sea or in mountain resorts for periods of a month or so every year. A certain amount of mutual visiting enabled contacts to be kept up and plans to be laid. Meanwhile Stalin relaxed – enough on one occasion to say to Kamenev and Dzerzhinsky, 'To choose one's victim, to prepare one's plans minutely, to slake an implacable vengeance, and then go to bed ... there is nothing sweeter in the world.' In my book *The Great Terror*, I cast mild doubt on the authenticity of this story, on the purely general grounds that it might be unlikely for Stalin to have expressed himself so openly. That consideration carries some weight: all the same, he does seem to have spoken in those terms, and Bukharin was later to recall this 'theory of sweet revenge'.

Unity against Trotsky did not, even now, amount to total and amicable unanimity on all issues in the triumvirate. Zinoviev was not so foolish as to fail to see the changes in the concentration of power in Stalin's hands. In the late summer, Zinoviev and Bukharin were on holiday in Kislovodsk in the North Caucasus, and discussed getting organizational matters under political control. They assembled a disparate group, including the Stalin loyalist Voroshilov, and met in a nearby cave (the Cave of the Dead Mule) – a detail which was later used to make the whole affair sound like a sinister, though also semi-comic, conspiracy.

One idea was that a committee of senior Politburo members – perhaps Zinoviev, Stalin and Trotsky – should be jointly responsible for the Secretariat. In the end they sent some such proposal to Stalin, who came down to Kislovodsk, eventually suggesting the entry of Trotsky, Bukharin and Zinoviev into the Orgburo – a move which in fact had little or no real effect. Stalin was later to represent the whole affair as an attempt to undermine the Politburo and put Zinoviev, Trotsky and himself in sole charge of the party. This is, of course, a backhanded admission that the man who already had the power which it was proposed to share was himself in a position.

2

If the summer had even so seen a certain lull in the political struggle, it soon picked up again. The triumvirate tried at a Central Committee plenum to weaken Trotsky by bringing some of his opponents into the Revolutionary Military Soviet. Trotsky, in a rage, offered to resign all his posts and go and fight in the German revolution. In a farcical scene, Zinoviev said he would do the same. The Central Committee forbade it. Stalin spoke moderately. In the ensuing heckling Trotsky left the meeting in a huff.

In letters and a collection of his writings, Trotsky now began to criticize the bureaucracy and the leadership's real attitude in something of the way Lenin had urged on him. And he even said that some of the factions Lenin had banned had certain useful ideas.

In October came a strong appeal against bureaucracy and for freedom of debate in the party – the 'Platform of the Forty-Six' – though without Trotsky's participation. The Forty-Six were an impressive array of Bolsheviks including prominent close allies of Trotsky like Pyatakov and Preobrazhensky, but also supporters of Shlyapnikov and his 'Workers' Opposition'. The Central Committee banned the document and censured the Forty-Six. But it was impossible to ignore this weighty group entirely, and the triumvirate changed its tactics and allowed discussion in the party in Moscow. The results were remarkable. Most of the cells, but especially in the army, the Komsomol and the university, sided with the opposition. The Politburo then dissolved the Komsomol Central Committee and removed the Trotskyite chief political commissar of the army, Antonov-Ovseyenko. Trotsky himself was ill, and the meetings of the Politburo were held at his bedside. In a manœuvre in which the hand of Stalin rather than those of his colleagues can be seen, they propounded a 'new course', taking over, though as it turned out in words only, the whole anti-bureaucratic programme. They even accepted Trotsky's amendments strengthening the text.

Trotsky soon saw that there was no intention on the part of Stalin and the others to carry out this new programme. He again raised the question publicly. This brought things into the open. And at the Thirteenth Party Conference, held in January 1924 to discuss the issues, Stalin's Secretariat successfully rigged the delegations, and the event was turned into a set of attacks on Trotsky – who was convalescing in the Caucasus. Trotsky had in effect attacked Zinoviev and Kamenev for their vacillations in November 1917 (and the former for the debacle of his recent attempt, through the Comintern which he headed, at a German revolution – a foolish project agreed to reluctantly by those on the spot, and called off imperfectly, amidst a blaze of incompetence). But if the two men could be attacked for their 'desertion' at the time of the Revolution, Trotsky had just as large a burden of past error – in his long, and often harsh, polemics with Lenin in earlier years. These were now raised against him in a series of increasingly vicious attacks. Stalin remained comparatively moderate – though speaking strongly enough about six 'errors' of Trotskyism, which amounted to a condemnation of Trotsky's 'proclaiming the freedom of groups. Yes, freedom of groups!' Trotskyite hecklers shouted that Stalin was intimidating the party, and he answered that he was only intimidating the factionalists.

And now, on 21 January 1924, Lenin died. He had been not quite fifty-three at the time of his incapacitating last stroke and was not yet fifty-four when he died.

There had been no reason to expect this sudden end. He had, indeed, been unwell: but so had others. The expectation until his last stroke was that he would have many years of political leadership. If he had lived only as long as Stalin, he would still have been ruling in the 1940s. If he had lived as long as Mao Tse-Tung or Tito, he would have survived until the 1950s.

Lenin's death had a number of consequences. First Stalin telegraphed Trotsky, away in the Caucasus, to tell him that the funeral would take place before it was possible for him to get back to Moscow, so that he might as well continue his cure. In fact it was held on 27 January, which would have given him plenty of time. Trotsky believed that Stalin had deceived him on purpose. At any rate, he was absent from the major ceremony of Leninist and party loyalty, and this did him no good.

On the eve of the funeral, various ceremonial orations took place. Stalin's was remarkable for its liturgical tone. It has struck many biographers of different views as embodying the full public self-image of Stalin and of Stalinism.

'Comrades! We Communists are people of a special cast. We are fashioned of special stuff. We are the ones who form the army of the great proletarian general, the army of Comrade Lenin.

There is no higher honour than that of belonging to this army. There is nothing higher than the calling of a member of the party whose founder and leader is Comrade Lenin. Not to every man is it given to be a member of such a party. Not to every man is it given to endure the tribulations and tempests that go with membership in such a party. Sons of the working class, sons of poverty and strife, sons of unparalleled privations and heroic struggles, these are the men who, first and foremost, are worthy to be members of such a party . . .

Leaving us, Comrade Lenin ordered us to hold high and keep pure the great calling of member of the party. We vow to thee, Comrade Lenin, that we will honour this, thy commandment.

Leaving us, Comrade Lenin enjoined us to keep the unity of the party like the apple of our eye. We vow to thee, Comrade Lenin, that we will with honour fulfil this, thy commandment.

Leaving us, Comrade Lenin enjoined us to keep and strengthen the dictatorship of the proletariat. We vow to thee, Comrade Lenin, that we will with honour fulfil this, thy commandment.

Leaving us, Comrade Lenin enjoined us to strengthen with all our might the union of workers and peasants. We vow to thee, Comrade Lenin, that we will with honour fulfil this, thy commandment.

Leaving us, Comrade Lenin enjoined us to strengthen and extend the union of republics. We vow to thee, Comrade Lenin, that we will fulfil with honour this, thy commandment . . .'

It was largely under pressure from Stalin that, contrary to the wishes of his widow and others, it was decided that Lenin should be embalmed and his tomb turned into a shrine. Krupskaya, in fact, publicly asked that there should be 'no external reverence for his person' and she urged Lenin's own attitude to such externals. But Stalin's attitude was different, as we can see to this day in Red Square. A different style of Bolshevism was being created.

Stalin also used the occasion to persuade the Central Committee to celebrate with a 'Lenin levy' of new mass admissions to the party. Thus the old party was further diluted, and to a large degree with entrants screened by representatives of the Secretariat.

But for Stalin the most critical result of Lenin's death was a matter outside his control. In May, just before the opening of the Thirteenth Party Congress, Krupskaya, exactly following Lenin's instructions, sent to Kamenev the so far secret Testament with a letter saying Lenin had 'expressed the definite wish' that the notes 'of 24–5 December 1922, and those of 4 January 1923, which contain personal appraisals of some Central Committee members' should be 'submitted after his death to

Gori church school: Stalin back row centre

Stalin's birthplace in Gori before restoration

Stalin at Tiflis Seminary

Stalin in exile at Monastyrskoye, with Spandaryan

The house in Kureika Stalin shared with Sverdlov

A group of exiled Bolsheviks, 1915: Kamenev, on Stalin's left in the back row, has been obliterated in the version published in the 1930s

Stalin in a tsarist police register

Nadezhda Alliluyeva aged thirteen, as Stalin first knew her

(*Left*) Stalin's first wife, Yekaterina Svanidze

(*Above left*) Stalin in 1911

(*Above*) Stalin in 1917

(*Left*) Stalin as a member of the Revolutionary Military Soviet of the Southwestern Front, 1918

(*Below*) Stalin in 1919

Lenin and Stalin in 1922

Krupskaya and Lenin not
long before his death

The Stalin leadership 1929: (*left to right*)
Ordzhonikidze, Voroshilov, Kuibyshev,
Stalin, Kalinin, Kaganovich, Kirov

The funeral of Kirov: Stalin, Voroshilov
(*left*), Molotov (*back left*) and Kalinin (*back
right*) carrying the urn containing Kirov's
ashes to the Kremlin Wall

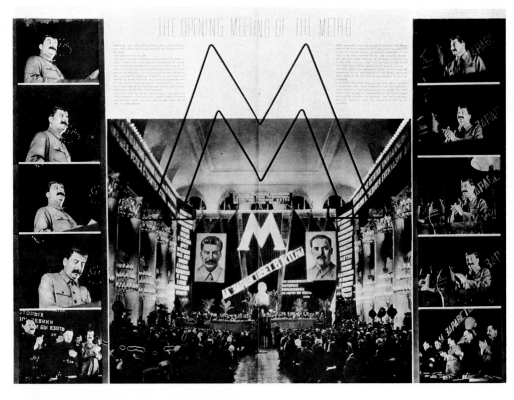

THE OPENING MEETING OF THE METRO

Opening the Moscow Metro, 1935

Stalin as children-lover (he later shot her father)

the next Party Congress for its information'. They were, as she put it, 'earmarked by Vladimir Ilyich for transmittal to the party'.

When Stalin had heard of Lenin's death, he was jubilant: 'I never saw him in a happier mood', he paced up and down 'with satisfaction written all over his face', his secretary tells us. But the Testament was another matter. He called Krupskaya an 'old whore', and when he read the document through he cursed Lenin too: 'He shat on me and he shat on himself . . .' At the Congress which followed he is quoted as saying to Sokolnikov, sitting next to him, 'He couldn't even die as an honest leader,' though by this he seems to have meant that the 'collective leadership' urged by Lenin was a fallacy, as indeed it was to prove.

When the Central Committee met to consider the documents, Stalin clearly realized that his affairs had reached a crisis. The Committee at this stage lacked any Stalinist majority, and if his rivals had insisted, they could probably have brought about his demotion. Kamenev read the Testament aloud. His secretary tells us:

'Painful embarrassment paralysed the whole gathering. Stalin, who sat on one of the benches of the presidium's rostrum, felt small and miserable. Despite his self-control and forced calm, one could clearly read in his face the fact that his fate was being decided.'

Zinoviev, however, saved him. He remarked that every word of Lenin's was sacred and that they would 'fulfil what the dying Ilyich commanded of us'. Well, not quite everything, for 'on one point, we are happy to say, Lenin's fears have proved groundless. I am speaking of the question of our General Secretary. All of you have witnessed our harmonious cooperation during the last months, and all of you, like me, have had the satisfaction of seeing that what Lenin feared has not taken place.' Kamenev too supported Stalin.

Trotsky sat silent, with a contemptuous look on his face. Stalin spoke, implying that Lenin had hardly been himself when he wrote, but 'a sick man surrounded by womenfolk'. The Committee decided that the Testament should not be read to the Congress (nor be published), and it was merely read to closed meetings of delegations from each province, with the comments of the Committee to the effect that Lenin had been ill and Stalin had proved satisfactory. Stalin submitted his resignation as General Secretary, which was unanimously rejected. He had weathered the storm.

The other event in Stalin's life immediately consequent on the death of Lenin was his delivery in April of a series of lectures, *The Foundations of Leninism*, soon printed as a book (112 pages in English in the Little Stalin Library edition). It is a perfectly sound exposition of the concepts behind the Communist autocracy, as far as it goes. It is written in a dogmatic and schematic fashion, and in the antiphonal style of all Stalin's work. It has not the theoretical coruscations of Trotsky's *Lessons of October*, or even Bukharin's *ABC of Communism*. Stalin was, as Bukharin put it, 'eaten up with the vain desire to become a well-known theoretician. He feels that it is the only thing he lacks.' The Old Bolshevik scholar Ryazanov had once told him openly that theory was 'not your field'. *The Foundations of Leninism* is his first serious attempt to compensate.

But its main interest lies elsewhere. It has now become clear that it was broadly, though not entirely, based on the work of his secretary F. A. Ksenofontov. Stalin acknowledged this in a private letter, but later forbade Ksenofontov to publish this, and advised him to give up his writings on Leninism (and in the 1930s had him shot).

Stalin had been taking bi-weekly lessons in Marxism from the Bolshevik philosopher Yan Sten, even studying Hegel's *Phenomenology of Mind*. Sten told a friend that Stalin found this hard going. But even if Stalin flunked in Hegel, he does seem to have rubbed up his general Marxism to the degree necessary to conduct the ensuing intra-party polemics at an adequate level.

3

It is hard to keep in mind that these struggles were not conducted among politicians in the ordinary sense. Their concern was not the immediate interests of the country. They considered only the transformation of that country, and in the long run of the world, according to the precepts of a particular dogma. And they viewed their party's retention of power at all costs as the only way of achieving these ends.

Every move had to be justified in terms of the dogma. Its essentials were that class struggle is the motive force of history; that the industrial working class, the proletariat, is empowered to defeat the earlier ruling classes; and that the result will be socialism, followed by communism, a society of total freedom and equality. Meanwhile, the Communist Party, 'representing' the Russian proletariat, has come to power and has the task of ruling in the name of this (admittedly small, dwindling and apathetic) class. In any case, Lenin continued to argue that other proletarian revolutions in the 'advanced' countries would save the day for the Russian Revolution.

This notion of the transcendental role of the industrial working class, the 'proletariat' in the Marxist scheme, was of course a central conviction of the Bolsheviks.

This idea had arisen early in the nineteenth century, when the industrial workers were indeed, at any rate to the eye of some academics, a new social phenomenon. Marx's class analysis gave this stratum the role of bringing history to its preordained conclusion, in first taking political power, previously held by other 'classes'; and thereafter creating the classless and otherwise ideal society.

In practice, the Bolsheviks made every effort to recruit the industrial workers as their main base. A huge Bolshevik effort went into organizing, and agitating to, a mass audience in the factories, and to committee-fiddling their 'representative' councils. At the time of the October Revolution, the organized skilled workers – printers, railwaymen and so on – had been solidly Menshevik, and in favour of a socialist coalition government.

But the big industrial enterprises in Petrograd like the Putilov Works were largely manned by 'proletarians' recently recruited from the peasantry, with all the political naivety that implied. In fact, as the writer Korolenko wrote to Lenin, the Revolution succeeded, at least among this stratum, not because of any Russian claim to unexpected maturity but precisely because of Russian backwardness. The Bolsheviks had turned to these workers, taken over their factory committees, and had used them. But they had done so sincerely, as their best, indeed inevitable, representatives under the Marxist scheme, or the Leninist interpretation of it. In replacing the old administration the Bolsheviks had to find a new cadre, and theory demanded that this should come as far as possible from the proletariat. The regime would then be validated in theoretical terms by its new class components. In fact, this Marxist attitude, apart from anything else, had failed to take into account the Russian anarchist Bakunin's objection to the whole Marxist view of these matters: 'Those previous workers having just become rulers or representives of the people will cease to be workers; they will look at the workers from their heights, they will represent not the people but themselves ... he who doubts this does not know human nature ...'

And this turned out to be the truth, against all the Marxist sentimentalities. Nevertheless, all through the first quarter of a century of Communist rule in Russia, the 'class origin' of party members was a major consideration (though exemption was somehow available to bourgeois Bolsheviks like Molotov – and Lenin). And the notion of 'class instinct' and a general innate superiority of the proletariat remained at least as a public piety – indeed it survived in a lesser degree almost to this day.

In the terror of the 1930s it was quite usual to hear denunciations without evidence accepted on the basis of class instinct. Children in the 1930s were praised for denouncing those suspected of thieving as 'kulaks' with kulak relations, since the children 'had learnt to speak the class language'. Even after the war Stalin was to rebuke Khrushchev, who had transmitted a peasant complaint, with, 'You have lost the pro-letarian class sense.' In fact, the notion of the 'workers' state', and of the priviligentsia as 'servants of the people' is still dying hard as I write – though glasnost has just released, for example, a complaint from seventy-odd building workers about the luxury of the apartments they are putting up for apparatchiks.

Lenin said, 'The victory of the workers is impossible without a temporary worsening of their situation.' In the first half of 1918, the Bolsheviks lost a large amount of the worker vote in factory soviets, in spite of their organizational effectiveness and their harsh exercise of power. In the Civil War they were able to appeal, however demagog-ically, to old class enmities against a restoration of the old regime. At the same time, the crisis empowered them to use their police powers against worker opposition. But as soon as this crisis was over, in 1921, great strikes swept the former factory strongholds of the Bolsheviks.

In the critical period early in 1921 Radek told war college cadets:

> 'We are now at a point where the workers, at the end of their endurance, refuse any longer to follow a vanguard which leads them to battle and sacrifice ... Ought we to yield to the clamours of working men who have reached the limit of their patience but who do not understand their true interests as we do? Their state of mind is at present frankly reactionary. But the party has decided that we must *not* yield, that we must impose our will to victory on our exhausted and dispirited followers.'

Lenin himself spoke of the necessity of 'revolutionary violence against the faltering and unrestrained elements of the toiling masses themselves'.

The Communists indeed recognized, as Lenin put it, that the pro-letariat had almost ceased to exist – those not incorporated into the state machine having largely drifted back to the villages where there might be (though there often was not) a bite to eat.

Within the party, groups favouring concessions to the working class sprang up illegally.

They attacked 'the new bourgeoisie' and spoke of 'the gulf between the party and the workers', the latter being 'deprived of the most elementary political rights'. The leaders were arrested, though in the end not sentenced to more than expulsion from the party. More formidable was the Workers' Opposition led by Shlyapnikov, who had been Lenin's leading agent in Russia during World War I. It was represented in the Central Committee, and when Lenin denounced and defeated it in 1921, he nevertheless thought it best to retain its leading members in that body, where they could be outvoted, but nevertheless continue to accept responsibility for party policy under the 'democratic centralism' concept. And, indeed, they fully supported the party when it moved to crush the Kronstadt sailors and workers ...

Whatever the situation in actuality, it remained an absolutely central point in Communist minds that the party represented the proletariat, and that its duty was to conduct on its behalf the class struggle against all other elements of society. In the political struggles within the party in the post-Lenin period 'the masses' were frequently spoken of as in some way the final court of appeal – though in fact the population, urban as well as rural, was now largely apathetic and exhausted.

Such were the furnishings of Stalin's mind – and, generally speaking, of the minds of most Communists. What we see henceforth is an evaporation of all substance from the 'proletarian' concept. This falsification, partly unconscious, partly semi-conscious, may be seen as the original rot at the heart of the Stalinist way of thinking, and the basis for the next half-century of Soviet delusions. Meanwhile, if the 'class' part of the idea of 'class struggle' was delusive, the 'struggle' part remained real and active.

4

In *Darkness at Noon* Arthur Koestler has his Old Bolshevik Rubashov saying:

'Before the Revolution and also for a short while after it, during the lifetime of the old leader, no distinction between "theorists" and "politicians" had existed. The tactics to be followed at any given moment were deduced straight from the revolutionary doctrine in open discussion; strategic moves during the Civil War, the requisitioning of crops, the division and distribution of the land, the introduction of the new currency, the reorganization of the factories – in fact, every administrative measure – represented an act of applied philosophy.'

Of course Rubashov, or Koestler, is presenting a highly romanticized version of the earlier Bolshevik debates. They had indeed been couched in doctrinal terms. But even at that level, Lenin had sometimes avoided philosophical controversy, when it had appeared necessary to seek a heretic's support for immediate pragmatic reasons. Nor was the Bol-shevik level of courtesy even in intra-party debate quite what one might expect of a congress of philosophers, however divided as to theory. Indeed, some of the more intellectual leaders, even Lenin, seemed to regard roughness as a sign of contact with the manners of the masses. Lenin's long indulgence of Stalin seems, as we have said, to have had some such roots. And in the debates of the immediate post-Lenin period, the coarseness and crudity of – say – Bukharin's style in attacking the oppositionists, until he himself became one, is not all that much better than Stalin's.

When Rosa Luxemburg had complained, in the first decade of the century, of the Leninists' 'Tartar–Mongolian savagery', she was speak-ing not only of their dictatorial attitudes, but of a built-in violence of thought and behaviour. Stalin of course contributed to a further low-ering of standards, but he was not the only one. Still, however coarse the manners of controversy, the matter was expressed in doctrinal categories.

It is a paradox that the Bolsheviks, almost uniquely among the opponents of the old regime, understood power when it came to com-peting with other parties and movements, but that they nevertheless – and particularly the intellectuals among them – considered the internal party disputes, partly at least, to be in a different category. The argu-ments and discussions under Lenin had been, in principle and to a large degree in practice, on the correctness of certain concepts of tactics, strategy and aims. They were, that is to say, conducted, however rudely, in rational terms. This was, indeed, within the confines of a doctrine which precluded certain rationalities normally expected of the inde-pendent human mind. But, granted the premises, the debates were in principle attempts to persuade the party elite on the merits of the cases in question. One ploy common to Lenin and all other Marxists was to claim, in Stalin's words, that one's own new style of Marxism was 'creative'. 'Creative' Marxists who created different novelties were called 'revisionists'. (Revisiónists can't win – that's not surprising/For if they win it isn't called revising.)

In the period after Lenin's death, almost all the Bolsheviks still followed this tradition. Time and again, over the next years, one is struck by the extreme concern of the non-Stalinist contenders to 'win' the argument. They appeared to believe, or half-believe, that if they presented a good case, it might prevail. Wordsworth, over a century before, had written that in putting a particular view, he did not entertain 'the selfish and foolish hope of *reasoning*' anyone into agreeing with him. In the intra-Communist polemics of the post-Lenin period, the impression is often given of just such a hope. But nor can we dismiss this attitude as merely silly. There was a large stratum of former Old Bolsheviks which did require persuasion, if only as part of their motivations for supporting one or another faction.

Thus, though the tactics of Stalinists often rode roughshod over the minimal decencies of debate, they still, up to a point, had to develop their policies, and shifts of policy, in terms of doctrinal argument. Their advantage was that they understood that the task was to win the debate at the level of the delegates they were appealing to; or, in the case of mere placemen, to provide enough doctrinal justification to excuse their prejudices. Preobrazhensky was ten times as intelligent as Voroshilov: but there were ten Voroshilovs to every Preobrazhensky.

5

It is naturally difficult in any given polemic within the party to say how much of any particular speech or article was based on genuine doctrinal belief (even if aided by rhetorical devices) and how much was convenient and conventional cover in the tactics of the struggle for power.

It certainly appears that Bukharin (for the Right) and Preobrazhensky (the leading mind of the Left) were not only fully convinced of the theoretical correctness of their analyses, but also that they truly hoped to convince others, at least in part, by logical argument.

Stalin seldom gives that impression (and nor does Zinoviev). Stalin's method of controversy is dogmatic assertion, supported by enough scriptural quotations from the Marxist classics, or from Lenin, to validate his views in the ears of an increasingly unsubtle stratum now rising within the party.

He combined this with increasing use of *ad hominem* argument, as indeed did some of his opponents, to a lesser extent. This period, in fact, shows a transition from the old idea of comradely discussion, however rough, to the idea (equally traditional in Leninism) of arguing merely to crush enemies: Lenin himself had said this was completely justified in the case of his attacks on Mensheviks.

But for Stalin, political opponents within Bolshevism were just as much 'enemies' as any Menshevik – and, as he was to show, in fact more hateful to him than those openly hostile to the whole Communist idea.

It is true that there were many factional, or political, or ideological differences among the leadership. But if we compare the post-Lenin period with the party struggles of 1917–23, we can see one major dividing wall. In the Lenin period a whole series of fierce intra-party disputes had occurred. But after each of them came what may be called a reconciliation, with the earlier disputes forgotten, or at least set aside. As early as the April Conference in 1917, when attacks were made on Kamenev for his policies of reconciliation with the Provisional Government, and there had been calls for his removal from the Central Committee, Lenin had said,

'Kamenev's activity stretches back over ten years, and it is very valuable. He is a valuable worker ... The fact that we argue with Comrade Kamenev produces only positive results. Comrade Kamenev's presence is very important and, in the same way, the discussions we have with him are very important. Having convinced him with difficulty, you realize that you are thus overcoming the difficulties arising among the masses.'

This assessment (not included in Lenin's *Collected Works* as published in Stalin's time), was to be applied to all the disputes which followed. Lenin's fury with Zinoviev and Kamenev for 'strike-breaking' just before the October Revolution itself was forgotten almost immediately; both men, having admitted error, were almost at once given important posts. And the same was true of the 'Left' Communists at the time of Brest-Litovsk; the Trotskyites over the argument about labour armies; and the rest. Even when Lenin had banned 'factions', in the crisis of 1921, at a time when maximum party discipline seemed to him to be essential, he in fact knew that divergent views and groups were inevitable. He had made the announced sanction dependent on a vote of two-thirds of the Central Committee. And he had personally worked to organize election to the Central Committee with the purpose of giving almost that critical one-third of the seats to members of the various defeated factions – the Workers' Opposition, and others, so that they could bring their talents to the common task without disrupting it.

To say this was not to be a feature of the Stalinist future is to put it mildly. But in the initial phases, it is worth recalling that this was the atmosphere the Bolsheviks were used to, and for a while the appearance of something like it was kept up.

6

Though the struggle was still in a sense fought in terms of ideas, the ideas became increasingly cruder and simpler – and so more, not less, convincing to the new cadres. Moreover, while the more intellectual members of the party like Trotsky continued to argue at a higher level, their very ideological loquacity often led, as we shall see, to their speaking in terms which could readily be misinterpreted.

Another way in which Stalin's attitudes, and even his speech, differed from most others was its lack (in practice if not in pronouncement) of the extravagant party-fetishism to be found among them. It is true that in his speech on the death of Lenin, for example, he made an obeisance vowing to the late leader to 'guard the unity of the party as the apple of our eyes'. But there is nothing that resembles Trotsky's famous 1924 assertion:

> 'None of us desires or is able to dispute the will of the party. Clearly, the party is always right ... We can only be right with and by the party, for history has provided no other way of being in the right. The English have a saying, "My country, right or wrong", whether it is in the right or in the wrong, it is my country. We have much better historical justification in saying, whether it is right or wrong in certain individual cases, it is my party ... And if the party adopts a decision which one or other of us thinks unjust, he will say, just or unjust, it is my party, and I shall support the consequences of the decision to the end.'

This notion, that the party (even if from time to time mistaken on a given point) somehow embodied a higher, because a collective wisdom, was even more obvious in some of the remarks of Pyatakov, Kamenev and others after they had recanted 'oppositional' ideas.

This conscious submission to an all-wise, or nearly all-wise, collective mind has obvious parallels in other political and religious movements. It suffers from the fault, boldly noted by the Polish poet Adam Wazyk in 1956, of similar claims by the Communist Party in his own country: that a group of stupid or narrow-minded people do not become more brilliant by pooling these qualities. If anything, indeed, the opposite: by a sort of Gresham's Law of Thought, original ideas are sooner or later driven out. The American black writer Richard Wright describes, in his *American Hunger*, his brief membership of the CPUSA:

> 'An hour's listening disclosed the fanatical intolerance of minds sealed against new ideas, new facts, new feelings, new attitudes, new hints at ways to live. They denounced books they had never read, people they had never known, ideas they could never understand, and doctrines they could not pronounce. Communism, instead of making them leap forward with fire in their hearts ... had frozen them at an even lower level of ignorance than had been theirs before they met Communism.'

This sort of incremental coarsening of the party mind is perhaps natural. At any rate, far from being an obstacle in Stalin's drive for power, it was a help.

In the West, and perhaps more particularly in America, there exists a tendency to think of members of militant revolutionary parties as perhaps wrong-headed, perhaps fanatical, yet driven by a desire to create a better society. Therefore, they deserve some sort of clearance as to their motivational virtues, a waiver of the scepticism usually applied to politicians. It is possible to disagree with this view, which the next thirty years of Soviet experience might have done something to dispel.

It is not the purpose of this book to trace the fine detail of all the disputes on policy, or to develop all the recondite manipulations of Marxism, or the small particulars of every factional manœuvre in the Central Committee – except to the degree that they are important to the understanding of Stalin's progress to power, and of Stalin himself. For his arguments were put, and were to be put throughout the Soviet period, in ideological terms. The Westerner is not used to this sort of thing – at least in this context. He may feel it a trifle comic, or childlike (as with Gosse as a boy noting that his father was a little embarrassed about his prospective new stepmother, and instantly seeing the probable doctrinal fault: 'Father, don't tell me she's a paedobaptist').

At least, we no longer have to argue, or at any rate not at serious and detailed length, that Marxism was a misleading mental addiction. We no longer have to write page after page refuting the Stalinist versions of various events in history, and in his own career.

7

Stalin, perhaps fortified by his dip into theory, became involved in several more or less theoretical disputes later in 1924. Meanwhile there was again something of a lull. Stalin's secretary of the period describes him at Politburo meetings, usually silent during the first phases of a debate, but eventually intervening on the side of the majority, with an air of one giving the decisive support. He would sit smoking his pipe, or pace about the room – some indication of the comparative informality of these small meetings. Indeed, in the intervals of polemicizing, there was a certain amount of heavy jollity, as between rough but good-hearted comrades – Trotsky alone holding somewhat aloof. For example, they derided the British Labour Prime Minister, Ramsay Mac-Donald, who had just given the USSR diplomatic recognition. Bukharin jested that the Communists now had their own man in London. But he was too stupid for the job, and Stalin and the others drew up a formal resolution transferring MacDonald to a proverbially backward small town in the Urals, and Mikhail Tomsky was appointed Prime Minister of Britain in his place.

Over the last part of the year, however, the polemics became public. In October 1924 Stalin, for the first time, started to denigrate, though not yet to dismiss entirely, Trotsky's role in the October Revolution. This involved a full-scale falsification which over later years was to become official history. Trotsky, Stalin noted, had not even been a member of the five man 'centre' appointed to conduct the seizure of power, though Stalin himself was on it. Since this centre never met, and is not known to have taken any action whatever, this was a breathtaking piece of impudence. Then, in December, came a serious and fundamental dispute.

We have to envision a Marxist sect, come to power in a country where almost nothing fitted their preconceptions. A country, moreover, whose economy had been almost destroyed, largely as a result of their own earlier policies. Their only true achievement, in fact, had been remaining in power, in spite of every obstacle. But now their rule was no longer at immediate risk and they had time to consider how they were to use their power.

It had been an axiom for Lenin, and for all his followers, that a proletarian revolution in backward non-proletarian Russia could only be successful if supported by proletarian revolutions in the West, where proletariats in sufficient numbers actually existed. Large efforts had been put into promoting these Western revolutions, but it was now reasonably clear that the results, if any, would not be soon or easily obtained.

Stalin now – on 17 December 1924 – adopted a truly major theoretical innovation, 'Socialism in One Country'. He argued, with specious quotations from Engels and Lenin, that Russia could in fact achieve socialism without the expected, but unforthcoming, aid of the Western revolution. It might, indeed, prove difficult, but revolutionizing the West was proving even more difficult. The world revolution would, of course, arrive eventually, and Russian socialism would encourage it. Meanwhile, the Russian workers wanted an achievable aim.

As Stalin expected, and no doubt hoped, his argument was attacked by the astonished Trotskyites. After all, Stalin himself had accepted the orthodox view as recently as in his *Foundations of Leninism* (from whose later editions this point had to be removed). They were, in fact, right in theory, and if the matter had been argued before a court of specialists in doctrine, they might have won. But, as was to be usual, they had mistaken the real issue. Logically, as Stalin pointed out, their 'Left' position entailed the following: that socialism in Russia would fail without the revolution in the West; that, therefore, the regime should concentrate all its efforts on promoting those revolutions; *and*, if those efforts failed, the Soviets should give up power.

Yes, this was indeed the logic of the knotty processes of Marxist thought. Stalin simply cut the knot, with the merest pretence of theoretical justification. What his opponents failed to realize was that the party no longer consisted of the doctrinally initiated. The general mood was that inside Russia it could do anything, however difficult in theory. And above all, any proposal which implied, or seemed to imply, risking the abandonment of power was uncongenial to the decisive stratum for whom power had become a way of life. Moreover, the old cosmopolitan intellectual cadres were out of touch with the new pragmatism, and

Russocentrism, of the second level of the party, let alone the 'party masses'.

Thus, the ideological struggle was in large part a matter of interpreting the Marxist runes in favour of one or another group or policy and, as in all similar disputes, rhetorical assertions of orthodoxy and denunciation of heresy were more prevalent than anything remotely resembling rational argument. And all that really need be said about Stalin's conduct of these controversies is that while his analyses have often been faulted by Marxist purists, and were often less sophisticated than those of his opponents, they were adequate to the occasion.

Stalin in fact provided enough Marxism to sugar the pill for the dialecticians on his side of the debate. He also threw them a bone in the form of a more recondite attack on a forgotten theory of Trotsky's – that of 'Permanent Revolution', which had involved Trotsky in polemics with Lenin. It was now linked, rather perfunctorily, into the main dispute: all the more effectively because the original texts were not available, nor reprinted for the audience supposed to judge them – an early example of mature Stalinist controversial methods.

Zinoviev and Kamenev were now engaged in even fiercer disputes with Trotsky. In January 1925, Zinoviev and Kamenev urged in the Central Committee that Trotsky be expelled from the Politburo. Stalin made several alternative suggestions, including merely removing Trotsky as War Commissar (from which post he had in fact just offered his resignation). This was carried. As Stalin was to say later:

'We did not agree with Zinoviev and Kamenev because we knew that a policy of decapitation is pregnant with great dangers for the party; we know that the method of axing and blood-letting – for blood is what they were demanding – is dangerous and infectious. Today you cut off one man, tomorrow another, the day after tomorrow a third . . . and what shall we have left of the party then?'

Over the next couple of years, Trotsky, while still a member of the Politburo, remained aloof from the new struggles now developing. He was replaced as War Commissar by Mikhail Frunze, a moderately successful Civil War commander whose sympathies were Zinovievite. In November Frunze was ordered by Stalin in the name of the Politburo to undergo an operation for ulcers, and died as a result. There were rumours right from the start that the operation was unnecessary, and in fact little less than murder. The most recent investigations in the Soviet Union fail to support this view, and its interest is largely that it was thought plausible so early in Stalin's career. It received particularly wide publicity a few years later with Boris Pilnyak's novella 'Tale of the Unextinguished Moon', in which the naive writer recounted the story in fictional form. (Curiously enough, Stalin had quoted Pilnyak approvingly in *Foundations of Leninism*; not so curiously, he was to have him shot in 1938.)

Frunze, in his turn, was succeeded as War Commissar by Stalin's old colleague Kliment Voroshilov.

All this time Stalin was building up his position. He had long had close ties with Ordzhonikidze and Voroshilov, and these had been much strengthened by the Georgian and Tsaritsyn events.

Other allies too gravitated to him. Molotov, related by cousinhood to his pre-pseudonym namesake the composer Skriabin, was himself able to play the violin. His own father was a salesman and he himself was sent to high school in Kazan, but became a Bolshevik there at the age of sixteen. Underground work prevented further education, apart from a one-year course in economics at the Polytechnic in Moscow. By 1912, at the age of twenty-two, he was involved in editing *Pravda*. And as we have seen, in 1917 he took a line which was at first overridden by Stalin and Kamenev, but which later turned out to have been 'correct'. Over the next few years he became valuable to Lenin with his organizational talent, and – always as a subordinate – an ally of Stalin's against the rhetoricians of revolution. Though one of the few 'educated men' among Stalin's entourage in later years, he was never to be one of those put forward to present intellectual analysis, or even justification, of Stalinism.

It is hard to find any description of Molotov except in the most neutral tones, as a colourless orthodox Marxist-Leninist, as a humourless bureaucrat (he was known as 'stone-bottom' even in the 1920s). He was to live into the 1980s, long since disgraced as an accomplice in terror though also (twice) nearly a victim as well: Churchill was to say of him, 'How glad I am at the end of my life not to have had to endure the stresses which he had suffered; better never be born.' He provided an air of solidarity and of Old Bolshevik credentials from his time at the pre-revolutionary *Pravda*.

Even Molotov had a stronger educational background than most of the rest of the rising Stalinists. Kaganovich, born into a poor Jewish family in the Ukraine, had become a worker at a shoe tannery at the age of sixteen and soon, with two brothers, entered the Kiev Bolshevik underground. He seems to have been taken up by Stalin, like Voroshilov, though in different circumstances, when Stalin was on his missions to the south.

Fairly similar backgrounds were usually to be found in almost all the second-level political figures who, by efficiency and ruthlessness, had hacked out careers over the Civil War period. They were from the hardest level of underground action, or of workers' circles, and of worker or near-worker origin. They had not been to universities, nor lived in studious exile in Geneva or Zurich. They had not been at the centre of things, producing *Pravda* or organizing the Bolshevik representation in the Duma. So long as policies seemed right, they were not much concerned with issues of intra-party democracy, as raised by Leftists like ex-prince Obolensky-Ossinsky. In fact they seem to have distrusted the intellectual fireworks of both the left and the right and preferred the simpler arguments of Stalin.

These are generalities, and the various factions contained a spread of both social and intellectual backgrounds. Nevertheless, it was the solid, hard, unsubtle, half-educated faithful who provided the bulk of the new Stalin group. Another emerging supporter was the Latvian Yan Rudzutak, farm boy become steel worker, and long an inmate of tsarist jails, who became a member of the Central Committee as early as 1921 (and whom Lenin seems to have considered for General Secretary). Other future leaders of the faction include Mikhail Kalinin, who inherited Sverdlov's position as Head of State in 1919, peasant-born and later a worker, and generally lacking in any political personality; Anastas Mikoyan, candidate member of the Central Committee in 1922, full member in 1923; Stanislav Kossior, candidate member in 1923, full member in 1924; and Sergei Kirov, candidate member in 1922, full member in 1923. Valerian Kuibyshev became a member of the Secretariat with Molotov and Stalin in 1922, and in 1923 was also head of the newly combined Rabkrin and Central Control Commission. He came of rather different stock. He was an officer's son, sent to a local Samara cadet school at the age of ten, and then to the Military Medical Academy from which he was expelled at the age of eighteen, having become a revolutionary.

Such figures were men of repute in the party, though on the face of it they were outweighed by the Trotskys and Zinovievs. Neglecting their potential and their present power not merely to vote under the influence of speeches made *de haut en bas*, but actually to form or maintain their own opinions, was a mistake made by his opponents, but not by Stalin.

For it is important to note that, although Stalin's position as General

Secretary from 1922 gave him a great deal of power in selecting provisional secretaries, packing Congress delegations and so on (which also contributed to overbearing his lower-level opponents), he could not have won power without carrying with him forty or fifty Old Bolsheviks at this higher level. They were, in fact, men whom Lenin had valued on their records alone rather than for their theoretical contributions. Now the constituency which a new leader had to win, they were the increasingly secure base of Stalin's rise to power. This stratum was wholly committed to the idea that the prime necessity was the elimination of the market system and of all producers independent of the state; and that 'class struggle', in the villages and elsewhere, was the necessary mode of procedure. But they also accepted Lenin's compromise with the peasantry as a temporary necessity.

Years later (in November 1937) Stalin spoke in private to a group of intimates about the problem of power in the 1920s. In those days he said, Trotsky was far better known than he was. Trotsky's reputation and that of the other famous figures – Zinoviev, Kamenev, Bukharin and Rykov, supported moreover by Krupskaya – far outweighed those of his own allies, Molotov, Kaganovich, Voroshilov and so on. He himself was a nobody in the party compared with Lenin. His rivals were better orators than he was, and all he had was the organizational machinery. But the oppositionists did not reckon with the party, especially 'the middle element – that is, the backbone of the party'.

In the last year of Lenin's life its leading departments were in the hands of Stalin's supporters – Organization and Instruction under Kaganovich, Records and Assignments under Syrtsov, and Agitation and Propaganda under Bubnov.

Stalin had a group of 'Assistants of the Secretariat of the Central Committee' under his direct orders. First was I. P. Tovstukha, who had been head of his personal secretariat before he became General Secretary, and who was made chief of the 'Secret Department' but in addition Stalin's principal subordinate. He was away at the Lenin Institute for a time, with Nazaretyan, another of the Stalin staff (later shot), apparently acting in his absence.

Other leading assistants included Boris Bazhanov, who defected to the West in 1928, and wrote interesting memoirs. More important was Lev Mekhlis, who had started as a Zionist, became a Menshevik, then a Bolshevik, had been with Stalin in the Civil War, and had a fearful Stalinist career ahead of him. We also note, as a junior, the young Georgi Malenkov, later to be Premier of the USSR. And the long-serving assistant who was to remain in charge of Stalin's office until 1952, Alexander Poskrebyshev. He was in the apparat in 1922, and was an Assistant by 1924. Poskrebyshev once suggested to Stalin that Tovstukha – a sick man suffering from some form of tuberculosis – might have touched some plates brought in for his dinner. Tovstukha was transferred to the Institute of Marxism-Leninism, and Poskrebyshev took his place. Poskrebyshev worked a sixteen-hour day. His main gift was a phenomenal memory; and his personality was so crude that he had no serious prospect of higher political employment. He was frequently drunk, and invariably used the coarsest possible language.

More important was the fact that, as some foreign observers already noted, Stalin's apparatus was by far the most effectively organized body in the country. In it were gathered, and increasingly so, the threads of all the political potentials in the party and the state.

8

At this time Stalin and his wife had an apartment in the Kremlin, and later a fine country house not far from Moscow, called Zubalovo after its former owners, whose flourishing oil business in the Caucasus had seen some of the strikes of Stalin's early career. Stalin constantly rebuilt this 'further' dacha, as it was to be called, to distinguish it from the one at Kuntsevo (the 'nearer') where he was to spend most of his later career.

In these homes, Nadezhda lived as the wife of a leading Bolshevik, though she never became a spoiled member of the 'new class' now arising. We are told in a recent Soviet biography of Stalin that she 'quickly adapted to the atmosphere of endless conferences, meetings, struggles, travel, in which her husband lived', and (in spite of his now adequate staff) did some of his secretarial work. She bore him a son, the to-be-notorious Vasily, in 1921, and an equally famous daughter, Svetlana, in 1926. Moreover, her stepson Yakov, Stalin's son by his first wife, who had been brought up in Georgia by his Svanidze grandparents, came to live with them at this time. Nadezhda got on well with him, but Stalin resented Yakov, whose knowledge of Russian needed a good deal of work, and who was thus a constant reminder of Stalin's Georgian background. Moreover, Yakov's uncle (till now in effect his guardian) had been fairly prominent among the unruly Georgian Communists – in fact he was local Commissar of Foreign Affairs – though not as intransigent as some.

Stalin also disapproved of Yakov's first marriage, and then of his second marriage (to a Jewish woman), Yakov's 'gentleness and composure', we are told, infuriated Stalin. When Yakov attempted suicide after a few years of this, his failure led to Stalin's comment, 'Ha! He couldn't even shoot straight.' After that Yakov went to live in Leningrad with his stepmother's family, the Alliluyevs.

Nadezhda herself was not endlessly patient with Stalin's way of life. She often complained, 'Your children, your family, are of no interest to you'; and he often answered rudely, sometimes with a curse. In 1926, she went back to her parents in Leningrad, though she eventually returned. But the life continued to weigh on her, and in the late 1920s she went to Berlin, where her brother Pavel was then stationed, to consult a neurologist. There seems to have been some family predisposition to depression; both her sister Anna and her brother Fedor were at various times hospitalized for psychological problems.

But marriage to Stalin was problem enough. By the late 1920s she had her own bedroom, and Stalin usually slept either in his office or in a small room of his own.

Though Nadezhda had reproached Stalin with his lack of interest in his family, she herself said several times that she was bored with everything, 'even the children'. In fact, though Stalin had little time for his young son and daughter, he seems to have had a more affectionate manner towards them than their mother's. In any case the children were largely looked after by nurses and governesses, like (presumably) their predecessors in the dacha, the children of the Zubalov oil magnates.

In their rows over this and other matters Stalin sometimes became enraged. Occasionally he lost his temper for other reasons, once throwing a cooked chicken out of the window of his Kremlin apartment as a complaint about the cooking; once tearing a telephone from the wall when he could only get a busy signal. On another occasion, his daughter recounts, he was pacing the apartment, smoking and spitting as was his custom. A parrot started to imitate the spitting and he angrily hit it on the head with his pipe and killed it.

Nadezhda objected to his drinking as well as to his temper. In fact, he does not seem to have been a real boozer, and drank only wine, usually Georgian. Occasionally he is reported as much the worse for drink, but usually he was more concerned with establishing a 'drinking bout' atmosphere.

This was in accord with a very marked side of his behaviour, and not only at home. Throughout his career we find an attempt at an atmosphere of good fellowship, often painful in its artificiality, but evidently representing something he in some way aspired to. His favourite picture, Repin's 'The Reply of the Zaporozhe Cossacks to the Sultan', of which he had a reproduction in his bedroom, looks rather like his idea of a meeting of some ideal Politburo: crude, drunk, broad-humoured, heroic.

This is not to say that the occasional drunkenness had no significance. But what significance? And how drunk was he? In some cultures it is considered socially appropriate in some festive circumstances to behave more drunkenly than you really are. One woman guest saw Stalin aboard his motorboat on the Black Sea, drinking and then dancing, or rather 'staggering and stamping' round the cabin out of time to the music. This seemed not only coarse and vulgar, but, she adds, so bizarre as to appear 'a kind of sinister threat', for Stalin 'still seemed sober enough to observe my reactions to his conduct'.

In any case, Nadezhda did not like this sort of social occasion. On the other hand, there were times when, with Bukharin and others, the hospitality was more to her taste, and she made a number of friends, in particular Molotov's wife Polina, Kaganovich's wife Maria, Andreyev's wife Dora, and Bukharin's (second) wife Esfiria.

Stalin's working hours, and his ideas of passing his spare moments, can have left little time for marital life. She persuaded him to go to various theatres (though after her death he visited only the Bolshoi – seeing one production of *Swan Lake* twelve or thirteen times). But when it came to films, by the end of the 1920s he was seeing one or two every week, in the small cinema in the Kremlin or in a room in his dacha. He once told some leading Agitprop figures: 'The cinema is only illusion, but life dictates its rules,' recalling Christopher Isherwood's remarks in his autobiographical *Lions and Shadows* where he is embarrassed at having to explain to friends why he excuses even bad films: it is, he realizes, because they have some relation, however clumsy, to real life.

As Stalin grew older he began to watch films which had no such relation, such as propaganda scenes from nonexistent happy collective farms.

9

In 1923 Stalin had been on the point of political ruin. In 1924 he was one among equals, but without any outright supporters in the full membership of the Politburo. Six years later he would be in unchallenged power, and all his quondam colleagues would have lost their posts.

Meanwhile, the beginning of the low-grade 'cult' attitude which had not existed under Lenin had found expression in one of the new era's most marked characteristics – the naming of towns (and mountains, and universities, and streets and anything remotely renamable) after the political leadership.

The renaming of Petrograd as Leningrad, in 1924, had at first been thought of as a special case. Besides, Lenin was dead. But now came a whole set of such changes – none of them permanent, though some lasted longer than others. Yuzovka, the mining town in the Ukraine, became Stalino in June 1924. It had previously been called after the Welsh entrepreneur Hughes, who had founded and developed it, but as a capitalist, and one without roots in Russian history, he was first to go.

To begin with it was a matter of small towns of this type. Yelizavetgrad became Zinovievsk at the same time, and thereafter the habit spread rapidly. There was even (briefly) a Trotsk – the town of Gatchina where, in 1919, Trotsky had won a *real* victory in the defence of Petrograd. Small towns were named for Kamenev, Rudzutak and others.

In April 1925 the city of Tsaritsyn became Stalingrad – a major advance, recording the rise of Stalin to a suitably higher level, well ahead of all competitors but not presuming to the status of Lenin and Leningrad.

The custom became common, and indeed lasted up to the 1980s. In the meantime, Yekaterinburg, where the murder of the Tsar had taken place, had appropriately been renamed Sverdlovsk; Sverdlov, with Lenin, had ordered the killing (as a Soviet analysis in 1989 makes clear). Then, as the cult developed, larger towns sacrificed their centuries-old appellations to Voroshilov, to Kirov, to Kalinin, to Kuibyshev, to Frunze, to Ordzhonikidze, to Maxim Gorki. Most of these blemishes have now been removed from the Soviet maps. Meanwhile over the years, the country had to endure not only Stalingrad and Stalino (eventually six Stalinos in all), but also Stalinabad, Stalinsk, Stalinogorsk, Stalinskoye, Stalinski, Staliniri (the capital of South Ossetia), Mount Stalin (the highest peak in the USSR – later to be joined by the highest peaks in Czechoslovakia and Bulgaria), Stalin Bay, the Stalin Range, and various villages simply 'name of Stalin' . . .

10

After the event, we now know the result of the political struggle which lasted from 1923 to 1929. In six years Stalin outmanœuvred a series of opponents; first, in alliance with all the rest of his colleagues, he opposed and demoted Trotsky. Then, in alliance with the Bukharin–Rykov 'Right' he defeated the Zinoviev–Kamenev 'Left' bloc, and then a new alliance between these and the Trotskyites. And finally he and his own following attacked their heretofore allies, the 'Rightists'.

At the time such an outcome seemed unlikely. It was not only that the small Communist ruling stratum, unpopular in the country as a whole, might be thought to need the employment of all its talent, all its thinly stretched cadres, to master its social environment. But, as we have seen, there was also no general feeling of Stalin's superiority over the others. Even those who foresaw something of his future eminence did not think in terms of the total personal supremacy he was to achieve. And few ever felt his rise to be inevitable. Radek foresaw its possibility, even its probability; but he struggled for five years to prevent it.

When we look at the position as it developed in 1923–4, our first feeling is of the political ineptness of the opposition to Stalin – at any rate its political ineptness as compared with Stalin. The Bolsheviks were, as we have said, a small and narrow sect. Except in out-and-out struggle with the old regime on the one hand, and ideological disputes settled by petty organizational intrigue on the other, they had little experience of politics proper.

Lenin, it is true, had been (as Trotsky put it) a 'pragmatist' of the most devoted sort when it came to tactics: that is, within the limits of his ideological commitments. Even he had blundered close to disaster in the policies pursued until 1921, saving the Communist state when it was almost too late. Still his skills in the pre-revolutionary intrigues had been, within those limits, of a 'political' nature.

But few of his followers had any experience of politics proper, of the balances of power within the *pays légal*, the manœuvres in the area of established power. Their experience had been limited. They were not 'men of the world' in such affairs. It was not a matter of intelligence in the abstract, but of lack of the right sort of knowledge and experience – or, lacking that, of instinct.

They had a crude, inchoate sense of limiting their rivals' power. But they had no sense of timing, of postponing action until the best moment. Bukharin was later to criticize Stalin as a master of 'dosing' – of getting his way in gradual doses. That this was supposed to be a damaging point is a measure of Bukharin's (and others') comparative incompetence.

People of political genius may indeed arise even among strange millennarian sects. The Mormon leader Brigham Young was an astonishing example, in a sect which many would regard as, at any rate at that time, very peculiar indeed. That most of the Communists did not have this talent is in part due to the fact that their politics had been almost entirely a matter of the intellectual acceptance of theory. It was academic. Lord Melbourne, future Prime Minister of the United Kingdom, wrote home while still at university that students with only the vaguest notion of real politics would ask 'with a supercilious sort of doubt, whether Pitt is really a good orator, or Fox has much political knowledge. This will wear off in time; though, to be sure, one of them is three and twenty ... You cannot have the advantages of study and of the world together ...' The younger intellectual Bolsheviks made their judgements on grounds almost as inept.

Trotsky was, in the eyes of his colleagues, a convert. This is a status which has always given trouble. Even Jesus Christ had to argue in favour of 'the sinner that repenteth' against the objections of those who considered themselves already saved. Converts have sometimes achieved success like, up to a point, the Apostle Paul, or, in another context, the Caliph Omar, at one time a leading enemy of Islam.

But Trotsky lacked one major Bolshevik habit – the constant worrying, like a terrier, over points of ideology or policy. This independent position had allowed him to pick and choose his controversies, to relax or even abandon the quotidian struggle. He had even (before the Revolution) attempted to reconcile the factions of the Social Democrats at a time when the Bolsheviks saw the doctrinal divergences as unbridgeable.

Stalin's own drive for power and reluctance to be inhibited, at any rate for long, by the wishes or interests of others was clear. It is true that he had shown a crude misunderstanding of the limits to which a seeker for power could push, though it was only towards the end of the Lenin period that he found he had gone too far.

But in the new situation in which genuine political manœuvre became undoubtedly necessary, he showed that he had learned his lesson. One recent biography notes that a modern games theorist has claimed that Stalin alone among the competitors had an adequate grasp of 'games theory'. In the sense that he was better able to sense the moment to move and the methods to use, this would be true. The theoretical formalization of the delicate, complex, shifting and sometimes unanalysable conditions at play is doubtless of interest to those whose taste is for formalization (though attempts to apply games theory to developments in the Politburo of the 1980s were singularly unfruitful – if only because even Politburo members themselves did not know which way they would jump in given circumstances). At any rate, Stalin had developed, and now increasingly developed, the skills needed for the rather less simple game as played in the chaos of reality.

11

The defeat of Trotsky, though not yet final, had been due to a virtually unanimous campaign by all the other leaders, his only support being the dying Lenin. Factional fighting in the Politburo was now, however, thrown open for all. Of the seven men elected as full members in June 1924, six would be killed by the lone survivor.

This membership now consisted of Zinoviev and Kamenev; Stalin; Trotsky; and Bukharin, Rykov and Tomsky.

The triumvirate, though without constitutional status, was now generally recognized as the leading core of this Politburo. It was always listed in the order Zinoviev, Kamenev, Stalin.

It later appeared extraordinary that a man like Zinoviev, with little prestige of his own in the inner party, and little political sense, should have appeared for a time to be the first man in the party and the state. He had, it is true, been Lenin's closest assistant in exile. But he had tarnished his record in opposing the seizure of power, and had acted with a combination of brutality and cowardice in Petrograd during the Civil War. In alliance with the more respectable figure of Kamenev he carried more weight, though Kamenev too had weakness in his record. Zinoviev was an effective orator, though his speeches left an aftertaste of lack of substantiality. Kamenev was a serious politician, and excellent as a chairman of party and government committees; he held, in Lenin's time, the chairmanship of the Politburo.

Zinoviev and Kamenev controlled the party machines in Leningrad and Moscow respectively. They had a number of prominent supporters – though far fewer outstanding Bolsheviks than the Trotskyites could muster. In contrast to the questioning and ideological minds of Pyatakov or Preobrazhensky, they represented a large stratum of traditionalist Bolsheviks who had reservations about the hitherto more peripheral figure of Stalin. Their supporters included above all Krupskaya, but also such respected political figures as Grigori Sokolnikov. In 1923 it looked as though they had a reasonable majority in the Central Committee.

In addition to their ideological investment in early world revolution they shared the 'Leftist' view that, in the interim, Russia should not let its rickety socialism leak away. This implied a rapid return to an attack on the errant classes. The means of attack was, indeed, usually not envisaged as mass terror, but the peasantry should at least be faced by taxation to provide the funds for reindustrialization. But Stalin, with his current allies of the 'Right', opposed this.

These 'Rightists', Nikolai Bukharin, Alexei Rykov and Mikhail Tomsky, carried less immediate weight than Zinoviev and Kamenev, but were more impressive as a political force. Bukharin, whom Lenin called 'the darling of the party', was an intellectual in the sense Zinoviev was not. Rykov, who had succeeded Lenin as chairman of the Council of People's Commissars, was more in the Kamenev mould. Tomsky (alone of the leaders) was actually a worker, and was now in charge of the trade unions, which Lenin had saved from Trotsky's notion of conscript 'labour armies'.

By late 1924 Zinoviev and Kamenev saw, though rather belatedly, that Stalin and his current allies were more of a threat to their position than Trotsky had been. They saw that Lenin had been right.

It was too late. In 1923 Trotsky had failed to push his advantage over the Testament. Kamenev and Zinoviev had defended Stalin, and realized his true nature only when they were in no position to defeat him. Now, through 1925, they started to mobilize their strength. As it turned out, their support was mainly a matter of inertia. It had little energy or vitality. Though thousands of old party members remained loyal Zinovievites through the ensuing struggle, the whole faction lacked the spark, or the weight, of any of the other factions. It was, throughout, a locus of dull conformism.

Its strength lay in its control of the dominant party machines of Leningrad and Moscow. With these bastions, Zinoviev and Kamenev had a chance in the play for power. But they were already outnumbered in the Politburo, as they had presumably not foreseen.

Zinoviev and Kamenev chose to fight on the issue of Socialism in One Country, Stalin's weak point doctrinally, but his strong point in practice – and, moreover, a position almost automatically implied by the mere existence of the New Economic Policy, and its seeking of economic stability.

Trotsky was meanwhile required to perform a humiliating 'service to the party'. The American leftist Max Eastman had published an account of Lenin's Testament in his *Since Lenin Died*, which came out in the West in 1925. The Politburo demanded not merely that Trotsky repudiate Eastman, but that he deny the existence of the Testament. They even dictated the terms; and Trotsky signed the statement that 'all talk about a "testament" allegedly suppressed or violated is a malicious invention and is directed wholly against Lenin's real will and the interests of the party of which he was the founder.'

Just before the Fourteenth Congress, in December 1925, Stalin secured the defection of Kamenev's hitherto trusted Secretary of the Moscow Party Organization, Uglanov. Stalin and Molotov had a series of more or less clandestine conversations with him, and he eventually came over, with his delegation, to the Stalin–Bukharin camp.

At the Congress Kamenev gave a remarkable and frank estimate of Stalin:

'We are against creating the theory of a leader; we are against making a leader. We are against having the Secretariat combine in practice both politics and organization and place itself above the political organ ... We cannot regard it as normal, and we think it harmful to the party to prolong a situation in which the Secretariat combines politics and organization, and in fact decides policy in advance. I must say what I have to say to the end. Because I have more than once said it to Comrade Stalin personally, because I have more than once said it to a group of party delegates. I repeat it to the congress: I have reached the conviction that Comrade Stalin cannot perform the function of uniting the Bolshevik general staff.'

This was 'the culminating point of the Congress', and Kamenev was interrupted with 'uproar' at several points. His last remark ends in the Stenographic Report with 'Various speakers: "A lie! Humbug! So that's it!"' And after a feebler counter-clamour from the Leningrad delegation, 'the delegates rise and cheer Comrade Stalin. Thunders of applause ... "Long live Comrade Stalin!" Loud and prolonged cheers. Cries of hurrah. Clamour' ...

Stalin himself, on the other hand, spoke up for moderation and collective leadership, in terms which required a good deal of amendment in later editions of his *Works*. 'You demand Bukharin's blood?' he said. 'We won't give you his blood!' And it was not only Bukharin that the

Zinovievites were attacking. He added: 'The party was to be led without Rykov, without Kalinin, without Tomsky, without Molotov, without Bukharin ... The party cannot be led without the aid of those comrades I have just named.'

Though the Leningrad delegation remained solidly under Zinovievite control, it was heavily outnumbered, and Zinoviev and Kamenev were defeated.

After the Congress Kamenev was reduced to candidate membership of the Politburo, and Kalinin and Voroshilov became full members. Though both – and especially Voroshilov – were generally speaking Stalinists, both had been on the right within that grouping, and were at this point thought of by Bukharin as just as much his allies as they were Stalin's.

Trotsky remained an onlooker. In fact, the new majority pointed to him as a model. The Leningraders were reproached for their extreme anti-Trotskyism. Mikoyan held Trotsky up as one who, in defeat, had accepted party discipline. Tomsky and Kalinin took the same line ...

12

In April 1926 came the third round in the struggle. Trotsky had not been on speaking terms with Zinoviev and Kamenev since 1923. Now, in private meetings with him, after many mutual exculpations, they attacked Stalin's intrigues. They joked about him, mimicked his accent and imitated his behaviour, rather to the annoyance of the humourless Trotsky. More acceptably, they described Stalin's cunning, implacability and ruthlessness.

According to Trotsky, they said they felt convinced that Stalin would like to kill all three of them, and that they had hidden statements in a safe place in case of such an event. Trotsky did not take this last seriously at the time.

In the early summer of 1926 the Trotskyites and Zinovievites formed a 'United Opposition'. Bukharin had attempted to persuade Trotsky that Zinoviev and Kamenev were not the best hope of the party. Trotsky accepted this, but argued that Stalin was even worse. Trotsky also pointed out that the Stalinists were now, in effect, carrying out anti-Semitic agitation in the Moscow party cells against himself and his two new allies.

In June Stalin launched an open offensive against the new grouping.

Trotsky and Zinoviev in the Politburo, and Kamenev in its non-voting membership, had no support except for a handful of Central Committee members, and a few thousand individual Communists. They did the best they could. Their meetings were broken up. Their emissaries were harassed. One famous meeting addressed by the Zinovievite Lashevich, who was still Deputy Commissar for War, was held in a wood outside Moscow.

The opposition was weaker than either of its factions had been a few years ago. As they started their struggle, they had already lost their only bastion, the Leningrad party organization. Over January and February 1926 there had been a massive operation, in which half the Politburo and other envoys of the Central Committee took part. By continuous pressure at every level of the local party they had finally broken the (as it turned out rather shaky) Zinovievite grasp in the city, and had Sergei Kirov, Ordzhonikidze's old accomplice in the subjugation of the Caucasus, 'elected' First Secretary.

The trio intervened formally in debate at a Central Committee plenum in July 1926. Zinoviev was immediately removed from the Politburo.

They continued to organize and appeal. But as one of their leaders, Radek, was to say later, they had in any case mistaken the whole battleground. They had thought theoretical propaganda would win the support which would in fact only have been forthcoming for practical and popular policies. But whatever their tactics, they were doomed. In October, under threat of expulsion from the party, they submitted and abjured their 'factional' activity on the understanding that no more would be required of them.

However, a few weeks later, during a 'stormy' session of the Politburo, at which many Central Committee members were present, Stalin went back on the agreement and insisted that the opposition was a 'Social Democratic deviation', and that they should now not merely accept party discipline but actually recant their views. Trotsky warned the majority that this must lead in the long run to the end of sincere disagreement in the party, and its eventual ruin. He then pointed to Stalin and said, 'The First Secretary offers his candidature for the post of gravedigger of the Revolution!' Stalin turned pale and got to his feet. It at first looked as if he would lose his temper and make a hot reply which might have been damaging to himself in the long run. At least, so he seemed to think, for he controlled himself with an obvious effort and went out of the room, slamming the door.

Next day the Central Committee voted to remove Trotsky from the

Politburo and Kamenev from his candidate membership.

The Fifteenth Party Congress followed. Stalin attacked the opposition in violent terms, citing both their record and their policies, and calling for a total repudiation of their views. Kamenev made a mild speech, in which he said amongst other things (wrongly as it turned out), 'We do not live in the Middle Ages. Witch trials cannot be staged now!'

Now the oppositionists – too late for it to do them any good – brought up Lenin's complaint that Stalin was too rude. Stalin with his overwhelming majority was now in a position to shrug off the accusation. Yes, he admitted, Lenin had indeed said this. And he read out the passage from the Testament about his rudeness, and other faults. He emphasized that the decision not to publish it had been unanimous, and on the essentials said, 'Yes, comrades, I am rude towards those who rudely and treacherously break their word, who split and destroy the party.' This had not, of course, been Lenin's complaint.

Stalin then reminded them that he had put in his resignation, and that all the delegates, Trotsky, Zinoviev and Kamenev among them, had voted for him to remain as General Secretary. It was not in his character, he added, to abandon his post, so he had continued to serve.

Bukharin was particularly ferocious against the Trotsky–Zinoviev group. In Isaac Deutscher's words, he 'assailed the opposition with reckless virulence, exulting in its plight, bragging, threatening and playing up to the worst elements in the party'. Stalin shouted, 'Well done, Bukharin. Well done, well done. He does not argue with them, he slaughters them!'

Expelled from the Politburo, but still members of the party and of its Central Committee, though under threat of losing even these appointments, the opposition now made the formal retraction and repudiation of their views that Stalin had demanded. The whole episode was instructive. Stalin had agreed to a partial surrender, and when that was made, welshed on the deal and went on to demand further and fuller surrender, at a time when the opposition could hardly return to its original bargaining position. Some of the oppositionists were to go through cycles of accepting such assurances and then finding them worthless – including, in the end, assurances that their lives would be spared . . .

For the present, Zinoviev and Kamenev merely hoped, or half-hoped, that their demotion would be temporary, that Stalin would need them again. On New Year's Eve, they unexpectedly turned up at Stalin's apartment with bottles of brandy and champagne. Stalin treated them in the friendliest fashion.

In 1927, the Trotskyites and Zinovievites made one last effort. There were new issues about which no promises of silence had been made: in particular the progress of the Chinese revolution. It had been handled with the same combination of ignorance, arrogance and incompetence with which Germany had been treated a few years earlier – more so, in fact, as the ignorance was more complete and the slapdash incompetence greater. All factions in the Kremlin had mishandled the matter in turn, but those in power were naturally the culprits in the more recent debacle, which ended with the rout of the Chinese Communists in April 1927.

Stalin now brought Trotsky and Zinoviev before the Central Committee and the Central Control Commission with a view to their expulsion from the former. He was meanwhile breaking up the opposition by transferring its second-rank leaders to provincial posts or embassies. There was what amounted to an opposition demonstration to see Smilga off to a post in the Soviet Far East.

The opposition prepared a platform for the next Party Congress. This was forbidden. They then printed it illegally, and this was represented as a plot – and indeed, it was a genuine underground operation.

The hearings against Trotsky and Zinoviev were resumed, without even a pretence of judicial decency. Trotsky's defence was met with curses, howls and the hurling of inkpots, books and glasses. Stalin alone spoke in a controlled manner, though in a tone of 'coarse and cold hatred'.

On 7 November, the tenth anniversary of the Revolution, the opposition made a last effort, joining the official demonstration groups but with their own slogans. They were attacked by police, 'activists' and others who had been mobilized especially for this operation. Then Trotsky and Zinoviev were expelled from the party, and Kamenev and the others from the Central Committee.

The Zinovievites now surrendered, being admitted to the Congress to speak of themselves as 'wrong and anti-Leninist'. Bukharin told them, 'You have done well to make up your mind – this was the last minute – the iron curtain of history is just coming down.' But they were, as yet, refused reinstatement in the party.

The Trotskyites refused to surrender and were deported to Central Asia and Siberia early in 1928 – Trotsky himself was sent to the Kazakh capital Alma Ata.

By the middle of 1928, Stalin had completed the political ruin of the various factions of the left. Over the next two years he was, by different tactics – and in different political circumstances – to defeat in turn his current Rightist allies. Meanwhile, in August 1928, Bukharin came to see Kamenev and Sokolnikov.

Bukharin was in a very nervous state. Stalin, he said, had now finally obtained a Politburo majority, with only Tomsky, Rykov and Bukharin himself holding out. Stalin's policies would lead to a 'police state' and to 'famine and ruin'. 'We consider Stalin's line fatal to the Revolution. This line is leading us to the abyss. Our disagreements with Stalin are far more serious than those we had with you.'

Bukharin expressed regret that Zinoviev and Kamenev were no longer in the Politburo. He compared Stalin with Genghis Khan, and said 'He will slay us.' Stalin's tactics were to make verbal compromises but, 'He is an unprincipled intriguer who subordinates everything to his lust for power'; and 'Stalin knows only vengeance ... the stab in the back.'

Bukharin's approach to Kamenev, which he insisted should be kept secret, of course became known to the secret police almost at once. Bukharin was desperately seeking possible allies for a future struggle; but Kamenev felt that the Zinovievites now had no choice but to submit to the party's actual leadership. Thus the political results of this strange meeting were nil. Its interest lies, rather, in Bukharin's view of Stalin; but even more in the fact that he had only now come to hold it. Stalin had again succeeded in hiding his real characteristics from the Rightists, all through the manœuvres of the past five years. This is in itself an astonishing political feat, and a reflection of profound elements of his personality.

Meanwhile, Bukharin can be seen as yet another in the chain of supposedly intelligent men, from Lenin to Roosevelt, who did not understand Stalin's real nature until it was too late.

Chapter 9

Towards Supremacy

One thing Bukharin now saw was that Stalin had obtained a Politburo majority. Bukharin had thought that Voroshilov and Kalinin would support the right, as most of their speeches implied. But Stalin, Bukharin said, had 'some special hold on them that I do not know of'. Ordzhonikidze 'came to me abusing Stalin in the most violent fashion, but at the decisive moment he betrayed us'. Bukharin had been outwitted, and he knew it. The political situation of the Right had become desperate.

The other and even more important thing he had now realized was that Stalin no longer intended to pursue the gradualist policies of the New Economic Policy. On the contrary, he clearly planned to launch the party on an adventurist class-war, policy of crash industrialization and collectivization, adventurist beyond even the most extreme of the plans hitherto rejected as beyond the pale for their Leftism.

The Communists were in what amounted to a doctrinal, political and psychological impasse. As we have said, they had taken power on the basis of a theory of class struggle as the motive force of history, with the proletariat's victory leading the way to the abolition of classes and the arrival of utopia.

They had justified their rule in a country with a small and shrinking proletariat, quite obviously unprepared on doctrinal or any other grounds to exercise its dictatorship, by the notion that the industrial countries of the West would soon also become Communist, and provide enough working-class masses for everybody. When this failed, or rather when it had to be admitted that it had failed for the immediately foreseeable future, and they had nevertheless decided on Socialism in One Country, they were faced with unpalatable facts.

First of all, their attempt to bring in 'socialism' by force had failed. The policy known as War Communism from 1918 to 1921 was not, as the phrase implies, a mere reaction to the events of the emergency of the Civil War. As Lenin later said on several occasions, it had been an attempt to effect an immediate transition to the new order. It was, he admitted, 'an attempt to attain Communism straight away ... generally, we thought it possible ... to begin without transition to build up Socialism.'

In a longer analysis he said:

'We calculated ... or we presumed without sufficient calculation – that an immediate transition would take place from the old Russian economy to state production and distribution on Communist principles; and, on the specific policy of requisition we made the mistake of deciding to change over directly to Communist production and distribution. We sought to obtain a sufficient quantity of grain from the peasants by the way of the *razverstka* [compulsory grain delivery quotas], then to apportion it to the industries, and that thus we would obtain Communist production and distribution. I would not affirm that this was exactly how we visualized it, but we did act in this spirit.'

This had to be given up, barely in time, when (as Trotsky said) 'the middle peasant spoke to us with naval guns' in the Kronstadt uprising – and with shotguns in the vast belt of peasant insurrections which, as a leading Soviet historian put it, 'almost totally encircled' central Russia.

But what were the Communists to do? They had rid themselves of the landlords and the capitalists – and though NEP allowed the rise of a number of small merchants and so on, this was an easily controllable phenomenon. But in the countryside the huge peasant majority of the population remained entrenched. They had received the land of the landlords in 1917–18, they had fought down the Bolshevik expropriations, and they were strongly established in a stubborn wish to work their own farms.

The Communist handling of the peasantry had been crass, but it had also been shot through with doctrinal delusions which still subsisted. Marxists had always regarded the peasantry as a backward class, and looked forward to the fulfilment of the Communist Manifesto's agrarian programme:

'The abolition of property in land ... the improvement of the soil generally in accordance with a common plan. Establishment of industrial armies especially for agriculture. Combination of agriculture with manufacturing industries; gradual abolition of the distinction between town and country.'

In Russia in particular the peasantry was regarded by most progressives as a drag on the modernization of the country, as the 'dark people' still mentally in the Middle Ages. Their stubborn refusal to accept the schemes of the urban intelligentsia is seen throughout Russian revolutionary literature as a fearful obstacle to change. Though the Marxists sometimes saw, as Lenin did, that some way must be found to neutralize, or bamboozle, this vast majority of the population over the short term, the attitude to be found in most of the advanced literature is one of little less than exasperated rage and hatred towards the dull rustics. Stalin, the small-town lad educated and literate beyond the dreams of the ploughboy, shows this as strongly as anyone.

Under the Marxist class scheme the mass of the peasantry were 'petit bourgeois', owners of private property but not exploiters of the labour of others. Lenin elaborated this into a triple division – the poor peasant with little or no land (together with the full-time agricultural labourer or 'village proletarian'); the middle peasant, constituting the bulk of the peasantry as defined above; and the rich peasant or 'kulak' who exploited the rest economically.

During the Soviet period, tactics varied with circumstances. The party was concerned to establish its hold in the villages through the poor peasant, to neutralize or convert the middle peasant, and to direct rural class war against the kulak. But the idea that a class-conscious village poor existed, able to play a role in the countryside comparable to the proletarian in the cities, was an ignis fatuus. The 'village proletariat', supposed to be particularly reliable, were few in number, and often the local ne'er-do-wells and drunks – as village Communists often complained.

Indeed the whole scheme was totally fallacious. First of all, the idea of the exploiting kulak was a false one. There had indeed been a rich peasant stratum, usually farming seventy or eighty acres and employing a few village 'proletarians'. There is little sign that even they had been much resented by their fellow villagers, and in the seizure of the landlords' land in 1917, they had survived untouched. But in any case,

Lenin's first wave of class struggle in the countryside in 1918–20 had eliminated them.

In fact in the 1920s there was almost no real class differentiation in the villages. Even the authorities found it impossible to define 'kulak' and 'middle peasant'. The poor peasant everywhere looked up to the richer. Sometimes he did part-time work for his richer neighbours or cousins, while the 'kulak' in turn saw him over hard periods with grain and food.

As the countryside grew more prosperous, efficient farmers who had started off poor became a little richer. In particular, those who had served in the Red Army, often a lively section of the village to start with, had come to learn of newer seeds and techniques, and were especially likely to flourish. Communists in the villages – not that there were many of them – were at this stage often the strongest supporters of NEP, and had nothing against the kulak.

And it is worth noting, to any for whom the word 'kulak' still conjures up a rich exploiter on the grand scale, that the most prosperous peasants in 1927 had two or three cows and up to ten hectares of sowing area, for an average family of seven people. This richest peasant group received only 50–56 per cent greater income per capita than the lowest.

Throughout the duration of the NEP, there was a continuous pressure of party controversy about what to do with the kulaks, and their built-in class menace to 'socialism'. If agriculture was to recover, and to maintain its recovery, the more efficient farmers had to be encouraged. Bukharin even told the peasants, 'Enrich yourselves.' This was generally felt to be going too far in its effusiveness, but the policy it expressed, too crudely for the more sensitive party palates, was maintained, though combined at times with various persecutions and harassments of the kulaks which contradicted it.

When the NEP came in, a common opinion in the West (but also among many in Russia itself) was that the Bolsheviks, having seen that their social and economic ideas led to disaster, had learnt the lesson, and would in future pursue sound policies without further attempts at solutions based on force and terror. This was to underestimate the power of strongly held ideas, however fallacious.

There were, as it turned out, several things wrong with the simple-looking Marxist scheme. While conflict between different economic groups had been understood as far back as Greek times to be politically important, to see it as the overwhelming element in society was not borne out by past history – and was not to be borne out by future history either. Second, the supernal role of the industrial proletariat as history's chosen fulfilment was, to say the least, unproven. Still, this was what the Communists believed, and, as we have seen, they saw themselves, even into the late 1980s, as in some sense the representatives of the 'working masses'.

But the party had its Mission as well as its Myth. It had to 'build socialism'. If we look merely at the social and economic forces operating at this time, we fail to take into account the restless dynamic of the party. Its members, and of course Stalin in particular, were by temperament suited not to compromise but to struggle, not to reasonable approaches but to confrontation. They were very far indeed from being economic pragmatists or realists. Sobered briefly, like Lenin himself, by the total disaster produced by strict adherence to doctrine, they remained unhappy with the compromise.

We have already spoken of the ideological preconceptions of the Communists, including Stalin's. We have not yet developed two points. First, the degree to which they held these principles, their intensity and determination in pursuit of these doctrinal goals. Second, the particularly harsh contradiction between their beliefs and the realities of Soviet society.

It is, of course, impossible to say at which point, and with what mixture of motives, Stalin came to the conclusion that the only sure way of securing his power was the launching of the party into a new civil war, against the peasantry. We cannot even tell if he consciously thought of it in such terms, or anything like them. He may really have believed that there was a hostile kulak class, as against a more or less acquiescent peasant majority, and that history required the destruction of the former, upon which the latter would accept the new order in agriculture.

It is certain, at least, that throughout the ensuing period he spoke as though these propositions were true.

2

The struggle over which Bukharin had expressed his desperation to Kamenev was thus of a different nature from those between Stalin and his previous opponents.

It involved a dispute about a major shift in political-social policies which was not merely pragmatic, like the argument about Socialism in One Country; nor peripheral like the argument about China; nor pettifogging, like the argument about Permanent Revolution. It was about the rapid transformation of the whole Soviet Union into a new type of social order, at the cost of enormous suffering and of the installation of Stalin as supreme ruler.

All the leaders were to various degrees committed to the New Economic Policy, and the reconstruction of the economy by concessions to the market. All wanted, as Lenin had wanted, to end this as soon as might be feasible and return to 'socialist' policies. They held a variety of opinions on when and how to accomplish this, and in addition none of them had really sorted out their ideas on the matter. There was a good deal of shifting of ground and general havering.

Stalin had been one of the firmest, if not the most totally committed, supporters of NEP. He had constantly attacked the Left for their idea that the country could be brought to socialism by a crash industrialization programme and a confrontation with both the richer and the middle peasants, saying, for instance, 'We hope to realize collectivization with reference to the peasants, little by little, by means of orderly economic, financial, cultural and political measures.' He added the thesis that:

> 'Collectivization will be complete when all peasant enterprises have been transformed on a new technical basis of electrification and mechanization, when the majority of working peasants have been organized in cooperatives, and the majority of villages contain agricultural associations of a collective character.'

And he even asserted that the peasant should be 'guaranteed the land he cultivates ... even for forty years'. As for the left's penchant for grandiose plans of crash industrialization, he said they 'will certainly ruin us' and 'inevitably lead to ... a great increase in the price of agricultural produce, a fall in real salaries and an artificially produced famine'. Few of the Left had gone as far as Stalin implied, but they certainly stood for a less leisurely policy than that of the NEP as thus far intepreted by Stalin and Bukharin.

But the party as a whole, and in particular the old militants, even when they supported Stalin against the Left, were also inclined to be restive about too long an acceptance of the market system and the individual 'petit bourgeois' peasant farm. For after all, the whole raison d'être of the party was the elimination of private ownership of the means of production, including peasant ownership of the land.

The contradiction was deep-seated. The party wanted economic recovery, but hated its inevitable product – prosperous peasants and small merchants. The recovery was, in fact, slowed down by constant harassment from the Communists. As Bukharin said, 'The peasant is afraid to install an iron roof for fear of being declared a kulak; if he buys a machine, then he does it in such a way that the Communists will not notice. Higher technique becomes conspiratorial!'

Over the next two years policy changed radically. What was going on in Stalin's mind? And in the minds of the Communist leadership in general?

We can probably not distinguish between the motivations of doctrine and of power in Stalin's mind. But from his point of view, simply as a matter of power, how would it have benefited him to rule the party if he did not fully control the country?

Still, gradualism might have been adequate to the outlook of the party, and of Stalin himself, for a longer time than it actually persisted, if the economy had continued to advance smoothly. But economies do not advance smoothly. And the leaders, suspicious of the market anyway, were liable to panic when it went into quite normal movements.

Moreover, the economic knowledge of the party elite was low – in most cases, including Stalin's, almost nonexistent. There were trained economists, often of non-Bolshevik backgrounds, and their advice was sought, though increasingly ignored as the decade went on. Moreover, the economic information available to the government was extravagantly inaccurate. Trotsky had noted that 'about 80 per cent of our calculations are unfounded', and many similar comments were made by economists and planners.

The main and clumsy weapon of intrusion into market processes was the setting of prices in the grain purchasing programme. When prices were set too low, at the end of 1927, as one of Stalin's experts wrote, 'The kulaks organized the sabotage of grain collection ... they refused to sell it to the state at the price laid down by the Soviet government.'

This resulted in what was seen as a crisis – though in fact the deficit was, as even pre-glasnost Soviet scholars noted, greatly exaggerated as to quantity, and easily rectifiable by a small increase in prices.

The government panicked and, by a unanimous vote of the Politburo, in January 1928 ordered grain requisitioning to make up the deficit. Stalin himself saw the whole problem as one of war with the kulak foe. He seems already to have come to the conclusion that he must, as soon as might be politically feasible, undertake the crushing of this mythical class enemy. Meanwhile, in 1928, he went to the countryside – the last time he was to do so in his whole life (if we omit dachas and villas). He made a much publicized descent on Siberia and insisted on the most ruthless measures of requisition, as in the period of War Communism. The Right, who had rather inconsistently supported the requisition as an emergency measure, complained that it had been enforced by illegal means, and that the peasantry had been alienated en bloc.

This was, of course, true. But economically the requisitioning was in any case a disastrous policy. In principle it was merely an emergency measure, and the government was in general to rely on the market. But from the peasant point of view the market was no longer to be relied on, since at any given moment it could be replaced by requisitioning. And the Communists remembered the successful requisition, without reflecting that it was the requisition of grain which had been produced with the incentive of the market.

Stalin's immediate task was in one way or another to win the top levels of the party – its activists and the bodies whose decisions were binding on them – to his new intentions. In principle, this was not so difficult. As he had said himself at the height of his support for the NEP, 90 per cent of party members instinctively favoured tough action against the kulaks.

The main body of second-line Old Bolsheviks had accepted the market and the free peasantry as a necessary, if temporary, compromise on the way to socialism. The Left had appealed to them too soon, when both party and country were still exhausted. Moreover, the Left's theoretical concern for immediate world revolution appeared to risk what had already been won.

But, as the economy revived, the party membership began to fear a restoration of capitalism. The Rightists' prescription of gradual voluntary collectivization of the land looked increasingly chimerical. All the same, it was with difficulty, and by dint of careful timing, that Stalin first defeated the right wing organizationally, and then used this victory to accelerate his new policies gradually through 1929, hustling the less enthusiastic of his allies bit by bit into the plans for crash collectivization and deportation of the kulaks.

3

With Stalin's new effective leadership of the Soviet state, and of the international Communist movement, he begins to emerge as a public personality. In the struggle for power, he had been known at first only to a limited circle, and later as little more than the point round which a rough and ready majority of the party had rallied. Though his influence had become more and more personal as he came into contact with wider and wider circles, he was still to a great extent a banner, or a slogan, rather than a unique leader. For many at the higher level he was first among equals, or near equals – as of course he was from the point of view of the party constitution. He himself, though claiming to be the spokesman for the true party line, put himself forward as no more than Lenin's successor and executor.

Khrushchev tells us that probably 90 per cent of the Party Congress listening to him in 1956 had heard or known 'very little about Stalin before 1924'. He had only built himself into a true public figure over the following five or six years. As we have said, this progress was in part due to his careful manipulation of the party apparatus, but his way of speaking also built up something of a rapport with larger audiences. The silent deputy in the 1917 Soviet, the unforthcoming intriguer of the early 1920s, had evolved through the necessities of the political struggle into his own style of demagogy. The ritualist incantations of the speech at Lenin's funeral always remained. But a more populist style began to accompany them.

A sympathetic observer describes his style of public speaking:

'He is definitely not what one would call a great orator. He speaks hesitatingly, not at all brilliantly, and rather tonelessly, as if he found it difficult. His arguments come slowly: they appeal to the sound common sense of people who grasp a thing thoroughly, but not quickly. But above all, Stalin has a sense of humour, a circumstantial, sly, comfortable, often cruel peasant's sense of humour ... When Stalin speaks with his knowing, comfortable smile, pointing with his forefinger, he does not, like other orators, make a breach between himself and his audience; he does not stand commandingly on the platform while they sit below him, but very soon an alliance, an intimacy is established between him and his listeners. They, being made of the same stuff, are susceptible to the arguments, and both laugh merrily at the same simple stories.'

Though expressed in excessively admiring terms, this description is sound enough.

4

From early 1928, Stalin began his main campaign against the Right. The set of manœuvres which followed over the next two years demonstrates a very different technique from that Stalin had used against the Trotskyites and Zinovievites. Until they were totally defeated, there were no public attacks on Bukharin, Rykov and Tomsky, and to begin with, while maintaining constant pressure, Stalin withdrew and made verbal concessions whenever the Rightists seemed to be on the point of boiling over. At first it was a matter of general attacks on 'pro-kulak' attitudes to be found in unspecified sections of the party.

In June 1928 Bukharin sent Stalin a letter protesting against the way the party was being led, with 'neither a line nor a common opinion', so that it was becoming 'ideologically disorganized'. Stalin saw Bukharin, and said to him, 'You and I are the Himalayas. The rest are nobodies.' When Bukharin repeated this at a Politburo meeting, Stalin hotly accused him of inventing the story to alienate the Politburo from him.

Over the rest of 1928 Stalin accepted most of the Rightists' amendments to policy documents, while moving against them organizationally. Stalin attacked junior Rightists, and spoke of those 'reluctant to quarrel with the kulaks', and so on. But he continued to assert that no split or deviation existed in the Politburo.

Bukharin and Tomsky now offered their resignation from the Politburo. Stalin is reported receiving it 'with trembling hands', and they were induced to withdraw.

Even now the party as a whole, or its middle echelons, was not yet quite prepared. But over the winter of 1928–9, Stalin, who had equally attacked right and left deviations, was saying that the right was now 'the chief danger'.

In February 1929, Bukharin with the other Rightists had to face the true accusation that he had had a surreptitious conversation with Kamenev. Even then, the Control Commission, though censuring him, refused his resignation and imposed no penalty. Stalin now complained that this was being too soft. At the Central Committee plenum in April 1929 he accused the three men of dangerous deviations and lack of party discipline. The Central Committee then, finally, removed Bukharin and

Tomsky from their posts – editorship of *Pravda* and chairmanship of the Comintern in Bukharin's case, leadership of the trade unions in Tomsky's. It allowed Rykov to remain as head of the government, and demanded that all three remain on the Politburo, and that the matter not be publicized, though Stalin had spoken of Bukharin's 'treacherous behaviour'.

It sometimes appears as though Stalin's successive victories over left and right were intellectually incompatible, or based only on a fragmentation of the power struggle. This makes sense as far as it goes, but does not cover one of the most important reasons for victory in both cases. The pro-Stalinist militants in both cases were led by the feeling that they were entrusted with a struggle against immense but overcomeable obstacles, which their opponents dared not face. The Trotskyites, and later the left as a whole, had had as a major weakness their opposition to Socialism in One Country. That is, they had argued that the task was, on theoretical grounds, beyond the capacity of Russia's Bolsheviks. Then in 1929–30 the right had similarly argued that the huge challenge of destroying the independent peasantry was beyond the party's powers. In both cases there was, for men like Kirov, an air of defeatism, a lack of trust in the party's ability to overcome every political and social obstacle.

As he moved against the right, Stalin continued to strike at the left. In February 1929 (against the opposition of Bukharin, Rykov and Tomsky), Trotsky, who refused to abjure political activity, was expelled from the Soviet Union. Stalin was later to say in private that this had been a mistake. It certainly enabled Trotsky to survive several years longer than his former colleagues in Lenin's Politburo.

But meanwhile, the shift leftwards had begun to win over most of the more distinguished Bolsheviks who had followed Trotsky. First Pyatakov and Krestinsky, then even the theorist of the left, Pre-obrazhensky, and a whole range of others almost as well-known, such as Radek, made their peace with Stalin and were readmitted to the party. They felt, and in a sense were justified in feeling, that their view had triumphed over the Bukharinites. Zinoviev and most of his followers were also readmitted to the party. Except for Zinoviev, Kamenev and Sokolnikov they were of little weight. But the Pyatakovs and Krestinskys had considerable value in the eyes of the second level of the party. Stalin's base became firmer than ever.

Meanwhile Stalin had been taking other actions which seen in retrospect foreshadowed later events.

In the autumn of 1928 Stalin took up a case which is often considered to mark the beginning of the use of the supreme penalty against party deviationists. In 1923 the prominent Tatar Communist Mir Said Sultan-Galiev, who had given much the same offence as Mdivani and the Georgian Communists with his ideas for an autonomous, or sovereign, Turanian republic in the Urals, had been arrested, with the agreement of Zinoviev and Kamenev. He was later released, though expelled from the party. In 1928, accused of illegal organization and counter-revolutionary plans, he was rearrested and sentenced to death. This has always been represented as a turning point in the treatment of deviant Communists. Kamenev is quoted as saying that it was now that Stalin first tasted blood – at any rate Communist blood. It was only in 1989 that the full facts were published: the sentence was commuted to ten years in the Solovki. Later released, Sultan-Galiev was rearrested in 1938 and shot only in January 1940.

5

Early in 1928, Stalin initiated a major manœuvre to heat up the damped-down fires of 'class war' in the cities as well as the countryside.

The local OGPU chief, Ye. G. Yevdokimov, reported a vast sabotage organization of veteran engineers in the city of Shakhty and its area. Yevdokimov had been a common criminal, freed from jail by the Revolution, when he had joined the party and distinguished himself in the Civil War. He became Stalin's special crony, was much decorated, and went with him on his vacations for several years running. Stalin, though without the legal power to do so, gave Yevdokimov *carte blanche* and the engineers were arrested. Menzhinsky, head of the OGPU, supported by Rykov and by Kuibyshev (naturally concerned as chairman of the Council of National Economy), objected. However, even Rykov accepted that they should not be concerned with justice towards the accused, but with the political advantages or disadvantages!

Stalin countered with a telegram from Yevdokimov hinting that attempts would be made in Moscow to hush the matter up. No decision was taken, but the case went ahead.

Stalin's political motive was to discredit the Bukharinite line of peaceful cooperation with non-party specialists, and to have 'proof' that the class struggle was getting sharper. He was to draw the specific lesson; 'We have internal enemies. We have external enemies. This, comrades, must not be forgotten for a single moment.'

The case came to trial in public in Moscow. The presiding judge, Andrei Vyshinsky, was to be one of Stalin's most despicable accomplices. He had been a Menshevik until the Bolsheviks consolidated their power, and had worked for the Provisional Government against Lenin. Thus he was particularly vulnerable. But Stalin had saved him and recruited him. They had been fellow inmates in Baku prison in 1907, and Stalin knew his man. The details of the Shakhty case are worth recording, as typical of the whole series of such trials which were to be central to Stalin's regime. What he thought plausible, or at least acceptable, is quite astonishing. (When opportunity arose, he was to promote the Shakhty secret police interrogation team to key posts all over the country.)

The trial opened in the huge Hall of Columns amid a press campaign of 'Death to the Wreckers!', the twelve-year-old son of one of the accused featuring among those who demanded the death penalty. Fifty Russian and three German technicians and engineers in the coal industry were charged with sabotage and espionage. Ten of the prisoners made full confessions, and six others partial ones. No other evidence was produced. A slight hitch was immediately evident. One of the prisoners, 'the accused Nekrasov', did not appear in the dock. He had, his counsel explained, gone mad. The written confessions were read out in court. They implicated all those present, including some who had not confessed.

Then Krylenko, the prosecutor, 'narrowing his eyes and twisting his lips into a sneer', viciously attacked the engineers. One accused, Benbenko, tried to withdraw his confession. He had been in the hands of the GPU for almost a year: 'I scarcely knew what I signed ... I was driven to distraction by threats, so I signed ... I tried to withdraw before the trial, but ...'

Krylenko gazed at him and finally said quietly, 'Do you want to say that you were intimidated, threatened?'

Benbenko hesitated, and then said, 'No.'

Another of the accused, Skorutto, had denied his guilt from the beginning. One evening he was reported too ill to attend. Next morning he appeared, 'an ash-grey trembling figure', and said that the previous night he had confessed his guilt and the guilt of others. There was a woman's cry from the public benches, 'Kolya, darling, don't lie. Don't! You know you are innocent!' The prisoner burst into tears and collapsed into a chair. After a ten-minute recess he was brought back and said

153

that though he had confessed he had withdrawn his confession earlier that morning. Krylenko went into the attack. Under intense badgering, Skorutto said that he had not slept for eight nights, and finally he had lied about his friends as they had lied about him. He had hoped that the court would be more lenient if he pleaded guilty. But he was not guilty. Next morning, Skorutto reaffirmed his confession and said that it had been his wife's outcry which had shaken his resolve to admit his guilt.

Another of the accused failed to appear and it was announced that he had committed suicide.

Rabinovich, a man past seventy, 'all but worsted the terrifying and heretofore invincible prosecutor Krylenko in brain-to-brain combat'. When another witness spoke of his sabotage links, Rabinovich went up to him and glared him down saying, 'Why do you lie, eh? Who told you to lie?' Krylenko looked crestfallen.

Another old man, Imineyetov, firmly maintained his innocence to the last. He boldly asserted that one day another Zola would write another *J'accuse* to restore their names.

An American present, Eugene Lyons, remarked that these flashes of illumination – the madness, the suicide, the withdrawals and reassertions of confession – 'left us limp with the impact of horrors half-glimpsed ... How did men like Krylenko, who sneered and snarled while the world looked on, behave when there were no witnesses and no public records?'

Eleven death sentences were announced, of which six were commuted because of the prisoners' cooperation.

Although the public trial was not a complete success as a production, Yevdokimov and his subordinates had constructed a pilot model which was to serve as a basis for the trials which would be a staple of Stalinism. More important still, a technique had been found for Stalin. Once criminal charges were being investigated by the secret police, using methods no one in political circles was in a position to inquire into effectively, any attempt to oppose such action at once took on the air of defending criminals and attacking the state and its investigative organs. It was not an easy brief even for Politburo members to argue to. And later, when the oppositionists were in the hands of the NKVD, Stalin had only to say that the investigation was not completed and might result in their acquittal, thus postponing the substantive argument, and then, after the confessions were in, say that the investigations had proved their guilt.

Meanwhile, the political significance of this horrifying spectacle lay in a vast intensification of propaganda against the 'class enemy'. And over the next few years came the removal of 'bourgeois specialists' in every field – engineers, teachers, all the others of pre-Revolutionary background who had accepted, and were serving, the new regime.

The result, of course, was a collapse of standards. We are told, for example, that by 1930 more than half the 'engineers' in the Soviet Union had no proper training: only 11.4 per cent had had higher education, and some had not even been put through crash courses.

This too indicates a central characteristic of Stalinism, and of Stalin's mind, which we have already noted in connection with his attitude to the military 'specialists' of the Civil War. He seems to have believed, or to have instinctively felt, that the professionally qualified could easily be replaced by fresh cadres of sounder political loyalties. The results were always disastrous.

The tradition of the Shakhty trial continued. In November–December 1930 came a trial of the so-called 'Industrial Party' – mainly high economic officials, who had allegedly undermined the Soviet economy on the instructions of President Poincaré of France, T. E. Lawrence and others. In March 1931 there was a Menshevik trial: only a few of the accused were Mensheviks, though they included the interesting figure of N. N. Sukhanov. He had indeed been a prominent Menshevik (though it was his flat that his Bolshevik wife had, without his knowledge, provided for meetings of the underground Bolshevik Central Committee in 1917), but he was better known for his 'grey blur' characterization of Stalin in 1917. He was now only jailed, though shot later.

Like the 'Industrial Party' the ex-Mensheviks were accused of sabotage in their posts in the economic sphere. So were the next batch, in the Metro-Vickers trial of April 1933 of British engineers working in Russia and a number of their Soviet contacts. This was less of a success, as most of the Britons withdrew their confessions, and said in open court that the whole thing was a 'frame-up based on the evidence of terrorized prisoners'.

All these trials were reported as great public events, and the accusations accepted as true by the whole Soviet press and propaganda system.

It will be seen that their political aim was twofold – to provide scapegoats for economic failure and, even at the cost of skilled assistance, to increase class hatred, partisan hatred and xenophobia. These sentiments clearly took precedence with Stalin over more material considerations.

6

It is difficult to know quite what Stalin really believed about the prospects of collectivization, by which the peasants not deported as kulaks were deprived of their property in land and livestock, and brought under full state control. It is certainly clear that he did not foresee the economic disaster which ensued. He seems to have had the notion that a socialist transformation of the countryside would really produce a great advance. This was to some extent based on another marked characteristic of the Bolsheviks, though not only of the Bolsheviks – an almost transcendental view of the machine. There had been a certain amount of this in the West too at an early stage, for example with the Railway Mania.

In Russia, the machine would haul a backward country into a new era. When Lenin said that socialism was 'soviets plus electrification', this was the sort of perspective he had in mind. In the villages, the tractor was to be the means of transformation, as Lenin had also said. The art, the posters, the fiction, even the poetry of the period (and later), are full of romantic treatment of urban and rural mechanization.

Even when it was clear that tractors would not be available on any scale, Stalin asserted that the 'simple pooling of peasant implements of production' would have – was already having – 'results of which our practical workers never dreamed': his Agriculture Commissar even called for 'a doubling of the productivity of the horse and plough'. (In the event the number of horses dropped by 47 per cent, and labour productivity shrank drastically). Butter consumption would soon match that of Denmark, as milch cows would increase in numbers by two and a half times, and their yield by three to four times ...

Stalin also subscribed to the aim of the large collectivized 'agricultural factory', and came out in favour of 'giant kolkhozes', saying, 'The objections of "science" to the possibility and expediency of organizing large grain factories of 50,000 to 100,000 hectares have been exploded and turned to ashes.' This formulation was indeed toned down when Stalin's *Works* appeared years later, to '40–50,000'; but meanwhile Stalin went so far as to predict that, by these methods, 'Our country will, in some three years' time, have become one of the richest granaries, if not the richest, in the whole world.'

It is sometimes argued in the West that the actions taken by Stalin and the party, of which he was now unchallenged head, were rational, at least within their social concepts. But the extent to which the whole attitude was centred on broader ideological myth is apparent in another of the main accompaniments of the collectivization drive and the 'cultural revolution' against the ex-bourgeois specialists. This was the simultaneous attack on religion. Anti-religious propaganda and action had been a powerful accompaniment of the Bolshevik conduct of the Civil War, but under the New Economic Policy there had been a certain relaxation.

Starting in 1928, the campaign resumed. On 22 May 1929 the constitution, which had permitted 'freedom of religious and anti-religious propaganda', was amended to read, 'freedom of religious worship and anti-religious propaganda'. In 1929 the Central Committee held a special conference on anti-religious matters.

Over the next years priests were imprisoned, churches were closed on a mass scale, architecturally irreplaceable ancient monasteries and cathedrals were destroyed. Above all a vicious and dogmatic atheism accompanied all the other horrors inflicted in the villages. We can hardly fail to see Stalin's own animus in this campaign, though such an attitude was largely shared by many other Communist activists.

7

Over 1929, with Stalin controlling from afar on a prolonged Black Sea holiday for the best part of the summer and autumn, the latest grain crisis was used for the further intensification of propaganda for mass collectivization, with the proposed figures increasing weekly.

At this point, the bulk of the Soviet economists were making complaints about the unreal industrial as well as agricultural aspects of the Plan. They were attacked as 'bourgeois-kulak ideologists' and removed from their posts, mostly to be shot a year or two later (and rehabilitated in the 1980s).

Stalin and his closest supporters claimed that the idea of collectivization was becoming ever more popular with the 'middle peasant' and now he pretended that their mass entry into the new kolkhozes was voluntary. Perhaps he really believed this, in some sense. But even granting his ability to believe what he wanted to believe, it was clearly untrue, as was to be seen shortly.

In November a 'decisive advance' to be accomplished in the next four and a half months was announced. The Right was again condemned and Bukharin was expelled from the Politburo for having 'slandered the party with demagogic accusations' and for having 'maintained that "extraordinary measures" had pushed the "middle" peasant toward the kulak'.

In December 1929, Stalin was able to celebrate his fiftieth birthday amid hitherto unprecedented adulation, the first great climax of the 'cult'. Its terms varied, but he was at lowest *the* leader of the party, the heir of Lenin.

At the end of the year Stalin finally announced his aim of 'the liquidation of the kulaks as a class'. Meanwhile, the remainder of the peasantry were to be almost entirely collectivized within a year.

Possibly the NEP perspective might have lasted. It certainly seems unlikely, in view of all other experience, that the peasantry would ever have willingly become collective farmers under state control. Mutual arrangements in pooling labour resources and farm machinery, traditional village arrangements about fallow and common land, cooperative marketing arrangements, have indeed been practised successfully, sometimes in Russia. But a willingness to work for, and on the assignments of, a party-controlled plan and its emissaries was never a likely prospect.

As it was, in the villages the party could in fact only rely on some of the local unemployables and psychopaths on the one hand, and some of the teachers on the other; the latter were often educated to the degree of accepting party dogmas, but no higher. They were assisted, or rather led, by the 'twenty-five-thousanders' sent by the party from the cities and almost all totally ignorant of agriculture, but strong on propaganda and terror.

Such a policy could not have been imposed without the maximum employment of force. This required an 'enemy' – the kulak, as representing the leadership of the villages. At the same time, economically speaking, his removal meant the destruction of precisely the most productive element in the villages.

Over the next two years a ruthless struggle, with millions of deaths, was waged in the countryside. First the kulaks, defined now to include 'subkulaks' – that is, peasants too poor to be called 'kulaks' by any standards whatever – were deported. One of the Soviet Union's most prominent agrarian scholars has lately told us that more than 15 million human beings, men, women and children, were uprooted. About two million (he adds) were transferred to industrial projects, and the remainder simply deported to the Arctic – a million of the adult males among them direct to labour camps.

A further element of the Stalin system was now also in the process of development – the forced labour camp. There had been concentration camps since the early days of the regime, but these were on a fairly small scale, with probably no more than about 30,000 inmates even at the end of the 1920s. But in 1928 Naftali Frenkel, a former millionaire, originally from Turkey but now serving a sentence, wrote to Stalin with a scheme for avoiding the low productivity of slave labour, which had been noted by Marx as well as most other economists. In brief, Frenkel proposed a linking of rations to output. This account has lately been confirmed in the Soviet Union, with the additional detail that Frenkel said that in this way six months' work would be got out of a prisoner, after which he could be written off.

At any rate, Frenkel was released and was given high posts in the new system. Forced labour, with a heavy death rate, was to become a central feature of the Stalinist order.

The circumstances of the kulak deportation were frightful. In fact it was only possible to carry it out by inciting a hysterical lynching mood in the party. Vasily Grossman, the Soviet Union's leading recorder of the Nazi death camps (in which his own mother perished), makes the comparison flatly:

'They would threaten people with guns, as if they were under a spell, calling small children "kulak bastards", screaming "bloodsuckers!" ... They had sold themselves on the idea that the so-called "kulaks" were pariahs, untouchables, vermin. They would not sit down at a "parasite" table; the "kulak" child was loathsome, the young "kulak" girl was lower than a louse. They looked on the so-called "kulaks" as cattle, swine, loathsome, repulsive: they had no souls; they stank; they all had venereal diseases; they were enemies of the people and exploited the labour of others ... And there was no pity for them. They were not human beings, one had a hard time making out what they were – vermin evidently.'

And again:

'What I said to myself at the time was "they are not human beings, they are kulaks" ... Who thought up this word "kulak" anyway? Was it really a term? What torture was meted out to them! In order to massacre them it was necessary to proclaim that kulaks are not human beings. Just as the Germans proclaimed that Jews are not human beings. Thus did Lenin and Stalin proclaim, kulaks are not human beings.'

They were dumped in the Arctic forests or tundra, where they had to build their own huts and, after a short interim, to produce their own food. These were territories which had not been settled, for the obvious reason that they were extremely inhospitable. The death rate was very high; 15 or 20 per cent, mainly infants and children, had already died in the packed cattle trucks or forced marches.

And now the falsehood of Stalin's claim that crash collectivization was popular emerged in the reality of the villages. At the beginning of 1930, over 14 million peasant households had been herded into the new farms. Rather than allow their cattle to fall into the hands of the state, they had slaughtered half the country's herd. By March it was plain that disaster had overtaken the countryside.

Stalin now issued his famous 'Dizzy with Success' statement. The policy had been correct and popular, but some Communists had been forcing peasant collectivization. This was wrong, and peasants should be allowed to leave the kolkhozes. In spite of many obstacles still put in their way, nine million households then left. Stalin's policy was in ruins. But the Rightists, thus proved correct, did not stand forward in opposition, as would have happened under any other political system. Bukharin had made some criticisms in the autumn, before his removal from the Politburo in November 1929. But now, accepting party discipline, he and the others had warmly and publicly supported the new line! And Stalin's defeat in the countryside was accompanied by final victory in the Politburo. Tomsky and Rykov were out by the end of the year, the latter also losing his chairmanship of the Council of People's Commissars, now taken by Molotov.

Through 1930-1, by more continual pressures, the mass of the peasants was forced back into the kolkhozes with Stalin still keeping up the verbal pretence that this was a voluntary movement. In fact, we may see this major falsification as crucial in the evolution of the Stalinist 'reign of the lie', which Pasternak took as the essential of the system.

By now the whole countryside was at the bare edge of subsistence. With almost no incentive to produce, and with scarce and ill-cared-for livestock, the peasantry was no longer a productive force. However, with what crop there was now under the control of the party's intruded collective-farm organizers, and guarded in the collective barns, it was easily accessible to the government. And it was laid down that the government's demands must be met before the peasant got his share.

Meanwhile, a vast effort went into industry. The pace of industrialization was killing, though Soviet economists have lately made it clear that at least as high a rate of real advance could have been achieved under NEP – indeed was already being achieved when NEP was abandoned. The claims made for the new Five-Year Plan were far higher than the actuality. This was to some extent concealed by huge prestige-enhancing enterprises like the Dnieper dam, which appeared to show a new level of industrialization. Conditions in the cities, and especially in the new construction areas like Magnitogorsk, were miserable, if not as miserable as in the villages. The labour force now had to be controlled by internal passports (which had been denounced by Lenin as a sign of the worst in tsarism) and labour books in which indiscipline was registered. Change of employment without permission became illegal. Higher and higher penalties were enacted for offences against the new economic order.

Not only economically, but also intellectually and morally, the country was in a dreadful condition. Politically too, in that discussion in reasonable terms, even at the level that had been possible under Lenin and up to the late 1920s, was crushed.

Though the Politburo was now completely Stalinist, the spirit of criticism was not quite extinct. Over 1930–2 there were several minor revolts among the second-level Communist cadres. In 1930 Stalin's protégé, Sergei Syrtsov, newly promoted to candidate membership of the Politburo, had to be expelled from his post (though not from the party) for an 'unprincipled left-right bloc' with the Georgian Old Bolshevik Lominadze and others: they had complained about the 'feudal' approach to the peasantry, and described the new industrial showpieces as eyewash.

A far more significant case, especially as regards Stalin himself, came from a lower-level group. Ryutin, who had formerly been a party secretary in Moscow, was in trouble in 1930 for a memorandum arguing that Bukharin had been right as to policy, and Trotsky as to the intolerable regime within the party. He called for the suspension of collectivization, and a return to a rational industrial policy; and he censured Bukharin and his colleagues for their capitulation. Ryutin was arrested, but released for want of any evidence of criminal intent, and even readmitted to the party with a warning. But in 1932 he and a small

161

group issued an 'Appeal' to all members of the party, attacking the destruction of the countryside, the collapse of genuine planning, the lawlessness in both the party and the country as a whole, the crushing of opinion, the ruin of the arts, the transformation of the press into 'a monstrous factory of lies'; it called for the removal of Stalin and his clique as soon as possible, adding that they would not go voluntarily so would have to be forcibly ejected. (Ryutin is now held up in the Soviet Union as a model of resistance to Stalin, as against the submission of Bukharin and the others.)

Stalin treated the 'Ryutin Platform' as the worst embodiment of everything hostile to his rule. Over the rest of the decade it was represented again and again as the great focus of opposition plotting and villainy. When Ryutin was rearrested Stalin made a strong personal effort to have him sentenced to death.

This was a crucial moment, the first serious dispute between Stalin and his closest personal clique on the one hand, and those members of the Politburo who had supported him out of conviction but were not ready to agree to intra-party killings. In Ryutin's case (and in several other lesser instances including that of Stalin's own former secretary Nazaretyan), Kirov, with Ordzhonikidze, Kuibyshev, Kossior, Rudzutak and, apparently, Kalinin, formed a solid majority against execution. Ryutin was sentenced only to ten years' imprisonment. Another case, a few months later, involved the Old Bolshevik A. P. Smirnov and others who had never been associated with any opposition. Stalin commented: 'Of course, only enemies could say that to remove Stalin would not affect matters.' This time, again, his attempt to shoot the offenders was blocked by a Politburo majority.

But though these cases are worth recording, and certainly show a strong degree of revulsion in some veteran circles, on the whole Stalin's grip on the party and the country was greatly strengthened by his extreme policies and the obvious emergency situation which had resulted from them. He had secured the support of the bulk of the party for these measures, even if some of them may have felt that they had been hustled too rapidly from one stance to another during 1929. In the crises two things greatly favoured Stalin. First, the doctrinaire militants felt that once again they were in the thick of the revolutionary fight. As Kirov, typically, remarked, 'The Rights are for socialism, but without particular fuss, without struggle.' And struggle, desperate struggle, was both a deep-set belief and a way of life to the ordinary Communist Kirov spoke for.

Loyalty to Stalin at the time was, as one official put it, 'based principally on the conviction that there was no one to take his place, that any change of leadership would be extremely dangerous, and that the country must continue in its present course, since to stop now or attempt a retreat would mean the loss of everything'. Even a Trotskyite could comment: 'If it were not for that so-and-so ... everything would have fallen into pieces by now. It is he who keeps everything together ...'

Nevertheless, the qualms arising in the Politburo itself were, or were seen by Stalin to be, a hindrance to his rule.

8

A new way of counting the grain crop came in – the 'biological yield'. This was an estimate of the grain as it stood in the field, rather than a measurement of it in barns after harvesting. In 1953 Khrushchev revealed that it had produced an exaggeration of over 40 per cent. There was even a decree forbidding the collection of data on the grain actually threshed, 'as distorting the picture of the actual condition of the crop'. This further importation of fantasy and falsehood into the economic processes had one immediate result. The government actually decreed the size of the crop – in principle by applying the maximum theoretical yield to the maximum utilizable area. It could then take its share of the produce on that basis, leaving a minimal, or nonexistent, residue to the peasant.

In 1932, Stalin launched his most deadly blow yet against the peasantry, and especially against the peasantry of the Ukraine and adjoining grain-growing areas, which had been most militant in resisting the collectivization drive. He refused to accept that productivity had gone down and, on the basis of wholly invented figures, demanded grain deliveries larger than the total crop. This was ruthlessly enforced, and the result was, in many ways, the greatest known tragedy of the century. Certainly not fewer than five million, and more probably at least seven million, died of starvation over the winter. As one of the activists who enforced the programme wrote later:

'Here I saw people dying in solitude by slow degrees, dying hideously. They had been trapped and left to starve, each in his home, by a political decision made in a far-off capital around conference and banquet tables. There was not even the consolation of inevitability to relieve the horror.'

The activists operated by searching houses, probing with crowbars, seizing every last grain. The amounts secured in early 1933 were negligible, and the requisition theoretically decreed was never reached – because no more grain existed.

Stalin personally drafted the notorious law of 7 August 1932, 'On the Safeguarding of State Property', defining all collective farm property as such – cattle, standing crops, produce. Any offence against them was to be met by execution or, in extenuating circumstances, not less than ten years' imprisonment, with confiscation of property. Tens of thousands were sentenced for such crimes as 'stealing' a few ears of corn. Stalin personally ordered that no pardons should be granted for these offences. Kaganovich, for example, condemned a judge who said he could not bring himself to sentence a peasant to ten years for stealing four cartwheels. In fact such a sentence was common for even lesser crimes, such as 'stealing ten onions', while the 'theft' of 25 pounds of wheat gleaned by his ten-year-old daughter resulted in the death sentence for a peasant. Such are fairly typical stories.

It was a fight to the death against the peasantry – and, blended with it, against the Ukrainian nationality. When Stalin was engaged in a fight to the death, there was always plenty of death to go round.

The famine was the focus of what was up till now the greatest and most massive of the falsifications of Stalinism. While millions starved to death, it was simply denied that any famine existed. This line was taken not only to the outside world, but even in the Soviet Union itself. It was only a few years ago that the famine was finally admitted. Even then it was for a time ascribed to drought (though Soviet books on droughts do not record them in the relevant period). Then it was conceded that it was due to government orders, but that these were mistaken rather than consciously designed to create famine. In 1988–90, the truth came out, and it is now usual to read such summaries as (in *Novy Mir* no. 9, 1989): 'The premeditated famine of 1932–3 was organized by the Stalin leadership, a famine selected as one of the most effective methods of struggle against the peasantry, which was resisting the forcible imposition on it of "higher forms of cooperation".' Or as *Sovietskaya Kultura* (1 October 1988) put it: 'Stalin organized this famine completely consciously and in a planned manner.' 'Dislike of, distrust of the peasantry was the root of the famine policy,' writes another (*Sobesednik* no. 49, November 1988). And it is flatly described as a 'murder famine' (*Literaturna Ukraina*, 18 February 1988).

There seems no doubt, either, that it was Stalin's personal decision simply to deny the existence of the famine. A number of his leadership cadres had actually seen the appalling results. At the beginning of 1933, the Secretary of the Kharkov Provincial Committee reported in Moscow that famine was raging in the Ukraine. Stalin retorted:

'We have been told that you, Comrade Terekhov, are a good speaker; it seems that you are a good storyteller, you've made up such a fable about famine, thinking to frighten us, but it won't work. Wouldn't it be better for you to leave your post of provincial committee secretary and the Ukraine Central Committee, and join the Writers' Union? Then you can write your fables and fools will read them.'

The truth simply became unsayable. Even in the starving villages it became an offence bringing ten-year sentences, or sometimes death, to speak of the famine. In fact, Stalin's whole system, and his whole technique of rule, was increasingly dependent on falsehood on a scale so vast that it seems fair to call it unprecedented – in any normal thinking it sounds impossible, impracticable. Stalin's rule was based in various ways on departures from anything that had been done before, or even imagined. Forcible collectivization itself was, on the face of it, impossible. Yet Stalin achieved it. In general, he seems never to have regarded precedent, or common-sense argument, as carrying much weight.

9

We are sometimes told, even now, of the enthusiasm, and other supposedly positive qualities, of the emissaries, or even the leaders, in Stalin's campaign. It is particularly distasteful to hear this, as one occasionally does, from Western academics who treat any threat to their own tenure, let alone life and liberty, as unbearable inhumanity.

As far back as the 1930s, the deans of Western sociology, Sidney and Beatrice Webb, were writing that 'something like a million families' had been ejected from their homes, and commenting, 'Strong must have been the faith and resolute the will of the men who, in the interest of what seemed to them the public good, could take so momentous a decision.' Momentous decisions about other people's lives have been taken often enough in the past century. The Nazi Holocaust can of course be justified in precisely the Webbs' terms.

When it comes to the enthusiasm of the men on the spot, we are on interesting territory not only morally, but also evidentially. It is clear that there were large, or largish, numbers of people who had accepted the morality of the local activist leader in Sholokhov's *Virgin Soil Upturned*, published with acclaim in Stalin's USSR: 'Yes ... You could line up thousands of old men, women and children and tell me they'd have to be crushed into dust for the sake of the revolution, and I'd shoot them all down with a machine-gun.' This was very much the mood felt, or at any rate acted on, by the party's emissaries to the villages. Or rather, it is that of those who survived – for we have many accounts of Communists who refused to carry out the brutal instructions of the centre, particularly against children. As Bukharin was to complain, though not publicly, one of the worst results of the whole four-year struggle in the countryside was that it inculcated even more deeply the idea that 'terror was henceforth a normal method of administration, and obedience to any order from above a high virtue'. What he saw was 'a real dehumanization' of the apparatus: in fact, its increasing Stalinization.

Why 'enthusiasm' should in itself be accounted a virtue, any more than with the Hitler Youth, is a mystery – even if the commentator accepts the Stalinist rank-and-file's mechanism of self-justification. It is less repulsive when cited of the young Stalinists who were sent to build the new industrial centres like Magnitogorsk, though even the working class (in such areas mainly peasants who had fled from the villages) was treated abominably.

But a further question remains. How far are we to accept common assertions that enthusiasm, even at this crude level, was indeed pervasive?

First of all, the peasants, still the majority, overwhelmingly loathed the system. The intelligentsia, or a large part of it, had little use for a regime which suppressed all but a particular orthodoxy of thought. The supposedly favoured 'workers' lived a miserable existence, mainly in hovels and huts around the new blast furnaces.

The regime had been accepted in the 1920s, not because of enthusiasm for it, but out of general civil exhaustion, combined with its newly tolerant economic stance. When the latter disappeared, there is no reason whatever to think that Stalin, and his ruling group, were supported by more than an atomized population controlled and made to appear enthusiastic by an apparatus of sneaks and bullies – with a fairly small stratum of doctrinaires of the older generation, and a rather larger group of younger people indoctrinated more or less to the point where their elders had lost faith, though unable, in the circumstances, to convey that to their children.

The struggle in the countryside produced its quota of much publicized heroes of Stalinism. Often they were informers, of whom a large quota had existed since the early days of the regime, but who now pullulated on an ever-increasing scale. One of the most lauded exemplars throughout the Stalin period – and indeed until quite recently – was not only a hero, but also a martyr: the fourteen-year-old Pavel ('Pavlik') Morozov, whose case, and Stalin's private reaction to it, we noted in the first chapter of this book. Morozov was not the first parent-denouncer. The son of one of the Shakhty accused had violently denounced his father, and changed his name to Shakhtin – though this was after the father's arrest, rather than a cause of it. The children of later accused were invariably required to denounce and renounce their parents in public sessions at their schools. After Morozov, a whole cycle of young delators of mothers and fathers was celebrated in the Soviet press, and entered in the Pioneer 'Book of Honour'. The whole theme is central to the idea of the Stalinist state.

Even within the ruling caste, it was the nastier children and students who controlled, manipulated and censured their fellows. The loyalty this produced was resentful, though it often seems, as in other spheres, to have taken the traditional Russian view that 'if only Stalin knew', things would have been different – that is, that the regime in itself was not to blame. Indeed, this attitude can be found among the activists who crushed the peasantry. Several of them, writing in the West many years later, say that they saw the horrors as due to local malpractice, while thinking that overall things were going well: a product of the control and perversion of information.

There is little reason to accept a view now found almost solely in certain Western circles, that Stalinism enjoyed broad, let alone warm, popular support. (I write this in the aftermath of the collapse of the East German Communist regime which, we were frequently told by such commentators, was fairly successful and in any case widely accepted by the mass of the population...)

Did Stalin himself think that he and his system were popular? Presumably he knew that the peasantry hated him and it. But, in fact, there is no reason to suppose that he cared one way or another whether they or any other section of the population were happy and contented, let alone grateful. At least, his whole conduct over the years that followed is that of one who recognizes that he is not regarded with more than the most reluctant acquiescence by any section of the population, including even the higher levels of the party itself. The personality cult had its effect among the young semi-educated class, and was also a conscious rallying cry of the victorious party militants. But it may be seen more importantly as a matter of ritual, or dogma: something of which enthusiastic acceptance was the minimum requirement for membership of decent society.

In one sense, Stalin now required the apparent quasi-unanimous support of party and people. At the same time, he demanded a constant struggle against an endless succession of enemies who, given the slightest tolerance, would (in his view) have shaken his rule to its foundations. Whether we look at this as a psychological or as a political attitude – or both – it persisted throughout his reign, and was an important element in the long distortion of anything resembling normality in the Soviet Union.

The memoirs we have, the interviews, written or given years later, show that a proportion did indeed feel allegiance to the party, and to Stalin personally, in the 1930s. These are largely from members of the 'new class' intelligentsia, the only real beneficiaries of the regime. Though devoted Stalinists fell with the others, those who showed any signs, however faint, of disagreement or disillusion perished in their millions, so that our sample is in any case comparatively skewed.

It is surprising to read the confident assertions still being put forward about the extent of the enthusiasm, on such a feeble basis of evidence. Still, we can certainly see an adequate stratum of enthusiasts, or fanatics, who had accepted the falsehoods and excused or ignored the terror of the whole Stalinist phenomenon, and, increasingly over the 1930s, a stratum of devotees of Stalin personally. Many of them were bound to the regime by complicity in terror and denunciation. But we should not ignore the effect on the entire population of the continuous pounding-in of the Stalinist line, of the complete absence of any expression of other ideas or truths. The effect was, as many modern Soviet writers tell us, psychologically disorientating in the extreme. People became, as it were, mentally deafened by the strident vociferation of the state.

10

Stalin had learned of the famine in its earliest stages, when it might yet have been prevented, from a source close to him. His wife Nadezhda, bored with her family life, had been allowed to take courses in textile production at the Industrial Academy. There, from fellow students who had been sent on assignment as activists in grain collection, she learned about the terrible conditions in the Ukraine, the forced seizures, the starving children, the cannibalism. She reported this to Stalin and there was a stand-up row. The students, who had hoped that with their information to Nadezhda they would reach and touch Stalin, were arrested.

Very soon afterwards, on 8 November 1932, there was a dinner after the Revolutionary anniversary celebrations, given by the Voroshilovs in the Kremlin.

Stalin was insufferably rude to Nadezhda. Accounts vary slightly, but the mildest has him shouting 'Hey, you!' and telling her to drink up. In one story, he threw a lit cigarette at her, which went down her dress. At any rate she got up and left. Her friend Polina, Molotov's wife, walked her home to her Kremlin flat, and left her in a reasonably calm mood. But she shot herself later that night, leaving a note to Stalin which though largely personal was 'partly political'.

Late in 1989 a fresh piece of information on the events of this night was published in Moscow in the hitherto suppressed section of Khrushchev's memoirs. After Stalin's death they questioned his long-serving head of bodyguards, Nikolai Vlasik, about the affair. Vlasik said that Nadezhda telephoned some time after dinner and asked where Stalin was. He had gone back not to the Kremlin apartment but to the 'nearby' dacha. She asked who was with him, and the duty officer, understandably characterized by Vlasik as a stupid dolt, told her, 'Gusev's wife.' There had always been rumours of some extramarital activities by Stalin. Molotov speaks of Nadezhda being jealous of, for example, a woman barber who shaved Stalin. This latest incident may perhaps register the final humiliation which drove her to suicide.

When Stalin returned to the flat he was deeply shaken. Nadezhda first lay in the building off Red Square which is now the GUM department store. When Stalin came to view the coffin he was seen to make a gesture of rejection, and heard to say, 'She left me as an enemy!' This was the only time tears were ever seen in his eyes. But stories of his often visiting her grave at the Novodevichiye cemetery are a myth.

Stalin to some extent blamed the suicide on Michael Arlen's novel *The Green Hat*, which Nadezhda had been reading, and which is replete with suicides by people leading meaningless lives. But though Arlen was an Armenian (and thus notionally subject to Soviet power), Stalin took no action against him, and this seems to have been no more than a minor element in his feelings. More broadly, he saw the suicide as yet another sign and symbol of the pervasive presence of 'the enemy'. It also represented an enormous personal rebuff. He had quite clearly failed in an important part of his life, and some of his later remarks show that he could not come to terms with this.

Hereafter, even the modicum of a normal life, which had been provided by his wife, was absent from his existence. He left the Zubalovo dacha and moved permanently into the 'nearby' Kuntsevo dacha, only eight kilometres from the Kremlin. Here, over the next twenty years, he organized terror and war, in a social ambience of coarse and squalid soirees.

Chapter 10

Terror

The year 1933 marks an epoch, not only as the culmination of Stalin's lethal victory over alien classes and party waverers, but also because it was then that Hitler took power in Germany – an event which was to be full of significance for Stalin's future.

Since the death of Lenin, internal affairs had to a large degree crowded out foreign policy in the concerns of the leadership. Moreover, their knowledge of foreign affairs was minimal, with Marxist stereotypes replacing real countries and populations in their minds.

The outer world had nevertheless to be coped with. The Comintern had to be deployed, and the leadership of its component parties had to be purged to rid them of representatives of successive oppositions, when first Zinoviev and then Bukharin were removed as leaders of the organization. And, as we have said, the sequence of defeats of the Chinese Communists, first when they used United Front tactics and then when they tried the appeal to force, had to be explained, and blamed on heads other than Stalin's. By 1930 this had been successfully accomplished.

There had been a certain amount of resistance to the Stalin style of political manœuvre. In May 1927, for example, with Stalin present, the Executive Committee of the Comintern was asked to condemn a document of Trotsky's on the Chinese question. They were about to do so, when the Italian delegation, consisting of Togliatti and Ignazio Silone, said that they had not seen the document. Nor had any of the other foreigners present. The Italians then objected that Trotsky was no doubt in the wrong, but that they could hardly be expected to issue a formal condemnation of something they had not read. Even when they were told that the Soviet Politburo thought it unwise to circulate it, and they were put under pressure during adjournment, they still refused. Stalin then, in typical style, withdrew the motion ...

As the foreign delegations got used to the new tone, the objections disappeared. By the early 1930s, the Stalinization of the Comintern was reasonably complete; though many defections were yet to come. Stalin had a powerful instrument for political and propagandist intervention in the West and in the world as a whole.

'Socialism in One Country' had never implied the abandonment of the World Revolution, and Soviet Communists were often rallied with its slogans. We cannot tell quite the drift of Stalin's thoughts, or feelings, on World Revolution. He certainly sneered at the Comintern in private from time to time. His spokesmen in the post-war period promulgated the view that a Western revolution could only succeed in conjunction with Soviet armed intervention, as in Eastern Europe. But in the early 1930s, Soviet military support of such an effort was not remotely plausible. Partly owing to Stalin's own policies, the German Communists had never looked like winning power, and were effectively destroyed as a real force in 1933. Elsewhere too, until 1936, the Communist Parties remained small minorities.

Was it merely whistling to keep up their spirits that Communists everywhere still spoke, as Georgi Dimitrov did at the Reichstag Fire Trial, of going forward to a World Federation of Soviet Republics? There is one sign that Stalin, in however vague a sense, still nourished the old hopes. Karl Radek, by now a devoted adulator, published an article in 1934 describing Stalin with his closest comrades at the May Day demonstration, while towards his calm figure mount 'waves of love and trust, waves of confidence that there on Lenin's tomb was assembled the staff of the future victorious World Revolution'.

But for the moment the Soviet Union was still weak and vulnerable. One of the reasons for Stalin's excessive appetite for grain in 1932–3 was to build up a 'strategic grain reserve' – which was to play a large part in causing the country's inadequate supply of foodstuffs right into the 1980s. Meanwhile, to starve millions of potential army recruits while alienating the rest was itself an irrationality.

Over the late 1920s, there had been various war scares. The French, or other Westerners, were supposedly on the point of aggression against the Soviet Union. In 1927, Stalin summarized the latest Soviet propaganda campaign with a set-piece article in *Pravda*: there was a real and immediate danger of imperialist attack. The People's Commissar for Foreign Affairs, Georgi Chicherin, knew there were no signs of any such preparations, and had asked what was going on. A colleague explained: 'Sh. We know that. But we need this against Trotsky.' The main purpose of the scare was, in fact, to trap Trotsky into saying he would oppose the Stalin leadership even in wartime, as Clemenceau had opposed the inept French leadership in 1914; thus handing Stalin on a platter the opportunity to call him a traitor. But now in the early 1930s, a real danger was perceived: this time from Japan. And indeed, one of the options before the new militarists in Tokyo included an attack on Siberia.

Earlier the USSR had actually sent troops and fought the 'White Chinese' to protect the Chinese Eastern Railway, at this time still operated by the Russians. But in 1935, Stalin sold the railway, now in Japanese-occupied Manchukuo, for a small sum to the Japanese. This can certainly be seen as intended to reduce frictions and excuses for war. (But towards the end of the 1930s, the Japanese made a series of probing attacks on the Far Eastern frontier.)

The Comintern was now in what is sometimes called the 'Third Period', marking Stalin's full control. The policies laid down were based on the idea that the Five-Year Plan and collectivization would soon place the Soviet economy in a position of great strength, while capitalism was on the point of terminal crisis. The tactics thought suitable were based on the idea that capitalism had a choice of two last hopes, almost equally obnoxious – Social Democracy and Fascism. The former, as a rival for the allegiance of the working class, was to be the main target of attack. Stalin personally wrote supporting this thesis as late as 1933.

This had such strange-seeming results as Nazi–Communist cooperation in the Prussian referendum of 1931 and the 1932 transport strike. The general policy forced on the German Communist Party – to refuse to cooperate with the Social Democrats, or anyone else, against the Nazis – is commonly blamed for Hitler's victory in 1933. As Ronald Hingley puts it, whether the Nazis 'would have obtained power in 1933 without Stalin's aid we cannot say. Certainly they would have found it more difficult to do so.' The whole Nazi–Communist relationship, and the light it casts on Stalin's political personality, though not only on his political personality, is a complex phenomenon, as was to appear more strikingly a few years later.

Hitler divided his enemies into supporters of the bourgeois regime – *Das System* – and the Communists, whom he called 'enemies outside the system'. Even during the war, he was to praise Stalin's planned economy and his political organization, as against the unemployment-ridden West. And though he hated 'Jewish' Communism, he did not hate Communists. As he said himself: 'I don't blame the small man for turning Communist ... When one thinks of that riff-raff of bourgeoisie, even today, one sees red ... I find our Communists a thousand times more sympathetic than Stahremberg [the Austrian right-wing leader], say. They were sturdy fellows.' He criticized Franco:

> 'Later on, the Reds we had beaten up became our best supporters. When the Falange imprisons its opponents, it's committing the gravest of faults. Wasn't my party, at the time of which I'm speaking, composed 90 per cent of left-wing elements? I needed men who could fight. I had no use for the sort of timid doctrinaires who whisper subversive plans in your ear.'

Indeed, in 1934 the British ambassador to Berlin noted that the ex-Communists in the march-past were the smartest of the SA units.

Hitler had also said, in one of several similar comments:

> 'In our movement the two extremes come together: the Communists from the left and the officers and the students from the right. These two have always been the most active elements, and it was the greatest crime that they used to oppose each other in street fights. The Communists were the idealists of socialism.'

When the totalitarian parties had eventually settled down into their final shapes, they gave the impression of having maintained a long and formal mutual hostility. It is more to the point to remember that the early career of Laval, France's leading collaborationist, was as one of the few anti-war pro-Lenin socialists of France in 1914–18; that Jacques Doriot changed from being a leader of the French Communist Party to heading the most pro-Nazi of all French organizations, and so on. On another tack, Gramsci, for example, was one of Mussolini's closest comrades, right into the latter's 'defencist' phase. Both Lenin and Trotsky are quoted as privately expressing great regret that Mussolini, held by both to be the one man who could have brought about a revolution in Italy, had diverged into Fascism. And, in fact, the earliest leaders of the Fascists were almost entirely from the left. This had started to change fairly rapidly. But, in Mussolini's last phase too – the 'Salo Republic' of 1943–5 – he instituted a rule which on all the usual criteria was the most 'radical' in all Europe. Like Mussolini, Hitler – in both cases rightly – felt at that time that they had been endangered by 'reactionary' elements. After the attempted coup of 20 July 1944, the

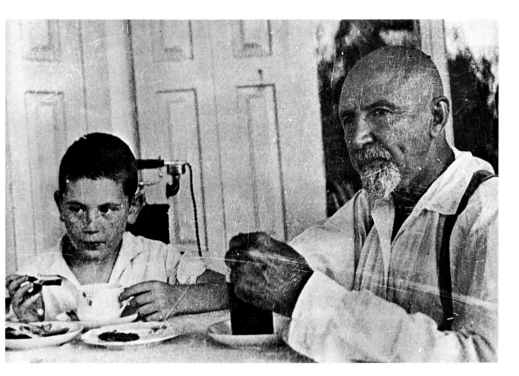

Vasily Stalin with Sergei
Alliluyev

Svetlana Stalin with
Lavrenty Beria, c. 1934

Nadezhda Alliluyeva, 1932

Nadezhda Alliluyeva's grave

Lenin,
died 1924

Trotsky,
murdered 1940

Kamenev,
shot 1936

Zinoviev,
shot 1936

Bukharin,
shot 1938

Rykov,
shot 1938

Tomsky,
suicide 1936

Stalin,
survived

Stalin with Poskrebyshev

Stalin with Yezhov, Molotov and Voroshilov at the opening of the White Sea–Baltic canal

Stalin and Ribbentrop at the signing of the Nazi–Soviet Pact

Stalin's mother in old age

Vasily and Svetlana in wartime

Stalin's son Yakov as a German prisoner of war

Stalin kissing the Sword of Stalingrad, presented to him by Winston Churchill, Teheran, 1943

Roosevelt, Churchill and Stalin at dinner, Teheran, 1943

Celebrating Stalin's seventieth birthday, 1949

Stalin exhibition in Budapest, 1967

Stalin lies next to Lenin in the Red Square
mausoleum

Nazi radios raved against 'the blue-blooded swine'.

Unlike Mussolini, Hitler did not himself emerge from the leading ranks of left-wing socialism; but he did emerge from the general 'radical' ambience of semi-intellectual café discussion. Indeed, we should remember that nationalism (in its modern version) has the same roots – as does eugenics, which was fashionable even with the Fabians, with all its racialist implications. But the central element was precisely the 'radical' extremist attitude, with its assumption of the total destruction not merely of the present order, but also of all its principles, moral, social, religious.

In such a context Hugh Seton-Watson notes that Hitler's Nazis were 'fanatics with an ersatz religion', who rejected not only Christianity but also traditional morality as such. Nazism's central feature was 'moral nihilism', and Seton-Watson adds, 'Moral nihilism is not only the central feature of National Socialism, but also the common factor between it and Bolshevism.' This is not to deny other resemblances, in particular the roles of ideology and the party.

Hitler had also said that while Communists could easily be converted to Nazism, Social Democrats could not. (It is a curious irony that, for example, Koch, Hitler's dreadful Gauleiter of the Ukraine, was a former Communist – it is odd, too, that he did not get a death sentence, but served the rest of his lifetime in a comparatively unlethal Polish Communist prison.) Hitler's estimate is supported by the number of leading European Communists who became Fascist or pro-Fascist in the 1930s, from Bombacci in Italy to Doriot, who even led a French pro-Nazi formation on the Russian front in World War II.

In *Life and Fate,* Vasily Grossman's leading character thinks to himself, 'To me a distinction based on social origin seems legitimate and natural. But the Germans obviously consider a distinction based on nationality to be equally moral.' He concludes that, in effect, 'We therefore have the same principle' – a man's individual qualities do not matter, merely his 'category'. When the orthodox Communist character Mostkovskoy is being questioned in a prisoner-of-war camp by the intelligent SS Obersturmbannführer Liss, he has no counter to the latter's insistence that the two movements do not differ in essentials and that whichever wins will incorporate the essence of the other. Liss is in fact repeating what Goebbels and other Nazis had said earlier. And at the end of the war a number of Fascist voices called for Communist rather than Allied victory, at least to destroy the corrupt capitalist order.

On the other hand, for the Communist the moderate socialist had always represented the class enemy in his most insidious guise. There was no error in doctrine in Stalin defining them, as 'Social-Fascists', as merely an alternative style of finance-capital rule. Lenin had, after all, similarly disrupted the Italian left during its struggle against the rise of Mussolini. It could, of course, be argued that Stalin (and Lenin before him) had been tactically mistaken, but there was no reason to fault them in principle. Meanwhile Stalin could at least feel some satisfaction, and a precedent for the future, in the fact that the German Communists had obtained millions of votes while slavishly following instructions from Moscow.

For a time, the Nazi triumph (and the crushing of the German Communist Party) was represented as a victory for the Communists in the sense that capitalism had been driven back on its last resort, naked force, so that the masses would soon mobilize to overthrow it. This view lasted until mid-1934, when Hitler's suppression of his own left deviationists in the June 'Night of the Long Knives' much impressed Stalin, and he accepted that Nazism was not about to collapse. On hearing of the purge of the SA leaders, Stalin is quoted in a recent Soviet account as saying of Hitler: 'Have you heard what's happened in Germany? Hitler, what a lad! Knows how to deal with political opponents.'

Thus, in spite of the virulent hostility at the overt level between the Hitlerites and the Stalinists, with each claiming to be the only true salvation from the horrors of the other, one can certainly sense an undertone of mutual understanding.

2

Stalin had won leadership. He had, in a devastating campaign, defeated the peasantry and imposed his system on the countryside. He had forced through his crude and ill-considered industrial policies. It might have been thought that he could now at last relax as the acknowledged victor and leader.

Such was not Stalin's nature. There remained what he evidently saw as a challenge to his authority. The opposition in the party had submitted – except for Trotsky, expelled and powerless. But they were still alive, mainly restored to party membership and holders of various posts of the second or third rank. As for the Bukharinites, they had surrendered even before the question of expulsion had arisen and they too held minor posts. It was not impossible that a change in events might bring at least some of these intrinsically hostile figures back into the struggle for power (as was to happen later in Communist countries, with Deng, with Gomulka, even with Dubček).

More immediately unsatisfactory was the fact that, as we have seen, it had so far been impossible to get a majority of his own, Stalinist, Politburo to accept the execution of party groups which had not, however hypocritically, surrendered to him and adulated him, but had openly called for his overthrow.

There seems now, and not on this issue alone, to have been a feeling among an important section of the leadership that the class struggle had been won, socialism had been achieved, and that reconciliation, both in the party and between the party and the people, would be the best way to consolidate the victory. The long alienation between the regime and society could now (they appear to have considered) be relaxed. The new social order could settle down. As for the party, the former oppositionists, already reintegrated into the movement to which (whatever their errors) they had given so much service, would be a useful resource for administration.

Thus it was in a mood of frustration that Stalin approached the Seventeenth Party Congress in February 1934 – the 'Congress of Victors'. As to intra-party matters, as he said in his keynote speech:

> 'At the Fifteenth Party Congress it was still necessary to prove that the party line was correct and to wage a struggle against certain anti-Leninist groups; and at the Sixteenth Party Congress we had to deal a final blow to the last adherents of these groups. At this Congress, however, there is nothing to prove, and, it seems, nothing to fight.'

And in fact all his former opponents spoke, admitting they had been wrong, praising him enthusiastically, and promising total support for the party line: Zinoviev and Kamenev; Bukharin, Rykov and Tomsky; Pyatakov, Radek, Lominadze ... Kamenev, in the typical tone of the defeated factions, spoke of the Ryutinites as 'kulak scum' who had needed 'more tangible' rebuttal than mere ideological argument.

But behind the scenes, the new resistance, which had already manifested itself over Stalin's attempts to shoot Ryutin and the others, was beginning to organize. These were loyal Stalinists, some of them ruthless executors of the terror against the peasantry, but seeking, as it were, post-crisis normalization. The idea emerged among a group of leading figures that Stalin, who had led them to victory, was too militant to cope with the new phase, and should remain in a more decorative post, giving up the General Secretaryship to Kirov.

This does not seem to have been because anyone thought that Kirov was a born political leader – on this all commentators (including Molotov in old age) are unanimous. On the contrary, in fact: he would be ideal as a representative of a collective leadership, with no claim to supremacy.

A number of leading figures – Petrovsky, Ordzhonikidze, Vareikis – seem to have approved this idea. Sheboldaev, who had been Stalin's chief agent in the terror in the Kuban, went to Kirov with their proposal. Kirov rejected it, on the grounds that such a change was bound to call in question the whole policy of the party. But when he spoke of it to Stalin (who had learned of it already) he said that it was partly Stalin's own fault, because 'after all, we told you things couldn't be done in such a drastic way'. Thus Kirov joined the ever-lengthening list of Communist leaders who misunderstood Stalin ... In the voting for the new Central Committee at least 166 Congress delegates (out of 1,225) seem to have crossed Stalin's name off in the ballot for the new Central Committee. Stalin, it is now said, was left with a feeling of 'revenge against the delegates, and, of course, against Kirov personally'.

Stalin, supporting Kirov's election to the Secretariat, tried to insist on his giving up his Leningrad job – that is, his power base – and coming to Moscow. Kirov refused, remaining both Secretary of the Central Committee (in name) and Secretary of the Leningrad Party organization. Meanwhile a certain political relaxation took place, of which Stalin outwardly approved.

3

Now we come to one of Stalin's most astonishing deeds. At some point in about mid-1934 he seems to have reached the conclusion that there was only one way to prevent a relaxation of the regime, and restrictions on his freedom of action. Kirov must be got rid of.

In the summer, Kirov was invited down to Sochi, where Stalin again suggested he should give up Leningrad and come to Moscow, and was again rebuffed. His other main request to Kirov was that he should undertake a new historical work on early Bolshevism in Transcaucasia. Previous historical accounts, even those in recent years written by such men as Stalin's friend Yenukidze, had already given Stalin a far weightier role than the facts warranted. But Stalin wanted further departure from the truth, to show him as 'the Lenin of the Caucasus'. Kirov had worked for a few years in Vladikavkaz, on the mountains' northern slopes. And even if he had taken no part in the events of Stalin's early years in Georgia and Azerbaijan, he had served there as a leading Bolshevik in and after the Civil War – and even been Soviet ambassador to Tiflis before the Soviet invasion. So his name would lend weight to the new version.

Kirov excused himself, on the grounds that he was no historian, and Stalin had (the following year) to turn elsewhere.

Back in Moscow, Stalin and Kirov had various quarrels. Kirov had to some extent dragged his feet over collectivization, with a smaller proportion of farmers in his area collectivized than elsewhere; Stalin had to withdraw his insistence on the campaign in Leningrad province being completed by the end of 1933, and to allow this to be amended to 1934.

Kirov and Stalin also had a direct confrontation, with angry words (witnessed by Khrushchev) over Kirov allotting extra food to the Leningrad workers (on the grounds that this would improve productivity, a logic far different from Stalin's own).

At any rate, Kirov was an obstacle, and he represented a mood hostile to any increase in Stalin's power. Moreover, this mood was in accord with that now beginning to take hold in the party; while in the country as a whole there was, of course, a great longing for something approaching normality.

Stalin's decision was that Kirov had to be killed. As Khrushchev was to write, in a section of his memoirs only published in 1989, Stalin evidently gave verbal orders to NKVD chief Genrikh Yagoda. There is no 'documentary' evidence against Stalin – though in 1989 the Soviet prosecutor's office released a statement that 'objective proof' was available on Yagoda's responsibility.

The present writer has given as full an account as was so far possible in his *Stalin and the Kirov Murder,* of which a recent Moscow article notes that it presents all the evidence now available. In brief, Kirov was shot on 1 December 1934 by the assassin Leonid Nikolaev. Nikolaev had made two previous attempts to get suspiciously close to Kirov, had been arrested and found to have a revolver in his briefcase, and had then been released. On 1 December, Nikolaev was able to get, with his revolver (and cartridges from the local NKVD sports club), into the third floor of the Smolny Institute in Leningrad, where Kirov worked. He waited for some hours. When Kirov arrived, his personal bodyguard Borisov was detained at the front door, and Kirov was unprotected when the assassin fired. Borisov was to be killed in the back of a truck by two NKVD men two days later, when they brought him to testify at the inquiry into the crime. The Leningrad NKVD chiefs were given short sentences for 'criminal neglect' of their duties, and even these they served as, in practice, chiefs of concentration camp administration. They were, however, shot in 1937–8.

Such are the bare bones of the story. Since no motive has ever been seriously advanced for Yagoda wanting Kirov dead (or thinking he could get away with killing him) it is clear enough that Stalin gave the orders.

Writers, including myself, have written of this operation to the effect that it constitutes, even by Stalin's standards, an abysmally black deed,

> 'Murder most foul, as in the best it is;
> But this most foul, strange and unnatural.'

Yet, on consideration, was it any worse than forcing other old colleagues, by torture and similar methods, to confess to imaginary crimes, and then killing them?

At any rate, Kirov had by this time plainly become, in Stalin's mind, an 'enemy'. And in Stalin's mind the distinction between a personal enemy and an 'enemy of the people' no longer existed. We probably need to envisage some such scenario as Stalin informing Yagoda that Kirov had been proved to his, Stalin's, satisfaction to be a concealed enemy agent. It was politically disadvantageous to make this public in current circumstances. So, as a highly confidential operation, Yagoda was entrusted with liquidating this enemy. The other NKVD men concerned (believed to number five or six) must have been given a similar story.

At Kirov's funeral, Stalin bent and kissed the cheeks of the corpse, who was certainly more useful to him dead than alive. For the assassination was the key moment in Stalin's drive to total power. As a recent Soviet commentator put it, history trembled in the balance, until 'Stalin threw Nikolaev's smoking gun into the scales'.

As soon as Stalin was told that Kirov was dead, he set out for Leningrad with an entourage of his allies, of NKVD men and of prosecutors. On arrival at the station in Leningrad, he slapped the local NKVD chief on the face, then drove to the Smolny. There he personally interrogated Nikolaev and various connections of Nikolaev's who had been pulled in. Nikolaev made it clear that he knew the NKVD had used him, and was hustled out of the room.

Stalin had meanwhile drafted an emergency decree on terrorism. All terrorists were to be tried as quickly as possible, and executed without appeals being considered.

In Leningrad, in addition to Nikolaev's own acquaintances and relations, a group of former Zinovievites who had nothing to do with the affair (and have lately been rehabilitated) were nominated by Stalin as the 'Leningrad Terrorist Centre' and arrested. They, and Nikolaev, were shot at the end of December.

In the new Stalinist style, Nikolaev's wife, ex-wife, sister-in-law, and one brother were also shot, while a sister, a cousin, another sister-in-law, and his sixty-four-year-old mother (a semi-literate cleaner at the Leningrad tramway depot) were given lesser sentences.

Meanwhile Zinoviev, Kamenev and many of their closest supporters were arrested. Tried in January in closed session on charges of having at least indirectly inspired the murder, they were sentenced to various terms of imprisonment – ten years for Zinoviev, five for Kamenev. From now on, they were never out of jail until released by execution.

4

Stalin had emerged even more slowly in the consciousness of the outer world than at home. A few – a very few – foreigners had reported quite early that he was a man to watch. But as a member of the first triumvirate he was still largely in the shadows; and even in the period of alliance with Bukharin, he only gradually attracted attention outside informed circles. It is in 1929, with his political victory, that he begins to be an international as well as a national figure. He had, of course, had contact with foreign representatives on the Comintern, and had received odd 'labour delegations' – to whom he had spoken in the most formal manner, merely as a mouthpiece of party views.

By the early 1930s, however, he had a number of extended interviews with foreigners, for practical purposes his first. These may, in a sense, be viewed as his only serious preparation for his later encounters with Ribbentrop, Roosevelt and Churchill.

One of the first to see Stalin was Eugene Lyons, the United Press correspondent, long an enthusiast, but now already sceptical about

Communism – he had been present at the Shakhty trial. He was later to be one of America's most vocal and effective anti-Stalinists.

Like all the other foreign correspondents in Moscow he had long since applied for an interview with Stalin. In November 1930, he was suddenly called by Stalin's secretary and asked to come round to the Kremlin. There had been rumours that Stalin had been assassinated, and Lyons thinks this may have been the motive for such an appearance before a certified Westerner. At any rate, they had a long interview.

Stalin put Lyons at his ease, and answered even rather provocative questions without arrogance. Was he a dictator? 'Stalin smiled – "No, I am no dictator. Those who use the word do not understand the Soviet system,"' and so on. He let Lyons use a Latin script typewriter in another room to get the interview on paper. He then read it to Stalin who made a few minor suggestions and wrote on it, for the benefit of the censor, 'more or less correct, I. Stalin'.

Lyons, though later so hostile politically, always admitted that personally, 'I like that man.' What he thought he saw was 'simplicity', 'nowhere a note of falseness or affectation'. He notes, indeed, that another American correspondent who later met Stalin had an impression 'completely at variance' with Lyons's own, and much closer to the 'public' record of the General Secretary. But at any rate Stalin had shown considerable political or tactical skill.

Another early interviewer was received in December 1931 – the German journalist Emil Ludwig, whom we have quoted in another context. Later, in a generally favourable book, he wrote of Stalin:

'He has no liking for a dialogue of short, excited questions, answers and interruptions, but prefers to string together slow, considered sentences. Often what he says sounds ready for press, as if he were dictating. He walks up and down while he is speaking, then suddenly approaches you, pointing a finger, expounding, didactic; or, while he is forming his considered sentences, he draws arabesques and figures on a sheet of paper with a blue and red pencil.

Stalin speaks without embellishment and, moreover, can express complicated thoughts simply. Often he speaks almost too simply, accustomed as he is to formulating his thoughts so that they will be understood from Moscow to Vladivostok. He has perhaps no wit, but he most certainly has humour; and his humour can be dangerous. Now and again he laughs a soft, dull, sly laugh. He is at home in many spheres, and he quotes extempore names, dates and facts accurately.'

More generally, this observer's impressions of Stalin, though in the main admiring, included some attitudes which were to require a little, though not a lot, of modification at later appearances:

'Stalin – we may well say it at the outset – makes a cold and alien impression; there is nothing about him that attracts. He does not come halfway to meet you; he is not open; he is cautious, unresponsive and, for the most part, sombre. When he laughs, it is with a grim, dark laughter, which comes up from the depths. Among the rulers of our time – and I have seen most of them – he is the most impenetrable. Everything about him, speech, walk, gesture, is slow and heavy. There is nothing to indicate trust in men or friendship for them . . .

You should always have before you the picture of an ordinary man, a plebeian without pose, uncommunicative by nature, even embarrassed by strangers – a man of medium height in a grey, military mantle, who seldom meets the gaze of his interlocutor. The forehead is low, the hair, growing down close, is barely touched with grey, the mouth, which sometimes holds a pipe, close-locked. The reader must think of this man's voice as quiet; the manner of delivery, in the answering of questions, utterly serene and self-confident. Stalin is firm and logical, but no argument can move him even to reconsider his views . . .

As he talks, Stalin lets syllables fall like heavy hammer blows. His answers are short and clear, not those of a man who over-simplifies things before a public audience, but those of a logical thinker whose mind works slowly and without the least emotion.'

In his answers to Ludwig's questions Stalin kept his end up most creditably. He explained that force alone could not possibly keep the Communists in power and that they would have been overthrown but for the fact that they always told the truth; that he was no more than a continuation of Lenin; that in any case all decisions were taken in 'our Areopagus', the Central Committee.

Over the next few years Stalin received a number of Westerners, often in a blaze of (from them) huge publicity. The journalistic interviews were as nothing compared with Stalin's reception of more distinguished foreign guests, such as George Bernard Shaw, whose conduct in the Soviet Union is understandably characterized by Ronald Hingley as having claims to being 'the most frivolous episode in recorded history'. Shaw, who also much admired Mussolini, swallowed everything the Soviets told him. Of Stalin he said: 'There is an odd mixture of the Pope and the Field-Marshal in him: you might guess him to be the illegitimate soldier-son of a cardinal with perfect manners, if only he had been able to conceal the fact that we amused him enormously.'

The 'we' consisted of Shaw and Lady Astor, the (American) first woman to take her seat in the House of Commons, the scourge of alcohol and of British military-sponsored brothels in the Far East. She was a little less impressionable and asked Stalin how long he was going to go on killing people. After the interpreter had reluctantly translated this, Stalin answered unperturbed that he would go on 'as long as is necessary', adding that 'the violent death of a large number of people was necessary before the Communist state could be firmly established'. Perhaps impressed by this frankness Lady Astor first lectured Stalin on the defects of Soviet educational methods (another of her fads) and then contributed to the clowning by going down on her knees, in what she felt to be the traditional Russian fashion, on behalf of the wife and children (still in the USSR) of an émigré professor. (The result seems to have been the arrest of the unfortunate family.)

All these experiences were doubtless useful to Stalin in assessing the credulity and irresponsibility of the Western educated classes. There were a number of later interviews of the same type, the lowest point being reached with the German writer Lion Feuchtwanger, whose book on *Stalin and the USSR* really deserves to be read, indeed reprinted, for the pathos of its idiocy.

The most striking of Stalin's conquests was, however, H. G. Wells, who arrived in Moscow in 1934 full of hostility to Communism and to Stalin personally, whom he saw as a despot, 'a sort of Bluebeard'. But the interview changed all that. Stalin, it is true, 'looked past me rather than at me', but this was 'not evasively'. He asked Wells's permission to smoke his pipe, and in this and other ways soon changed Wells's hostility to frank admiration:

'I have never met a man more candid, fair and honest, and to these qualities it is, and to nothing occult and sinister, that he owes his tremendous undisputed ascendancy in Russia. I had thought before I saw him that he might be where he was because men were afraid of him but I realize that he owes his position to the fact that no one is afraid of him and everybody trusts him.'

Such personal misapprehensions about Stalin's personality ignored Lenin's wise saying that there is no such thing as a 'sincerometer'. It is reasonable to suppose that they encouraged Stalin in the massive array of falsifications so central to his regime and its successors.

On more formal occasions Stalin did not feel quite at home. Ivy Litvinov, widow of the former People's Commissar for External Affairs, once told me of her first meeting with Stalin in the early 1930s. He was brought forward at a reception to shake hands with the Finnish Minister's wife. He started to shake hands with Madame Litvinov instead, and when turned in the right direction appeared thoroughly embarrassed and abashed at his mistake. But such occasions, and gaffes, were rare (and in no way harmful). On the whole Stalin had learned how to handle outsiders.

And, of course, even important foreigners who did not meet Stalin were being deceived about the whole nature of the system, and the realities behind the scenes. I have covered this at some length in my books *The Great Terror* and *The Harvest of Sorrow*, and here I will only cite one story which concerns Stalin directly. Julian Huxley, British zoologist and public figure, reports enthusiastically in his *A Scientist Among the Soviets* that volunteering to help unload railway trucks is common among 'highly placed personages' in the Soviet Union, adding, without comment, 'One is told that Stalin himself sometimes comes down to the Moscow goods sidings to help.'

5

Of course when Stalin told Ludwig and others that there was no terror and that the only people who were frightened were a small class of kulaks (and they were frightened not so much of the state as of the poorer peasants) – when Stalin put forward this breathtaking Big Lie to his foreign visitors it was no more than an expression of the propaganda picture now being put out for Russians and foreigners alike. A prisoner once explained the internal importance of the suppression of the truth, including the truth of the famine, as follows:

'You don't understand the importance of revolutionary propaganda. If the truth about the famine had been openly discussed we shouldn't have survived in 1931 and 1932. A fact which is openly proclaimed has an electrifying effect. Peasant insurrections would have swept us away. The first attempts to found a socialist order of society would have been drowned in the flood of counter-revolution.'

On smaller events, Stalin had been falsifying for some years. As we saw, as early as 1924 he had told delegates that he had belonged to the 'centre' in charge of the October Revolution and Trotsky had not. This centre, as we have seen, was of no importance, and indeed never met. Moreover, in 1918 Stalin had himself fully acknowledged Trotsky's decisive role. This was only a beginning. As we have seen, the Shakhty and other trials were total falsifications. Now came further massive faking in which Stalin played a personal role.

One of the 'gigantic' projects of the Five-Year Plan was the Baltic–White Sea Canal. Started in 1930, it was built entirely by the OGPU, with slave labour. The workforce at its largest seems to have been about 300,000, mostly 'kulaks' constantly replenished, who hacked it out of the earth and rock under appalling conditions – deaths are reckoned at about 200,000. It was, as it happened, practically useless, and only barges were able to go along a waterway originally intended to link the Baltic and the Northern Fleets.

It was finished, as far as it ever was to be, in May 1933. In July Stalin himself, with Kirov, Yagoda, Voroshilov and others, visited the canal and went on a short boat trip. This was the occasion for a vast public build-up of the project as not merely an industrial but also a moral triumph, in that the Soviet penal system was born humane and rehabilitatory. Many prisoners were quoted as expressing their joy at having been saved and turned into decent citizens. A group of writers, including Maxim Gorki, was sent to the canal, and a ludicrous book emerged. Gorki seems to have been genuinely taken in.

Stalin was, in fact, engaged in a campaign to harness Gorki to the Stalin myth. He lured him back from 'Fascist Italy', where the old socialist had preferred to live, and tried to induce him to undertake a Stalin biography. This would indeed have been a great coup. But Gorki, though a dupe, was not such a dupe as that, in spite of Stalin visiting him, and calling a mediocre poem of Gorki's adolescence 'more powerful than Goethe's *Faust*'.

None of this worked – not even the changing of the name of Nizhni Novgorod to Gorki. Part of the trouble was that Gorki had always been on friendly terms with Kamenev. By the middle of 1934 he was living in what amounted to protective custody, with his NKVD-appointed secretary Kryuchkov screening and often turning away visitors.

However, though Stalin from time to time had hints sent about the proposed biography, nothing came of it.

The clumsy adulation Stalin showered on Gorki seems yet another sign of the intense drive for validation which is to be found, in one form or another, throughout his life.

It also seems to show another of Stalin's traits – a respect for, even awe of, literature. It is notable that in almost all of his various letters rebuking writers, he uses a tone quite different from that of his intervention in other fields. He often disguises his opinion in the phrase 'some comrades consider' or says that he speaks only as an amateur. Not that this was a reliable or continuously operating attitude – Stalin was to kill off writers in large numbers. He had himself, of course, been a poet (and at the turn of the decade was to allow a reference to and praise of his verse, and later a four-line quotation, to appear in Tbilisi in Russian – though he never referred to it himself). He was to have poets executed, including one of the two leading Georgian poets, Titsian Tabidze (the other, Pavel Yashvili, shot himself); but they had committed the serious offence of telling the truth about the history of Georgian Bolshevism. On the other hand, when he learned of a new translation into Russian of Rustavelis's *The Knight in the Tiger Skin* he had the translator, Shalva Nutsubidze, released from prison, and went over the text with him, eventually ordering its publication.

As to Russian poets, it is a curious fact that none of the most important actually received death sentences. Gumilev had been shot before Stalin came to power. Blok had died of starvation. Mayakovsky and Yesenin – and later Maria Tsvetayeva – committed suicide. Pasternak and Anna Akhmatova survived, though silenced. Zabolotsky was sent to camp, and lived through it. Osip Mandelstam, also sent to camp, died there of hunger and cold.

That was some years later. But Mandelstam and Pasternak now enter Stalin's life in a very striking way. Mandelstam (his widow tells us) had concluded that the aim of the regime was the total destruction of independent thought. He now, most imprudently, wrote a short poem attacking Stalin.

> We live, deaf to the land beneath us,
> Ten steps away no one hears our speeches,
>
> But where there's even half a conversation
> The Kremlin mountaineer will get his mention

His fingers are fat as grubs
And words, final as lead weights, fall from his lips,

His cockroach whiskers leer
And his boot-tops gleam.

Around him a rabble of thin-necked leaders –
Fawning half-men for him to play with.

They whinny, purr or whine
As he prates and points a finger,

One by one forging his laws, to be flung
Like horseshoes at the head, the eye or the groin.

And every killing is a treat
For the broad-chested Ossetian.

Mandelstam recited this to half a dozen friends, one of whom informed on him. Yagoda, who is said to have been so struck with it that he had it by heart, informed Stalin.

Stalin had (temporarily) spared the prose writer Boris Pilnyak, at Gorki's intercession, after the extremely libellous 'Tale of the Unextinguished Moon', about Frunze's death. But that was a decade earlier. In 1934, there was almost nothing to stop him destroying Mandelstam.

Instead, he telephoned Pasternak for his opinion of Mandelstam's talents. When Nadezhda Alliluyeva's death was announced, the Union of Writers had sent a routine message of condolence; but Pasternak had written a strange letter saying that 'On the evening before, I found myself thinking profoundly about Stalin for the first time from the point of view of an artist. In the morning I read the news. I was shaken exactly as though I had been present, as though I had lived through it and seen everything.'

Some commentators believe that this letter, and the effect, almost superstitious, that it may have had on Stalin, accounts for Pasternak's survival through the period. But their only direct contact was this telephone call. Pasternak, instead of answering Stalin's question about Mandelstam, tried to speak of the problems of life and death. Stalin cut him off with a remark to the effect that he had expected a proper defence of his colleague Mandelstam.

Various figures interceded for Mandelstam through Bukharin and Yenukidze, rightly insisting that the poet was non-political and eccentric. Perhaps it was this which led to his being sentenced merely to three years' exile in the small town of Cherdyn. There he attempted suicide, and his wife appealed to the authorities, who let him move to the pleasanter city of Voronezh. Stalin can hardly have been pleased with Mandelstam's very hostile poem. But he seems to have been restrained, for now, from harsher action in part because he hoped, as with Gorki, for a favourable poem from Mandelstam. And such a poem Mandelstam, now understandably terrified, did indeed write. It was not a success and was never printed.

The appeal to Yenukidze by Mandelstam's friends is interesting. At the time Stalin's old comrade still seemed to be in favour. He was continually at Stalin's dacha, and retained his high position. But he had by now annoyed Stalin in several ways. He had earlier said of Stalin to his old friend Serebryakov, with whom he remained on good terms in spite of the latter's prominence in the old left opposition, 'What more does he want? I am doing everything he has asked me to do, but it is not enough for him. He wants me to admit that he is a genius.'

Yenukidze had continued to intercede not only for poets, which at a pinch might be tolerable to Stalin, but also for various party purgees. Yet his worst offence was his history of pre-revolutionary Bolshevism in the Caucasus. In it, Stalin is given a prominence far greater than the facts warranted, but this was no longer enough. In this, as in every other area, Stalin's appetite increased all the time.

6

Gorki's ewe-lamb, the White Sea Canal, illustrates some of the fallacies of Stalin's industrialization. He was primarily concerned with vast projects, not economically better than a number of smaller ones, but far more usable in propaganda. Some, like the Canal, were a waste of investment; others, like the Dnieper dam, probably took an excessive share of the national product, but were of great use.

As we have said, the intra-party opposition saw these huge projects as so much 'eyewash'. And a more balanced approach would have been better. But Stalin, whose knowledge of economics was slight, was committed to the idea of enthusiasm and compulsion rather than incentives, and to the wholly unrealistic Plan. Moreover, constant slogans calling for each factory to 'overfulfil' its target were nonsensical even in terms of the Plan itself: for where were the extra raw materials to come from, unless from another sector in need of them? The pressures were intense and, to some degree as with the struggle in the countryside, a wartime atmosphere was created, in which Stalin and his fellows could demand discipline and attack all failure as sabotage and treason. This may be seen as the central element of the Stalinist construction policy.

The results in industry were not as negative as in agriculture. But vastly excessive claims were made, both at home and in Soviet propaganda abroad. Indeed, it is astonishing how deep the myth penetrated in Western circles. Most of the figures then touted were in fact falsified. Current Soviet estimates for the 1930s are that instead of the alleged fivefold increase in production over 1929 to 1941, the true figure is about one and a half. This was about the same rate as in Germany. Moreover, as we have noted, the industrial advance was distorted in the direction of the prestigious and away from the profitable.

Still, some of the efforts most publicized, and patronized by Stalin personally, were by and large successful. One of these was the Moscow Metro, symbol of the transformation of the capital. Built largely by forced labour, including that of the Spanish Republican general 'El Campesino', it was and remains an excellent piece of work. It was, of course, not unique to Moscow. I remember in the late 1930s a Russian refusing to believe that the London Underground had opened its first line in the 1860s; but, as a song in a New York left-wing revue of the time had it, there was a difference:

> Moscow Metro Underground!
> – Underground!
> Built for the workers' gain
> Not for the bosses' gain!

More generally, the Soviet Union was building industry, exemplified in the huge enterprises, and building it in a socialist manner. Russia had indeed been backward, but under Stalin it would overtake and surpass the old capitalist countries in fairly short order. Anything good in the Soviet Union was thought of as a wonderful achievement, and anything bad as a wonderful sacrifice.

It was only the physical paraphernalia of industry which resembled that of capitalism (and even then the new plants were on a more grandiose scale). Mechanical progress had been made by socially superior methods, with scientific planning supported by huge popular enthusiasm. Much was made of the supposedly unprecedented training of the previously raw peasants who were transferred to the new enterprises for the less skilled industrial jobs – as had naturally been true in every previous industrial revolution.

Few of these ex-peasants seem in fact to have been enthusiastic. But, as we have said, enthusiasm was available for the Plan. The cadres of the party now had a revolutionary task, a challenge. A large corps of young activists, trained in the new party's attitudes, was 'fighting on the industrial front'. The elan, though partly factitious, was partly genuine and was channelled above all into the acceptance of Stalin and his decisions. It was to be seen, in the service of modernity and the machine – though in each case supported by forced labour – in all the new efforts from Magnitogorsk to the Moscow Metro.

Equally typically, Stalin's other contribution to Moscow's modernization was the destruction of scores of cathedrals, churches and monasteries everywhere; of the Iversky Gates and Chapel on the Red Square (to facilitate 'demonstrations'); of the old quarters of Moscow, the Kitaygorod and the Okhotny Ryad; and above all of the Cathedral of Christ the Saviour, between the Kremlin and the Moscow river, a 'monument of the nations' and 'the pride of Russia', as his latest Soviet biographer puts it, which was destroyed 'for atheist and architectural reasons' with the intention of replacing it with a Palace of Soviets.

This was decided on in the summer of 1931, as part of a programme 'for the reconstruction of Moscow'. Stalin's chief architect, B. Yofan, explained the plans. 'In 1931 the cathedral of Christ the Saviour still stood on a large square by the Moscow river. Huge and massive, glittering with its gilded spires, reminding one of the cake and the samovar ... a landlord-merchant fane. The proletarian revolution will boldly confront this massive architectural structure, symbolizing the power and taste of the rulers of old Moscow.' When in December Stalin heard the explosions of the demolition squad he said to his secretary Poskrebyshev, 'What's that cannonade?' Reminded of the decision, he calmed down.

The Palace of Soviets which was to replace it would have been four hundred metres high, topped by a statue of Lenin in aluminium which Stalin proposed should rise a further hundred metres. It would then have been the tallest building in the world. Its main hall would have had 21,000 seats. As things turned out, the soil could not have supported such a structure, and the area is now a public swimming pool.

Though such problems, and the interruption of the war, prevented for a time the achievement of a 'new' Moscow, the idea did not die. As Khrushchev, then the City Committee's First Secretary, told the Central

Committee in 1937: 'Rebuilding Moscow, we must not be frightened of pulling down a wood, or some little church, or this or that cathedral.'

7

How, if at all, had Stalin changed by the mid-1930s? Could a preliminary assessment have been made?

While in the 1920s he had often led the discussions and in the 1930s had intervened frequently at Politburo and other confidential meetings, Stalin now seldom took the chair, but sat to one side smoking his pipe. He usually let the others speak first and then 'in a low, but strong and assured voice' he summed up and dictated the resolution.

Not that this is a rare or secret notion. A member of the British diplomatic service once told me the formula, passed down for decades by successful candidates, for getting high marks at the 'weekend' seminars which formed part of the procedure for passing into the Foreign Office. First, buy a pipe; second, sit through the seminar puffing at it; and towards the end 'sum up' with a 'balanced' assessment of the arguments. No oriental cunning is in fact required (and the fact that Stalin always smoked British – Dunhill – pipes is no more than coincidental).

A former Soviet official notes that on these occasions, in Stalin's face only the eyes were alive, watching the smallest movement and expression of the other speakers. 'He smiles quite often, but it is a stereotyped smile, a dead smile ...' For the section of the party which had voted for him he was indeed, very largely, a stereotype, the expression or embodiment of simple ideas, of a simple momentum towards the social fantasy they nourished as their main motivation. The diary of the Old Bolshevik Fedor Raskolnikov, who defected in 1939 when Soviet ambassador to Bulgaria, and had moved in the highest party circles for decades, became available recently. It includes a long and thoughtful characterization of Stalin at this time. Of course, it stresses Stalin's 'fundamental psychological trait' as 'his unusual, superhuman strength of will' which, as Raskolnikov puts it, was able to 'suffocate', to 'crush' not only the 'soft and weak-willed' Kalinin, but 'even such wilful people as Kaganovich'. He goes on:

'A narrow sectarian, he proceeds from a preconceived scheme. He is the same kind of schematist as Bukharin, with the difference that Bukharin was a theoretically educated man. Stalin tries to force life into a ready-made framework. The more life resists being forced into the narrow Procrustean bed the more forcefully he mangles and breaks it, chopping limbs off it. He knows the laws of formal logic, and his conclusions logically follow from his premises. But he has never shone intellectually ... He is poorly educated ... like all semi-intellectuals who have picked up scraps of knowledge, Stalin hates the genuine intelligentsia.'

As to his tactics, Stalin had once told Raskolnikov: 'In as much as power is in my hands, I am a gradualist.' But Raskolnikov's most interesting observation is that:

'He lacks the realism that Lenin possessed and, to a lesser degree, Rykov. He is not farsighted. When he undertakes some step, he is unable to weigh its consequences. He is after-the-fact. He does not foresee events and does not guide the spontaneous flow, but drags at the tail of events, swims with the current. Stalin lacks the flexibility of a man of state.'

Thus, at the profoundest level Stalin had so far shown a very ordinary mind. Some characteristics, however, were well developed. He obviously had an insatiable drive, an overwhelming will-power, and he is every-where reported – after a certain maturing up to his achievement of power – as having that talent or gift for swaying others found, in different forms, among many charismatic leaders of all times and regimes.

As Trotsky wrote:

'Extraordinary historical circumstances invested his ambition with a sweep startling even to himself. In one way he remained invariably consistent: regardless of all other considerations, he used each concrete situation to entrench his own position at the expense of his comrades – step by step, stone by stone, patiently, without passion, but also without mercy! It is in the uninterrupted weaving of intrigues, in the cautious doling out of truth and falsehood, in the organic rhythm of his falsifications, that Stalin is best reflected as a human personality.'

One of his great characteristics was a phenomenal memory, at least in the matters which concerned him most. And he had the ability to master the facts in a variety of fields. He mistook this, as laymen often do, for the ability to understand at least the essentials of any field whatever and make informed judgements. He was to decide not only questions of economics, in which he was barely competent, but also

193

crucial issues of, for example, biology, on which his knowledge was no more than comparable, at best, to that of an all-purpose journalist called upon to write an article, or a lawyer required to 'brief himself' for a week or two on some technical problem.

This attitude, which led to such absurdities, must in part be based on the Communist principle that a dogma transcending other knowledge had been discovered, and that political leadership, and political considerations generally, are on a higher and more comprehensive plane than all other elements of life and society, and are empowered to make final decisions. It allowed Stalin to decimate, and more than decimate, his engineers, his physicists and so on. When the Kharkov Physics Laboratory, one of the best in Europe, was destroyed by the arrest of almost all its leading staff, one of its departmental heads commented: 'You need five years to train an engineer, and even then the government had a very great deal of trouble before it could get suitable engineers for its new factories. But a capable physicist needs from ten to fifteen years' training.'

The most crucial area in which Stalin failed to appreciate the need for specialists was, however, to be military science. Here, as we have said, he clearly believed that he himself had shown high talent in spite of a total lack of training. His destruction of the military cadres, which nearly resulted in disaster in 1941–3, was a natural result.

8

The removal of Kirov was the action Stalin had needed to break the deadlock and go forward to the achievement and consolidation of complete autocracy. There were still obstacles, which required pressure and manœuvre to reduce. Over 1935 Stalin's advances appeared to be minor or partial. There were various secret trials. The old leaders of the Democratic Centralists and the Workers' Opposition were dealt with, though only by imprisonment. Yenukidze was suddenly demoted to what was purportedly a high post in the Caucasus, but which turned out to be a minor job at a spa. In June he was expelled from the Central Committee for 'personal and political dissoluteness'. His Caucasian Bolshevik history was superseded by a new one, authored by the new Secretary of the Transcaucasian Party, Lavrenti Beria (though in fact written by an assistant called Begia, shot not long after). This represented

Stalin as 'the Lenin of the Caucasus', and remained orthodox until Stalin's death.

Meanwhile the Society of Old Bolsheviks and the Society of Former Political Prisoners were liquidated, and Politburo members were given to understand that any memoirs they might be writing would not be welcome. The Politburo itself was now more amenable than ever. Kirov's ally on such issues as the Ryutin case, Valerian Kuibyshev, had died suddenly – though this death was very probably (not certainly) natural.

The attack on Yenukidze, in the part of it not then made public, was that he had, in his general supervisory capacity as Secretary of the Central Executive Committee, allowed former aristocrats to take jobs in the Kremlin. The museums and libraries in the Kremlin were indeed, naturally enough, partly staffed by educated people from an earlier stratum.

During 1935, with virtually no publicity, a new fake trial was built up – the so-called 'Kremlin Affair'. For many years there were rumours about it, including the fact (now confirmed) that two men were shot. We still do not know precisely what the charges were. Rumour in high party circles in the 1930s had it that a girl of aristocratic origin working in one of the Kremlin libraries had attempted to kill Stalin by putting poison in a book he was scheduled to take out. Since all the accused have now been rehabilitated, it seems clear that there was no real attempt; but Stalin's suspicious mind may have thought that one or another of these unfortunate women was, or might be, the active expression of the millions who wanted him dead.

There was another Kremlin connection useful to Stalin. Kamenev's ex-sister-in-law, Nina Rosenfeld, worked in the Kremlin library. So Kamenev was incriminated without difficulty, together with five of his relatives including his ex-wife. Trotsky's son, Sergei Sedov, who was totally unconnected with any of this, but a nephew of the Kamenevs, was also arrested.

After a secret trial Kamenev got ten years, and nine cleaners, a porter, a telephonist, eighteen librarians (mainly women) and an assortment of other Kremlin functionaries and their wives and acquaintances, 110 in all, were sent off to prison or exile.

This was very much Stalin's personal affair, involving people he saw every day. But we can also see Stalin's hand in various decrees and appointments and other matters of 1935. Not only had Yenukidze been purged. Gorki too had come, for the first time since 1918, under severe criticism from *Pravda*. And Nadezhda Krupskaya was also under pressure. She is reported attending a Politburo meeting during the 1933 famine and, though courteously received by Stalin, being in effect told to mind her own business. In 1935, she is reported joining in the efforts of the Society of Old Bolsheviks and others to argue against the death penalty for Kamenev. It seems to have been at this time that Stalin told her that if she did not conform the party would nominate another widow for Lenin: the party, he is supposed to have added, 'can do anything'. This story was reported in the West quite early on, and was naturally doubted. But Khrushchev confirms it in his memoirs. Stalin, he says, more than once raised the possibility in his presence. The proposed new widow was apparently to have been Yelena Stasova. Incredible though the idea might sound to non-Communists, there would have been nothing impossible about it. History then was being rewritten on a large scale, and in this case all that was needed was an announcement that the divorce and remarriage had been kept confidential at Lenin's request, but that in view of Krupskaya's anti-party activity the Central Committee now found it necessary to publish the truth.

We can certainly see Stalin's hand in a decree of 7 April 1935, extending all penalties, including death, down to twelve-year-old children. This made very bad propaganda for the USSR in the West: the French Communists were reduced to arguing that people matured so quickly under socialism that by the age of twelve they were already fully responsible citizens.

But the decree could have been passed and kept unpublished. The purpose was clearly to put heavy pressure on the oppositionists with children, like Kamenev and Zinoviev. The public announcement was a sign that the state's intention was serious. The decree would be put into force in a number of cases. The light it throws on Stalin's ruthlessness is obvious. It also serves to illustrate the distinction between his words and the reality: in August 1936 he publicly rebuffed any idea that in Soviet circumstances children should answer for their parents' sins. A few weeks later dozens of relatives of Zinoviev and others were arrested, and many were shot. This is only one of many occasions in which Stalin's pronouncements were very different from his practice. It is deplorable to have to record that there are still Western academic historians who take his disinformatory speeches as genuine indications of policy.

The terror machine was now also being fine-tuned, with Yagoda,

Vyshinsky and Yezhov controlling the secret police, the Prosecutor's Office and the party machine respectively.

It is not the purpose of this book to trace the whole story of the Great Terror of 1936–8, which is the central and essential event of Stalinism. In it he finally crushed not merely opposition but any trace of overt independent thought.

We may find it appropriate to look at this fearful series of events not merely as the general expression of his will, but also to consider his day-to-day role. Some biographers have suggested that he merely gave the general idea, and that Yezhov and the others saw to the details. Documents recently published in the Soviet Union show, on the contrary, how concerned he was with every detail of the major cases of the period.

In 1936 came the first great faked public trial of ex-oppositionists, with Zinoviev, Kamenev, Ivan Smirnov and others in the dock. Early in the year Stalin personally gave the order that a great conspiracy needed uprooting. He saw to it that promises were made to Zinoviev and the others that their lives would be spared if they confessed. He chose the list of accused, making several changes at the last moment. And it was he who ordered the death sentences to be carried out.

During the last quarter of 1936, it was on Stalin's order, sent from his customary long holiday in Sochi, that Yezhov replaced Yagoda as head of the NKVD, which Stalin alleged was four years behind schedule in uprooting enemies. Pyatakov and Radek and the rest of the personnel for the next great trial were arrested. Tomsky committed suicide. But Bukharin and Rykov, still candidate members of the Central Committee, were temporarily cleared. Over the autumn, Stalin played a cat-and-mouse game with Bukharin. At the 7 November 'demonstration' – the nineteenth anniversary of the Revolution – a soldier came up to Bukharin in one of the minor stands. Bukharin expected arrest, but it was instead an invitation from Stalin to come up and join him at the main stand. Later NKVD officers arrived to search Bukharin's flat. Stalin 'chanced' to telephone, and on hearing of it ordered the NKVD men to leave at once.

In December 1936 the Central Committee, at its plenum, heard a series of violent attacks by Yezhov and others against Bukharin and his rightist plotters. Stalin intervened and suggested that the question should be postponed until the next plenum.

Over the next few weeks Bukharin and Rykov were called to 'confrontations' with those already confessing, like Pyatakov, in the presence of Stalin and the Politburo.

Meanwhile, under a barrage of public speeches, and of secret Central Committee letters to the party branches drafted by Stalin himself, a hysterical wave of 'vigilance' and denunciation was sweeping the country. In Kiev, Stalin's emissary Pavel Postyshev tried to block the worst excesses. Stalin, relying on a local delator called Nikolaenko, started to undermine Postyshev. Nikolaenko was typical of the worst of the lunatic sniffers-out of enemies of the people. When Khrushchev became First Secretary of the Ukraine she came to him with various new denunciations – including Khrushchev's new deputy, Korotchenko. Khrushchev told Stalin that he thought she was wrong. Stalin became angry and said that distrust of such a person was 'incorrect'. He added, 'Ten per cent truth – that's already truth, and requires decisive measures on our part, and we will pay for it if we don't so act.' Nikolaenko eventually denounced Khrushchev too as a Ukrainian nationalist plotter, and Stalin finally agreed that she was off her head. Khrushchev tells us that this should have been obvious from the start. (Another of Stalin's denouncers, Mishakova, who caused Kosarev and the Komsomol leaders to be shot, was also plainly 'psychologically defective', in Khrushchev's words.) Meanwhile Nikolaenko had several thousand deaths on her conscience, even though people had long since gone to any lengths to avoid even meeting her, since to know her at all was to court arrest.

'On her conscience?' But revolting though her conduct was, Khrushchev implies a verdict of, in the old phrase, 'guilty but insane'. What about Stalin's conscience? Nikolaenko, it is true, intensified the atmosphere of terror in party and public circles in Kiev, but things were much the same throughout the country. Stalin did not strike Khrushchev as insane, in the sense that Nikolaenko did. He was indeed (in Khrushchev's words on another occasion) 'sickly suspicious'. But the idea that one only has to believe a tenth of an accusation to act on it is, at least apparently, different from a full belief in it. Stalin's attitudes seem to have been that though Nikolaenko's precise allegations were perhaps untrue (and certainly unsupported by evidence), she nevertheless had some special sensitivity to otherwise undetectible signs of inner disloyalty. It is as though Stalin had an almost superstitious respect for what he regarded as some sort of primitive instinct.

Such a notion was indeed to be found in some party circles. Vyshinsky himself instructed his junior prosecutors that evidence was less important than 'political flair'. There are many cases in which (in this case at an academic meeting) accusers are reported as saying, 'When class instinct speaks, evidence is unnecessary.'

And in one sense Stalin, Vyshinsky and the others were right. When no overt expression whatever of disloyalty is possible, and opposition is confined to internal thoughts, these thoughts can only be observed in deeply, but not quite perfectly, concealed facial expressions, or tones of voice. And the intenser the terror, the more tenuous the signs become.

Stalin's exculpation of Khrushchev is also interesting. Khrushchev, as a Russian, was an implausible Ukrainian nationalist plotter. But implausibilities abounded at this time (and he could easily have been transferred to some other category of guilt). What Khrushchev achieved, both now and later, was to give Stalin the *appearance* of innocence, much more important than innocence itself. He seems to have done this in the tradition of his Russian peasant ancestors – by, whatever his true feelings, always showing every sign of naivety and frankness when confronted by the unpredictable *vlast*. Sometimes, indeed, as Khrushchev tells it, he appears to have been consciously acting the Holy Fool. Stalin, with little or no experience of this older Russia, seems to have accepted this more or less at its face value, even in the midst of his blackest moods of suspicion.

9

At the end of January 1937 came the Pyatakov trial. Once more Stalin chose the list of accused (and again made last-minute changes). He also himself insisted on the inclusion of a flight by Pyatakov from Berlin to Oslo to meet Trotsky and receive his instructions on terror, sabotage, espionage and so on. The Norwegians at once issued a statement that no aircraft had used Oslo airfield in the month in question, so this raised qualms.

Moreover, Ordzhonikidze had been promised that Pyatakov would not be shot. Like Postyshev, Ordzhonikidze had become opposed to the excesses of the purge; and he was a full member of the Politburo. He had already complained of an error at the Zinoviev trial, when an alleged meeting of conspirators had taken place in a Copenhagen hotel demolished nearly twenty years previously. He had not joined in the December 1936 attacks on Bukharin. Stalin was already moving against him, having had his brother arrested. And over January and February came a series of violent rows between the two men. Ordzhonikidze was at first told that Pyatakov had not really been shot, though this pretence could not be kept up long. And Ordzhonikidze was supposed to give the report on the economy to the Central Committee in late February, at what was to be the famous 'February–March plenum'. Stalin returned his draft speech with coarse comments scrawled on it. Ordzhonikidze planned to make trouble at the plenum, hoping for the support of Postyshev, and perhaps Chubar and Kalinin. However, after another flaming row with Stalin, he was found dead of a gunshot wound on 18 February, the day before the plenum was supposed to open. His death was announced as a heart attack: nowadays it is generally written of as a suicide, though some Soviet analyses imply, or even say, that murder is equally likely. If indeed a suicide, it was a suicide little different from murder, on the basis of 'shoot yourself or else . . .'

The plenum was postponed a few days. When it opened, it first condemned Bukharin's announcement that he was on a hunger strike. Stalin assured Bukharin that he would not be expelled; and Bukharin gave up (and apologized for) his hunger strike. The plenum then considered the 'case of Bukharin and Rykov'. The two were shouted down by Voroshilov, Molotov, Yezhov and others. A commission on their cases heard three proposals – from Yezhov to shoot them, from Postyshev to arrest them without shooting, and a moderate one from Stalin, accepted by the Commission, to arrest them and await the result of the investigation. Bukharin was told that he could prove his innocence in jail. This, under Stalin's new system of interrogation, was easier said than done.

Meanwhile Postyshev had voiced objections to the purge at the plenum, and had been silenced by a rough interjection by Stalin.

Over the next months Stalin had other targets. First Yagoda and his team of NKVD leaders was arrested. Then came the blows at the army with the arrest of leading generals, including Stalin's bugbear of the days of the invasion of Poland, Marshal Tukhachevsky. The officers first pleaded innocent, then confessed under torture (there are forensically identifiable bloodstains on Tukhachevsky's interrogation record). All the documents were sent to Stalin, who saw Yezhov almost every day, and 'took a direct part in the falsification of charges', as it was recently put in an organ of the Central Committee.

After the arrests, but before the 'trial', Stalin assembled the Supreme Military Soviet, and spoke viciously of the arrested officers, and of a number who were shortly to follow them. He saw Ulrikh, chairman of the Military Collegium of the Supreme Court, and Vyshinsky just before the 'trial', and gave them instructions. Tukhachevsky and the others (who had been promised their lives) were of course shot. Stalin had asked how the military members of the Court had behaved, and when told that none but his old companion Marshal Budenny had shown any enthusiasm, he cursed them. Meanwhile he had written on Yakir's appeal for his family to be spared, 'scoundrel and prostitute'.

A recent Soviet analysis of the results of the purge in the army points out that the military education of a General Staff major takes a minimum of ten to twelve years, and of an Army Commander twenty years: 'and they were almost all annihilated. Even Zhukov at the beginning of the war in no way matched Tukhachevsky or Yegorov in his training.'

Stalin required not only acquiescence but also complicity. Early in 1938, he drafted a circular for the armed forces saying that not only 'enemies' but also 'silent' ones who did not adequately denounce the enemy must be purged. In this (which was by no means confined to the army), Stalin was following earlier despots. Gibbon condemns an edict of Emperor Arcadius who decreed 'that the knowledge of mischievous intention, unless it be instantly revealed, becomes equally criminal with the intention itself; that those rash men who shall presume to solicit the pardon of traitors shall themselves be branded with public and perpetual infamy'. Enthusiasm was particularly demanded. M. M. Landau, the editor of the army newspaper, said at the June meeting of the Supreme Military Soviet, 'We are vitally interested in fulfilling in the shortest possible time Comrade Stalin's directive at the February plenum – to restore the significance of the Bolshevik printed word.' Stalin answered, 'Weak, weak,' and Landau was arrested.

It was not until March 1938 that the third of the great public trials, that of Bukharin, Rykov, Krestinsky, Yagoda and others, took place. Stalin actually watched part of the proceedings from an alcove where at one point a trick of the light left him plainly visible. He had at the last minute intruded into the charges of terrorism, espionage and so on an accusation that Bukharin had planned to murder Lenin, a particularly mean smear.

When the proceedings opened, Krestinsky repudiated his confession. Stalin told the interrogators, 'You worked badly with that filth,' and Krestinsky was worked on again overnight. Next day he confessed as required.

There was a peculiar episode at the very end of the trial. The Old Bolshevik Rozengolts, for whom Stalin seems on other evidence to have nourished particular hatred, was recalled and asked about a charm his wife, a religious woman, had sown into his pocket, and which was found there on his arrest. Vyshinsky read it out in a sneering voice –

verses from the Sixty-Eighth and Ninety-First Psalms.

LXVIII

1. Let God arise, and let his enemies be scattered: let them also that hate him, flee before him.
2. Like the smoke vanisheth, so shalt thou drive them away: and like as wax melteth at the fire, so let the ungodly perish at the presence of God ...

XCI

1. Whoso dwelleth under the defence of the Most High: shall abide under the shadow of the Almighty.
2. I will say unto the Lord, Thou art my hope, and my stronghold: my God, in him will I trust.
3. For he shall deliver thee from the snare of the hunter: and from the noisome pestilence.
4. He shall defend thee under his wings and thou shalt be safe under his feathers: his faithfulness and truth shall be thy shield and buckler.
5. Thou shalt not be afraid for any terror by night: nor for the arrow that flieth by day;
6. For the pestilence that walketh in darkness: nor for the sickness that destroyeth in the noon-day ...

It is impossible to think of this episode otherwise than as an idea of Stalin's. And it casts a light on his feelings. As the final word in a long series of confessions to fearful crimes, it amounts to very little, or nothing. As a demonstration of the power of the state as against the impotence of God it makes sense. There is also the feeling that Stalin himself, who must have remembered the psalms well (and whose own style was hieratic, even psalmodic), was making a personal as well as a political demonstration – perhaps even reassuring himself, in what may be thought a strained and excessive manner.

That these dreadful spectacles were planned and overseen by Stalin personally is clear enough. He gained from them first, the physical destruction of all former or potential political leadership; second, a great intensification of the mood of terror throughout the party and the country; and third, the opportunity to blame the accused for anything economically, politically or otherwise deplorable in the country. (Thus, all shortages were due to sabotage. And the Kirov murder was now, rightly, attributed to Yagoda – though acting on Yenukidze's, not Stalin's, instructions.)

Yenukidze had meanwhile, it was announced on 20 December 1937, confessed at a closed trial held on 16 December and been shot. We now know that he and his fellow accused had in fact been executed at various dates over the autumn, and were not alive at the time of their trial. Why Stalin practised this peculiar deception is unknown. Perhaps to show that 'the party can do anything'.

As Yenukidze's fate indicates, the major public trials were only the tip of the iceberg of terror. Over the years Stalin received and signed for execution, with Molotov countersigning, 383 lists of names, divided into 'general', 'military', 'NKVD' and 'wives of enemies of the people'. Over 1937 to 1938 these lists are reported as having included some 40,000 names (and over the whole Stalin period we are now told that 230,000 appeared on such lists). On 12 December 1937 alone, Stalin and Molotov approved 3,167 death sentences, and then went to the cinema.

The level at which a victim became important enough to reach Stalin's lists is fairly clearly deducible from a remark of his a few years before: 'If we have in mind the leading strata, there are about 3,000 to 4,000 first-rank leaders whom I would call our party's corps of generals. Then there are about 30,000 to 40,000 middle-rank leaders who are our party's corps of officers. Then there are about 100,000 to 150,000 of the lower-rank party command staff who are, so to speak, our party's non-commissioned officers.'

His 'phenomenal memory' for such things would presumably mean a reasonable acquaintance with at least a thousand-odd of the upper level, with his (or Malenkov's) card index providing the connections, and hence the suspicious affiliations, of the rest. At the least, Stalin must have considered the cases of all of the Central Committee, the High Command, and the Provincial Secretaries past and present. In cases he was directly concerned with, he received reports on how the executions went, and sometimes made comments. A well-known story which circulated in the NKVD tells of a party for senior police officials late in 1936. After a good deal of drinking all round, K. V. Pauker, who had been present at Zinoviev's execution in his capacity as head of the NKVD Operative Department, gave a comical rendering of that event. Himself acting the part of Zinoviev, he was dragged in by two other officers. He hung from their arms moaning, 'Please, for God's sake, Comrade, call up Iosif Vissarionovich.' Stalin laughed heartily, and when Pauker repeated the performance, adding as his own invention,

'Hear, Israel, our God is the only God'! Stalin was overcome with merriment and had to sign to Pauker to stop.

It is certainly true that Stalin had no feeling that death deserved any dignity. (Nor that it closed the account. For example, various people, such as Army Commander S. M. Kamenev, no relation of the politician, were posthumously disgraced.) Indeed, it is clear that Stalin regarded despair and horror as part of the penalty deserved by his opponents.

Meanwhile, those going to the execution cellars without public trial, sometimes without any trial at all, included the majority of his own followers. Some, such as Krylenko, he telephoned to reassure that all would be well the very day before their arrests, though this may have been not for malicious pleasure, but to discourage suicide. His old Politburo allies, Rudzutak, Chubar, Postyshev, Kossior and Eikhe, all had confessions tortured out of them and Eikhe, for one, was viciously tortured *after* his trial, just before his execution. On one occasion Krupskaya, who had with Pyatnitsky made a last effort against the NKVD at the June 1937 plenum, was brought before the Politburo to listen to a 'witness' against Pyatnitsky. At another 'confrontation' Stalin, to demoralize Petrovsky, had Yezhov produce Kossior. Kossior, addressed throughout as 'Prisoner Kossior', confessed in a mechanical way that he was a Polish spy. When Petrovsky tried to get him to say he was innocent he was removed. Stalin turned to Petrovsky and shouted that he, Petrovsky, need not think he would be spared because he had been a member of the tsarist Duma. But he was in fact spared, as were all the other Bolshevik Duma members – which, as I have suggested elsewhere, shows once again a respect for legitimation, however indirect, arising from Stalin's own insecurities.

But throughout the period Stalin's public persona contrasted remarkably in its benignity with his pitiless and hatred-sodden dealing of death. For example, there was a famous and much reprinted photograph of Stalin holding in his arms the little daughter of a Buryat Mongol Communist, Ardan Markizov. It was even turned into a sculpture, and continued to appear after Stalin had had the father shot.

Stalin seldom indulged in the usual despot's caprice of unexpected pardon. But he did sometimes, at least up to a point. Khrushchev tells of a Soviet trade delegate in South America who had talked to a local about life in the Soviet Union, though mainly about horsemanship there. The local turned out to be a journalist, and printed this harmless material. Sent back, the Russian appeared before the Politburo and appeared doomed. But Stalin said, 'Well, he was too trusting and fell victim to gangsters, pirates,' adding: 'The case is over. In future be more careful.' This greatly pleased and impressed Khrushchev. There are several similar stories.

Then again (though this was in March 1936, when, the Soviet historian who recounts it suggests, Stalin might not yet have 'matured'), there is the case of the Zinovievite Central Committee member A. S. Kuklin, serving a sentence of ten years' imprisonment. When assured that Kuklin, a sick man, was at the point of death, Stalin permitted his immediate release. (On the other hand a few months later Yuri Gaven, a similar case, was taken out on a stretcher to be shot.)

There are several such stories. But the one most obviously due to a caprice was his sudden release from labour camp in 1940 of the Georgian Communist S. I. Kavtaradze, who was brought straight from prison to Stalin, and after a friendly conversation was immediately made Deputy People's Commissar for Foreign Affairs – Stalin adding at the end of the interview, in a gloomier tone, 'Still, you planned to kill me.' What can this signify about Stalin? That he knew Kavtaradze to be innocent and just made his last remark as some sort of justification for his earlier treatment? Or that he still thought Kavtaradze to be guilty, and was explaining, even to himself, the extraordinary extent of his forgiveness?

In general, in any case, Stalin's conduct throughout the period of the Yezhov terror is as the originator and director of the whole huge bloodbath. His known interventions behind the scenes are almost all dreadful. At the June 1937 plenum he ordered the NKVD to stop 'coddling' prisoners. When the Old Bolshevik Beloborodov failed to confess, Stalin wrote, 'Can't this gentleman be made to speak of his foul deeds? Where does he think he is, in a prison or a hotel?' And above all, we have the famous confidential telegram on torture sent out in January 1939 when, after Yezhov's fall, some officials were hoping for more humanity. It is worth quoting in full, since it bears every mark of Stalin's personal style, and of his way of thought, or at least argument:

'The Party Central Committee explains that application of methods of physical pressure in NKVD practice is permissible from 1937 on, in accordance with permission of the Party Central Committee ... It is known that all bourgeois intelligence services use methods of physical influence against the representatives of the socialist proletariat and that they use them in their most scandalous forms. The question arises as to why the socialist intelligence service should be more humanitarian against the mad agents of the bourgeoisie, against the deadly enemies of the working class and of the collective farm workers. The Party Central Committee considers that physical pressure should still be used obligatorily, as an exception applicable to known and obstinate enemies of the people, as a method both justifiable and appropriate.'

10

The terror of 1936–8 was an almost uniquely devastating blow inflicted by a government on its own population, and the charges against the millions of victims were almost without exception entirely false. Stalin personally ordered, inspired and organized the operation. He received weekly reports of, as a recent Soviet article put it, not only steel production and crop figures, but also of the numbers annihilated. He personally examined and signed, it is true, only the top-level death sentences. But slaughter was not left to local authorities. Yezhov, by telegram and by actual visit, would order the execution of ten thousand or thirty thousand enemies of the people. It is not conceivable that this was done without Stalin's orders. Over the years, the whole political attention of the country and of the party was focused on enemies of the people, and in particular on the great public trials, which provided at this time the overwhelmingly dominant theme of Soviet indoctrination and publicity.

What is sometimes neglected by those of us who never faced such things, is the extreme intensity with which the terror bore down not only upon its victims but upon the population as a whole. Millions lived year after year in an insane world of denunciation and hysteria. As Soviet writers tell us today, people's whole psychology was distorted in unnatural and inhuman ways – to the degree that even now the recovery has not yet been complete.

The massive system of threats and rewards – at least the reward of survival – conditioned the minds of millions into an almost Pavlovian submission to the state's insistences, and not seldom an acceptance, with relief, of the state's false enthusiasms. More independent minds were reduced to despair and apathy. Such are usual psychological concomitants of life in completely abnormal conditions.

Nor, given the frightful pressures, is it psychologically unprecedented that at least some of the victims and political victims developed an attachment to Stalin, as the only stable point in sight – rather as the hostages of terrorists sometimes became emotionally attached to their captors.

Besides, as usual having it both ways, Stalin to a large extent avoided the public responsibility. Even intelligent people thought his subordinates were to blame. The producer Meyerhold said, 'They conceal it from Stalin.' Pasternak, meeting Ilya Ehrenburg one snowy night in the Lavrushevsky Lane, lifted his hands to the dark sky and exclaimed, 'If only someone would tell Stalin about it.' For who else was there to turn to?

Even if Pasternak and Meyerhold were not politically sophisticated they were men of the highest intelligence. The picture is thus one of people who abhorred the terror and prevalence of vicious denunciation, and who yet exempted Stalin from blame. This is a measure of his achievement in projecting, at least in some ways, a benign personality.

In less intellectual spheres, similar attitudes were to be found. Robert C. Tucker quotes a Russian telling him years later how he had wept in tears of gratitude when Stalin abolished bread rationing at the beginning of 1935! When true information about responsibility was wholly absent, much could be got away with.

Generally speaking (if we omit the myriads disillusioned by their own or their relatives' arrest), survivors have given differing accounts of their thoughts at the time. A section of the indoctrinated young, and not only that stratum who were simply beneficiaries and accomplices of the regime, continued to believe in Communism and in Stalin personally. Many more participated, however reluctantly, in a life in which no other public thought existed, and adjusted with much psychological strain to the necessities of the situation. It appeared that Stalin had indeed by and large succeeded in atomizing society.

The terror was directed against the population as a whole, with a million-odd executions of which the mass graves are now being discovered all over the country; millions more were sent to die in the Arctic camps. But it also devastated the party: half its membership was arrested, and over a million died by execution or in camps. Of the Central Committee itself, 70 per cent perished.

It is not clear when Stalin decided to wind up the superterror and revert to what were by comparison normal levels of repression. By the middle of 1938, he had killed, or had in prison ready for execution, the great majority of the Central Committee elected in 1934, and also the great majority of the generals. At a slightly lower level the terror had also reached a certain limit. For instance, on the Byelorussian railway system it was plain that any further arrests would lead to total break-down. The big factories had lost almost all of their properly qualified engineers. The economy was heading downhill. The mere number of the population was sixteen or seventeen million fewer than the Plan had projected. The NKVDs of the republics were simply being ordered to shoot tens of thousands for no reason but to keep the terror going.

Over the autumn of 1938 Stalin set up a commission to investigate the NKVD. It reported adversely, as was no doubt intended. In December Yezhov was replaced by Beria. Over the next few months many of Yezhov's men were shot. But Yezhov still remained in at least one of his various posts – People's Commissar of Water Transport. And he appeared on the platform at Lenin's birthday celebrations in February 1939. At the informal Council of Elders which met before the Eighteenth Party Congress in March to decide on a new Central Committee, he was present as a current member of that body. When his name was suggested from the chair, there was at first no objection, and in fact speakers noted his loyal service, until Stalin, puffing his pipe, walked from the corner where he was sitting to the front table and called Yezhov forward:

'Well! What do you think of yourself? Are you capable of being a member of the Central Committee?'

Yezhov turned pale and in a broken voice answered that his whole life had been devoted to the party and to Stalin, that he loved Stalin more than his own life and didn't know anything he had done wrong that could provoke such a question.

'Is that so?' Stalin asked ironically. 'And who was Frinovsky? Did you know him?'

'Yes, of course I knew him,' answered Yezhov. 'Frinovsky was my deputy. He –'

Stalin cut Yezhov short, asking who Shapiro was, what Ryzhova had been (Yezhov's secretary), who Fyodorov was, and who others were.

'Iosif Vissarionovich! You know it was I – I myself! – who disclosed their conspiracy! I came to you and reported it ...'

Stalin didn't let him continue. 'Yes, yes, yes! When you felt you were about to be caught, then you came in a hurry. But what about before that? Were you organizing a conspiracy? Did you want to kill Stalin? Top officials of the NKVD are plotting, but you, supposedly are not involved. You think I don't see anything? Do you remember who you sent on a certain date for duty with Stalin? Who? With revolvers? Why revolvers near Stalin? Why? To kill Stalin? And if I hadn't noticed? What then?'

Stalin went on to accuse Yezhov of working too feverishly, arresting many people who were innocent and covering up for others.

'Well? Go on, get out of here! I don't know comrades, is it possible to keep him as a member of the Central Committee? I doubt it. Of course, think about it ... As you wish ... But I doubt it!'

And that was the end of Yezhov. Arrested a few days later, he was shot on 4 February 1940.

11

Stalin called writers 'engineers of the human soul' – a totally meaningless phrase to be much quoted for its wisdom and depth in certain circles. His uneasy feeling for their importance was perhaps in part due to his own memory of the effect Rustaveli and Schedrin and the others had had on his youth. Theirs was, in fact, another source of power, at least over the mind. A truly logical Stalin would have suppressed the great writers of the Russian past – Tolstoy, Turgenev, Chekhov, Dostoevsky and the others, all in their different ways bringing before the Soviet reader values fundamentally subversive of orthodox Communist belief. (Indeed, in one view, it was this literature as much as anything which in the long run wrecked the attempt to create a new and cruder morality.) Yet Stalin was unable to produce a better literature, a higher Soviet creativity, from his hacks, and he knew it. Alexei Tolstoy, nephew of Leo, was obviously mediocre in his sub-Tolstoyan socialist realism. Stalin tended to prefer Sholokhov, unorthodox enough in his earlier books; or Bulgakov, quite unassimilable to orthodoxy; or the erratic Ehrenburg.

Stalin could, of course, rely for actual control of the intellectual world on an intellectual stratum more narrowly fanatical than himself. Chekhov, coping with the already highly intolerant left-wing editors of earlier times, had written:

'Under the banner of learning, art and persecuted freedom of thought Russia will one day be ruled by such toads and crocodiles as were unknown even in Spain under the Inquisition. Yes, you just wait. Narrow-mindedness, enormous pretensions, excessive self-importance, a total absence of any literary or social conscience: these things will do their work ... will generate an atmosphere so stifling that every healthy person will be nauseated.'

The humiliations forced on the good writers – Mandelstam's poem on Stalin, Pil'nyak having to take Yezhov as a collaborator on a novel – were constant. When Isaak Babel bravely spoke of the current necessity for the 'heroism of silence' he was violently denounced. Every writer's meeting, every literary journal, was full of vicious accusations. Submission, and self-abasement, usually only earned a reprieve. The great majority of the Union of Writers were shot or sent to labour camps.

Stalin's deep concern with this whole sphere may be seen in dozens of interventions. He attended a performance of Shostakovich's opera *Lady Macbeth of Mtsensk* and condemned it; he had the Politburo severely reprimand Margarita Shaginyan for the novel *Ticket to History* (though that was for misrepresenting Lenin). Stalin personally told the leading Soviet historian Tarle what to write about Talleyrand and Napoleon, threatening otherwise to have him sentenced to another term of exile. (He had just been amnestied.)

As we saw in his crash course with Sten, Stalin was taking a direct interest in correct history – and philosophy. The 'philosophical front' was the subject of special decrees, under which Sten and his colleagues were denounced (and later mostly shot). Stalin had continuously asked Sten, as he listened to Sten's complicated expositions (made even more indigestible by Sten's 'monotonous voice'), what a given lesson of Hegel or Fichte or Kant 'signified from the point of view of the class struggle'. What it all signified was that Stalin, with his limited grasp of these matters, abetted by a few third-rate hack denouncers like Mitin, defined the truth. Above all, he said that 'it is not only possible, but absolutely necessary' to link all theoretical disputes with the political deviations in the party.

It is worth noting in this connection that Stalin's regular reading included extracts from all the nine main émigré journals, and that his library had copies of many of the émigré books, including Trotsky's. Indeed, it is presumably Stalin's hand which is seen in the answers of one of the accused at the Pyatakov trial, when asked what he thought of Trotsky's *My Life*: 'I said that from the literary point of view he, as a journalist, wrote well, but because of the infinite number of "I"s in it, I did not like it.' At any rate, it is true that Stalin was sparing with his "I"s: now more often than ever referring to himself as 'Comrade Stalin'. 'It is impossible to deceive Comrade Stalin' was a common usage of his.

In this period, too, we see the flowering of another intellectual phenomenon profoundly symptomatic of Stalinism, and of the thinking of Stalin himself. In the world of science, the Bolsheviks had long inclined to crackpot, quick-fix theories. Lenin himself had more than once warned against the nostrums of Bolshevik doctors ('Really, in ninety-nine cases out of a hundred, doctor comrades are asses'). After he died several 'unorthodox' medical notions got attention in high places.

In the 1930s the absurd linguistic theories of N. Marr, who believed that all words derived from the sounds 'rosh', 'sal', 'ber' and 'yon', were declared orthodox, and his opponents vanished to execution or labour camp – though Stalin was to abandon this particular theory in 1950.

In biology this attitude reached its extreme. The charlatan Trofim Lysenko, though not in full control until after the war, devastated the field with his supposedly Marxist theory of the inheritance of acquired characteristics. There is no doubt that Stalin was deeply interested in, and convinced by, this notion. It is sometimes argued that Lysenko had had some practical successes – that he possessed what amounted to a green thumb – and that this led Stalin to believe his theories. But Stalin was not such a low-level pragmatist as to accept a theory on such superficial grounds. It was clear, and became clearer, that he really believed in Lysenkoism.

This attachment to eccentric ideas was to grow greater in the 1940s and 1950s. Nor was it always just a matter of Stalin personally. Under the strain of the Stalin-style economy, officials at every level sought for some quick way, unorthodox by bourgeois standards, in which difficulties might be solved, or decisive savings made. This would be accompanied by vast publicity until it failed, after which no more was heard of the patent method.

It is tempting to view all this, and Stalin's own addiction to such things, as part of the revolutionary mentality. Marxism promised a quick and all-purpose solution to all the problems of history. The mind which accepted that, it may be felt, was also prepared for final breakthroughs in all other areas of thought.

12

Meanwhile the Stalin cult reached new heights, or depths. In 1938 the rewriting of history was expanded to the whole Bolshevik and Soviet past with the publication of the famous *Short Course* history of the All-Union Communist Party, which became the bible of High Stalinism.

It was printed in over 40 million copies all over the world, and represented the truth in the whole international Communist movement – 'an encyclopedia of basic knowledge in the field of Marxism–Leninism', and so on. It amounts to a vast and breathtaking deception, in which all the oppositionists (and the non-Bolsheviks) are represented as agents of imperialism, and Stalin is credited with leading the Bolshevik underground, organizing the Revolution, crushing treason, creating prosperous agriculture and, in general, being the leader of the world proletariat and its best Marxist.

The *Short Course* was written by a commission of the Central Committee. This was originally put as its having been written by this commission 'under the direction of Comrade Stalin and with his most active personal participation'. In a later version we read that it was 'written by Comrade Stalin and approved by a Commission of the Central Committee'. When the Director of the Museum of the Revolution asked for pages of the manuscript of the *Short Course,* Stalin answered that he had burned it.

Among this farrago, which became the keystone of the whole imposition of systematized falsehood on the minds of a generation, we find a short chapter on Marxist theory, believed to have actually been written by Stalin. Schematic in form and hieratic in tone, it is nevertheless (as the veteran oversubtilizer Georg Lukacs was to concede in his post-Stalinist days) a useful summary. In its context it is doubtless to be seen as a statement of belief justifying the rest of the book.

The *Short Course* had its place as the central text of Stalinism, but its role was the assertion of theory and of supposed facts, and its tone was comparatively restrained. On the broader scale it is hardly possible to convey by mere quotation and example the overwhelming pervasiveness of the hysterical and obsequious outpourings which increasingly accompanied all reference to Stalin.

'Leader of Genius of the Proletarian Revolution', 'Inspirer and Organizer of the Victory of Socialism', 'Supreme Genius of Humanity', 'Experienced Proletarian Commander', 'Theoretician of Genius and Organizer of Collective Farm Construction', 'Leader of Genius of the Toilers of the Whole World' (from a single speech, if by a particularly servile local secretary). All this was accompanied, as its practical result from the point of view of politics, by (in Roy Medvedev's words), 'illusions, autosuggestion, the inability to think critically, intolerance towards dissidents, and fanaticism'. People said, and wrote, that they had fainted, or gone into ecstasy, on seeing or hearing Stalin.

Intellectuals contributed. Quite early on Alexei Tolstoy was naturally writing such stuff as 'Thou, bright sun of the nations / The unsinking sun of our times / And more than the sun, for the sun lacks wisdom.' The proletarian writer Alexander Avdeyenko, after a reprimand for having inadequately praised Stalin in a speech to the Writers' Union, felt obliged, the next time he spoke, to conclude, 'When a son is born to me, when he learns to speak the first word he utters will be "Stalin",' prefiguring a similar promise for a piglet in Orwell's *Animal Farm*.

Not only in the spoken or written word but also in the visual arts, falsification and glorification flourished. In film after film, Stalin's role before, during and after the Revolution was fictionalized. Paintings showed him leading strikes, or advising a complaisant Lenin. Almost every office or workshop, and many private houses, had idealized portraits of the Leader hanging prominently – as icons, less prominently, had done in the past. A recent Soviet article shows a deluded citizen of the period pressing kisses on such a picture out in a public park. Flypasts of fighter planes, parades of gymnasts, were deployed to form the name Stalin.

Some results were as absurd as they were dreadful. At a provincial meeting there was an ovation when Stalin's name was mentioned, and no one dared to be the first to sit down. When, finally, an old man who could stand no longer took his seat, his name was noted and he was arrested next day. When one speech of Stalin's was published on gramophone records, the eighth side was devoted entirely to applause ...

Did Stalin believe (and if so, in what sense) all this adulation? His daughter puts it in this way: 'Did he perceive the hypocrisy that lay behind "homage" of this sort? I think so, for he was astonishingly sensitive to hypocrisy and impossible to lie to.' A veteran Soviet diplomat and soldier wrote: 'Anyone who imagines that Stalin believes this praise or laps it up in a mood of egotistical willingness to be deceived, is sadly mistaken. Stalin is not deluded by it. He regards it as useful to his power.'

But, the human mind being what it is, it seems that he both disbelieved it and believed it, either simultaneously or in different moods.

Publicly, up to a point, Stalin was able to have it both ways. He had told Feuchtwanger that adulation was distasteful to him, but forgivable in the circumstances. For the Soviet people, as well as for foreigners, he gave various examples of his 'Bolshevik modesty' (as Mekhlis put it at the February–March plenum). More privately, he prevented publication of a book called *Tales of Stalin's Childhood* as not only 'full of factual errors' but also as instilling a 'cult of personalities of leaders': but in this case perhaps the 'errors' loomed largest. Similarly he stopped Malenkov and Poskrebyshev from sponsoring a Russian translation of his youthful poems; here too, he may have wished not to lay himself open. On a slightly different note, early in 1938, citing 'workers' suggestions', Yezhov proposed to the Politburo that Moscow should be renamed Stalinodar. Stalin pronounced against this.

But when the otherwise devoted American journalist Louis Fischer wrote in an article that Stalin could and should restrain the cult, Stalin's private reaction was to snarl, 'The swine!' In general, his sporadic and ineffectual criticisms of the cult may be seen as a ploy to add modesty to the rest of his panoply of virtues. The consciousness of the whole country was in any case adequately swamped in an ocean of adulation.

13

When the miserable period of the early 1930s became a little less miserable – with malnutrition but no actual famine, and an easing off of the terror to comparatively tolerable proportions, the scorpions for the time being put aside and whips alone being used to chastise the population – a slogan was issued, and was soon to be seen everywhere: 'Life has become better, comrades, life has become more joyful. Stalin.' An artist was sentenced to five years' imprisonment for adding a 'u' to one of these placards, making it read: 'Life has become better, comrades, life has become more joyful *for* Stalin .'

This proposition seems not to have been true. After Nadezhda's death, Stalin's private and social life became increasingly gloomy and limited. Khrushchev strongly suggests that an alleged 'governess' of Svetlana, 'a young and beautiful woman', was in fact selected on other grounds. And the British traveller Rosita Forbes, who visited Stalin, reports a woman present who appeared to be his wife. A woman originally sent to the dacha as a waitress, Valentina Istomina, became established as his housekeeper, never joining in the conversation, but remaining for the rest of his life. She was more or less accepted as the widow when he died.

He now lived mainly at his 'nearby' dacha at Kuntsevo, though he occasionally stayed overnight at the flat under his office in the Kremlin. His waking and working hours grew more eccentric. He usually rose around noon, went to his office and worked until six or seven, then had dinner with his political cronies – increasingly a scene of coarseness and squalid jests – and often saw a film afterwards.

Stalin was, of course, carefully guarded. The Operative Department of the NKVD, headed by K. V. Pauker until his disappearance in 1937, had the security of high officials as one of its main responsibilities. Several thousand operatives might be assigned to cover particular movements of Stalin. Under Pauker, the actual head of Stalin's bodyguard (as he had been since the Civil War period) was Nikolai Vlasik. Stalin's daughter describes him as 'incredibly stupid, illiterate and uncouth', though in later years he intervened in artistic and other matters far beyond his ken. Anyone visiting Stalin had to go through Vlasik's security check.

At the dacha, and sometimes in his flat, Stalin still from time to time entertained his closer companions and his relatives – the in-laws still coming over for some time after Nadezhda's death. But Stalin began increasingly to see her as having gone over to the enemy, and only started speaking more kindly of her to his daughter very late in life.

He remained on affectionate terms only with Svetlana, though occasionally he lost his temper with her and used foul language (the abuse was limited 'essentially to his tongue'). He was angry, for example, when she wore, even at the age of ten, dresses he thought too short and, soon afterwards, tight sweaters.

In general he was still an affectionate father. They played a rather heavy-handed charade of her being 'Housekeeper' and he her 'Secretary No. 1', with her giving him written instructions, and his countersigning 'I submit' with either his own name or 'little papa'. In the eyes of occasional visitors like Khrushchev, Stalin had behaved 'very humanly' in the early 1930s, and there was much chaff and laughter. But Stalin's usual companions and guests at home were limited to a few individuals or families. Bukharin had for a time been one of them. Avel Yenukidze, that old comrade from Caucasian days, had been a frequent guest. Another guest was Moscow's police chief, Stanislav Redens, who was married to Nadezhda's sister Anna; and sometimes Kirov.

215

These more or less personal relationships petered out. Bukharin, who had even wrestled in fun with Stalin, ceased to be a visitor, and was soon to perish, as were Kirov, Redens and Yenukidze.

By 1938 Stalin's political circle, much less intimate than before, included the personalities who were to survive until the end of his rule – though in the last days it was a near thing for some of them. The inner circle was now Molotov, Kaganovich, Andreyev, Voroshilov, Mikoyan, Khrushchev, Kalinin, Zhdanov, Beria and Malenkov. Younger men were to rise and fall in the interim, but through the forties and early fifties this core of Stalinists was to remain in place. This is a remarkable contrast to the vicissitudes of the 1920s and 1930s, and marks, in a sense, the stabilizing of Stalinism as a system.

In my book *The Great Terror* I suggested that Stalin showed a certain reluctance to have women, at any rate women Old Bolsheviks, shot – unless they were also 'wives of enemies of the people'. And in fact there was a surprisingly high ratio of survivors. Even Lenin's secretary, Fotieva, who had been deeply involved in his last manœuvrings against Stalin, survived. So did Yelena Stasova, almost as close to those events. Various others included R. S. Zemlyachka, a pre-revolutionary Central Committee member. Alexandra Kollontai, one of the former stars of the Workers' Opposition, remained as Ambassador to Sweden long after thirteen other leaders of the faction had been jailed (in 1935) and later shot. Of the 1934 Central Committee neither of the women full members was executed: K. I. Nikolaeva (a former Zinovievite, too), and Nadezhda Krupskaya. Krupskaya was of course a special case; and she was denounced by Yezhov (certainly on Stalin's initiative) at a meeting of the Central Control Commission in 1938. He called her an accomplice of Trotsky's, and accused her of hastening Lenin's death, adding that 'only respect for the memory of Lenin' prevented him 'turning her over to Vyshinsky and Ulrikh, as he had other traitors'. Krupskaya fainted and had to be sent to a sanatorium. She died, still only seventy years old, at the end of February 1939, not long before the Thirteenth Party Congress. There have always been rumours that she was poisoned.

We have just learned that the only woman candidate member of the Central Committee, A. S. Kalygina, was indeed shot, so we are speaking more of a tendency to spare such women than of a rule. Neither of the two women who appeared as implicated 'witnesses' in the Moscow trials was then sentenced to death, as all the men were – though one of the women, the prominent ex-'Left' Communist Yakoleva, who received a prison sentence, seems to have been shot, like all the surviving accused still in prison, in 1941. The other, Ivan Smirnov's ex-wife Safonova, survived. (Later, in the 'Crimean Affair' of 1952, the only defendant not to receive a death sentence was the only woman, Academician Shtern.)

We can be quite certain that Stalin himself made the decision in all these cases. On the only occasion when Stalin is known to have crossed a name off a death list, it was that of a woman, Lili Brik – though the reason he gave was that she was the (common-law) 'widow of Mayakovsky'. Molotov, on the other hand, once changed a woman's prison sentence to death on his own account, and does not seem to have been overruled.

Of course the NKVD tortured and shot many women. But at the higher level, some faint vestige of restraint seems possible and may perhaps represent a flicker of the old Caucasian chivalry.

As to his own family connections, for a time Pavel Alliluyev, Nadezhda's brother, continued to visit. But, he told a friend, he began to feel increasingly estranged, and on Pavel's sudden death in 1937 Stalin did not even sign the obituary. Stanislav Redens (Svetlana's 'Uncle Stan') lasted only a little longer; in 1938 he was removed from his post as head of the Moscow NKVD and demoted to Kazakhstan, but soon shot. His wife Anna, Stalin's sister-in-law, pleaded for him, but Stalin told her that his accusers knew what they were doing. Afterwards she would not believe he had been shot, and Stalin personally assured her that Redens had indeed been executed. Anna went half-mad.

Thus life went on more and more drearily, in the cases where it went on at all.

14

The end of the Yezhov period coincided with the crucial steps in foreign policy which were to lead to the spectacular Nazi–Soviet Pact in August 1939.

As early as October 1933, Stalin had initiated confidential contacts with the Hitler regime. He does not at first seem to have regarded Nazi Germany as a major problem. But then some rethinking seems to have taken place. Stalin never gave up on the possibility of agreement with

Germany. Hitler's fanatical anti-Communism seemed to be a decisive objection, but (as it turned out) this was not insuperable. A representative of the NKVD Foreign Department, reporting to Stalin in August 1935, presented a pessimistic analysis of the possibilities, but saw that it made little impact.

Stalin now proclaimed a foreign policy, and a Comintern policy, based on the idea of forming a strong anti-Nazi coalition from which he could, if convenient, negotiate from strength. The Comintern gave up its anti-'Social-Fascist' stance in favour of United Fronts, later 'People's Fronts', stretching yet further to the right. In diplomacy, Maxim Litvinov, People's Commissar for Foreign Affairs, was a proponent of alliances against the Nazis. Stalin at this time once put his arm around Litvinov's shoulder, and said that it seemed they could now agree. 'Not for long,' Litvinov answered.

For three years, in fact. While Stalin did not cease to seek contact with the Germans through his own men in the Soviet Embassy in Berlin, the official policy was now alliance with the West. Over the period there were many strong Soviet statements and speeches condemning the Nazi principle of expansion, especially in the East, as provided for in *Mein Kampf* and never repudiated. Stalin himself spoke apprehensively, but moderately, on the issue. At the Seventeenth Party Congress in 1934, Stalin put out the first of various feelers. He remarked, 'Of course we are far from enthusiastic about the Fascist regime in Germany. But Fascism is beside the point, if only because Fascism in Italy, for example, has not kept the USSR from establishing the best of relations with that country.'

But even in the speeches of Molotov attacking the dangerous tendencies in Germany there were usually escape clauses, readily readable in Berlin. In January 1936, after a powerful attack on the German menace, Molotov told the Central Executive Committee that 'side by side with' Berlin's reckless anti-Soviet policy, the German government had proposed, and the Soviet government had accepted, two hundred million marks of credits, and that negotiations for more were still afoot. In March he gave an interview to *Le Temps* saying, 'There is a tendency among certain sections of the Soviet public towards an attitude of throughgoing irreconcilability to the present rulers of Germany, particularly because of the ever repeated hostile speeches of German leaders against the Soviet Union. But the chief tendency, and the one determining the Soviet government's policy, thinks an improvement in Soviet–German relations possible.'

218

This was at the time of Hitler's remilitarization of the Rhineland and the absence of any French reaction to it.

In the summer the Spanish Civil War started. Stalin became involved to the extent of sending supplies including 648 aircraft and 407 tanks. Three thousand Soviet military 'volunteers' served in Spain, and the Comintern organized the 42,000 genuine volunteers of the International Brigade commanded by the supposed Canadian 'Kleber', in fact Red Army Corps Commander M. Z. Shtern. At the same time, the Spanish Communists were in effect encouraged to take over the Republican government, mainly because the genuine leadership resisted Stalin's most obviously personal requirement, the total (rather than partial) suppression of the allegedly Trotskyite POUM, in whose militia George Orwell served. This was, over the first half of 1937, the overwhelming concern of the Soviet ambassador, of the representatives of the NKVD, and in effect of Soviet policy in general. As to the war effort, Stalin lost interest when it became obvious that the Republican cause was unwinnable, and reports in the Soviet press shrank in both size and intensity, as Ilya Ehrenburg tells us.

At the time of the Pyatakov case, when the accused were charged with having plotted with the Nazis through Trotsky, envoys of Stalin several times let it be known to the Germans that this accusation was not to be taken seriously – a point not to be admitted to the Soviet or the world public, though the Germans of course knew the facts anyway. And on the last day of the trial itself, Stalin's personal envoy (and former schoolmate) David Kandelaki, speaking from a prepared text in the name of Stalin and Molotov, assured Schacht that the Soviet Union had no anti-German intentions, and was ready for political negotiations at any time.

Meanwhile, through 1938 Hitler's political offensives went forward. Austria fell. Then, in the autumn, the Munich agreement awarded the German-speaking territories of Czechoslovakia to Germany. Finally, in March 1939, Hitler seized the rest of Czechoslovakia.

Now the Western powers, double-crossed at Munich, determined to resist, and they offered guarantees to Hitler's next obvious victim, Poland, which was certain to provide military resistance.

Stalin's alternatives presented themselves starkly – an alliance with France and Britain to block Hitler, or a deal with Germany. For the moment Stalin kept these options open. But as Robert C. Tucker puts it: 'Stalin's collective-security diplomacy was a calculated effort of coalition-building in Europe. He earnestly sought to bring about the formation of a strong politico-military anti-German grouping based on France and Britain. But, *it was not a coalition in which he wanted the Soviet Union to participate when war came.*'

In his report to the Eighteenth Party Congress Stalin said that the Western powers had abandoned collective security, and that Soviet policy would 'not allow our country to be drawn into conflicts by warmongers who are accustomed to have others pull the chestnuts out of the fire for them'. This overture was understood in Berlin, and by Hitler personally, as was the removal of Litvinov and the appointment of Molotov to the Foreign Commissariat on 3 May.

Later in May Hitler took the decision to attack Poland, even if it meant war with Britain and France. By the end of the month the Germans decided to negotiate seriously with Moscow. The Western Allies now also began to put out feelers to Moscow. As Churchill thought, and as the British General Staff and the majority of the Cabinet were now convinced, a full Anglo-Franco-Soviet military alliance without conditions was the only thing which might deter, or alternatively defeat, Hitler. With reluctance on Chamberlain's part, arrangements were made to discuss a security treaty. France and Britain have been cogently criticized for their comparatively low-level delegation, which arrived in leisurely fashion by boat on 11 August and made all sorts of reservations about Soviet freedom of action in the Baltic states, and for their negotiating too slowly (though as to the last, it was the Soviets who confined military discussions to one meeting a day).

Such a treaty could only have been negotiated at the price (eventually paid anyway) of granting effective Soviet dominance in Poland and the Baltic states. Nor is it certain that it would have stopped Hitler. At any rate, Stalin might have faced at least the possibility of early war, with the French motionless behind the Maginot Line. An arrangement with Germany offered both peace, at least for a time, and unopposed expansion of Soviet territory. Thus it is by no means obvious that Stalin would have preferred the West even on the best terms it could offer. As it was, the Westerners were hobbled by many considerations, some of them of weight.

First, they did not trust the Soviets, and were of course shown to be right when it came to the observance of later agreements, such as Potsdam and the Balkan peace treaties. Second, they did not believe in the Red Army's ability, at this stage, 'to maintain an effective offensive', as Chamberlain put it; a few months later the Finnish debacle proved them right. Third, they wrongly thought (as did Stalin) that the French

Army would prove a match for the Germans, at least defensively. But more important, in Britain at least, public opinion had been mobilized against Hitler because of his seizure of the Czech lands, and a Stalinist occupation of the Baltic states had no higher justification (though perhaps this could have been fudged). Then, Poland remained a problem. Polish acceptance of Russian troops in their territory was, naturally enough, by no means a foregone conclusion, and would in any case have led to friction.

Worst of all, the West offered a prospect of collective security which might or might not deter Hitler, or, alternatively, Soviet involvement in an uncertain war. Hitler offered large territories, peace, and the chance of he and the West being worn down in a long and evenly balanced contest in which the USSR would be the *tertius gaudens*.

Once the Germans had decided on a settlement with the USSR, there was little real chance of any Soviet–Western agreement. The British and French negotiations were fizzling away, with every point having to be referred to Stalin personally, while spokesmen like Zhdanov were put up to cast doubt on Western intentions. At the end of July diplomatic conversations between Soviet and German trade representatives in Berlin established that the Nazis would give the USSR what it wanted in Eastern Europe. By 18 August, Hitler's planned war in Poland was only days away. The Germans insisted that Ribbentrop be received in Moscow by 23 August.

Stalin acceded. Ribbentrop arrived. The pact was signed and announced that evening, though the secret protocols on the division of the loot were not referred to. The public communiqué as originally drafted by Ribbentrop appeared too effusive to Stalin, who said that since the two countries had been 'pouring filth over each other' for years, a slightly more restrained tone would be appropriate. He also told Ribbentrop that the British would fight 'stubbornly and cunningly', thus apparently assuming that England and France would after all fulfil their treaty obligations to Poland. Stalin assured Ribbentrop on his personal honour that the Soviet Union would faithfully observe the pact. He even added, if rather unconvincingly, that if Germany were forced to her knees he would send a hundred divisions to the Rhine to help her. And at the reception following the brief negotiations he stood and proposed a toast: 'I know how much the German people loves its Führer. I would therefore like to drink his health.'

221

Chapter 11

With Hitler

Whether or not Stalin, or Hitler, had been quite certain that the Western Allies would honour their commitment to Poland, the astonishing speed of the German blitzkrieg was a surprise in Moscow as well as in London and Paris. Hitler had demonstrated that he had a first-class military machine. But France and Britain, however ineffectively at this stage, were now at war with Germany.

On 9 September Molotov telephoned to congratulate the Germans on the capture of Warsaw. On 10 September Stalin started a partial mobilization and attacked Poland on 17 September. By this time the Polish Army was in a hopeless situation, and Stalin tried to convey the idea that he was only intervening in view of the collapse of the Polish state. He evidently feared that France and Britain might consider him too as guilty of an attack on their ally. He was unable to get German agreement to a formal announcement that Russian troops came to Poland only as liberators. But in Paris and London there was at this stage little but relief that Hitler had not taken the whole country.

Stalin had not, of course, taken a naive and ingenuous view of the pact, or of German intentions. He remarked to the Politburo (most of whose members had not been consulted at any point), 'Hitler wants to trick us, but I think we got the better of him.' He now began showing, or at least pretending, the extreme suspiciousness which was also to be seen in his relations with his later allies.

On the very day of the Red Army's move, he told the German ambassador that on the Soviet side there were 'certain doubts' whether the German high command would observe the pact, and withdraw to the line laid down in the secret protocol. He even added that there might be people in Berlin who suspected that the USSR would support the defeated Poles against Germany. A few days later Molotov told the ambassador how Stalin was 'astounded' at the Germans' 'obvious violation' of the pact. There was nothing whatever in these suspicions. Hitler meant (for the present) to carry out the pact in every detail and not quibble, or fight, over territory. Stalin's fears, or his way of expressing them, appear very small-time.

A few days later Stalin again saw the German ambassador, and now suggested a change in the secret protocol. Originally the USSR was to receive a large part of ethnic Poland – the Lublin province and some of Warsaw province – while the Germans were (eventually) to get Lithuania. Stalin proposed an exchange.

This has been interpreted as the straightening of a strategic line. But political considerations seem to have been the real crux. A main point was that the three Baltic states formed, as it were, a single meal, and a division was likely to cause competition among the two occupiers. More important, the Soviet public line became one of merely taking from Poland lands which were Ukrainian and Byelorussian by population, and which had, in the main, been considered as not part of Poland by Western negotiators in the post-World War I period.

This was reasonably defensible to Western opinion, while a direct annexation of indisputably Polish land would not have been. Thus the risk of either immediate or eventual effective Western hostility was much reduced. Moreover, what would Stalin have done with his ethnically Polish territory? In principle he must have given it some sort of 'autonomous' status, in the Soviet usage of the term. But a 'Polish Republic' manned by the few Polish Communists surviving Stalin's purge would have constituted a provocation to the German occupiers on the other side of the Vistula.

It is odd that Stalin had considered neither of these points earlier. But the pact had been signed in a hurry, and we must remember that this was Stalin's first real immersion in a serious and immediate matter of foreign policy.

On 27–8 September Ribbentrop flew to Moscow for the further negotiations suggested and, after hours of discussion on various points, the two parties agreed that Germany should get all ethnic Poland, and Lithuania should go to the USSR. Stalin specifically asked that the Germans should not create any sort of subordinate Polish state on their territory. He also told Ribbentrop that he intended to settle with the Baltic states immediately, and expected German support.

The redivision of the loot was, of course, registered only in another secret protocol. The public side was celebrated in a Treaty of, now, not merely Non-Aggression but also 'Friendship'. It was accompanied by a joint declaration that with the collapse of the Polish state, there was no longer any reason for the war to go on, but that if the efforts of Germany and the USSR to procure a general peace on this basis failed, this would show that 'England and France are responsible for the continuation of the war'; in which case Germany and the USSR would consult on 'necessary measures'. Stalin personally drafted the text, in terms Hitler found superior to the German original.

At the celebrations afterwards Ribbentrop and his colleagues were made to feel at home – it was like being in a 'circle of old party comrades' of the NSDAP, one Nazi delegate reported. As to Stalin personally, the strongest impression the Germans took away with them was of his 'charm'.

2

The Soviet Union now provided Germany with vast amounts of raw materials – oil, grain, cotton, manganese, chromium. Stalin watched every detail, personally negotiating quite small matters with junior German officials, and having the last word in lifting embargoes on goods especially needed by the Nazis. The Germans were given good credit terms, only being required to pay six months after delivery. They often paid, moreover, later still, and with obsolescent or obsolete war materiel. And when the Germans complained of delays and other matters, sometimes even roughly rejecting 'the views of Herr Stalin as unworkable in practice and contrary to the Agreement', Stalin replied, as Adam Ulam puts it, 'meekly'. The Soviet Union also acted, in effect, as a middleman in the world market, to enable Germany to evade the British blockade. In a dramatic satire attacking British 'non-intervention' in the Spanish Civil War, the English Communist writer Edgell Rickword had argued:

> 'Euzkadi's mines provide the ore
> That feeds the Nazi dogs of war.'

He did not now find it necessary to write:

> 'Baku's wells provide the oil
> To bear the bombs to British soil ...'

Stalin had particularly high hopes of German collaboration in enabling him to build a battle fleet. Here, once again, was a subject of which Stalin knew little but on which he had strong opinions. The Soviet navy had been purged (eight of the nine senior admirals were shot in 1937–8; the survivor, Galler, was to follow them after World War II). They had been accused, among other crimes, of opposing the creation of a large surface fleet, and their removal had been greeted as making it possible to create 'a most mighty attacking force'. Stalin had personally ordered the 'severe punishment' of anyone opposing heavy cruisers, but his new admirals were still dubious, especially about the usefulness of capital ships in the narrow waters of the Baltic. Stalin got up from his chair, stuffed his pipe with the tobacco of a couple of cigarettes, and said, 'We will gather the money penny by penny and build them,' measuring each word and staring sternly at the doubters.

This was a capricious hobby-horse, and an extremely expensive one at that. He wanted from the Nazis more than he got, but he did obtain the unfinished hull of the heavy cruiser *Lutzow,* and some other naval equipment. On several occasions he personally joined German–Soviet conferences on these matters, even as late as February 1940 – the last of his direct contacts with Nazi officialdom apart from meetings with the German ambassador.

At these talks the Germans were impressed by his knowledge of engineering details (and by his excitable complaints about delays, for which he later apologized). But his idea of himself as a naval strategist was one of the worst of his misconceptions about his ability to master any subject. The Soviet fleet was to play a very small role in the years ahead.

Meanwhile, Stalin provided the Nazis, in naval and other matters, with evidence of good will far beyond necessity. 'Base North' for U-boats was established in a bay near Murmansk – with fuel and repair ships. (It never actually became operational – the two U-boats on their way to use it were sunk by the Royal Navy, and the German invasion of Norway thereafter made it unnecessary.) The Soviets also escorted the Nazi commerce raider *Komet* through the Northern Sea Route, and it did a lot of damage to Allied shipping in the Pacific.

A more extraordinary act of Stalin's was to order the sending back to Germany of several hundred German Communists who had been political refugees in the Soviet Union. They were handed over on the bridge at Brest-Litovsk, Gestapo and NKVD officers checking the lists together. Most of them went straight to Nazi concentration camps.

As soon as the pact was signed, the whole vast Soviet propaganda machine reversed itself. Stalin told Mekhlis, as head of the army's Political Administration, that the military press should stop irritating the Germans, and give up writing about 'Fascism'. The rest of the media followed. The German ambassador was able to report as early as 6 September, not only that current press coverage had totally changed its tone, but that anti-Nazi books had disappeared from the shops. Anti-Nazi films like *Professor Mamlock* were withdrawn. (Two sixteen-year-olds, a boy and a girl, who naively ordered it for showing at their school, were sent to labour camp.)

Beria issued an order forbidding NKVD men to abuse prisoners as 'Fascists'. One Soviet diplomat got a five-year sentence for using the word in an offensive sense. Stalin seemed, moreover, to have foreseen something of a convergence of Nazism towards the Communist position, as indeed was logical enough. A recent Soviet article, in one of the party's most authoritative journals, tells of his remarks at a dinner following the 7 November 1939, parade:

> 'He said that in Germany the petty-bourgeois nationalists were capable of a sudden turn, that they were flexible and not connected with capitalist traditions, in contradistinction to bourgeois leaders such as Chamberlain, etc. I.V. Stalin added that it was necessary to abandon routine and not to stick to established rules, to see what was new, dictated by changing conditions. Because of this, the supposition is born that I.V. Stalin envisaged a Nazi evolution from their current attitudes.'

The effectiveness of Stalinist control of the Comintern now also became evident. Everywhere, with few and temporary exceptions, the Communist Parties accepted the pact. The interests of the Soviet Union, as interpreted by Stalin, were taken as supreme. With what amounted to masochistic discipline, the shift of policy even took place (as in the Palestine Communist Party's organ) between morning and evening editions. For the first few days, most foreign Communists took the line that by Stalin's bold stroke peace had been saved. This naturally had to be abandoned within a few days, on the outbreak of war. For a short time some Communists now became disoriented. The Communist Party of Great Britain at first supported both the Nazi–Soviet Pact and the war against Fascism. In a few weeks, former leaders Harry Pollitt and John Campbell had to confess that this was a mistake, while Britain's best known Communist, Willie Gallagher MP, who had in fact supported them and their anti-Fascist line, was represented, in the party's interests, as actually having voted the other way. The British Communists, and Communists everywhere, finally accepted the thesis that this was an imperialist war with nothing to choose between the two sides – with the proviso that the British and French governments were the main obstacle to peace.

The switch of loyalties over the period September 1939 to June 1941 was remarkable. A German Communist in exile in Sweden was to be a little taken aback when a comrade broke in on a committee meeting with an excited shout of 'We've taken Paris!'

In Britain, after the fall of France, the Communists launched a 'peace campaign' based on a new front organization called the People's Convention, and supported by figures like the pro-Soviet lawyer D. N. Pritt, MP and the actor Michael Redgrave. A book by the party's leading theoretician, Palme Dutt, was announced, with the title *For a People's Peace*; it had not actually appeared by the time of the Nazi invasion of Russia, and was replaced by an equally persuasive work by the same author urging fiercer prosecution of the war ...

An American friend of mine chanced to see two or three prominent New York Communists of his acquaintance in Washington Square in June 1941, and asked them what they would think if Hitler attacked Russia. The idea, they replied hotly, was a typical Western imperialist provocation. He was then able to show them the early edition of the *New York Times* with news of the attack. Once again, though this time with relief, Stalin's international apparatus changed its line overnight.

3

Immediately after the 28 September 1939 agreement with Germany, Stalin personally undertook negotiations with Lithuania, Latvia and Estonia. He forced them to accept Soviet garrisons, while still reassuring them in new treaties that their sovereignty would be respected.

In October Stalin also approached the Finns. While his approaches to the Baltic states had been crude and threatening, his tactics with Finland were, at first, very courteous. He demanded merely, on the one hand, the moving of the Finnish frontier further from Leningrad, with compensation from Soviet territory further north. The Finns were inclined to compromise on this; but Stalin's further point, in his role as a naval strategist, was to demand a base near Hango, far to the west, from which Soviet artillery could, he argued, cover the approaches to the Gulf of Finland in conjunction with the new Soviet bases on the Estonian coast (though when the German invasion came in 1941 the Soviet batteries by that time established on the Finnish coast proved almost useless).

After nearly two months of negotiations, the Finns were still refractory, and on 30 November Stalin attacked Finland, installing at the village of Terijoki just across the border a new Government of the Democratic Republic of Finland, headed by his Comintern henchman Otto Kuusinen (whose wife was now in a labour camp). The new republic was to take in all Finland, plus the Soviet Karelian areas.

It is not clear whether Stalin had always wanted war, or really felt obliged to follow his naval fantasies about the Gulf, where he had won his own first fairly uncontroversial (and fairly naval) laurels by storming fortresses from the sea. But now, it seemed, he was committed to taking the whole of Finland. Soviet troops were told how to conduct themselves when they reached the Swedish border. It is evident that Stalin expected something like the same success the Germans had had in Poland. Though some officers warned that the campaign might present difficulties, the view prevailed that it would all be over in ten or twelve days.

Of course, this proved a major miscalculation. The Red Army performed very badly. Disastrously defeated on the minor fronts to the north, it was for months repulsed in its attempts to break through in the Karelian isthmus.

But not only was Stalin's military weakness exposed. The long struggle gave time for Western pro-Finnish sentiment to build up, and with the Western Front static the idea of military aid to Finland, and even of Western intervention in the Caucasus, began to be heard. The Germans, according to Soviet diplomatic reports, were working for a 'final breach between Moscow and the West'; and Stalin himself said privately that the Red Army's prolonged failure against a weak opponent had encouraged anti-Soviet efforts. The danger Stalin had feared in connection with Poland, of premature involvement in the main war, seemed to loom again, at least as a possibility. The Finns played their cards brilliantly: when the Red Army began to break through by mere weight, they negotiated terms worse, but not very much worse, than those proposed in November. The 'Democratic Republic' was tacitly forgotten. (The territories thus lost by the Finns were regained within weeks in 1941 when, but for the Winter War, Finland might have remained neutral.)

Now the Germans struck in the West. In December Hitler had sent

Stalin birthday greetings, and Stalin had responded with a message of confidence in Soviet–German friendship which, he pointed out, had been 'sealed in blood' – Polish blood. Now it was Stalin's turn to congratulate Hitler, first on his success in Denmark and Norway. On 10 May, when the Germans notified Molotov of their invasion of Holland and Belgium, Molotov expressed Soviet understanding of the Germans' need to protect themselves, and hope for their success.

The fall of France was almost as great a disaster from Stalin's point of view as from the West's. He too had miscalculated. On the continent, no military force to counterbalance Hitler now remained. Only the hard-pressed fighter squadrons of the RAF stood between Hitler and air supremacy over southern England and possibly successful invasion. But even if Britain survived, it possessed no land force capable of serious offensive action in Europe.

Stalin cursed the French and British. He now had no option left except the appeasement of Hitler. As France fell, he made his final moves into territories reserved for him under the pact. The Baltic states were annexed. Romania was forced to cede Bessarabia and the northern Bukovina, to which the Germans agreed.

These gains were as much less substantial than the Nazi expansion in the West as the Finnish War had been less impressive than the Nazi war on Poland.

4

Meanwhile, there had been a chance for Stalin to shed more Polish blood. In April 1940 came one of the most offhandedly ruthless of all Stalin's acts – the massacre at Katyn and elsewhere of about 15,000 Polish officers and others, prisoners of war from the 1939 campaign. This act did more to poison international life, and to corrupt the truth, than anything similar the Soviets had done. It was only in 1990 that it was admitted in Moscow that this was a crime of Stalin's and not, as had been maintained for nearly half a century, of the Nazis. A recent Soviet investigation links it to a conference of Gestapo and NKVD officers on action against Polish nationalism which took place at Zakopane, in German-occupied Poland, in the winter. Photographs have recently appeared in the Soviet press of Gestapo and NKVD officers going for a spin in a sleigh between sessions.

It seems to have been undertaken with the idea of destroying, as far as possible, the national leaders of Polish independence. Stalin's view of the Poles had some peculiarities. He more than once said to American correspondents that American economic classes were not as rigidly differentiated as those of Europe, because America had no burden of an earlier feudal or 'landed aristocracy'. The obverse of this idea was, however, Stalin's notion that in Poland and Hungary the nationality principle was especially deeply rooted because, unlike other East European countries, they had a long-established independent gentry class. It was perhaps this conception which lay behind Stalin's 'decapitation' of Poland by the 1940 massacre. It was to give him a great deal of trouble later, as we shall see.

5

In the summer, Stalin had one further triumph. On 20 August 1940, Trotsky, after various approaches and attempts, was finally murdered in his home in Mexico by an NKVD agent using an ice pick.

Trotsky had been ruthlessly hunted for several years. Trotskyites had been kidnapped and killed in France and Spain. In an earlier attempt in Mexico, the Communist painter David Siqueiros and a gang of twenty gunmen had raked Trotsky's house with tommy-gun fire and left incendiaries and dynamite, but failed to kill their victim. The simpler one-man approach had long been prepared in case Siqueiros failed.

The whole thing had been planned in the Lubyanka, where the files and operation rooms on Trotsky spread over three floors. Beria's chief aide in the project was Pavel Sudoplatov, of the Foreign Administration of the NKVD; under him was Gaik Ovakimian, then undercover NKVD 'Resident' in the Soviet Consulate General in New York, who organized access to Trotsky through a New York contact. The highly experienced Naum ('Leonid') Eitingon was the operator on the spot in Mexico. All three became generals in 1945. (Sudoplatov and Eitingon were imprisoned as Beriaites in 1953, but later released; Sudoplatov is still alive in Moscow.)

Ramon Mercader, the assassin, was represented in Stalinist propaganda as a dissident Trotskyite acting on his own. He was arrested and served his term in a Mexican prison, denying any Soviet involvement. His mother, a close colleague of Eitingon's, escaped, and was given the Order of Lenin on Mercader's behalf. (When he was released and came to Moscow in the 1960s, the award was confirmed, but he was instructed not to wear the insignia in public.)

Stalin's theory of sweet revenge had finally taken out the last of his Politburo colleagues and rivals. It is clear that, as against Hitler, Trotsky was an enemy past redemption. It must have been a moment of unalloyed pleasure for Stalin, who had expelled his enemy from the Politburo, from the party, from the country, and now from life itself.

6

While Stalin had good reason to avoid or postpone trouble with Germany, for Hitler the opposite considerations applied. His military intelligence estimated the Red Army as a formidable opponent, but lacking the necessary leadership at all levels, which it could, however, reconstitute in a few years' time. This meant, from the German point of view, that an attack on Russia must be made as soon as possible. Hitler had already virtually decided on this as early as July 1940. Meanwhile, a final diplomatic effort was made. Ribbentrop wrote to Stalin, inviting Molotov to Berlin for a general discussion of Soviet–German relations. Molotov came in November, and had much discussion with Hitler. Stalin's instructions gave Molotov little leeway, and he was tenacious in seeking an explanation for the presence of German troops in Finland and Romania. Hitler was evasive, as was natural enough, but held out to the Soviets the prospect of a share in the 'bankrupt' British Empire's Asian assets.

The Russians, as Hitler was informed by his own agents, were concerned to find out 'which military men' were opposed to Ribbentrop's pact policies and in general 'which German personages were opposed to collaboration with Russia'. Stalin, who certainly gave the instruction, believed (as he appears to have briefly believed even after the outbreak of the German–Soviet war) that only some militaristically inclined Germans, and by implication not Hitler himself, were a danger to the pact. Stalin seems to have felt that for the more prudent Germans the risks of a war in Russia would appear overwhelming. The offer of parts of the British Empire seems to have confirmed Molotov, and presumably Stalin, in the view that Germany wanted to entangle Russia in a war with Britain – a reasonable analysis as far as it went.

However, when Molotov returned bearing the German offer, Stalin sent Berlin his agreement to join the Tripartite Pact with Germany, Italy and Japan, and to accept expansion 'in the direction of the Persian Gulf'. But he made it a condition that the Soviet Union should also be given military bases in Bulgaria and the Straits, and that German troops should withdraw from Finland. By this time Hitler was not interested enough even to go through the motions. The proposal was left hanging. On 8 December Hitler signed the formal order for his invasion of the Soviet Union – Operation Barbarossa – which was to be ready for launching by 15 May 1941.

But one strange result may have emerged from these November discussions. Hitler suggested at one point that the difficulties could only be resolved by a meeting 'at the highest level'. A Soviet diplomat present at the talks in Berlin and at the reporting to Stalin, says that Stalin was evidently much struck by the idea of what was later to be called a summit, and that over the next months he quite clearly hoped for arrangements to be made for such a meeting, at which, perhaps, he would be able to sort things out with Hitler. The diplomat is convinced that this played a very important part in Stalin's misperceptions over the months that followed.

7

Meanwhile the Finnish war had brought one advantage to the Soviet Union. It was now clear to Stalin that the Red Army was in no condition to fight a major war. That army was still not to be anything like adequate in June 1941, but without the partial rethinking and reorganization which followed the Finnish debacle, it would have been in worse condition yet.

On 4 May 1940 Voroshilov was replaced as War Commissar by Timoshenko; and competent officers like Zhukov and Meretskov took high posts – though several incompetents from Stalin's Civil War entourage like Marshal Kulik were also given major positions. The dual command system of political commissars was abandoned in August 1940, and Stalin's agent, Mekhlis, was removed from the Political Administration of the army in September – though he remained available to procure disasters in the German–Soviet war.

Moreover, Stalin did not cease to persecute the army. Early in 1941 Meretskov, as Chief of Staff, made a very inadequate presentation at the Supreme Military Soviet, and was shortly afterwards replaced by Zhukov. In June Meretskov was under arrest as a British spy, together with the Commissar of the Defence Industry, Vannikov – who had offended by opposing a decision by Stalin to have a gun he remembered with admiration from the Civil War installed in Soviet tanks, for which it was quite unsuited.

Other senior officers were also implicated. The young commander-in-chief of the Air Force, Rychagov, was criticized for the number of aircraft involved in crashes. He lost his temper and said that the reason was that he was being given not airplanes but flying coffins. Stalin replied, 'You should not have said that,' and then repeated the phrase, abruptly closing the meeting. Rychagov, arrested that night, was joined in jail by his two predecessors as air force chiefs, Generals Loktionov and Smushkevich (under the pseudonym 'Douglas' the Soviet air ace of the Spanish war), together with General G. M. Shtern, who had led and won the fighting against the Japanese in 1938, and a number of air and artillery commanders. Meretskov and Vannikov were later released and put to good use. The others were shot.

Over the first half of 1941 Stalin, whatever his motives or beliefs, had sunk into a sort of torpor punctuated by irrational sallies. The most striking case occurred in April 1941. The then pro-Axis Yugoslav government was overthrown by a military coup. Stalin immediately signed a treaty of friendship with the anti-German administration – and was actually photographed, all smiles, with the Yugoslav ambassador. Within a week the Germans had invaded Yugoslavia and the new government went into exile in London. Stalin then rapidly withdrew his earlier recognition of it.

The Yugoslav coup had an unforeseen effect. The fighting there, and later in Greece, led to the postponement of Barbarossa from mid-May to mid-June – as it turned out, this was probably crucial to its success or failure.

Stalin now relapsed into a policy, if such it can be called, of complete 'appeasement'. In April, as he saw off the Japanese Foreign Minister at the station, having signed a non-aggression treaty, he warmly embraced the German ambassador and said to the German military attaché, 'We will remain friends with you in any event.'

An event bizarre enough to fan suspicion even in minds less prone to it than Stalin's now took place. On 11 May 1941 Rudolf Hess, one of Hitler's closest comrades, flew to England.

It seems that Hess, no mean fantasist even in an era of strange beliefs, was acting on his own initiative, with the idea that if he could discuss matters with a duke considered to be not unfriendly to the Germans, the British government would hasten to discuss peace terms. Stalin, from his point of view understandably, thought that Hess was indeed an emissary of Hitler's, with this plan in mind; and that the British and Germans might well do a deal against the Soviet Union. It was a long time, even during the war period of Anglo-Soviet alliance, before he even partly gave up his belief that the British had seriously been considering the proposal – as, of course, he would himself have done in their position.

Meanwhile evidence was now piling up that the Germans were concentrating troops in Poland. Stalin personally wrote to Hitler expressing concern, and Hitler replied, also in a personal letter, that the troops were resting outside British bombing range, and giving his word that he would observe the pact. Stalin took no further action, except that on 6 May 1941 he became chairman of the Council of People's Commissars, having not held any government appointment for nearly twenty years. Ulam suggests that though this appears to represent a concentration of power, it may also be read as a signal to the Germans that Molotov, seen as less friendly to them, had lost his leading position. It may also, of course, have been thought a prerequisite for a summit.

Earlier in the year Stalin had confidentially told his generals that war with Germany was possible. But over May and June, when information came in from all sides about the German plans to attack, Stalin ruled that this was a British provocation. His military intelligence chiefs are often accused of concealing the truth from him. But on the whole they gave him the information about German plans to attack with the proviso, dictated by his own stance, that it might have been planted. A report from the head of the NKVD's Foreign Department, Fitin, gave him the same data from Soviet espionage sources in Berlin. Stalin merely replied that he trusted no German source, apart from the future head of East Germany Wilhelm Pieck. On the eve of the invasion Beria ordered some of these agents who had returned to Moscow to be 'ground into dust' in labour camps, for 'systematic disinformation' as 'abetters of international provocateurs', and he wrote Stalin asking that the Soviet ambassador and military attaché in Berlin be disciplined for sending similar reports. Beria ended, 'I and my people, Iosif Vissarionovich, firmly remember your wise assessment: Hitler is not going to attack us in 1941.'

Not only was Stalin's assessment erroneous. His system of rule also prevented alternative counsels being put forward. His colleagues either accepted his superior wisdom, or had to behave as if they did. The necessary minimal level of free discussion had long since disappeared from the Kremlin. Meanwhile members of the Politburo had started to take their summer holidays.

Stalin could hardly, by this time, ignore the mere fact of German troop concentrations on his border, and the continuous German reconnaissance overflights of Soviet territory which now took place, but he seems to have hoped that this was merely a threat which would be used to extract concessions from him – and he was ready to give way on these on a large scale. He also seems to have thought that any counter-mobilization would lead only to earlier crisis.

So Tass on 16 June carried a statement, clearly drafted by Stalin himself, saying that responsible circles in Moscow had authorized the announcement that rumours of war were obviously absurd, that German troop movements were due to 'motives having nothing to do with Soviet–German relations'; and that in general, 'according to evidence in the possession of the Soviet Union, both Germany and the Soviet Union are fulfilling to the letter the terms of the Soviet–German Non-Aggression Pact'.

Even on the evening of 21 June, with war only hours away, Stalin told Zhukov that the question 'might still be settled by peaceful means', and muttered, as if to himself, 'I think Hitler is trying to provoke us. He surely hasn't decided to make war?' When the attack came, Stalin still maintained for a while that it might be due to 'provocative' acts by insubordinate German generals. His first thought was to contact the German ambassador. But the German ambassador now presented Molotov with the official declaration of war – and Molotov could only ask, 'What have we done to deserve this?' Stalin reacted to the news with a long silence, broken by Zhukov asking for orders to fight. Stalin then ordered the army to destroy the invaders on Soviet soil, but not to pursue – still implying that full-scale war could be prevented. There is something very peculiar about the thinking here: in particular, after long timidity in the face of the threat, the reversion to the long-established Soviet propaganda theme that the Red Army, the best and most socialist in the world, could give a 'stunning rebuff' to any invader.

The reality was quite different from what Stalin's order implied. The Germans overwhelmed the frontier defences immediately and were soon driving deep into Soviet territory.

Chapter 12

War

Stalin's whole position was now in grave and imminent peril, as it had been twenty years earlier at the time of Lenin's strokes. And, once again, Stalin's first reactions were ill-considered, even irrational.

He was, of course, faced with an extremity of crisis which was largely his own fault. He had miscalculated on a gigantic scale.

The Nazis had been able to concentrate most of their forces to attack him. Britain had, it is true, survived. British planes were hitting at German industry; dozens of German divisions had to be kept in the West against all eventualities, together with a major part of the Luftwaffe; a large German production effort was being diverted into the U-boat fleet; and so on. But the great bulk of the German land forces were now striking into the Soviet Union.

It is true that the Germans had little advantage in mere numbers; and that they actually deployed fewer tanks and aircraft than those opposed to them. But the army Stalin now had was otherwise immensely inferior to its adversary. By late 1940 not a single regimental commander had taken the normal course at the Frunze Academy. And not only was there a disastrous shortage of trained officers at every level as a result of Stalin's purge of the army, but the purge and its 'vigilance' had made the remaining commanders timid and ruined their sense of initiative. The tactical methods which had replaced Tukhachevsky's more modern conceptions were based on slow-moving masses and tanks tied down to the infantry.

All that was bad enough. But Stalin had robbed his crushed and hobbled army of its best chance of successful defence, when he had refused to mobilize. He seems to have been influenced by the idea that it had been Russia's mobilization in 1914 which had been the occasion for the German ultimatum, and war. Stalin's military advisers had suggested partial mobilization some time earlier, and after the German attack on Yugoslavia the situation in the Balkans would have been a sound excuse for such a move on the Soviet part.

But not only was there no mobilization. Owing solely to Stalin's insistence on avoiding 'provocation', even the most elementary orders for combat readiness only reached some of the troops after the war had already started. In the 1890s von Schlieffen had written that a surprise attack on Russia was no longer possible. Halder now wrote, 'Surprise has apparently been achieved along the entire front.' What is more, no consistent Soviet plan for war existed.

In addition, the whole deployment was inherently faulty. The previous autumn the General Staff had made the assessment that if Hitler attacked, the main thrust would be directed towards Moscow. Stalin had said that, on the contrary, Hitler's first aim would probably be to attempt the conquest of the Ukraine, for economic reasons; and it was on this basis that the Soviet army was deployed. Moreover, in spite of Stalin's long insistence on an immense military-industrial effort, there was a shortage of the most elementary equipment. As Khrushchev later pointed out, the much criticized inadequacy of supply to the tsarist army after a year or two of World War I was to arise in the Soviet army almost from the start in 1941. Even rifles and machine-guns were not available in adequate numbers.

Stalin was severely shaken by the catastrophic turn of events, and it was Molotov who was sent to announce the war to the people on the radio. He made a speech promising early defeat for the Nazis, and defending the pact as having put the enemy in the position of aggressors before world opinion . . .

Stalin's first reaction after the quick debacle of his early attempt to see the invasion as unauthorized by Hitler, was to issue new orders to the Soviet forces to defeat the invader and carry the war into Poland and Germany. Orders were given to capture Tilsit, Lublin. If his policies towards Germany had proved mistaken, he would now retrieve them by using the army he must still have imagined capable of the task of routing the invader. The only result was a few local and fruitless counter-attacks. In reality the front had collapsed.

After a few days the facts penetrated, when Stalin learned that the Germans were near Minsk. As the full truth finally sank in, Stalin, as his most recent Soviet biographer puts it, 'went into prostration, nothing interested him, he lost initiative'. He retired to the Kuntsevo dacha, and for several days was not 'at his post'.

Khrushchev first told of this dereliction. Doubt has since been cast on Khrushchev's account, because some military memoirs published under Brezhnev's reStalinization report Stalin giving rational orders at this time: but fuller and more recent Soviet research has shown that these passages were not in the manuscripts of the memoirs, but merely inserted by the authorities for reasons of historical morale. The fullest of today's Soviet biographies of Stalin (that of General Dmitri Volkogonov) gives a full and circumstantial account of these lost days, which are also covered from different points of view in other recent Soviet publications.

Meanwhile, orders were issued under various signatures as the generals and politicians, deprived of central leadership, tried to cope. Not that any orders from Moscow now meant much to the trapped or shattered divisions to the west.

So Stalin, who in the Civil War had prided himself on his ability to deal with emergencies beyond the scope of most leaders, was now faced with the failure of the policies in which he had invested so much of his own prestige, and following that was seeing the disastrous results of his belated military endeavours. The word 'shock' is used over and over again in the most recent Soviet studies, and it is clear that, psychologically, Stalin was simply unable to cope, and was in a state far beyond anything that had ever before happened to him.

In any other country, the leader responsible for these fiascos and disasters would have lost power. But such had been Stalin's thoroughness that no alternative leaders of real credibility remained alive. Those now trying to handle matters without him had long been little more than puppets. Moreover, even if one or more of them considered any other action, Beria and his apparatus were ever-present, and Beria had no alternative candidates.

On 29 June a junior figure, Nikolai Voznesensky, proposed to Molotov that they should all go and see Stalin. When they arrived at Kuntsevo, he remained seated in a corner by the window and asked, 'Why have you come?' The question struck Mikoyan as odd – it was Stalin who should have summoned *them* to council. Odder still was a 'strangeness' about Stalin, almost as if he expected them to dismiss him, or even arrest him.

But what they proposed was the setting up of a Supreme Defence Council with Stalin as chairman, to take control of the country's effort. Stalin simply replied, 'All right.'

His 'paralysis' (as Molotov put it) now wore off, and he pulled himself together, though he was still gloomy. It was at the first Politburo meeting since his absence that he made the well-known remark, 'All that Lenin created, we have lost.' (Or, in a more recent Soviet version, 'Lenin left us a great inheritance and we, his heirs, have fucked it all up.') On 3 July he finally made a major public appeal on the radio in terms very unlike his previous self: 'Brothers and sisters! I turn to you, my friends ...' This speech, Ivan Maisky tells us, was not a success, being delivered in 'a dull colourless voice' with Stalin 'often stopping and breathing heavily'. The impression given was that Stalin 'was at the end of his strength'. However, the speech ended with a strong call to unite for certain victory.

One of the strangest things noted by foreign observers in Moscow on the day of the announcement of the outbreak of war was that there were no demonstrations of public patriotic feeling, such as have usually marked such occasions – including that of Russia in 1914. People had been told that war was impossible. For nearly two years the Nazis had been getting favourable treatment in the press. The country was in any case psychologically exhausted from the years of Stalinist terror. It was only when the Nazis' brutality declared itself openly in their conduct in the occupied areas, and when the war itself came to be seen as patriotic and liberating, that the mood changed.

In fact, Stalin's having to 'appeal' to the citizenry he had maltreated made things seem desperate. Yet the speech also constituted the beginnings of a drive for genuine solidarity. It still, indeed, spoke of rallying 'round the party', but over the next few months the Communist theme was downplayed in favour of patriotism. As Stalin said to the US envoy Averill Harriman a few months later, the Russians were fighting 'for their homeland, not for us'.

Meanwhile, Stalin was applying his traditional methods in an attempt to restore the military situation. The Western Front commander, Army General D. G. Pavlov, is usually said not to have been up to the demands of his position. He had been a tank officer in Spain only four years previously, and had won Stalin's favour by agreeing that Stalinist tank tactics had proved successful there. He was now, with his staff, made the scapegoat for disaster. He was arrested at the beginning of July at the behest of Stalin's emissary, the worthless Mekhlis (himself later responsible for a less excusable disaster, and then only demoted one rank). On 22 July Pavlov, his Chief of Staff, his Signals Commander, and the Commander of the 4th Army, were charged with an anti-Soviet conspiracy designed to undermine the army, and sentenced to death. Stalin approved the sentences but told Ulrikh, chairman of the 'court', to remove all the 'rubbish about conspiracies'. Thus, by a remarkable innovation, the four generals were shot only for, in effect, criminal negligence – though theirs had clearly been less than Stalin's, judged by exactly the same criteria. At least fifteen other generals were now arrested, though in most cases we do not know their fates.

Thus Stalin resumed full control. It may have appeared that the worst defeats were over. The army was by now mobilized, and the Germans might be expected to slow down. In fact, however, the worst defeats of 1941 were yet to come.

Stalin's style of command was marked by his extremely rude and peremptory tone both directly and in telegrams – except to his close adviser Marshal Shaposhnikov, the former tsarist colonel who was the one survivor of Stalin's original appointment of army commanders in 1935: Stalin always addressed him courteously as 'Boris Mikhailovich' and never raised his voice even when they disagreed; he was the only man allowed to smoke in Stalin's office. With Zhukov, who was to be his leading fighting general, he was often rude; but sometimes, and particularly in real crises, he let Zhukov overrule him.

His generals were all impressed by Stalin's extraordinary memory. Through the war he knew the names, Marshal Vasilievsky tells, of 'all the front and army commanders and there were more than a hundred of them, but also of some of the corps and divisional commanders'. This was, of course, a talent he had previously employed with the upper nomenklatura of the party machine. It now led him to frequent interventions, often at inappropriate moments, to replace commanders in mid-battle. He also mastered a great deal of information about the location and availability of even quite small units, and of supplies of war materiel. This again often led him to petty interventions.

But the rebirth of his conviction that he had mastered military affairs showed itself at first mainly in orders to hold untenable lines or to make impossible counter-attacks, culminating in his refusal to allow the evacuation of Kiev in spite of the urgings of the field commanders. This resulted in the greatest single defeat of the whole war, and the loss of half a million prisoners, at the beginning of September.

2

Stalin's attitude to these, and to the three million-odd other prisoners now falling into German hands, was characteristic. When the Germans approached the Soviets, through Sweden, to negotiate observance of the provisions of the Geneva Convention on prisoners of war, Stalin refused. The Soviet soldiers in German hands were thus unprotected even in theory. Millions of them died in captivity, through malnutrition or maltreatment. If Stalin had adhered to the convention (to which the USSR had not been a party) would the Germans have behaved better? To judge by their treatment of other 'Slav submen' POWs (like the Poles, even those surrendering after the Warsaw Rising), the answer seems to be yes. (Stalin's own behaviour to prisoners captured by the Red Army had already been demonstrated at Katyn and elsewhere. German prisoners captured by the Soviets over the next few years were mainly sent to forced labour camps.)

As to the Soviet soldiers now fallen into German hands, Stalin simply ruled that they were traitors. Order No. 270 of 16 August 1941 announced that officers and political workers taken prisoner were to be regarded as 'malicious deserters' and their families should be 'subject to arrest', while the families of rank-and-file soldiers in like condition were to be 'deprived of state assistance' – that is, of rations. Mekhlis, issuing the instruction 'Everyone who has been captured is a traitor to the Motherland', added that they should all have committed suicide rather than be taken alive. As a result, the survivors who came back after the war were almost all sentenced to labour camps. Stalin made a personal issue of the capture of certain generals. Lieutenant-Generals Kachalov and Ponedelin, commanding the 18th and 12th Armies respectively, which were overrun in August 1941, were sentenced to death for collaboration in October 1941. Kachalov had in fact been killed when his command post received a direct hit from a shell; his family were treated as relatives of an enemy of the people until 1956. Ponedelin had been captured unconscious, and conducted himself stoutly in captivity. However (and in spite of the death sentence), he was on return only sentenced to five years in labour camp; in 1950 he was retried and shot.

Even soldiers who had not been captured at all, but had evaded the Germans or successfully broken out of encirclement, were suspect. Stalin approved Beria's plan to set up fifteen special camps to screen them.

Among the millions of prisoners the Germans were now capturing on various fronts was Stalin's son, Senior Lieutenant Yakov Dzhugashvili.

The Nazis tried to exchange him, but Stalin merely said he had no son called Yakov. However, he ordered Yakov's surrender to be investigated, and Yakov's wife Yulia Mel'ster was arrested and held in prison for two years, though she was later released.

Yakov, who remained an orthodox Communist and stood up to his German interrogators, was in various officer prison camps. On 14 April 1943, in a suicidal mood, he ran to the barbed wire fence and was shot by a guard.

Another relative of Stalin's failed to survive the war – his brother-in-law Alexander Svanidze, Yakov's uncle, who had been in jail for several years. In August 1943, the People's Commissar for State Security V. N. Merkulov told him, on Stalin's orders, that if he confessed he would not be shot. He replied that he was innocent, and had nothing to confess. He was shot, and Stalin commented to members of the Politburo, 'Well, what a proud man Alyosha turned out to be! I didn't expect it.' The charge against him is said to have been that he had been 'planted' on Stalin by German intelligence – that is, presumably, back in the first decade of the century when their relationship began.

Meanwhile, the loyalty of fighting troops was covered by a great increase in the size and powers of the army's security apparatus, soon to become known as Smersh. The Prosecutor General of the USSR, Vyshinky's successor V. M. Bochkov, was put in charge of their operation on the Northwestern Front, while the Byelorussian NKVD Commissar, Tsanava, was appointed to the same duty on the Western Front. Their 'military tribunals' operated incessantly.

3

It is not within the scope of the present book to cover the multitudinous events of the four years of the Soviet–German war, to portray in detail the dark and tremendous background against which Stalin was now silhouetted. Yet each phase brought out something of his nature.

His military position remained desperate all through the autumn of 1941. Nor, however well informed he might be, was his selection of commanders always helpful. At first, in fact, it was disastrous. He named to lead the three fronts now organized against the Germans Voroshilov, Timoshenko and Budenny, all of old Tsaritsyn days. Timoshenko was competent, the other two virtually worthless. Others of Stalin's old entourage, including the second-rate Tyulenev and the grotesque Kulik, held important commands. And Mekhlis, in the army's political leadership, in effect overrode commanders in the field with sheer uninformed stubbornness. At the same time, while regiments at the front were being commanded by lieutenants, there were 300 experienced officers in jail in Moscow.

For Stalin was now much concerned to eliminate the last remnants of suspected opposition, political or military. On 5 September he signed a list of 170 people for execution. The survivors of the great trials of the 1930s, Rakovsky and the others, were retried and shot, as was the famous former Socialist Revolutionary leader Maria Spiridonova. In October Generals Rychagov, Loktionov, Shtern and Smushkevich were shot without trial, along with a dozen others including two former members of the Central Committee – one of them, Goloshchekin, having served on that body before the Revolution. And throughout the camps this prophylactic measure was widely used on possible troublemakers.

4

One major result of the outbreak of the German–Soviet war was that Stalin, who since 1939 had had little contact with foreigners apart from Ribbentrop's two visits, became personally a central figure in international negotiation.

Throughout this period he continually pressed the Western leaders for his maximum demands and, though not quite achieving them, nevertheless did far better than the objective conditions required. He was almost always very well briefed on the points at issue.

But his main advantage was not so much in his negotiating skills as in the weaknesses of the British and Americans, though it is fair to say that on the whole he exploited these weaknesses to good advantage. The Allied leaders showed themselves vulnerable in different ways. Generally speaking, Roosevelt thought he could trust Stalin, while Churchill, not quite so naive, was yet inclined to give in to Stalin's demands on what amounted to sentimental, or chivalrous grounds – the Russians were bearing the brunt of the fighting and Churchill felt a moral obligation to support them to any feasible degree.

The British Foreign Office, it is true, contained an influential group which was broadly pro-Russian, and though other views were taken, the Foreign Secretary, Anthony Eden, was also largely of that persuasion. In the US State Department, things were if anything worse still, with an internal coup bringing the well-informed Soviet experts of its Eastern division under the control of the ignorant or pro-Stalin European division; there was even an attempt to destroy the Eastern division's records. Other British and American representatives, such as Lord Beaverbrook and Harry Hopkins, shared the general ignorance and euphoria. The Allied military men, who had to deal with the practical side of co-operation with the Soviets, were, both Americans and Britons, much in favour of a far firmer policy; they became very tired of their role of providing large-scale assistance in return for continual abuse for not providing more.

On 18 July Stalin wrote to Churchill, calling on him to establish fronts against Hitler in the Arctic and in France. He urged that:

'A front in northern France could not only divert Hitler's forces from the East, but at the same time would make it impossible for Hitler to invade Great Britain. The establishment of the front just mentioned would be popular with the British Army, as well as with the whole population of southern England.'

This extraordinary appeal to supposed popular feeling in England is an extension of Stalin's frequent references to what the Soviet people wanted, or would be disappointed if they didn't get. As with these, what we find here is Stalin substituting for his own wishes or concern the alleged feelings of the 'people', though in this case a foreign people he was even less entitled to speak for.

How little he understood the British situation is shown by his demands for large invasions of France (held by forty German divisions) by the small British forces not already engaged in other theatres of war – and again in September, when he asked Churchill to send him twenty-five or thirty divisions to fight on the Russian Front. It alarmed Churchill that Stalin was 'thinking in terms of utter unreality'; it was 'almost incredible that the head of the Russian government with all the advice of their military experts could have committed himself to such absurdities'.

The United States, of course, was not yet at war, and was not to be until the bombing of Pearl Harbor in December. But Roosevelt was already prepared to help Russia, as he was helping Britain, with equipment. Roosevelt's personal emissary, Harry Hopkins, who was later to ask a State Department expert if he belonged to the 'anti-Soviet clique', arrived in Moscow at the end of July.

Stalin was frank with him about the disastrous situation, and asked for 20,000 anti-aircraft guns, a large quantity of aluminium sheeting for aircraft production, machine-guns and rifles. He even wrote this list on a piece of paper and handed it to Hopkins – the meeting's only document. And he asked Hopkins to tell Roosevelt that he would welcome an American army on the Soviet Front. Hopkins said that if America entered the war, it was unlikely that troops would be sent to Russia, but that he would pass on the request.

Stalin also spoke bitterly about the German breach of the Nazi–Soviet Pact. 'There must,' he said, 'be a minimum moral standard between all nations.' The Germans had failed to observe these standards. But, Stalin earnestly told the American, 'nations must fulfil their treaty obligations, otherwise international society will be unable to survive'. He was himself, of course, in breach of a whole series of treaties with every one of his European neighbours. And indeed, his rule over his native Georgia was in breach of just such a solemn treaty ...

He seems to have impressed Hopkins both by his moralizing and by his efficiency. At least, on his return to Washington Hopkins was responsible, or partly responsible, for the development of Roosevelt's attitude to Stalin. The former American ambassador to Moscow, William Bullitt, told Roosevelt that the Soviets were imperialist by nature, and that in exchange for Lend-Lease, the United States should ask for definite public pledges against Soviet expansion in Europe and Asia. Roosevelt replied that he did not dispute the logic of Bullitt's reasoning, but that 'I just have a hunch that Stalin is not that kind of man. Harry [Hopkins] says he's not ... I think if I give him everything I possibly can and ask for nothing in return ... he won't try to annex anything and will work with me for a world of democracy and peace.' When Bullitt pressed his point Roosevelt said, 'It's my responsibility, not yours ... and I'm going to play my hunch.'

Roosevelt's analysis, if such it can be called, must be among the crassest errors ever made by a political leader. The wholly uninformed Hopkins's subjective impressions and Roosevelt's 'hunch' were given precedence over Stalin's record and the fund of knowledge of the Soviet Union available among experienced figures in the United States Foreign Service. Stalin had won an important victory, and in part at least by his treatment of Hopkins.

In late September, an Anglo-American supply mission arrived in Moscow, headed by Lord Beaverbrook and Averill Harriman. They had three meetings with Stalin. Beaverbrook, as if to show that the British could be as asinine as any Hopkins, started by asking the British ambassador, Sir Stafford Cripps, to leave, and Harriman felt he had no choice but to ask the American ambassador, Steinhardt, to do the same. Beaverbrook's motive was, it appears, to start 'with a clean slate', in order to overcome 'a lack of mutual confidence'.

This first meeting was cordial. Stalin again gave a realistic account of the fighting, and asked for tanks, anti-tank guns, medium bombers, armour plate, fighter and reconnaissance planes, barbed wire. Harriman told him that Roosevelt was concerned about religious freedom in the Soviet Union, but Stalin did not seem to take this in; Molotov later asked Harriman if Roosevelt, being an intelligent man, really was as religious as he appeared, or whether it was all for political purposes ... Stalin was soon to relax the pressures against religion, and even to receive Metropolitan Sergei; there was what amounted to a concordat, and prayers were said for Stalin. As far as can be seen, the motive was the same as with Stalin's ever-increasing appeals to Russian national tradition – the utilization of all available solidarities against the Nazis. But pleasing Roosevelt may have played a part.

The second meeting was quite different. Stalin was discourteous, and complained about only being offered a thousand tons of steel armour plate by the Americans, who produced millions of tons. Harriman, who was highly knowledgeable about the steel industry, explained the technical problems. Harriman then mentioned an American offer of five thousand jeeps. Stalin asked for more, and when Harriman said he might get armoured cars, Stalin said he didn't want any.

Harriman described the evening as 'pretty hard sledding'. But next day Stalin was all smiles. He was particularly enthusiastic about the list Beaverbrook gave him of what the British would send, having no doubt thought that the hard-pressed British industrial base could not extend to such aid – or perhaps that the memory of the large-scale supply of materiel he himself had sent Hitler right up to 22 June for his war against Britain might rankle and incline them to be niggardly.

As to American aid, at dinner that night Stalin toasted the President, as 'giving more assistance as a non-belligerent than many countries in history have given as allies'. There were thirty more toasts. Beaverbrook noted that Stalin always referred to Leningrad as Petersburg; but in other ways was less observant. Very influential in Britain not only as Minister of Aircraft Production, but also as owner of mass-circulation newspapers, he reported that Stalin struck him as a 'kindly man'. Over the next years his weight was thrown into pro-Soviet (and anti-Polish) campaigns. The head of the British Military Mission, General Ismay, took a view of Stalin different from Beaverbrook's:

'He moved stealthily like a wild animal in search of prey, and his eyes were shrewd and full of cunning. He never looked one in the face. But he had great dignity and his personality was dominating. As he entered the room, every Russian froze into silence, and the hunted look in the eyes of the generals showed all too plainly the constant fear in which they lived. It was nauseating to see brave men reduced to such abject servility.'

Stalin had observed to Harriman that the war would be decided by the petrol engine and that the country with the most would win. On this score he had little to complain of (though he was to complain continually). As recent Soviet sources have confirmed, the West supplied the Soviet Union with over fourteen thousand aircraft. And, while the army's artillery and tanks were for much the greater part Soviet (even if they sometimes carried American armour plate), the transport, including the gun-towing vehicles, was overwhelmingly American – Studebakers, Dodges, Chevrolets, jeeps, half-tracks. Without them, as Stalin saw, victory would have been dubious or impossible. Nowadays Soviet writers say frankly that without Western supplies the Soviet army could not possibly have fought a successful war.

5

Late September and early October saw further disasters on the western approaches to Moscow where the front had for a time seemed stable. Stalin was again severely shaken. In an extraordinary outburst he telephoned the new front commander, Ivan Konev, and said, 'Comrade Stalin is not a traitor, he is an honourable man, his only mistake is that he believed the cavalry generals too much, he is doing everything to put right what has occurred.'

The 'cavalry generals' – Budenny and Voroshilov – were indeed removed. The order dismissing Voroshilov has recently been published. He was charged with incompetence in the Finnish war, and with more recent 'serious errors' as commander-in-chief of the Northwestern Front defending Leningrad. Some of these errors smacked of the Civil War attitudes defended at the time by Stalin. Voroshilov had ordered that commanders of home guard units should be elected, not appointed, and wasted time on 'workers' battalions' armed with light weapons, neglecting the artillery. Stalin, who had himself ordered cavalry attacks on the Nazis in June, was learning the realities of modern war.

By mid-October the Germans were at the gates of Moscow.

On one account it was at this point (though other versions make it in the early summer) that Stalin ordered Beria to make contact with the Nazis through the Bulgarian ambassador to Moscow, Stamenov, and he was apparently brought to see Stalin and Molotov. In terms described by Molotov as of the same necessary boldness that Lenin had shown at Brest-Litovsk, Stalin offered Hitler the Baltic states, the Western Ukraine and Byelorussia, Bessarabia and 'other territory' in return for peace.

The Germans, who at this time had every hope of winning a good deal more by their own efforts, could hardly have been expected to take this seriously. It is interesting mainly as indicative of Stalin's pessimism about the military outcome. It is also to be seen in the context of frequent Soviet allegations both during and after the war that the Western allies were in secret negotiation with Hitler. (The post-war Middle School *Atlas of the History of the USSR* deals with the Western powers in its key to the general war map up to 1943 solely under the heading: 'Breaches by the Anglo-Americans of their obligations as Allies'. There are two subheads: 'advances of the Anglo-American armies in second-rate and unimportant theatres of war', and 'Berne – place of secret negotiations between representatives of the USA and Fascist Germany'.)

On 16 October came what Andrei Sakharov calls 'the notorious Moscow panic'. Sakharov describes what he saw: 'As office after office set fire to their files, clouds of soot swirled through streets clogged with trucks, carts and people on foot carrying household possessions, baggage and young children ... we found the Party Secretary at his desk; when we asked whether there was anything useful we could do, he stared at us wildly and blurted out, "It's every man for himself!"'

The secret decree on evacuating Moscow, issued the previous day, has just been published. The government was to go to Kuibyshev immediately, and 'Comrade Stalin will be evacuated tomorrow or later, depending on circumstances.' He still hoped for the arrival of fresh divisions from Siberia. His villa at Kuntsevo had been mined and booby-trapped by the NKVD against German occupants. When the government officials arrived in Kuibyshev, they started high-handedly requisitioning all available luxuries, throwing locals out of their own flats and so on; hearing of this, Stalin spoke heatedly of 'that damned caste'. Molotov went to Kuibyshev to supervise.

Stalin himself now planned to leave on 18 October. A train and planes were ready. After considering the matter he came to a decision. Zhukov assured him that Moscow could be held. Meanwhile the direct German blow at the city had failed to materialize; the enemy were regrouping for an encirclement from the north and south. Stalin is reported to have thought that his leaving Moscow would be a severe moral defeat.

The French government had, it is true, left Paris for Bordeaux for a few months in 1914 when the capital was in danger, without the outcome of the battle being affected. But the circumstances were different. Joffre had actually wanted his government out of the way, so that he could fight his battle without looking over his shoulder. In the case of Moscow it was Stalin himself who represented the whole military as well as political effort. The symbolic effect of his departure would have been great. And even if a fight for Moscow could still have been put up, the morale behind it would have been lower: and it was to be a very near thing ...

Stalin decided to stay. What is more, he ordered the 7 November parade to proceed as usual: fortunately the sky was overcast enough to prevent Nazi bomber attacks. Later, in the Kirovskaya Metro station, now a giant air-raid shelter, he made a strong and effective speech.

At one critical point in the long battle, Stalin lost his head briefly, though only over a minor matter. He was told that a village called Dedovsk, only fifteen miles from Moscow, had fallen, and ordered Zhukov to go in person and retake it. Zhukov found that it was not Dedovsk which had fallen at all, but another similarly named but more distant village called Dedovo. Stalin refused to listen, so on 1 December Zhukov and two other senior generals had to leave headquarters and organize an attack by an infantry company and two tanks to recapture Dedovo.

The Nazis were now making their final effort against Moscow. The weather conditions were appalling. And, with both sides now fielding front-line forces very weak compared with those available a month or two earlier, Zhukov won his promised victory.

Stalin believed that he now had the opportunity to destroy the German forces. Over the winter of 1941–2, again against the advice of Zhukov and others that the time should be spent in reorganization, Stalin insisted on a counter-offensive. This made deep penetrations here and there, though it also suffered important defeats. But in spite of heavy losses it failed seriously to shake the German position.

6

In December 1941 Anthony Eden, the British Foreign Secretary, came to Moscow and saw Stalin. He had had an interview with him in 1935. Stalin had then 'impressed me from the first: his personality made itself felt without effort or exaggeration. He had natural good manners, perhaps a result of his Georgian inheritance. Though I knew the man to be without mercy, I respected the quality of his mind and even felt a sympathy which I have never been able entirely to analyse.'

At that time Stalin had confirmed to Eden Molotov's formulation that 'the Soviet government has no desire to interfere in any way in the internal affairs of the British Empire'. And to Eden's surprise, Stalin had mentioned that German firms had been allowed to accept Soviet arms contracts – presumably an early example of the playing off of Britain and her allies against Germany, which had in the long run produced such extraordinary results.

Eden, with his erratic and egocentric political character, was to play a large role in the appeasement of Stalin. At this December 1941 meeting, Stalin asked for British recognition of the Soviet annexation of the Baltic states and the territory taken from Finland and Romania, with a more indirect reference to the borders with Poland, astonishingly adding that this was 'the main question for us'.

To make this more acceptable to Britain, Stalin put forward a suggestion which once again shows his staggering ignorance of Western ways. In return for the Soviet claims in Eastern Europe, Britain should receive military and naval bases on the French coast, such as Boulogne and Dunkirk, while Belgium and Holland should be allied with Britain on terms guaranteeing British bases in those countries too – an offer later repeated to the British through the Soviet ambassador in London, and thus clearly not just one of Stalin's passing fancies. As to the particulars of the boundary agreements, these should be in a secret protocol, while the public Anglo-Soviet Treaty would consist of high-minded generalities. Stalin also said that he meant to declare war on Japan during 1942.

Eden had no authority to discuss the Soviet boundary claims – indeed, Churchill had long since announced that Britain would not recognize any territorial changes made in the war. Still, when Eden got back, he put it that, 'We shall not succeed in removing M. Stalin's suspicion of ourselves and the Americans unless we agree to these claims. It is true that the claims seem difficult to reconcile with the first three clauses of the Atlantic Charter ...' – that is, with the West's war aims!

Eden had, in effect, been taken in by Stalin, and henceforth urged that if Soviet demands were not met collaboration with Stalin 'would be limited to matters on which they require our help and that of the USA'. As Stalin in fact anyhow made such limitations, this merely meant that the West must gratuitously and without recompense give him what he wanted, however morally or politically inadmissible. Field Marshal Alan Brooke, the British Chief of General Staff, saw that as a result of Eden's tactics the Russians 'despise us and have no use for us except for what they can get out of us'.

Churchill was at first angry at this blatant blackmail. The Russians had not only done nothing to help Britain in its extremity, but had actually added to its troubles, and now, 'They are fighting for self-preservation and have never had a thought for us. We on the contrary are helping them to the utmost of our ability because we admire their defence of their own country and because they are ranged against Hitler.'

But in the long run Eden's view largely prevailed. He laid it down that, 'Our refusal to satisfy Stalin's demand may be the end of any prospect of future cooperation and may cause Stalin to revert to the pursuit of purely selfish aims.' Stalin had, of course, done nothing whatever in pursuit of any other aims, and was never to do so. He was fighting the Germans, but not in order to help or please the West. And Eden, unlike Roosevelt, could not plead ignorance, unless we are to accept that Stalin possessed the gift of instilling hypnotic blindness by some psychological method as yet uninvestigated.

Stalin now sent Molotov to the West. The British would still not agree to accept the Molotov–Ribbentrop frontiers. Though Molotov at first argued the point stubbornly, Stalin finally telegraphed to say that it could be dropped, since the frontier problem would in the end be 'settled by force'.

So an Anglo-Soviet treaty was signed on 26 May 1942 without any reference to the border question. Molotov then somehow obtained from the Americans a suicidal joint communiqué on the urgent task of creating 'a second front in Europe in 1942'. The British, who at this point would have had to have provided most of the troops, told him, 'We can give no promise in the matter.' But the damage had been done.

Henceforth, at every meeting of Stalin's with Westerners, and also in the propaganda of every Communist Party in the West, the Western obligation to open a second front in Europe was a constant pressure. Though the Western leaders were not in fact prepared to launch their armies prematurely into certain disaster against all the advice of their generals, they still felt at a disadvantage vis-à-vis Stalin.

As political realism, this was all absurd. It is true that it was in the Allies' interest that the Soviet Union should not be defeated by Hitler. But it was even more in Stalin's interest! His ability to extract advantage from a situation in which it was he who was in the most disadvantageous position is a remarkable tribute to his ability as a bargainer, and as an exploiter of his allies' weaknesses. At least in this sense, he must by now have seen how much better it was to be allied to the West than to a more sceptical Nazi Germany – though his daughter tells us that even after the war he often said, 'Ech, together with the Germans we would have been invincible.'

In August 1942, Churchill and Harriman arrived in Moscow. At this first meeting with Stalin Churchill had to tell him that there would be no second front that year. Stalin retorted, 'That is to say the English and American leaders renounce the promise they made to us in the spring.' Churchill explained the obvious objections. Stalin said that without risks a war could not be won. Why were the British so afraid of the Germans? Churchill controlled himself, and then explained the Allied plan for the invasion of North Africa. Stalin became interested and understanding. However, Churchill saw Molotov next morning and told him that Stalin should not 'be rude' to him and his party, who had come all this distance to help him.

In any case Stalin was rude again at the next meeting with remarks such as 'When are you going to start fighting?', and he again accused Churchill of breach of faith in not invading France. Churchill now got up and banged his fist on the table, repudiating these attacks, and saying he had come around Europe in the midst of his own troubles hoping to meet the hand of comradeship and was bitterly disappointed not to have met it. Stalin, not waiting for a translation, grinned and said he did not understand what was being said but he liked 'Churchill's spirit'.

The dinner that night, at which several Soviet leaders showed the effects of drink, was less of a success. Stalin, very oddly, gave a toast to intelligence officers who, he said, could not reply. The American naval attaché Captain Duncan did, however, reply, with some wittiness. Stalin was so taken with him that he walked over, clinked glasses with him and took him by the arm and talked with him for a while – a strange scene (recorded, but often thought fictitious by viewers, in *The Winds of War*).

Churchill, still not in a friendly mood, finally said good night and was half way to the door when Stalin caught up with him, and walked with him almost 'at a trot', unlike his usual slow pace, through the Kremlin halls.

In the morning they had a last meeting, and afterwards went to Stalin's private flat for a drink. On the whole this last meeting was a success, until Stalin again could not resist asking if the Royal Navy had no sense of honour – because of the failure of one of the British convoys to Murmansk – convoys which, with great risk and heavy losses, were bringing the Russians free supplies (and to a point not far from where Stalin had given the Nazis a U-boat base).

In fact, the new phase of the Battle of the Atlantic was putting a strain on shipping capacity, which was also under pressure from the new operations in the Mediterranean, and Churchill had to take the necessary decisions, whether Stalin liked that or not.

One particularly rude letter of Stalin's included such passages as:

'. . . it would be inadmissible to have the supplies of the Soviet armies depend on the arbitrary judgement of the British side. It is impossible to consider this posing of the question to be other than a refusal of the British government to fulfil the obligations it undertook, and as a kind of threat addressed to the USSR.'

Churchill had this letter handed back to the Soviet ambassador as unacceptable. Allied naval cooperation raised various other troubles. The British naval personnel stationed at Murmansk to service the convoys were harassed by the Soviet authorities. Stalin had accused them of failing to obey Soviet laws. Churchill then showed that he was prepared to stop the convoys if the Royal Navy was not properly treated. As usual when standing up to Stalin, he won his point.

The United States Navy had to swallow, though (fortunately) while the war had not long to run, a much more physically damaging rebuff. The Russians had captured the German submarine experimental station at Gdynia, and refused access to American experts, who were thus prevented from discovering ways of protecting their convoys from the still very dangerous U-boat fleet. The head of the US military mission in Moscow wanted to suspend the American convoys to Murmansk until the Russians gave way – but was overruled, for fear of 'risking Soviet displeasure'.

Stalin's tactics, of rudeness punctuated by warmth, were sometimes counter-productive. But his general strategy was sound. As Clausewitz remarks, bad tactics can be redeemed by good strategy. And though

Churchill at least was alienated by Stalin's offensive attitude, even he was still susceptible to the feeling that Stalin had a genuine grievance while the Soviet Union was bearing the brunt of the war.

7

In May 1942 Stalin ordered a major offensive in the Ukraine. As with the Kiev battle the previous year, Stalin simply refused to listen to the objections of the commanders in the field. It was a disaster. The attacking armies were surrounded and once again Stalin forbade retreat, so that a further huge haul of Soviet soldiers went to the German prisoner-of-war camps. Moreover, the broken front lay open to the great Nazi offensive which now swept forward to the Volga and the Caucasus.

As the Germans pressed on, Stalin issued in August 1942, in his own name, an order to be read out at company level in all units, though not published in full until quite lately. He presented the truth about the German gains, said that Rostov and Novocherkassk had been abandoned 'without serious resistance and without orders from Moscow', and went on:

'Our country's population, which regards the Red Army with love and respect, is beginning to be disappointed in it, losing faith in the Red Army, and many curse the Red Army for sacrificing our people to the German oppressors while itself fleeing eastwards. Some unwise people at the front take consolation in the talk that we can continue retreating eastwards because we have a lot of territory, land, a large population and that we will always have plenty of grain; these people use the talk to justify their disgraceful behaviour. But this talk is utterly false, mendacious and advantageous only to our enemies.

After the loss of the Ukraine, Byelorussia, the Baltic area, Donbas and other regions we have much less territory, fewer people, less grain and metal, fewer plants and factories. We have lost upwards of 70 million people, more than 800 million pounds of grain a year and more than 10 million tons of metal a year. We no longer enjoy superiority over the Germans in either manpower or grain reserves. To retreat further would mean our ruin and ruin of our Motherland. Thus it is time to end the retreat. Not a step backwards! This must be our main call today.'

He went on to say that the great defect was lack of discipline; 'Panic-mongers and cowards must be shot on the spot', while even commanders showing 'instability' should be reduced to the ranks and sent to special penal battalions (from one to three of these per front) to be used 'in the most dangerous positions'.

Stalin had miscalculated again. The German plan of attack had fallen into the hands of Soviet intelligence, but he had preferred other sources, in fact Nazi plants, which gave Moscow as the objective of the summer campaign. But Hitler's new blow was, as Stalin now saw, almost as dangerous as when the Nazis reached the first station on the Moscow Metro the previous year.

In fact the stubborn defence of the Stalingrad bridgehead through the autumn left the Germans unable adequately to cover their northern flank. This time the counter-attack was devised by the Soviet High Command, and though Stalin interfered half-heartedly over detail, the generals were able to cut off the Germans at Stalingrad in November, in the battle from which, though the war lasted over two years more, the enemy never recovered.

Zhukov said that Stalin only really began to understand military matters at this point. But he still insisted on actions which, though not disastrous, brought unnecessary losses. The Germans in Stalingrad, who were in any case doomed, were attacked continuously until they surrendered in February. The advantage to the Russians was small, and meanwhile troops needed on the main front were diverted to what was now a sideshow. The rest of the German armies in the south retreated through the Ukraine. Stalin again pushed for an early decision, but a German counter-attack retook Kharkov, and the armies settled down for the summer campaign of 1943, and the superbattle of Kursk.

This saw Stalin at his best militarily. He accepted the experts' intelligence conclusions. Though himself inclined, as ever, to a preemptive counter-offensive, he gave in to the military's choice of a strictly defensive posture. The result was a great defensive victory, followed by the successful Soviet offensive of the late summer.

It was in August 1943 that Stalin paid his only established visit to the front. He had been under fire in the Civil War at least once, when his train was attacked by Cossacks. And in Moscow there had recently been air raids, though minor ones by London standards; in any case, he naturally had a well-equipped deep shelter. The present visit to the front was kept at least as safe.

Marshal Voronov was summoned back from near the actual front to

an urgent conference at his rear headquarters. On arrival, he found
Stalin. The headquarters cabin, which Voronov had made as comfortable as he could, was now far more front-line in appearance. The
furniture had been replaced by bare wooden chairs and table and a field
telephone. This became the scene of a photograph of 'Comrade Stalin
listening to a report in a front-line command post'. (A picture even more
often printed showed Stalin looking through field glasses at what was
said to be a German position: but the scenery does not appear to be
summery, and this may be of an earlier rumoured visit to the general
area of the front.)

8

Meanwhile, the Germans had discovered the mass graves at Katyn.

In the days of the great Soviet defeats in the early part of the German–
Soviet war, Stalin had resumed relations with the Polish government,
then in London. Stalin personally had three long interviews with Polish
representatives – first with the Polish ambassador Professor Kot; then
with Kot, the Polish Premier General Sikorski and General Anders; and
lastly with General Anders alone.

Each time there was general conversation: for example, Stalin asked
Kot what had become of the beautiful Polish Communist Vera
Kosztrewa. Kot replied that she had been shot in the Soviet purges.
Stalin said, 'A, zhalko' ('What a pity'). On most of the points raised,
Stalin was very forthcoming, smoking and doodling as was his wont.

For a time it had looked as though the Poles would not be able to
gain anything from Stalin. But, in the first place Stalin was, to say the
least, in a weak position militarily and diplomatically. He could and
did press the Western allies strongly for aid, but he could not expect a
favourable response from them to hostile action against a government
which had been fighting on their side for nearly two years. Second, he
had virtually no Polish Communists available, having shot them all in
1937–8. As it turned out, he needed time to raise even a minimally
adequate cadre.

Stalin seems to have hoped to postpone consideration of the Polish
issue proper until such time as he felt strong enough to deal with it.
Meanwhile, he planned to raise a Polish force to fight on the Soviet
Front. The question of what to do if the Soviets were victorious could
be put off until later – if this scenario had worked out doubtless the

Polish force would have been treated as their Home Army was to be later on.

Stalin evidently hoped that the Poles he now committed himself to releasing would forgive past Soviet treatment of them in the light of the dominating struggle against Hitler. When General Anders told him that he had been badly treated in Lwow NKVD prison, though less so in the Lubyanka, but that in any case prison was prison, Stalin merely said that it couldn't be helped, as such was the condition of things at the time. But the Poles were, of course, specially concerned with the absence among the Polish military now released of any of the 15,000 who had been in the camps at Kozelsk, Starobelsk and Ostashkov, including the bulk of officers captured by the Russians in 1939. Kot had had several meetings with Vyshinsky and Molotov in which this had been the major theme. They had both said that the officers, if they had not escaped, would be found and released.

All this was deeply disturbing to the Poles. But as General Sikorski said to his own Cabinet, 'We shall find them ... Gentlemen, you don't maintain that the Soviet government has simply murdered them? Absurd! Nonsense!' But he was wrong.

To Sikorski and his colleagues Stalin simply denied all knowledge of the 15,000 missing Poles. His suggestions of what might have happened to them – that they had escaped to Manchuria, that they were in camps whose chiefs had not received, or had failed to obey, orders – did not sound plausible. Moreover, when Stalin telephoned the NKVD and asked about the release of Poles, he listened for some time, then said that 'the Polish ambassador here with me maintains that all have not been released', and, after a further long answer, put the telephone down and changed the subject.

In March 1941 Stalin again received General Anders, who reported on the position of the Polish army he was forming, and again raised the question of the missing officers. Stalin said he had given instructions for their release. He added, 'I do not know where they are. Why should I want to detain them? It may be they are in camps taken over by the Germans and have been dispersed there.' The Polish reply was that this could not be the case without their having learnt of it. Stalin then, as on the previous occasion, changed the subject.

By allowing Anders to form his army, and later to take it out of the USSR, Stalin ensured that a great fund of knowledge about the horrors of labour camps and a great pool of anti-Soviet feeling was sent abroad. Even by the standards of the Gulag, the Poles had been treated with exceptional brutality, and had suffered an exceptionally high death rate. Stalin apparently nourished special malice towards the Poles, perhaps dating from their failure to let him defeat them at Lwow in 1920. This period of his extreme need between 1941 and 1943 is the only time in which he behaved with restraint in Polish affairs.

When the Germans announced the discovery of the graves in 1943, an International Medical Commission (including neutrals) reported that the deaths had taken place in April 1940 – a view supported confidentially by Western officer POWs brought to the site, and by representatives of the Polish underground. Stalin had no recourse but to further falsehood – that the Poles had been killed by the Germans after the invasion. He broke with the Polish government. And the Allies, in the interest of the war effort, ignored or disbelieved the facts.

The repercussions of Katyn were severe and long-lasting, and the truth is only now appearing in the Soviet Union as I write, getting on for half a century later. Stalin's attitude to human life, and to truth, let alone to international law, emerges very clearly. His precise state of mind when he decided on the executions in March 1940 is beyond our knowledge. In a broad sense he presumably thought, 'They might give trouble in future, so let us shoot them.' But it also shows something of the shortsightedness Raskolnikov had noted.

9

Early in 1943 Stalin had taken a decision on an operation against a section of those he had been fighting much longer than he had been fighting the Germans – his own citizens. In this case it was the smaller nationalities of the Caucasus and the Crimea who had, in Stalin's view, either welcomed or not opposed the Germans. They were now to be deported en masse.

Stalin had already, in 1941, deported the Soviet Germans, and suppressed the Volga-German Autonomous Soviet Socialist Republic which was their largest centre. It was now to be the Kalmyks, the Chechens, the Ingushi, the Karachai, the Balkars and the Crimean Tatars. After careful planning over late 1943 and 1944 these people were rounded up, packed into Lend-Lease Studebakers, and then sent crammed into trains to various areas of Central Asia and Siberia. Their autonomous republics and provinces were abolished.

If we include the Germans, Volga and non-Volga, the total thus transported was over two million. About a third of them died either in transit or in the first months in the desert or tundra in NKVD 'special settlements'. Stalin only regretted that he was not able to send the Ukrainians as well – but there were too many of them.

The effort put into these operations must have significantly affected the military effort at the front. First, for each of these deportations, large forces of NKVD troops employable, and often employed, at the front were concentrated for weeks in the minority areas – quite apart from several thousand security agents proper. (Each action was carefully prepared, and sprung upon meetings called ostensibly for other purposes in each village and town.) Second, moving these masses took a great deal of transport. For the Chechen–Ingush deportation alone, 6,000 lorries were used in the first phase; while overall, 15,200 railway wagons were diverted for over a month from the movement of troops or supplies.

It might have been thought that the deportations could have waited until 1945. That such considerations did not affect Stalin is all of a piece with the fact that some hundred thousand healthy NKVD men spent the war guarding the prisoners in the labour camps.

As for his attitude to nationalities, Stalin could find in the Marxist texts a number of references to some nations being 'reactionary', and of the necessity of opposing their 'national movements'. But this deportation en bloc, and their disappearance from the list of Soviet nations, was taking this logic further than had previously been envisaged.

10

Stalin had little leisure over these years, and his home life grew narrower and narrower. He saw little of Svetlana, though he sent for her once to meet Winston Churchill. However, over the winter of 1942–3 she gave trouble.

Her brother Vasily had developed into a semi-literate drunk, 'a beastly pampered schoolboy let out into the world'. He had done badly at the Kuchinsky Flying School, but had graduated with perfect marks, and was by now an Air Force colonel (and destined for higher rank still). Not that Stalin intervened for him. It was more that none of those Vasily served under dared fail to recommend his promotion. At the top level, where Stalin's wishes were better known, this did not apply. Malenkov once gave Vasily a sharp public dressing-down on a Stalingrad front.

Stalin paid little attention to him and at first evidently took it that his promotions were on merit.

Vasily gave patronizing parties for the Moscow intelligentsia. At one of these Svetlana met Alexei Kapler, a film scriptwriter. They had a love affair, though only meeting for a few hours, over a few months. Kapler was soon warned by Vlasik's deputy, Rumyantsev, to stop seeing Svetlana. When he refused he was arrested and sentenced to five years in labour camp. Stalin came into Svetlana's room. Spluttering with rage he demanded to see Kapler's letters. 'I know the whole story!' he added. 'I've got all your telephone conversations right here' – and he patted his pocket. 'All right! Hand them over! Your Kapler is a British spy. He's under arrest!'

She gave Stalin all the letters, photographs, a film script and said, 'But I love him!' '"Love!" screamed my father; with a hatred of the very word I can scarcely convey.' And now, for the first time, he twice slapped her face. He shouted to the nurse, 'How low she's sunk! ... Such a war going on and she's busy the whole time fucking!'

That evening Stalin called her in. He was tearing up Kapler's letters and photographs and throwing them into the wastepaper basket. 'Writer!' he said. 'He can't even write decent Russian! She couldn't even get herself a Russian!' Kapler was a Jew, which seems to have particularly rankled.

Kapler served his five years, but on his return paid a visit to Moscow, from which he was banned. He then got another five years. Beria explained to him, on the occasion of one or another of these sentencings, that Kapler should thank Beria for doing him a favour – five years being by NKVD standards hardly a sentence at all.

After this Stalin and his daughter were estranged for a long time, and their relationship never fully recovered.

By now Stalin's non-official life had settled down to a surly routine, ending with gloomy all-male dinners around midnight. Milovan Djilas, representing the Yugoslav Communists, who first visited Stalin in the spring of 1944, describes the heavy meals and dull potations of these dreary evenings – though on the whole Stalin himself drank sparingly.

Stalin had dissolved the Comintern in 1943, apparently in the belief that its continued existence might irritate Roosevelt, or at least give other Americans a handle against him. But he continued to treat foreign Communists (now Stalinists to a man) in a more 'comradely' fashion than he was employing with his new allies Churchill and Roosevelt, at such get-togethers.

11

There were sturdy voices in the State Department and the Foreign Office, and among the American and British military, who continued to warn against giving in to Stalin's bullying and wheedling. They were a minority fighting an uphill battle. But there was one issue on which appeasement of Stalin, or at least overt and abject appeasement of Stalin, remained difficult. The United Kingdom had gone to war over Poland. The United States was committed to self-determination.

But more influential assessments from the Foreign Office spoke of how wrong it was to offend the Russians 'in their agony'. This sensitive humanitarianism was not, however, applied to the Poles in *their* at least equal agony. The selective sanctimoniousness of the Stalinophile lobbies in London and Washington is even more repulsive than their political stupidity.

The Katyn revelations had made it almost impossible to give satisfaction to both Stalin and Poland. In what they felt to be the interests of victory, the Western allies urged the Poles to be silent – indeed in Britain the press was censored for anti-Soviet remarks. In Washington true reports of Katyn from a US officer simply disappeared from the files. By now Stalin had formed his own group of Stalinist and sub-Stalinist Poles who were to be the core of his quisling regime in Warsaw.

In the autumn of 1943 a Foreign Ministers' conference was held in Moscow. The Polish issue was still avoided. Stalin had written to Roosevelt and Churchill in a virulent tone about the decision to invade Italy rather than France at this point. He accused them of 'withholding' the expected support, and of 'disregard of Soviet interests'. He now bullied Eden, and dropped heavy hints to the American Secretary of State, Cordell Hull, about a separate Soviet–German peace.

He may have meant it, or at least have been using it, as a way of blackmailing the West into further concessions. As to his own connections with the Germans, after his attempted approach through the Bulgarian ambassador in 1941, the story of contacts between Moscow and Berlin is still obscure. It seems that odd unofficial approaches took place in Stockholm at the end of 1941 and again a few months later, and that hints about the possibilities were given to foreign Communist leaders. In addition there were Soviet articles suggesting that Germany should not be occupied or disarmed and might keep some of the territories gained in 1938–9 – and even a hint in Stalin's speech of 6 November 1942 that it was *not* the Soviet aim to 'destroy all organized military force in Germany'. It is not yet easy to explore Stalin's view of the options. In 1942–3, the Soviet Union was in a state of exhaustion, and German successes were still possible. There was certainly a pragmatic case for a separate peace – and rumours that this was contemplated now circulated in high Western circles.

One difficulty was, as in 1941, that the side that was winning had no interest in pursuing the idea. Nor is it clear that Stalin was prepared to deal with Hitler. On one view, his feelers were put out with the idea of settlement with a post-Hitler regime – either military or consisting of the more pro-Soviet Nazis. (Hitler himself, confronted in 1944 with Goebbels's suggestion that he might have to come to an arrangement with the West or with Stalin, said that if so he would prefer negotiations with Stalin, but did not believe that they would be successful.) Stalin's often expressed fear that the West might come to an arrangement with Germany had a rational enough basis – that he himself would have done so in the right circumstances. It was a natural part of his general suspicion of the Western leaders. He was to tell the Yugoslavs of the English, and Churchill in particular, 'There's nothing they like better than to trick their allies ... Churchill is the kind of man who will pick your pocket of a kopek if you don't watch him. Yes, pick your pocket of a kopek! By God, pick your pocket of a kopek! And Roosevelt? Roosevelt is not like that. He dips in his hand only for bigger coins.'

It was in November 1943 that Stalin finally met these two other members of the Big Three for the Teheran Conference. This was Roosevelt's first encounter with Stalin, and it is hard to see why Stalin summed him up as a pickpocket, at any rate a successful one. Stalin did well straight away, by persuading the US President to stay in the Soviet compound. In their first talks, with Churchill absent, Roosevelt spoke of a post-war world in which the French and British empires would have to be liquidated. Stalin's empire was not thus threatened.

Roosevelt had formed the impression that Stalin was 'get-at-able', by which he meant that personal persuasion would induce him to change his mind. This was a uniquely erroneous view: as Ronald Hingley has put it, 'The one consistent feature in the career of the elusive Stalin is – if we may adopt the President's own colloquialism – that of *un*getatability.' Roosevelt was to leave the conference with the feeling that he had won over Stalin. He wondered if training for the priesthood 'made some kind of difference with Stalin. Doesn't that explain part of the sympathetic quality in his nature we feel?'

Roosevelt's tactics in winning Stalin over consisted, when all three were together, of joining with him in teasing Churchill. As Roosevelt himself said later, when he started to needle Churchill 'about his Britishness, about John Bull, about his cigars, about his habits', Stalin became amused: 'from that time our relations were personal ... we talked like men and brothers.' This took an unpleasant turn at dinner in the British Legation, when Stalin proposed that after the war fifty thousand German officers should be shot.

Churchill, horrified, said, 'I would rather be taken out into the garden here and now and be shot myself than sully my own or my country's honour by such infamy.' Roosevelt, perhaps trying to deflate the situation, jokingly said they might reduce the figure to 49,000, and his son Elliott Roosevelt said he agreed with Stalin, and so would the US Army. Churchill rose and went off to his room. Stalin and Molotov came after him and Stalin explained that he was only joking. Churchill was not convinced of this. Indeed, it is hard to see in what sense it could have been merely a merry quip. It seems clear enough that Stalin, who had shot nearly as many of his own officers, and a comparable proportion of Polish officers too, felt his proposal to be perfectly reasonable.

As to the results of Teheran, the Western powers now in effect agreed to Stalin's frontiers. As Ismay put it, Stalin got 'exactly what he wanted', while the UK and the USA had a few vague promises in exchange.

12

When de Gaulle representing the new France went to Moscow in December 1944, it was for the purpose of signing a new Franco-Soviet Treaty. Stalin tried very hard to make it a condition that de Gaulle recognize the Soviet-sponsored Lublin Committee as the government of Poland. De Gaulle regarded the proposal as dishonourable, and simply refused the condition. Stalin struck de Gaulle as a cunning dictator, and a master of deception full of ambition and 'fierce' political passion. At the dinner which followed, Stalin proposed thirty toasts, mainly to his generals. Khrushchev says he got 'completely drunk'. Anyhow, he was in what passed for him as a joking mood. In one toast to a General of Supplies, he said, 'He had better do his best, otherwise he'll be hanged,' then he called heartily for a machine-gun to mow down the diplomats. He threatened in similar vein to send his own interpreter to Siberia because 'he knows too much'. To de Gaulle, he said that he hoped he would not put the French Communist leader Maurice Thorez in prison, or 'at least not right away'. De Gaulle noted that the Soviet guests did not look very mirthful.

Over the next months the West still hoped somehow to maintain Polish independence. But as D-Day approached, Cordell Hull summed up the Western view as follows: that they could not 'afford to become partisan in the Polish question to the extent of alienating Russia at the crucial moment'. Things had reached the stage that to take the Soviet side against the Poles was not to be 'partisan'.

Stalin managed the Polish question with a combination of falsehood and brutality, that is to say in his usual style. Adherents of the Polish government in London, that is the overwhelming majority of the population, had their underground troops and organizations declared anti-Soviet. Stalin's little Polish committee at Lublin was given full power. The Warsaw Rising was crushed by the Germans after over two months' fighting, under the very eye of the Red Army, with Stalin refusing help, and only belatedly allowing a few American arms-drop aircraft based in Italy to refuel on Soviet airfields.

When Churchill went to Moscow in October 1944, Stalin told him that while he and Molotov wanted a softer line on Poland, he was hampered by the harder views of other Politburo members. Nothing was achieved, but Churchill was pleased when Stalin accepted the idea that the major Nazi war criminals should be tried before they were executed.

When the Big Three met again at Yalta, in February 1945, it is sometimes believed that Stalin achieved his aims in part because a Soviet spy was present in the American delegation in the form of Alger Hiss, deputy director of the Office of Special Political Affairs. But on the record, the Westerners were already set on the course which now in practice finally gave Stalin his way in Eastern Europe.

On Poland, the Lublin Committee was recognized as the basis of a future government, but free elections were promised, as they were in the newly liberated, and soon to be re-unliberated, Balkan countries. Yalta ended on a euphoric note with warm speeches from Stalin, and Roosevelt at least was convinced that there would be peaceful relations 'as far into the future as any of us could imagine'.

But when it was over Stalin reverted to, or rather continued, his old ways. He deeply offended the Americans by refusing to allow them to send officers into Poland to look after American prisoners of war released by the Soviet advance. He seems simply to have wanted as few observers as possible in Poland, as well he might. For he now had the leaders of the Polish underground army and state arrested while under a safe conduct for supposed negotiations (and after months of interrogation submitted them to a public 'trial' in Moscow).

He soon infuriated Roosevelt with a barrage of accusations that the West was conducting secret negotiations with the Germans, intending to use them against the USSR. After a very nasty exchange, the dying President began to grasp Stalin's nature, and wrote to Churchill, 'We must be firm.'

When Roosevelt had argued that, in return for unconditional Allied aid, Stalin would help build a peaceful and democratic world, he had sanguinely relied on, as he put it, Stalin's sense of *'noblesse oblige'*. Now, only a few days before his death, he said in private, 'We can't do business with Stalin. He has broken every one of the promises he made at Yalta.'

Roosevelt was wrong, in the sense that Stalin had still a number of promises to break.

13

As the Soviet armies advanced, Stalin gradually recovered his confidence in his own military abilities. He started once again to order offensives to be undertaken before preparations had been made. Against a skilled and tenacious foe, this resulted in excessive casualties, as numbers were thrown in to rectify the defects of strategy. This culminated in enormous losses in the very last phase of the war, in the assault on Berlin.

When the Soviet armies swept into Germany, as so vividly described in Solzhenitsyn's poem *Prussian Nights,* there was an outbreak of raping and looting. There is no doubt that this was encouraged by Stalin. Not only were there orders from the High Command, and press articles, encouraging the utmost ruthlessness, but Stalin actively condoned rape, too, apparently from a primitive view of a soldier's rights. Nor was this only in connection with German women. When Djilas was again in Moscow with a Yugoslav Communist delegation, he complained to Stalin that, even in Yugoslavia, Soviet troops were acting so. Djilas added that friends of the Soviet Union had somehow to explain the fact that British troops were behaving much better.

Stalin was, of course, infuriated. How could Djilas compare the Soviet army with the imperialist British? Stalin pursued this obvious target with vigour. But he added that a soldier, after hundreds of kilometres of fire and death, was entitled to 'have fun with a woman or take some trifle'. He added that he had once intervened in the case of a Red Army major sentenced to death in such a case – on the grounds that the Soviet Union needed victories more than it did virginities.

However, when it came to Germany, Stalin is reported sending one curious order about a civilian. When Beria informed him that the widow of the Emperor Wilhelm II was living in East Prussia, he ordered that she should be protected.

Soviet military critics are now bitter about the fact that Soviet losses in the war were so very much higher than those of the Germans – four to eight times greater, according to various Soviet historians. But Stalin was now the victor. And he was shortly to write of himself:

'The advanced Soviet science of war received further development at Comrade Stalin's hands. Comrade Stalin elaborated the theory of the permanently operating factors that decide the issue of wars, of active defence and the laws of counter-offensive and offensive, of the cooperation of all services and arms in modern warfare, of the role of big tank masses and air forces in modern war, and of the artillery as the most formidable of the armed services. At the various stages of the war Stalin's genius found the correct solutions that took account of all the circumstances of the situation: Stalin's military mastership was displayed both in defence and offence. Comrade Stalin's genius enabled him to divine the enemy's plans and defeat them. The battles in which Comrade Stalin directed the Soviet armies are brilliant examples of operational military skill.'

His ego, and his sense of his own superiority in the military field, were based on the solid fact that he had indeed won the war. It might have been won more easily but for his mistakes both before and during the struggle. In a crisis largely of his own making, the Soviet Union was more than once on the point of collapse. But it was Stalin, when all was said and done, who had held the country together by the sheer application of will-power through this long and difficult period.

During the last phases of the war, he was still rebuking front commanders with, by now, splendid battle records, in the most abusive terms, charging them with being too cowardly to attack and otherwise using the rudest and most damaging language. This he seemed to find appropriate. As we have seen, he sometimes spoke in similar terms to the Western leaders, his allies. It came naturally to him.

14

In July 1945, Stalin came to the Potsdam Conference, the last of the Anglo-American–Soviet summits. He was at first going to fly, but at the last minute took a train – by now the details of the plot against Hitler were available, including the attempt to blow up his plane.

At Potsdam, while making 'concessions' when pushing and then abandoning various implausible claims to territory now in Allied or neutral hands – Libya, Tangier, a base in the Turkish Straits or at Dedeagach, a share of the Ruhr's industry – Stalin in effect secured his position in Eastern Europe.

Churchill still found him 'likeable'. But in mid-conference Churchill was replaced as Prime Minister by Clement Attlee. The new American President, Harry Truman, completed the changed trio.

Stalin was in a triumphant mood, and justifiably so. But it was now that revulsion began to set in on the part of his Western colleagues. Truman found him impressive, good-humoured, polite and willing to listen to views straightforwardly put. But Truman at once decided that the Soviet Union should not be allowed to occupy any part of Japan. Stalin asked again later, when the Americans had control of Japan, and was again refused, to which Stalin replied, 'I and my colleagues did not expect such a reply from you.'

Attlee too, said of Stalin, 'He was obviously the man who could make decisions, and he was going to be difficult ... I was under no illusions as to his readiness to cooperate or to his liking for us.'

During the conference the first atomic bomb was successfully exploded in Nevada. Truman informed Stalin in general terms that he had a very powerful new explosive. Stalin, who knew all about the project from Klaus Fuchs and other Soviet spies (as has recently been confirmed in detail in the Moscow press), merely said he hoped it would be used against Japan.

For nearly four years the Allies had, generally speaking, been acting on false principles. It is true that they did not give in to Stalin on every issue, and on some of those they finally conceded they put up some sort of resistance.

They might not have been able to stop Stalin imposing a Communist regime in Poland, but little advantage came of helping him cover up this breach of his promise by inducing the head of the true Polish government, Mikolajczyk, to return to Poland for a short and insecure tenure as Vice-Premier in a Communist-dominated regime.

Stalin had won every round. He had done so as in the past by contriving, at least part of the time, to be 'likeable'. He played the card of Russia's titanic battles to press for concessions from the West. In fact, he overplayed it, though the West usually forgave him. Stalin had told the NKVD, of the great trials of the late 1930s, that the West would 'swallow it'. He now practised other deceptions on the same principle, and again found dupes.

But, cunningly though he had used his psychological advantages, in the aftermath of Potsdam a point came at which they failed him. He had not understood that there were limits. Litvinov was to say later to another former Soviet diplomat that Stalin might have succeeded fully against the West if its leaders had been 'some sort of shahs or sheikhs', but as it was, they were bound eventually to turn against him.

15

After the defeat of Japan, Stalin took what had been promised him as long ago as Teheran – South Sakhalin, the Kuriles, Port Arthur and Dairen – the last two the legitimate property of his ally China. This represented exactly the earlier possessions lost by the tsars. In his speech on the victory, he said that people of his generation remembered the Russo-Japanese War of 1904–5, and had waited for forty years to avenge the Russian defeat.

It will be seen that this marks an astonishing transformation. In 1905, the Bolsheviks had unconditionally opposed the war, and had worked for and welcomed Russia's defeat. The Old Bolshevik now in charge was, on the contrary, openly and ostentatiously proclaiming himself the heir of the tsarist empire.

Chapter 13

Postwar: Cold War

After Hitler committed suicide, Stalin long believed, or pretended to believe, that he had in fact probably escaped by plane to Hamburg and thence by U-boat to Japan or Argentina, in spite of perfectly clear evidence provided by Soviet investigations on the spot in Berlin.

But Hitler was indeed dead, and Nazism with him. The swastika battle flags were paraded in Red Square, and thrown down in ignominy before Lenin's tomb. And with the victory over Japan those against whom Stalin had directed the Soviet armies were at last totally crushed. The world was at peace.

In the abstract, Stalin now had the option of civic reconciliation at home, accommodation with the West, the acceptance of Communist–democratic coalitions in Eastern Europe, and (a little later) cooperation in the Marshall Plan and a programme of economic recovery. But the pressures of war had not softened his character. In fact, Khrushchev said that 'in my opinion it was during the war that Stalin started to be not quite right in the head'.

The long struggle against the imagined internal foe and the real external enemy had worn him down. Now sixty-five, he had aged visibly. Soon after the end of hostilities he had a minor stroke; and then he spent over three months (from 9 October to 17 December 1945) resting and recuperating in his Black Sea dacha at Sochi.

If Stalin was exhausted, so was the country as a whole. For many the war itself with its real horrors had, as Pasternak tells us, come in some ways as 'an omen of deliverance, a purifying storm' compared with the cold-blooded, meaningless sufferings of the 1930s. For Russia it was, as its official title puts it, the Great Patriotic War; and, as the veteran Soviet novelist Vasily Grossman saw, many thought of themselves as fighting not only against the Nazis, but for a better Russia, without terror, without Gulag.

With victory it was widely felt that the titanic effort, the enormous sacrifice of life, could not have been in vain. In Pasternak's words, 'so many sacrifices cannot result in nothing' and 'a presage of freedom was in the air'. The mood of the country, as Andrei Sakharov recalls, was that 'we all believed – or at least hoped – that the postwar world would be decent and humane. How could it be otherwise?' The war, he says, had restored the nation's 'pride and dignity'. But the hope of social and political peace in Russia, and a cooperative international community, was a false one. In the event, says Sakharov, 'As the illusion faded, the nation disintegrated into separate atoms and faded away.'

In Sochi Stalin got, as it were, his second wind. If he had to some extent slowed down, he was still possessed by the old hatreds and suspicions, the vision of enemies everywhere. The mood of the country, the longings for a freer and fuller life, were for him not a guide to future policy, but an intolerable challenge to his power and his principles.

Returning to Moscow, he took steps not merely to restore but to consolidate his system. In some ways it was to become even more brutal. The labour camps received a flood of new inmates. Those who had served their time and been released were soon to be rearrested. The maximum sentence was increased from ten years to twenty-five. A new category of 'strict regime' labour camps came in where the inmates served in chains and without blankets. The exiled nations, but also the mass of individual exiles, were forbidden to return on pain of a twenty-year sentence. In the secret-police laboratories research was to go on into poisons, mind-bending drugs, assassination weapons. Important prisoners were to be tortured with red-hot irons in special trains circling Moscow.

2

The economy was in a desperate state. Agriculture had been disrupted, with a devastating famine in the Ukraine and elsewhere. When Kosygin reported the incidence of dystrophy in the areas affected, Stalin was angry, and for some time addressed him ironically as 'Brother Dystrophic'.

Stalin cared as little as ever for the fate of ordinary people. He is reported (not only by Khrushchev but also by his Minister of Finance,

Zverev) as urging higher taxes on the already indigent peasantry. Several Soviet analyses have lately pointed out that he was still, in effect, trying to ruin agriculture to help industry, though in fact industrial investment benefited little and the whole population was short of food. In fact he remained not just mistaken but disastrously ignorant about economic matters and the consequences of forcible methods. But, as Khrushchev was later to say, Stalin did have the power to make the people live at sub-minimum standards.

One rational solution would have been, as we have said, the abandonment, even if only temporarily, of confrontation with the West, with a view to obtaining Western aid. The American offer to extend the Marshall Plan to the USSR shows that this would have been forthcoming. As it was, Stalin accepted massive United Nations Relief Administration assistance in the immediate crisis of the postwar famine; but in the longer run, given the choice of autarchic poverty or economic and political cooperation, he chose the former.

But the internal problems were not (at least in Stalin's eyes) primarily economic. The war had in some ways shaken his and the party's grip. As the writer Konstantin Simonov, who spoke with Stalin a number of times at this juncture, puts it, the war effort had to some extent depended on using the soldier's qualities as an individual, 'his potential, his mother-wit, his intelligence, his courage'. But (says Simonov) these were just the qualities Stalin saw as dangerous now that peace had come.

Moreover, as Stalin viewed it, the soldiers who brought back stories of the incredible wealth of people in not merely Czechoslovakia or Austria, but even Poland and Bulgaria, had not properly understood the 'necessity' for the economic sacrifices they had made. They were in danger of being seduced by the riches of the West, as the intelligentsia was in danger of being seduced by its values. In Simonov's words, Stalin 'feared a new Decembrism. He had shown Ivan to Europe and Europe to Ivan, as Alexander I did in 1813–14 ...' That is to say, he saw a potential threat to his rule.

Stalin therefore took his decision on his next moves for pragmatic reasons, rather than being suddenly overcome by an ideological and nationalistic urge, as is sometimes supposed.

He first envisaged sending to labour camp a few hundred thousand army men (mainly but not entirely officers) – including those who had first contacted the Americans in the famous Meeting on the Elbe. In camp from 1946 on, they joined the already sentenced former collaborators with, and former prisoners of war of, the Germans.

Stalin felt his victorious generals too, though they showed fewer signs of becoming infected with Westernization, to be dangerous in their own right. Marshal Zhukov in particular had acquired popularity which might easily be translated into political terms. On 9 June 1946 Stalin signed an order referring to reports of Zhukov's 'unworthy' attitude to the Supreme Commander-in-Chief, and at a top-level meeting soon afterwards Zhukov was accused of 'awarding himself the laurels of the chief victor'. Soon evidence was concocted showing him to be a Western spy. But after long consideration Stalin did not order his arrest, merely expelling him from the Central Committee and transferring him to a minor territorial command.

Generals of less renown, including a number of Zhukov's closest colleagues, were not so lucky – Minyuk, Buchin, Telegin and others. This military purge continued, unpublicized, for several years. Early in 1948 five admirals, including the lone survivor of the Fleet Admirals of the 1930s, L. M. Galler, were sentenced as Anglo-American spies (Galler died in prison). In 1950 even Stalin's old (and disastrously incompetent) companion, the former Marshal Kulik, was shot.

3

While Stalin's preemptive blows against the rank-and-file soldiery and the generals were struck without publicity, he understandably decided that the war against Western ideas required a more outspoken campaign.

The insidious deterioration of ideological discipline had begun to exercise his mind even before his stroke. The party's doctrinal organ *Bolshevik* failed to appear for two months, and when the August 1945 issue finally emerged in October with a changed editorial board, its tone was far sharper and more dogmatic.

The political problems proper were quite different from those of the 1920s or 1930s. In the 1920s Stalin was engaged in a struggle against a series of open rivals; in the 1930s he still faced colleagues with reservations about his claims to supremacy. But henceforward we find no trace of opposition in the political sphere. There is no longer any threat to his power. His subordinates are entirely servile. The whole political world has shrunk to a simulacrum. The ideological arguments are pettifogging. The spotlight is now on a stage in effect empty except for the single figure of Stalin.

Events, especially at this public level, thus seem to be in a different key, as when Dante leads us from a circle of hell all flame and demons into another where the damned suffer in cold and gloomy silence. It is as horrible; but it is not as dramatic – though at the end of the period, the stench of brimstone again pervades the scene.

We must thus not expect the individual personalities and dangerous confrontations of the early period. All seems a tabula rasa on which the leader can act at will. Yet Stalin was still able by sheer will-power to strike sullen coruscations even from this unpromising material.

Bukharin and Trotsky, Kirov and Ordzhonikidze, had gone. The veteran Stalinists Molotov and Mikoyan, Kaganovich and Kalinin remained. But Stalin had long been relying on a younger cadre. Since the beginning of the decade, his chief henchman had been Georgi Malenkov, while Beria as head of the secret police had enjoyed almost equal trust.

Now Stalin decided that Malenkov, associated with comparative moderation, must be replaced, though not killed. Early in 1946, Andrei Zhdanov was brought from Leningrad to organize Stalin's new ideological offensive. Zhdanov (according to recent Soviet accounts) had been a worthless figurehead in Leningrad – even living under virtual house arrest – during the direct challenge of the German besiegers, and his duties had fallen to his Second Secretary A. A. Kuznetsov. At any rate Stalin brought in Kuznetsov too to join the Secretariat.

After Kuznetsov's appointment, Stalin summoned a Provincial Secretary, Patolichev – not a Zhdanovite though approved by Zhdanov – and in a strange charade showed him a decree folded so that he could only see its point 2. This appointed him too as Secretary of the Central Committee. Patolichev later found out that point 1 removed Malenkov from his Secretaryship. Patolichev took charge of party organization and personnel, which Malenkov had managed (at first as Yezhov's assistant) since 1934.

Malenkov was sent to Central Asia, though there was no public announcement of demotion. His ally, the head of the State Planning Commission, was replaced by the Zhdanovite Voznesensky. Beria, still at the centre, used what influence he had in Malenkov's favour. But Kuznetsov's responsibilities in the Secretariat were as the party's controller of government affairs: this included supervision of the police. In previous years such supervision had been a formality, but Kuznetsov now started demanding documents from State Security officials. Moreover, he had the Leningrad secret-police chief Kubatkin, with whom he

273

had developed close relations, transferred to the centre – all of this boding ill for Beria and his circle.

In fact, like Malenkov though to a lesser degree, Beria now appeared to be in some disfavour. He lost direct control of the police ministries in March 1946, though his closest colleague Merkulov remained head of what was now the MGB. But one day Stalin suddenly asked Beria why all his generals and security staff seemed to be Georgians. Beria answered that they were devoted and loyal. Stalin said angrily that not only Georgians but also Russians could be loyal.

Shortly afterwards a Russian, Viktor Abakumov, was appointed head of the MGB, and Beria's men were replaced not only in Stalin's entourage, but all through the higher levels of the secret police – though none were arrested and most were given tolerably prestigious posts outside. Beria remained a member of the Politburo, and his transfer from his police responsibilities 'to other duties' meant in fact control of the crucial Soviet atomic bomb project. Moreover Abakumov, though a Russian, was not hostile to Beria, nor close to the Zhdanovites.

Malenkov remained out of favour for nearly two years, though he was not removed from the Politburo. While thus preserving his options, Stalin now seemed committed to the Zhdanovites – Svetlana thought she would please him by marrying Zhdanov's son. He once spoke of Zhdanov as his successor, and when Zhdanov himself appeared unsuitable Stalin suggested, in front of others, that Voznesensky should succeed him as Premier and Kuzentsov as General Secretary. Whether this was even partly sincere cannot be known. Soviet historians tend to feel that it was said in order to fuel the jealousies within the leadership.

4

The new team's task was to correct the comparative indiscipline Stalin saw around him. There had been a certain amount of cultural contact with the West, and – or so it appeared to him – a softening of the necessary hostility to that alien order. His main public blow was therefore directed at the intelligentsia. Zhdanov is described by some who met him as 'comparatively' intellectual; though, as a recent Soviet account points out, 'like the whole of Stalin's circle, including at its centre the "genius" himself, he had no systematic education' – just a few courses at the Tver Agricultural Institute. This he made up for by a very good memory. At any rate, he seemed suitable to be chief agent in the struggle with the erring intellectuals.

On 9 August 1946, Stalin had the editors of two journals – *Zvezda* and *Leningrad* – brought before the Orgburo. He himself was present, his first attendance for ten years. And he personally launched the attack. The contents of the journals had, he said, been 'empty', written as if for children, full of cheap jokes. On 14 August came the announcement, amid vast publicity, of a Central Committee decision on the errors of the journals describing them as 'in ideological bondage'. *Zvezda* had published the satirical writer Mikhail Zoshchenko. The story objected to was of a monkey escaping from the zoo and after a day of mis-adventures in town returning in relief to his cage – the sort of story that might be written anywhere, but of course not complimentary to life in Leningrad. Zoshchenko was attacked for 'hooligan representations of our reality accompanied by anti-Soviet assaults'. Just as bad, *Zvezda* had printed the superb poetry of Anna Akhmatova – 'a female writer whose literary and sociopolitical physiognomy had long been known to Russian society ... a representative of empty ideal-less poetry alien to our people ... a decadent drawing-room poetess'. These two and others had as their aim 'disorientating our youth and poisoning its con-sciousness'.

This virulent diatribe set Stalin's tone for the whole Zhdanovshchina, as the period came to be known, and was at once felt by the intelligentsia as a severe shock – and a severe warning. However this time Stalin ordered no arrests. Both sinners were expelled from the Union of Writers. Zoshchenko lost his ration card (later restored). Akhmatova survived by scrubbing floors. Others, including Pasternak, were attacked in less violent terms, but the voices of independent literature were effectively silenced.

Zhdanov took up the hunt, jackal to Stalin's tiger: 'Lack of principle, looseness and slackness' had paved the way for publishing the 'literary hooligan' Zoshchenko, and the reactionary Akhmatova, 'half-nun and half-whore' with her 'insignificant experiences and religio-mystical erot-icism'.

Anna Akhmatova, especially, may indeed be seen as defining Stalinism and Stalin's own personality by its opposite. She did stand for the personal life and the personal conscience, for the autonomy of the individual and of art. Like most, she had not been exempt from the public events that had racked and were still racking Russia. Her first husband, the poet Nikolai Gumilev, had been shot as a counter-revolutionary in Lenin's time. Her second husband was a victim of

Stalin's. Her son by Gumilev had been arrested and this led to her magnificent (and long unpublished) cycle of poems *Requiem* which (in a sense Stalin would not have approved of) is profoundly political – the protest of the helpless individual against a politics designed to crush the personal life. She speaks of her mouth as one 'through which a hundred million people cry'. But what we may find in Akhmatova is not only her voice, but also that extraordinary toughness of mind which enabled the best of the Russian people, of the Russian intelligentsia, to outlast Stalin and Stalinism. And Stalin was right to see in her principles a fundamental threat to his system. Over the long run they helped to destroy it.

Literature and the arts suffered, and were brought under Stalin's new disciplines, because he rightly believed them to represent, or to affect, the thoughts and feelings of the most conscious section of the population. However, it was not only the writers who were under attack. In music the country's leading composers, Prokofiev and Shostakovich, were censured for (as Zhdanov put it) not writing tunes which could be whistled by every worker. The campaign to restore Stalin's Soviet Union to its pristine pre-war condition was now also directed at party philosophers who inadequately condemned non-Marxists, and at economists who held that the capitalist world was not on the point of collapse.

Science, too, was a major area of ideological, and hence political, conflict. The biggest scandal was in biology. The crackpot soil scientist Viliams had triumphed in this sphere in the 1930s, with the execution of a number of senior agricultural researchers. As we saw, the charlatan Lysenko, with an array of other pseudo-scientists, had been allowed to infest the scientific foundations, and to procure the dismissal of genuine biologists. This had culminated in the notorious case of the Soviet Union's leading biologist, Nikolai Vavilov, who had been arrested in 1940 and sentenced (for espionage on behalf of Britain) the following year. (Recently a denunciation of Vavilov by a fellow professor has been found in the Soviet archives. He called Vavilov a Rightist and saboteur who had managed to get previous denunciations of the Fascist tendency of genetic theory deleted from the official record of biological debates.) In 1942 Vavilov had been elected a Fellow of the Royal Society, and this seems to have led to some attempt to save him, but he was already near death from the results of dystrophy and ill-treatment in prison, and died there in 1943, as other geneticists had as early as the 1930s.

But Lysenko's theories had not yet become compulsory. A number of genuine biologists still pursued genetic research. It was not until 1948 that the Central Committee issued a decree, on Stalin's personal instructions, to condemn genetics proper as unMarxist. Prominent biologists who were also party members now said that they had taken the geneticist view while the question was open, but now that the party itself had spoken, they renounced it and promised to be good Lysenkoites. This saved some of them, but not their research institutes.

Lysenko's ideological attraction for Stalin was his claim that he could change plants by environmental pressure – that is directly and totally, not merely by breeding for good results. This theory promised the submission of the plant world to the orders of the party. Lysenko was able to tell his cowed audiences, over the weeks of ceremonial denunciation and confession, that Stalin had personally helped to draft his speeches. There had evidently been some political resistance to the full Lysenkoite triumph, which came as Zhdanov was dying; and Zhdanov's son, the husband of Svetlana Stalin, had to make a public apology for his errors as head of the Science and Culture Department of the Central Committee, in protecting genetics.

The results, for both science and agriculture, were of course negative. Even so, Lysenkoism long outlasted Stalin, since Khrushchev was also an addict. Lysenko's pseudoscience is generally believed to have appealed to Stalin and his like not only as regards the vegetable kingdom. The malleability of species also had a human application. Stalin's environment was creating the 'new Soviet man': Lysenkoism implied that the new characteristics would be biologically inheritable.

Genetics was publicly condemned as mystical 'idealism', founded on bourgeois ideology, and above all representing the alien thought of the imperialist West. In fact, error in every field, whether biology or psychology, literature or music, was denounced in terms of the struggle against the Western menace. Over these years the lesson was hammered in with a continual, deafening campaign in the press, over the radio, in speeches by the thousand. The secret police laid down new confidential categories for arrest:

VAT – Praising American Technique
VAD – Praising American Democracy
PZ – Abasement before the West

The press reported fearful suffering in the West – the machine-gunning of workers in London, children working twelve hours a day in sweatshops in New York. Inventions made in the West were reattributed to Russians – the aeroplane before the Wright brothers, the radio before Marconi, and others. The Moscow Musical Conservatoire even attacked an ensemble for using Robert Burns's song:

> Of a' the airts the wind can blaw,
> I dearly like the West
[which goes on, 'For there the bonnie lassie lives,
> The lassie I lo'e best'.]

5

For Stalin the West was of course not merely a source of subversive ideology, but also his great surviving antagonist in the struggle for world power. His hostility had been fairly obvious for some time, even in his wartime conversations with Western leaders. To foreign Communist delegations he had been franker still. When it came to his attitude to future conflict, he had told the Yugoslavs in April 1945, 'The war will soon be over. We shall recover in fifteen or twenty years, and then we'll have another go at it.' This did not in itself present the threat of an immediate war. But it very strongly showed the basic hostility with which Stalin viewed the 'imperialist' world. In fact, of course, expansionism was built into the Soviet system, and the war against Hitler had at the start been defensive out of necessity rather than principle. At the Eighteenth Party Congress in 1939, Mekhlis had said, in a part of his speech unpublished at the time, that one of the main tasks of the Red Army in a possible war was to increase the number of Soviet republics ...

The allies had agreed that Nazi war crimes should be punished, and in 1946 came the Nuremberg Tribunal. Soviet vulnerability on these issues was such that Stalin's agreement to Soviet participation might seem somewhat risky. However, he set up a special commission, headed by Vyshinsky, 'On the Organization of the Trial at Nuremberg', consisting of an equal number of Soviet judges and prosecutors on the one hand, and police officials on the other. It passed a secret resolution on 'issues which are inadmissible for discussion at the trial', and in particular the facts of Nazi–Soviet collaboration. Given the undoubted guilt for many atrocities of all or most of the accused, the tribunal's activities and verdicts were a great public success in West and East alike, though objections to the procedures were even at the time voiced by such observers as the American philosopher Sidney Hook.

For Stalin, it was more than a success. It validated Soviet law in that

278

with the three Western judges sat I. I. Nikitchenko, who had been a member of the court at the faked trials of Zinoviev and others, while the prosecution team openly included Vyshinsky's deputy Lev Sheinin, who had publicly signed many faked accusations. (Behind the scenes a secret-police team headed by the soon-to-be-notorious torturer Colonel Likachev operated.)

It was even the case that the charges on which Ribbentrop and others were found guilty included war of aggression. The USSR had been expelled from the League of Nations on precisely that accusation only six years previously – and, indeed, had participated in Hitler's Polish aggression: but attempts to submit the 1939 Secret Protocols as evidence were rejected. On only one ground was Stalin left unsatisfied. The charge sheet included Nazi responsibility for the Katyn massacre; and a number of Soviet witnesses repeated the Soviet story. But the crime was not mentioned in the verdict – a juridically astonishing procedure, though of course explainable politically.

As early as November 1945, when Litvinov was asked by Harriman what the West could do to satisfy Stalin, he replied, 'Nothing.' By June 1946 Litvinov (now Deputy Minister for Foreign Affairs) was warning Westerners that Stalin could not be appeased by concessions. The 'root cause' of the increasing confrontation (he told one American correspondent) was 'the ideological conception prevailing here that conflict between the Communist and capitalist worlds is inevitable'. The correspondent asked, 'Suppose the West would suddenly give in and grant all Moscow's demands? ... Would that lead to good will and the easing of the present tensions?' Litvinov's reply was, 'It would lead to the West being faced, after a more or less short time, with the next series of demands.' This was a clear analysis by a veteran Communist who had been in closest touch with Stalin, and was taking very grave risks in attempting to secure peace by turning the West to realism. Not everyone in the West was even yet so ready to face the facts.

But Stalin's policies in Eastern Europe had at least begun to convince serious Western statesmen that he was an implacable and unappeasable opponent. Democrat and Republican, Labour and Conservative, Socialist and Gaullist, all saw this; as Churchill put it in a famous phrase in his speech at Fulton, Mass., on 5 March 1946, 'An Iron Curtain has descended across Europe.'

Stalin had applied his method of 'doses' in Eastern Europe (in Hungary his satrap Matyas Rakosi called it 'salami tactics'). Stalin's idea was, as ever, to go forward against his opponents far enough to make solid gains, but just not far enough to produce really effective opposition. Starting while the war was still going on, he had removed the democratic and socialist parties one after another from the East European post-Nazi governments, occasionally retreating briefly, as when he got the Western allies to put enough pressure on Mikolajczyk, then head of the legitimate Polish government in London, to join the Communist-controlled rulers in Warsaw in what was hoped would be a moderate and not anti-Soviet regime. This and other manœuvres were brief and insubstantial, though remnants of democratic parties were allowed to vegetate in persecuted opposition even into 1947. When the Western powers joined the USSR in signing peace treaties with Hungary, Romania and Bulgaria, these guaranteed the legality of all anti-Fascist parties, and left the local heads of the diplomatic missions of the three powers as guarantors, to meet if there was any dispute on the matter. The Soviet ambassadors refused to meet their Western colleagues when they complained, on the grounds that no dispute existed. Paper guarantees never meant much to Stalin. By these and similar methods he gained control of Eastern Europe.

However, his tactics were a failure in one major respect. The doses had, after all, been given too quickly and the assaults came too soon. Stalin had seen the dupability of a variety of Westerners before the war, and to a lesser degree of their leaders during the war. He knew of the popularity in the West of the Soviet struggle against Hitler. But he greatly overestimated how far he could go in exploiting Western good will. The long-term result of his moves in the immediate postwar period was that American troops remained in Europe and that eventually the NATO alliance came into being.

In February 1948 the Stalinist seizure of power in Czechoslovakia, the showcase of Communist collaboration in a democratic government, was the last straw for Western opinion, and Stalin's last success in Europe. In June came the Soviet blockade of West Berlin. Communists were waging civil war in Greece. The Communist Parties in Italy and France undertook militant strikes, and declared that the Red Army would be welcome. The situation was intensely menacing.

But the Western governments kept their heads. The improvised airlift saved Berlin. And Stalin was not in fact ready for war, if only because the USSR still had not got the atomic bomb. Stalin said in public that the bomb would only frighten 'weak-nerved' people. But in private he expressed great admiration for it, as 'a very powerful thing, pow-er-ful!'

The Soviets had started, with Beria in charge, to develop the atomic weapon, in part using information from their espionage rings, during the last part of the war. At the same time, following the German V2 attack on Britain, Stalin became interested in long-range rocketry, and teams were sent to Germany (as they were by the West) to round up the rocket experts. Stalin told the aeronautics expert Colonel Tokaev that such a weapon would make it 'easier for us to talk to the great shop-keeper Harry Truman and keep him pinned down where we want him'. He added, whether from sincerity, or from self-justification, or from sensitivity to some expression on the independent-minded Tokaev's face, 'You see, we live in an insane epoch.' In fact, the German engineers were not of much use, and the Soviet rocket programme owed most of its success to the native genius of Sergei Korolev. But this was later, and meanwhile Anglo-American air superiority was overwhelming.

Stalin's thinking on international relations at this time had two contradictory strains. On the one hand, as Khrushchev tells us, he wished to avoid war with America. On the other hand, perhaps in other moods, all his international actions, while not enough to secure his victory outside Eastern Europe, were enough to provoke the maximum resistance and mobilization by America and the other Western countries. He got the disadvantage of confrontation, and few of its possible fruits.

This has, understandably enough, been described as irrational. He should, on this view, have compromised and waited. But that is to ignore a more profound motivation. The Cold War was being waged not only against the West and non-Communist countries everywhere, but also against non-Communist ideas in the Soviet Union. And this was in essence a single campaign necessary, or so Stalin thought, to his survival.

Stalin's conduct of this first phase of the Cold War had certain peculiarities. It was sometimes carefully prepared, though occasionally erratic. Its moves were always aggressive and led to critical situations, but after the danger had declared itself, a belated prudence held Stalin back from the brink. His sense of realism, though shaky, was still just adequate. He continued to watch for his opportunities while putting a huge investment into political campaigns aimed at disorientating the Western public.

6

In these postwar years, Stalin was aging ever more noticeably. People who had not seen him since the immediate postwar months were struck by a marked slowing-down. These beginnings of a deterioration in his health seem in part to be attributable to his style of living.

Apart from being a heavy smoker, of both pipe and cigarettes, he was increasingly confined to a cycle of work and relaxation far from conducive to fitness. He had always been accustomed to rising late, working through the early part of the evening, and then staying up to dreary and endless dinners with his often miserable cronies, only going to bed around dawn. (A recent Soviet account speaks of his insomnia.) And since the ministers thus had to observe his hours, the same applied to the ministries they controlled and hence to the whole higher apparatus whose members might expect a summons until late in the night. One result was what was called the 'Kremlin complexion', pallid but blotched with red, which Stalin himself increasingly showed over these years.

The routine was that after arriving in the Kremlin from his dacha Stalin would call a more or less official meeting in his office and discuss political matters. A film, or sometimes two films, would be presented by successive heads of the film industry. Sometimes the meeting in the office was dispensed with, and discussion took place between reels in the film theatre. Stalin liked cowboy films; Khrushchev tells us, 'He used to curse them and give them proper ideological evaluation, but then immediately order new ones.' And he also liked new Soviet films which showed him as the main hero of the Civil War, or gave a picture of immense prosperity in the collective farms. Other types of film were also shown. Khrushchev mentions a historical film about a pirate captain who manages to get rid of his comrades one by one, throwing them overboard. Stalin commented favourably on the captain's cunning way with political rivals.

Not that every single evening was spent in this way. Sometimes Stalin, with others of his entourage, went to the theatre or the opera, a difficult operation for the security forces, but usually decorous enough – though Shostakovich tells of a (non-public) occasion when Stalin, Voroshilov, Zhdanov and others, all drunk, sang with the soloists of the Bolshoi, Stalin conducting. But such outings were now rare and became rarer.

On the usual evening, the film would be over by one or two in the morning, and Stalin would then 'suggest' dinner. The group would go to the Kuntsevo dacha in their armour-plated cars, taking a different route each time.

There are a number of descriptions of these glumly festive evenings, made particularly unentertaining because, as Bulganin once remarked to Khrushchev when they were on their way to such an occasion, Stalin's subordinates never knew if they would end the night at home or in the Lubyanka.

There were never women among those attending the dinners. Waitresses served the meal, but Stalin was suspicious even of them. The Polish Stalinist leader Jakub Berman mentions one of them stopping for a moment as she served the dishes. 'Suddenly Stalin burst out: "What's she listening to?"' As Berman points out, it was an extraordinary sign of his mistrustful nature, as all these girls had been 'checked a thousand times over'.

Stalin would not take a dish until someone else had eaten a portion – though again, the security coverage of the food and its preparation was very thorough.

When the waitresses had gone, things became a little more relaxed. Endless toasts went round. Crude jokes were played, particularly on Poskrebyshev. Tomatoes were put on chairs people were about to sit in, and so on. Djilas mentions one occasion where they all had to guess the temperature, and drink a slug of vodka for every degree they were out. Beria was the life and soul (in so far as there was any life or soul) of the party. He sniggeringly recommended pepper vodka as stimulating the sex glands. He jeered at the older Bulgarian Communist Kolarov as a doddering veteran – though in fact Kolarov, whom the present writer met later, was mentally active, but merely depressed by his surroundings. Stalin (who himself drank comparatively little at this time) might now play the gramophone. Once he played a record with a coloratura singer accompanied by the yowling and barking of dogs. He laughed 'immoderately' and when Djilas failed to respond he said, 'Well, still, it's clever, devilishly clever.'

With the music on, there was womanless dancing. Stalin would occasionally jig a few steps, but did not join in though he appeared to enjoy the scene – where, for example, Berman danced with Molotov, the latter 'leading'. On this occasion Molotov took the opportunity to whisper to Berman a warning about being 'infiltrated by various hostile organizations'. And so the hours would slowly pass.

One New Year's Eve some time in this last period, Stalin drank more wine than usual, and he, Voroshilov, Kaganovich, Bulganin and

Khrushchev were dancing clumsily when (Khrushchev tells us) Svetlana Stalin came in and Stalin made her dance, though she showed little enthusiasm and soon left the floor. Stalin dragged her back (by her hair if Khrushchev has it right), and forced her to go on participating in the unwelcome fun.

Even the holidays in Sochi or elsewhere in the south were much the same (though not all the leadership would be regularly present). After watching a few films, 'the whole crowd would come to dinner, Beria, Malenkov, Zhdanov, Bulganin and the rest', his daughter notes, adding that it was 'dull and exhausting' to listen 'for three or four hours' to the same old talk. Once, when the Hungarian Communist leader Rakosi was with them in Sochi and complained of the drunkenness, Stalin managed to get him totally intoxicated, and was delighted at this success.

Except for these occasional outsiders, Stalin's circle was now limited to a set of Stalinists as narrow personally as they were doctrinally. Molotov and Kaganovich, Zhdanov and Beria and the other Politburo members were drab and servile conformists. The Yugoslavs noted that they still seemed to feel themselves to be, in some way, a conspiracy against their countrymen. Their fear of and 'vigilance' against external and internal foes was matched by their fear of, and vigilance against, Stalin.

Of course, they were themselves under constant security supervision. Stalin is reported insisting, if Poskrebyshev took more than five or ten minutes to make his tea, on having it tested by the chemical kit originally provided by Yagoda and now used by Beria's men. But this seems to have been more a way of bullying Poskrebyshev than a serious suspicion. In general, while occasionally losing his temper with Poskrebyshev, and setting him up as a drunken butt for his companions' humour in the evening, he continued to rely on him until late in 1952.

With Beria, Stalin's relationship was similar, if on a slightly subtler plane. The gruesome Beria was almost a master of ceremonies at the Kuntsevo soirees. He was on comparatively easy terms with Stalin, and was often quick-witted enough to evade Stalin's wrath. Not always. Stalin, like a bandit chief, liked to be free not only to curse, but actually to assault, at least some of his closest subordinates. He would sometimes insult Beria, slap his cheek, or throw tea in his face.

As to Stalin's rudeness and coarseness with subordinates, Khrushchev comments:

'Stalin's character was brutish, and his temper was harsh; but his brutishness didn't always imply malice toward people to whom he acted so rudely. His was a sort of inborn brutishness. He was coarse and abusive with everyone. I often experienced his rudeness myself. Stalin liked me. If he hadn't liked me or if he had felt the slightest suspicion toward me, he could have gotten rid of me anytime he pleased in the same way he got rid of so many people who were undesirable to him. More than once, after being rude or spiteful to me, he would express his good will.'

With the rudeness, at least the victim knew where he was. As Khrushchev implies, the sly provocations were more difficult to handle. In any case, Stalin preferred Beria's (and Khrushchev's) clowning to facing his inability to know what a subordinate really felt. In one of his moroser moods he would look at a man and say, 'Why are your eyes so shifty today?' or 'Why are you turning so much today and avoiding looking me directly in the eyes?'

Of course, he could hardly demand even mild frankness. It must have been irritating for him to see the sycophantic reaction when (to take a minor example) he spoke of his Siberian exile, and told of having come across a number of birds perched on a bough, shooting some of them, but (being short of ammunition) having to ski back for eight miles to get more, and on return finding the remaining birds in the same position and shooting them. No one made any comment, though when Stalin had left Beria said to Khrushchev, 'He's lying.' But (unless Beria was merely into a period-piece 'provocation') no one could have thought of it as a lie, rather than a tale not even expected to be believed, an old-fashioned example of the 'fisherman's story' type.

The atmosphere, in any case, was not one of off-duty banter and chat between comrades, and can hardly be seen as providing rest and relaxation.

7

As Stalin extended his rule over Eastern Europe he had to work through the existing Communist Parties. Their representatives with the Comintern in Moscow had been thoroughly purged in the 1930s. Indeed, the Polish Communist Party had actually been dissolved and all its Central Committee executed, and its reconstitution was a hard job.

In most cases local leaderships had remained and operated underground for years, not always in effective contact with Moscow, and in any case developing the habit of making decisions on the spot. All anti-Stalinist factions had long since been removed, and Stalin was for these parties the movement's world leader and hero; and they accepted the Stalinist dogmas. But they had still not fully absorbed the Stalinist spirit and habits of mind.

This was, of course, especially true of Yugoslavia, where Tito had built up his own partisan movement over several years of fighting, and brought it to power, in part but not wholly with Soviet help.

On 12 August 1947, Stalin wrote a letter to Tito criticizing a Yugoslav–Bulgarian pact which, he said, could only encourage further Western military intervention in Greece and Turkey. More generally, he seems to have felt that things were getting out of hand in Eastern Europe. To replace the defunct Comintern, at least up to a point, he now founded the Cominform, a supposedly consultative body of the Soviet, East European, French and Italian Communist Parties, with headquarters in Belgrade. It issued a periodical which Stalin personally christened *For a Lasting Peace, For a People's Democracy*, on the grounds that the Western press would have to repeat this slogan every time it quoted from it – though in fact it was always referred to merely as the *Cominform Journal*.

Early in 1948, Stalin summoned the Yugoslav and Bulgarian Communists to Moscow. He criticized the veteran Bulgarian leader Georgi Dimitrov for an idea he had made public without consulting Moscow, of an East European federation, 'chattering like women from the housetops whatever occurs to you', and he went on to denounce a phrase (from a Yugoslav–Bulgarian agreement) about action 'against all hotbeds of aggression', condemning this as 'preventive war – the commonest Komsomol stunt; a tawdry phrase which only brings grist to the enemy's mill' (not, in fact, a bad analysis). The Yugoslavs, to whom he had previously said that they could 'swallow' Albania if they wished, he now attacked for agreeing to send troops into Albania without Soviet consent. He also took them to task for supporting the Greek Communist rebellion: it had no chance because 'the United States is directly engaged there – the strongest state in the world'.

We may parenthetically consider this point. Greece was indeed strategically crucial to the West, and Stalin's later challenges were in areas he probably considered not vital to Western security – Berlin and Korea. But it is also striking that he refers to America as the most powerful state in the world, without reservations about the Soviet Union's power.

It would perhaps be a mistake to think of this merely as a matter of the atomic bomb, which in any case was soon to be in Soviet hands. Stalin's Marxism, and the experience of the war would certainly have led him (rightly) to view the USA as being the overwhelming economic power in the world, and hence, unless diverted or prevented, or outflanked, destined to remain the 'most powerful'.

Bulgaria was, in fact, firmly under control. It was the Yugoslavs who provoked Stalin's real suspicions. His attempts to secure full Stalinist power in Yugoslavia were failures. Tito and his entourage were loyal Stalinists, but resented clumsy efforts by Soviet ambassadors, secret policemen and others to take over their party and state and enforce every petty whim of Moscow's – in particular by creating their own faction in the leadership and elsewhere. Within weeks all sorts of minor incidents were provoked, and in March came the first of a series of letters, in Stalin's personal style, accusing Tito and his entourage.

First it was a matter of the undemocratic way the Yugoslav party was run, and the excessive powers of the secret police, together with anti-Soviet attitudes on the part of some Yugoslav officials. It developed into harangues about Tito's 'groundless denial of facts and documents' and warnings that 'in his time Trotsky also rendered revolutionary services ... We think that the political career of Trotsky is quite instructive.' And indeed, Tito became a major villain almost at Trotsky's level in Stalin's personal psychodrama.

The Cominform condemned or expelled the Yugoslavs, who continued to insist that they were good Stalinists, and to send greetings to Stalin from their conferences, until Moscow started attacking Tito and his colleagues as old Gestapo spies and agents.

When Stalin wrote the first of these letters he told Khrushchev, 'I will shake my little finger and there will be no more Tito.' In fact, there were total devotees within the Yugoslav party and its leadership (two members of the Politburo, the Chief of Staff and others) and Tito and his friends had problems. But Stalin had miscalculated. Nor were MGB assassination plans successful – one while Tito and his Politburo were playing billiards, one on the boat taking him to his favourite island resort.

Stalin seems to have thought of war on Yugoslavia. A leading Czechoslovak Communist definitely says that Rakosi in Hungary planned such a war, and of course not as an independent initiative. It is, in fact, reported that Stalin was given an invasion plan by his then Chief of Staff, but consulted more experienced officers now in semi-disgrace, and found their objections cogent. A mistake on the level of the Finnish debacle would have been disastrous.

The whole episode shows Stalin at his most incompetent. The Yugoslavs, while not totally servile, had been completely committed to the Soviet side. Tito, in fact, could never have become an enemy but for the steps Stalin took when he suspected that possibility. The Yugoslavs' forced defection weakened Stalin not only in Eastern Europe, but in world opinion everywhere.

There were to be failures with Yugoslavia in other spheres too. In 1952 Yugoslavia and the USSR were drawn to play against each other in the soccer Olympics. Moscow considered a boycott, but after Stalin's Komsomol chief, N. A. Mikhailov, had checked over the names of the Soviet team, and the organizers had promised victory, the game went ahead. The Soviets lost and the team was disbanded by Malenkov and Beria as having 'dishonoured themselves and the entire nation and all people working for peace'.

Stalin, meanwhile, had gone on to tighten his grip on the parties of the rest of the Soviet bloc. Everywhere, from now until the end of his life, large groups of plotters were exposed in their top leaderships. In purges supervised by high Soviet police officers, agents of Tito, of the West, and (earlier) of the Gestapo were exposed. Laszlo Rajk, Minister of the Interior, was tortured and made to confess at a public trial in Budapest. Traicho Kostov, Secretary of the Bulgarian party, was tried, but withdrew his confession in open court in Sofia – Stalin is said to have been very angry at this dereliction of duty, and as a result Kostov was tortured to death (in a fashion Dr Vaksberg, who has recorded the frightful beatings and bonebreakings meted out to the great Soviet theatre producer Meyerhold and others, cannot bring himself to describe). Wladislaw Gomulka, Secretary of the Polish Communist Party, had made a bad impression on Stalin when they met. 'He sits there all the time looking into my eyes as though he were searching for something. And why does he bring a notepad and pencil with him? Why does he write down every word I say?' He was now transmuted into a spy and a Titoite, and only avoided trial by failing to confess even as late as February 1953, just before Stalin's death.

Even the good Stalinists like President Bierut of Poland were not entirely satisfactory. Bierut more than once asked Stalin what had happened to missing Polish Communists in the USSR. Stalin, as with his answers to the London Poles about the Katyn officers, said that perhaps they were somewhere in the country, and ordered Beria to find them. The last time Bierut asked, however, Beria took him aside afterwards and said 'Why are you fucking around with Iosif Vissarionovich? You fuck off and leave him alone. That's my advice to you, or you'll regret it.' Bierut took the hint.

8

The break with Tito coincided with, and was in part connected with, a political upset in Moscow. By June 1948, Zhdanov had been replaced as 'second' secretary of the Central Committee, that is as Stalin's chief aide, by Malenkov. Zhdanov died within weeks – but though it was later alleged that he had been murdered, there is no credible evidence of this.

Zhdanov himself, like Yezhov before him, had had little personality of his own except for servility and cruelty, and had never been one of Stalin's boon companions. In fact, at a dinner in 1947 Stalin shouted angrily that Zhdanov was sitting there unsociably, 'looking like Jesus Christ'. Zhdanov, for reasons of health, could not drink, and Stalin liked his guests to drink freely, no doubt in part in order to loosen the tongues of potential troublemakers. He did not like non-drinkers for the same reason that Caesar, in Shakespeare, distrusted thin men. Let me have men about me that are drunk, might have been Stalin's motto.

Beria and Malenkov were now able to persuade Stalin to abandon the whole Zhdanovite group. No public trial took place. Voznesensky, Kuznetsov and the others were removed early in 1949, tortured severely, and shot in 1950 in the secret 'Leningrad Case' (one of the Leningrad party secretaries had had technical training in Britain, and hence was vulnerable as a 'British spy', though there were other charges too).

Stalin had abolished the death penalty in 1947, apparently to please Western opinion, though some executions seem still to have taken place. Early in 1950, 'in response to numerous demands by workers' he restored it, with a view to coping with the new wave of treachery in the top leadership.

The task Stalin had set the Zhdanovites in 1946 had in any case been fully accomplished. The manifestations of the popular longing for a normal society had been silenced and crushed. The system as now consolidated may be defined as High Stalinism; a state of things as near to the achievement of his political aims as Stalin was ever to reach.

9

By 1948 an ingredient that had always been latent in Stalin's mind started to be all-pervasive: anti-Semitism.

Stalin had shown some anti-Semitic tendencies early on. But these really began to develop during World War II. The Jewish Social Democratic Bund activist, Lucjan Blit, told the present writer that when he and his comrades were arrested in eastern Poland after the Soviet occupation in 1939, they were treated very badly by the NKVD, but the curses and imprecations never had any racial tone. When they were reinterrogated in 1942–3, anti-Semitic abuse had become the norm. This can hardly be seen as other than the effect of unofficial but clear signals from higher up.

The Bolsheviks had always politically opposed and repressed the Bund (though when its leaders, Ehrlich and Alter, were shot in 1941 it was on the more Stalinist – and less plausible – charge that they had urged Soviet soldiers to desert to Hitler). To the end Stalin maintained that he opposed Jews who were Bundists, or religious activists, or 'cosmopolitans', or secessionists, or Zionists, or agents of American–Israeli organizations, but was not against Jews as such. On the contrary, he had provided them with a Jewish Autonomous Region (in an inhospitable corner of Siberia, which attracted only a few thousand hopeful immigrants).

Stalin's attitude from 1942–3 seems to have been based in part on what he took to be Hitler's successful use of anti-Semitic demagogy. It was certainly also due to his increasing Russian nationalism, to which he felt most, or many, Jews were not truly assimilable. And the idea of a special Jewish predilection for capitalism is of course to be found in Marx.

During the war Stalin, as so often, had it both ways. A Jewish Anti-Fascist Committee was set up and its leaders visited the United States and worked to secure international Jewish support for the Soviet Union. But as early as November 1946, Mikhail Suslov sent Stalin a note on the Committee's 'harmful activity'.

A year or so later Soviet officials were, though not publicly, boasting that Zhdanov had 'purged all the Jews from the Central Committee machine', and that the Deputy Chief of General Staff, Antonov, had been 'exposed as being of Jewish origin'. Jews were barred from the diplomatic service and from judicial office, while quotas were set on Jewish entry to academic education.

It was early in 1948 that Stalin ordered in strict secrecy his first actual murder of a Jewish leader. Instructions were given to Lavrenti Tsanava, secret-police chief in Byelorussia, to liquidate Solomon Mikhoels, the great Yiddish actor and director whose world fame had led to prominence in the Jewish Anti-Fascist Committee and a visit to the USA under its auspices.

The killing of Mikhoels, together with his colleague Golubev, was represented as an accident, and he was publicly mourned, as Kirov had been. Stalin, striking this ruthless blow at Jewry, was not yet quite prepared for an open breach. This seems mainly to have been due in part at least to his current manœuvres to use Israel, whose statehood he had been the first to recognize, against the West.

In the autumn of 1948 Golda Meir arrived in Moscow as Israeli ambassador. A huge crowd of Jews turned out to greet her on Rosh Hashanah. On 8 November she was warmly welcomed at a diplomatic reception by Polina Molotov, herself a member of the Jewish Anti-Fascist Committee.

For Stalin this public and private demonstration of Jewish feeling seems to have been the last straw. One of the projects the Jewish Anti-Fascist Committee had undertaken was the joint publication in Russian, English and Yiddish of *The Black Book* on the Nazi Holocaust. The Soviet editors were Ilya Ehrenburg and Vasily Grossman. Its printing plates were now destroyed and it never appeared in the Soviet Union. As to the Committee itself, on 20 November 1948 it was abolished on Politburo orders, and most of its members were arrested.

This was all done without public announcement. But an open, full-scale campaign of attacks on Jewish culture and attitudes, and on Zionism, soon began in the press. The theme was that the country's values were being undermined by 'rootless cosmopolitans'. There was a particularly vicious assault on theatre critics, eventually described as an 'anti-party group'. When their Russianized names or pseudonyms were given, the original Jewish name was printed in brackets, and papers asked how anyone so named could understand Russian culture.

Meanwhile unpublicized arrests, especially of writers in Yiddish, continued, and there was a general growth of public anti-Jewish pressure.

Among those arrested at the end of 1948 was Polina Molotov.

10

It says something for the bizarre nature of Stalin's character, and of Politburo circumstances in general, that many of his *convives* had wives and relatives in jail or shot. Polina Molotov was not the first. Yekaterina Kalinin, wife of Mikhail Kalinin, who was Soviet Head of State until his death in 1946, was in labour camp after having been beaten unconscious by a woman NKVD officer in Beria's presence. Poskrebyshev's wife Bronislava was imprisoned for three years and then shot, in spite of his pleas. Kaganovich's brother, charged (though a Jew) with having been Hitler's nominee for head of a Fascist Russia, had managed to shoot himself in Mikoyan's lavatory. And several others, including Khrushchev, had relatives in jail. It does seem extraordinary that, highly suspicious as he always was, Stalin did not consider that such blows at their nearest and dearest might at a minimum cause a certain awkwardness, and more importantly turn his colleagues into implacable secret enemies. This does not appear to have happened, so to that extent Stalin was right. But it still seems odd that he did not think it necessary to play safe and either refrain from these arrests or remove the husbands from power.

One answer Stalin could have given any colleague protesting against the maltreatment of relatives was that at least he treated his own just as ruthlessly. When his brother-in-law Alexander Svanidze was arrested, his wife went too: their eight-year-old son shouted at them as they were carried off, 'You are enemies of the people, I disavow you!' But he was himself arrested when he was older.

On the Svanidze side Stalin's sister-in-law, Maria Svanidze (Alexander's sister), had been Yenukidze's secretary. She died in prison. As to the Alliluyevs, Nadezhda Stalin's sister Anna had, as we saw, become a little crazed after her unsuccessful pleas in favour of her doomed husband Stanislav Redens. However, in 1946 she published the reminiscences from which we have quoted in connection with Stalin's pre-revolutionary life. Though in no way hostile to Stalin, these were not in accord with recent presentations of him as a faultless paragon. However, it was over a year before *Pravda*, in a review entitled 'Irresponsible Fabrications' evidently drafted by Stalin himself, or from his notes, blasted the book, which was soon impossible to obtain.

In 1948 Anna was arrested, together with Yevgenia, widow of Nadezhda Stalin's brother Pavel. Stalin told his daughter that they 'talked too much'. But there were other charges, and they were both connected, through Jewish friends, to the new Jewish conspiracies. They both got ten years for espionage (and were released in 1954 after Stalin's death).

As to Stalin's family life with his close relatives, it hardly existed. He had reluctantly allowed Svetlana to marry a Jew, Grigori Morozov, as her first husband, but refused to meet him – and though much taken with his new grandson, seldom saw the baby or its mother. When Svetlana got her first divorce and married Zhdanov's son, Stalin had been fairly pleased, but made no trouble about the second divorce which followed.

When Svetlana was ill and reproached him for not caring he wrote her a warm letter, but the comparative intimacy of their relationship before her affair with Kapler was never restored. In 1948 Stalin told her that her first husband had been 'thrown her way by the Zionists'. When she said that the younger Jews cared nothing for Zionism he retorted, 'No! you don't understand ... the entire older generation is contaminated with Zionism and now they're teaching the young people too.'

In November of that year Svetlana visited Stalin on his holiday in the south. Once he lost his temper and called her a 'parasite' in front of everyone. The next day he started talking about her mother's suicide. 'What a miserable little pistol it was,' he remarked, showing her with his fingers just how small it had been. He spoke of Polina Molotov's bad influence. In 1951 Svetlana went down to Borzhomi for two weeks with her father, the last time he left Moscow. But, on each occasion, 'We had nothing to say to one another.' Still, she took her children to see him on his birthday on 21 December 1952, and found him more tolerant of her way of life, though the 'usual' people and talk and 'the same old jokes' depressed her.

As for Stalin's younger son Vasily, he continued to get undeserved promotion in the Air Force, becoming a lieutenant general at the age of twenty-nine – all this not because Stalin intervened for him, which he seems not to have done, but because it was seldom that anyone dared do otherwise. Bulganin, Malenkov, Beria and Kaganovich did him favours. He became a hopeless alcoholic, and fell in with a circle of crooks and adulators. In 1952 he grossly mismanaged the ceremonial fly-past, and Stalin personally had him removed from his post, referring to him as an 'ignoramus' and a 'dolt'. After Stalin's death he was imprisoned (under the name Vasil Pavlovich Vasiliev) though later released, reimprisoned, and finally allowed to live in Kazan, where he died of his excesses at the age of forty-one.

Vasily's character was simply not strong enough to stand the pressures and strains of being the son of the autocrat. There are many similar cases in history.

Svetlana's character was strong. But all in all it is difficult to dispute Khrushchev's surprisingly shrewd and sympathetic summing-up: 'He loved her, but he used to express these feelings of love in a beastly way. His was the tenderness of a cat for a mouse. He broke the heart first of a child, then of a young girl, then of a woman and mother.'

11

Stalin's running of the country by decisions taken at Politburo or cabinet meetings was erratic. Sometimes he was well briefed and would give careful consideration to the details and technicalities. Sometimes he was only told what he wanted to hear, very distorted versions of reality. One extraordinary example of the conflict between his wishes and the refractory facts was a vast project in the far north. In 1947 Stalin chanced to remark at a meeting of the Council of Ministers, that 'the Russian people had long dreamed of having a safe outlet to the Arctic Ocean'.

The result was what is now called in Russia 'the Railway of Death'. For more than four years, in subfreezing temperatures in winter, and swamps and mosquitoes in summer, scores of thousands of forced labourers worked at a railway to Igarka. There were more than eighty campsites, along a 1300-kilometre stretch of tundra. It was even planned to extend the whole project into an Arctic Trans-Siberian railway, right across the north. In the end 850 kilometres of rail were constructed, at enormous cost of money as well as lives. After Stalin's death the whole thing was abandoned, and the line and its equipment were left to rust in the snow – until the glasnost era, when photographs of this vast wastage, including derelict locomotives, appeared in the Russian press. There were photographs, too, of the endless cemeteries of those who, in the words of the organ of the Soviet government, died of 'intolerable toil, cold and starvation, unheard-of degradation and humiliation'.

As Lytton Strachey remarks, the acts of arbitrary government are apt to be 'disgraceful and absurd'. This was particularly so when big decisions were made in what can only be described as a frivolous manner. On one occasion in the Council of Ministers, Stalin handed round major economic plans and said sternly, 'Any objections?'; when no one answered he broke up the meeting to see a film, remarking gleefully to Khrushchev and the others that he had 'properly fooled' the governmental chiefs.

As ever, films played an important role in his daily life, in some ways more important than reality. But he was also concerned that a reasonable flow of ideologically and historically correct films should reach the Soviet public. The great director Eisenstein was summoned in February 1947 and strongly harangued about errors in his *Ivan the Terrible*. He had represented Ivan's frightful secret police, the *oprichnina*, in a bad light, while they had really been a 'progressive army'. Ivan himself had not been given enough credit as a 'great and wise ruler': in particular (unlike Peter the Great) he had excluded foreign influence. 'Ivan the Terrible was very ruthless,' said Stalin. 'One can show that he was ruthless. But you must show why it was necessary to be ruthless.' After various detailed comments Eisenstein was sent back to remake the film.

Ever-increasing attention was also given to modern films celebrating the Revolution and the 1941–5 war, with Stalin in major parts. The actor Mikhail Gelovani acted Stalin in several of these, and the strain, he complained to intimates, was intense, though he managed to satisfy Stalin – being, apart from anything else, a handsomer screen presence than the reality, as Stalin admitted. Stalin had certain sensitivities about his appearance – about his height, of course, but also on lesser points. When Djilas, back in Yugoslavia after his second meeting with Stalin, wrote an article about him, it was well received, but the Soviet representative conveying this praise added that 'in subsequent editions I ought to cut out the observation that Stalin's feet were too big'.

Stalin took special care to oversee army and air force films. On one occasion the head of the state film committee, Bolshakov, had the film *Zhukovski*, about the Russian air pioneer, ready for release by Air Force Day. He could not find Stalin (then in the Caucasus) to get his formal approval. When he asked Molotov and Beria, he was told to take his own decision. He released the film. Stalin, on his return, called a meeting of the Politburo, with Bolshakov in attendance. Stalin asked him on what authority he had released *Zhukovski*. Bolshakov, white and trembling, said he had consulted and decided.

'You consulted and decided,' said Stalin quietly but ominously. 'You consulted and decided,' he repeated. He got up, went to the door, opened it, and once again said, 'You decided.' He went out and shut the door and there was a tense silence.

After a pause, Stalin opened the door, looked back into the room and said, 'You decided correctly.'

12

In this way Stalin approached his seventieth birthday on 21 December 1949, a day of vast public celebration, with the image of his face projected on to a large blimp overhanging the Kremlin, and in myriad variants elsewhere in the country. Below or beside these dominating icons the citizenry demonstrated their gratitude and happiness in every city's main square and in every village's main street. Everywhere there were lengthy parades of soldiers and gymnasts, of happy girl Komsomols in their neckerchiefs, and merry workers in dungarees, with float after float without exception illustrating achievements and joys only achievable under Soviet rule, and gratitude for them to Stalin personally, like some monomaniac Mardi Gras. The newspapers carried hundreds of articles, the radios put out scores of programmes, about his whole career, from childhood in Gori to world leadership.

This was merely the high point in the constant campaign of which we have already seen the launching and spread. We may confine ourselves to two examples of the later period. Stalin authorized 33 tons of copper for a statue on the (slave-built) Volga–Don Canal. And, more remarkable than such local manifestations, he wrote himself into the Soviet national anthem:

> Stalin who raised us to trust in the people
> It was he who inspired us to great words and deeds ...

We have to envisage a cult so pervasive and inordinate that the whole party and country were swamped – and it spilled over into the outside world too.

One final monument to Stalin was never to be completed – a fully Stalinized city of Moscow. We have seen how the first steps in his style of modernization had been taken in the 1930s. Now much was changed to his satisfaction – and more was planned.

He is reported to have been irritated, looking out from his new office in the Kremlin, at the sight of the handsome old-style building of the British Embassy, just across the river. But in other directions there now rose the ring of tall buildings surrounding central Moscow – the university, the Foreign Ministry, the Ukraina Hotel and the others, all with his personal sponsorship.

This style is often called 'Stalinist wedding-cake'; that gives an impression, no doubt, of tastelessness, but yet of delicacy or sentimentality. On the contrary, these buildings look above all like heavy projections of inhuman power. They remind one of the cover of a science-fiction magazine of the 1930s showing, in full colour, fortresses from which implacable alien invaders have established their grip on earth's cities, ready with beam-weapons at the pinnacles to burn down any revolt. Such an illustration would combine the sense of mere un-arguable power with the idea of a totally non-human style, but neverthe-less a style. It is sinister and oppressive in the extreme (even though, in those stories, the yoke of apparently invincible aliens was usually, in the long run, overthrown by human effort).

Though Stalinism has gone, Stalinist architecture remains. But Moscow was spared the worst. A plan adopted by the Soviet government in 1935 had called for big changes in Red Square. Now, in June 1947, the official Committee on Architectural Affairs held a meeting to discuss the next stage. The whole area would be transformed. All the buildings surrounding Red Square, including St Basil's Cathedral, would be pulled down, and the Square and its extension renamed 'Mausoleum Prospect'. This would be dominated by a Monument to Victory, incorporating a 'statue of Stalin, personifying victory'. Some members of the Committee suggested that the Kremlin would have to go. Perhaps it would all have been ready for Stalin's eightieth birthday.

But Stalin was already noticeably far into the aging process. Though he retained his grip on matters essential to his power he began, for example, momentarily to forget the names even of close colleagues he was addressing. His brain, according to his autopsy in 1953, had been affected by arteriosclerosis for at least five years. He himself took to mentioning his aging to Politburo members, who always denied it and declared that he looked fine.

He became increasingly concerned with the prolongation of life, at least of his own life. He had earlier shown great interest in the 'longevity serum' of a Dr Alexander Bogomolets. Bogomolets claimed that a man like Stalin could live until he was 150 or so. Unfortunately Bogomolets himself died at the age of sixty-five – though it was explained that for some physiological reason he had been unable to take his own serum.

Other longevity studies became common, with a special Ger-ontological Institute in the North Caucasus set up to investigate the many aged people of the area. In the public media a more amateur optimism was even greater. A 1948 play about Stalingrad, *The Great Days* by Nikolai Virta, is reported to have been edited by Stalin himself; it says that he will live to be a hundred.

And now new experts came forward. In 1949 the particularly fraudulent G. M. Boshyan obtained wide state and party support for some work on the alleged crystallization of bacteria, and hence the origin of life – a field closely connected with longevity research. (At this time there was also work done not merely on longevity but actually on immortality in a Romanian laboratory favoured by the Soviets.) But the most remarkable new pseudoscience was that of the aged Old Bolshevik Olga Lepeshinskaya. Scientifically illiterate even by Lysenkoite standards, she had attended some courses for medical assistants in the 1890s. In 1949 she announced that the theory of cells as the basis of life, well established even before she was born, was a mistake, and that albumenous matter without cellular organization had living form – as Engels had vaguely held. Her theory affected Stalin in a personal way, for she was much concerned with 'rejuvenation', for which she recommended dissolving a bag of soda in one's bath or alternatively a soda enema. Lepeshinskaya herself lived until she was ninety-two, whether as a result of her prescription or not is unknown.

Stalin supported her. By 1951 her ideas were compulsorily promulgated by the Ministry of Education. She was awarded the Stalin Prize and elected to the Academy of Medical Sciences. No one dared oppose her, and a number of venal academics helped forward her cause.

Such incidents, and they occurred in many spheres of science, have their comic side indeed. But they were tragic enough for those who opposed them. They, and their terroristic enforcement, were extraordinarily damaging to Soviet science – and even, as in Lysenko's case, to the economy. Stalin's sponsorship continues to show a mind persuaded by erroneous argument in spheres he did not properly understand, obstinate in error, and error of a recognizable type – crackpot pseudoscience.

Physics was submitted to a milder variant of dogmatism. Relativity theory and quantum mechanics were attacked by ideological bullies as 'idealistic'. But when physicists working on the atomic bomb were asked their views of quantum theory, and replied that whether it was true or not its equations were useful in their practical work, they were not disturbed. It was even the case that this was virtually the only sphere where Jewish scientists of repute went almost untouched through the anti-Semitic period – a sign of the limits beyond which ideology and caprice still met pragmatic resistance in Stalin's mind.

Stalin also rejected Western psychological theory, and the work of the great Russian physiologist Ivan Pavlov was made central. Pavlov had in fact loathed the Soviet regime, and over the early 1930s, until his death in 1935, had written to Molotov and others to protest against 'repressions'.

His study of 'conditioned reflexes' was then regarded by the Soviet authorities as mechanistic rather than Marxist, failing to deal with the human consciousness. But in the postwar period a new Soviet psychology, strongly opposed to Freudian and all other Western schools, accepted the Pavlovian idea, merely adding that the consciousness, as well as 'animal' behaviour, could be conditioned by outside pressures, defined as 'social'. This of course was an academicizing of the Stalinist – or more generally Marxist – notion that socio-economic relations determine consciousness. Like Lysenkoist biology, it reflected the Stalinist doctrine that the new order was creating the 'new Soviet man' with characteristics different from, and superior to, those of others. This transformation of the human mind, of the human species, appears to have been among Stalin's most powerful aims and convictions.

In one sphere, to be fair, Stalin denounced pseudoscience and returned to science. As we saw, since the early thirties the pseudo-linguistics of N. Marr, who amongst his other absurdities held that language was a class phenomenon, had been accepted as the truly Marxist view. Stalin had so far only shown a mild interest in linguistics. For example, he had chanced to remark that the Azerbaijanis were obviously descended from the Medes. As a result linguists had worked for years trying to find Median words in Azeri. A Soviet linguist later explained: 'Eventually thirty-five dubious Median words were found, although the Median language itself is mythical.' All trivial enough. But in 1950 Stalin suddenly published, in his own name, a ten-thousand-word article on linguistics. He condemned the Marrists, not only for their views but also for ignoring 'the clash of ideas' and 'freedom of opinion' without which (he declared) 'no science can develop and prosper'. The Marrists, he was horrified to have to point out, had formed 'a closed group of infallible leaders' and 'acted in a wilful, high-handed manner'. The Marrists were at once removed from the many academic positions they had acquired. Stalin's own stand for freedom did not, however, cause a revival of independence in any other field.

The incident is mainly relevant to Stalin's career as curious evidence not so much of his amateur interest in the field, as in many others, but of long work and thought about what amounted to a hobby, to some degree distracting him from the rest of his acts and thoughts. It is true that his power and prestige were now such that he hardly needed to devote all his energies to the hunting down of the enemy. Still, while the indulgence of such diversions, or idiosyncrasies, as his linguistic studies are of interest in showing an aspect of his mind, they did not divert him substantially from his main concerns. Many men of action take up such hobbies when they retire. But the septuagenarian Stalin, far from having retirement in mind, was preparing further devastating blows against Jews, against his Politburo colleagues, against Eastern European Communists, against the West, and against the Soviet citizenry itself.

Chapter 14

Last Years

So Stalin enters his last phase, possessed even more than before by the demons of suspicion and implacability. He was beginning to have bouts of dizziness, and his psychological condition too continued to deteriorate.

In 1951, in a moment of insight, Stalin actually said in front of Mikoyan and Khrushchev, though appearing not to notice them, 'I'm finished, I trust no one, not even myself.' His daughter writes that in these last years he had forgotten all human attachments, he was tortured by fears which became a genuine persecution mania, and in the end his strong nerves gave way. But the mania was not a sick fantasy; he knew and understood that he was hated, and he knew why.

His anti-Semitism became even more obsessive. This and other signs of increasing paranoia did not, however, in any way shake his grip on power, right up to the end. And whatever his basic physical and mental condition, foreigners he received only a few weeks before his death saw him as reasonably sharp and fit, and only noted that he was doodling wolves on his notepaper.

2

Though he had been frustrated in Europe, Stalin found opportunities in Asia – in Communist tradition the vulnerable flank of imperialism. But there were problems as well as opportunities.

In 1949, contrary to Stalin's predictions (and, apparently, to his wishes), Mao Tse-Tung had won the civil war in China. Stalin's envoys with the Chinese Communists had long been reporting anti-Soviet tendencies among the Maoists. Though no open breach could have been advantageous to either party, a formidable rival to Stalin for the laurels of destructive megalomania had established his power in a large country, outside the sphere of Stalin's real control.

In 1950 Mao came to Moscow, amid public rejoicing, to sign a Sino-Soviet Friendship Treaty. This was not a great success. The amenities were preserved, and Stalin was even induced, against his will and with vast security precautions, to attend a banquet given in his honour by Mao at the Metropole Hotel.

But (as a recent Soviet account has it), 'Mao asks for the atom bomb. Stalin refuses. They understand each other well. Mao asks because he does not have trust. Stalin refuses for the same reason.' Nor did Stalin's attempt to impose on China the 'joint' companies by which he was exploiting Eastern Europe succeed. Moreover Stalin, by no means mealy-mouthed himself, was offended by Mao's scatological crudities.

However, for the time being a certain accommodation was valuable to both. Mao continued to pay public lip-service to Stalin as leader of the world Communist movement. And Stalin made one gesture of good will, in denouncing to the Chinese his own main agent in the Chinese Politburo, Kao Kang, who was soon afterwards shot. How Stalin would have coped with Mao in the long run is unclear. The Chinese leader was to give later Soviet leaders a hard time.

Other Asian Communists were also striving for power. At the beginning of 1950 Ho Chi Minh came to Moscow from Vietnam. He annoyed Stalin by asking for his autograph, which Stalin later arranged to be secretly retrieved from Ho's luggage by the MGB, or so Khrushchev tells us. Ho, though much less ambiguously Stalinist than Mao, was in general treated rather contemptuously by Stalin.

More important, in March 1950 the equally devoted Stalinist Kim Il Sung came to Moscow from North Korea to get permission and support for his planned invasion of the South. Stalin held a Politburo meeting which Kim attended, and 'gave him the green light'.

When the attack took place, Gromyko tells us that it was Stalin who, contrary to his own diplomats' advice, ordered the Soviet delegation to the United Nations to boycott, rather than veto, that body's condemnation of the North Koreans. This has always seemed a tactical error, in that the Americans and their allies were able to fight under the United Nations banner. But it appears that Stalin did not want, at this stage, to clash openly on such an issue with the massive majority now mobilized against North Korea in that body, while after the promised quick victory the whole thing could be forgotten. Macarthur's unexpected destruction of the North Korean army in 'the last Cannae', following Truman's almost equally unexpected decision to fight, destroyed any such hope.

The war, especially after Stalin had as a last resort arranged for Chinese intervention, was both enormously destructive and full of danger to world peace. But Stalin had from the start ruled out any direct Soviet involvement. And the war in fact remained localized, though it was not settled until after Stalin's death. It almost certainly represents his being tempted, without adequate thought, into what appeared to be the simple seizure of a vulnerable point in the outer world; and it was not accompanied by crises in Europe and elsewhere.

What it was accompanied by, like all Stalin's postwar moves against the West, was a vast propaganda campaign in favour of peace and progress. Stalin had hit at what he saw as pro-Western voices inside the Soviet Union, and they were by now effectively silenced. But pro-Soviet voices in the West had a free run, and Stalin was able to accompany his political and military pressures on the West with a lavishly funded, multifarious, highly-organized attempt to win over the Western public. That the struggle against Stalinism had as a vital component the struggle for the Western mind had been understood by responsible Westerners soon after the end of World War Two. And their resistance was successful. But this had not been obvious from the start. It did not seem foreordained that the Italian Communist Party, or even the French Communist Party, would remain a minority; it was not certain that its semi-pacifist wing would not take over the British Labour Party. And so on.

Stalin's effort did indeed have its successes. For example, some socialists still thought of the USSR as superior because socialist; and in the USSR itself denial of access to reality by foreigners had been much more systematically and efficiently organized than in the pre-war years.

What eventually decided the issue was first that the people who knew most about Stalin and his regime overwhelmingly provided informed opposition to it; and second that, as Orwell said in another context, whatever intellectuals might think, 'no ordinary man could be such a fool' as to believe that nice words cancelled hostile acts or that dictatorship could be a sort of democracy.

Stalin's idea of peace and the 'peace campaign' was also the subject of much internal propaganda in the Stalinist countries themselves, though with equal emphasis on the necessity for military preparedness, the crushing of pacifist moods, and so on. The campaign about Western warmongering certainly frightened many people, but others saw through it. The Anglo-Hungarian humorous writer Georges Mikes has a story about the 'Sleep Campaign', in which there are mass demonstrations with drums and trumpets in the streets all night, shouting, 'Sleep! Sleep! Sleep is good for you! Sleep! Sleep! Sleep!'

Or again, as a well-known Soviet joke put it:

'Comrade, will there be a war?'
'No, comrade, but there'll be such a struggle for peace that not a stone will be left standing.'

The campaign reached a climax with the famous Stockholm Peace Appeal, for which Picasso designed a special dove. It was signed by millions of people, including the whole North Korean Army just prior to its attack on the South.

We can be fairly certain that Stalin himself, who never showed the slightest trace of pacifism or even peaceableness, was well aware that the whole operation was a fraud.

3

In Stalin's anti-Semitic campaign up until 1951 the killings, the arrests, the dissolution of the Jewish Anti-Fascist Commmittee, had all been carried out without publicity. The attacks on the Jewish critics had been public, but only as part of an ideological assault. Now the whole theme of Jewish criminal guilt, of Zionist–imperialist conspiracy, became public.

In Czechoslovakia, a large group of high-level victims, including Foreign Minister Clementis, were ready for trial as Titoites. Stalin had managed the affair, as he had the Rajk and Kostov trials, through MGB officers sent as 'advisers'. In Prague two of Abakumov's senior subordinates, Likachev and Komarov, oversaw the operation. Stalin became greatly interested in the identity of a Czechoslovak figure referred to in a supposed CIA document as 'The Great Sweeper'. This mystery man was, or so Stalin came to believe, a CIA agent at a very high level who was still at large.

Stalin began to drop hints to the other Czech leaders that the Sweeper was none other than the Jewish Secretary-General of the Czechoslovak Communist party, Rudolf Slansky. His name started appearing in the interrogation protocols, on the interrogators' instructions, in the spring of 1951, and at the same time the basis of the conspiracy began to be changed from bourgeois nationalism to Zionism. One of the few survivors of this purge, Deputy Foreign Minister Artur London, later wrote of his surprise when a 'high police official' shouted at him, 'You and your dirty race, we shall eliminate you! You are all the same! Not everything that Hitler did was bad, because he killed the Jews and that was a good thing. Too many escaped the gas chambers. What he did not finish, we shall complete . . .' And these words, London comments, came from a man wearing a party badge, in the presence of three other officers: 'All this by a security official in a socialist country, a member of the Communist Party.' London's brother, mother, aunt and uncle had perished in Nazi camps.

In the autumn Stalin sent Mikoyan to Prague to convey orders for Slansky's arrest, and to supervise the new political line. Slansky and the other Jewish member of the Czechoslovak politburo, Geminder, were arrested in November, together with a number of other Jewish officials. The Czechoslovak press, warmly echoed in the Soviet press, at once embarked on a virulent campaign in which Tito and the CIA and MI6 and the Gestapo still figured among the villains, but in which Zionism was by far the most emphatic target. Of the group of fourteen now allotted to public trial eleven were Jews. Needless to say they were veteran Stalinists and fervent anti-Zionists. But it was said of Slansky (whose family's original name Salzmann was often appended) that he was 'by his very nature a Zionist' because of his Jewish-bourgeois origins.

4

In the late summer of 1951 Stalin replaced Abakumov as Minister of State Security, and had him and his chief aides arrested. (Abakumov, who had directed a whole series of fearful brutalities, was soon writing letters to the Politburo complaining of inhumane treatment.) The new Minister, Semyon Ignatiev, was a party official with no previous secret police connection. Beria thus lost his last clear link with his main power base.

One of the reasons for Abakumov's fall was that he had discouraged the head of the MGB's key Section for Investigating Specially Important Cases, M. D. Ryumin, from expanding the case of one of the Jews under arrest. This was Professor Ya. Eitinger, who had treated Zhdanov's brother-in-law Party Secretary Shcherbakov (dead of cirrhosis in 1945). Eitinger was soon dead in jail, whether because of torture or as part of a cover-up by Abakumov is not clear. But anyway Ryumin went straight to Stalin, who supported him. Other denunciations of doctor poisoners were soon coming in from the MGB-affiliated anaesthetist Lidia Timashuk. And so the Doctors' Plot started.

Meanwhile in Georgia, the arrest was ordered of a number of Mingrelians high in the state and party apparatus. Mingrelia is the coastal strip of Georgia north of the river Rion. It was the home area of a number of Georgian officials including, most importantly, Beria himself. Among several hundred junior Georgians, Second Secretary Baramiya and others were arrested, among them Tsanava, who had organized the murder of Mikhoels. This murder was now interpreted as plotters silencing one of their fellows who had talked too much, and the Jewish and Mingrelian purges were thus conveniently linked. When Stalin died Beria ostentatiously rehabilitated Baramiya and most of the other Mingrelians, and gave them high appointments. It is clear enough that they were his men, and that he had indeed been under attack. In fact Stalin personally instructed the interrogators, and told them not to forget about 'the big Mingrelian' – an oblique but obvious reference to Beria.

But now Stalin seems to have lost control of, or lost interest in, the matter. He sent Beria himself down to Georgia to conduct the purge, in accordance with an old Stalinist tradition of using a leader to crush his own followers. Beria carried out orders, but at the same time managed somehow to confuse the issue, in part by removing the local MGB chief in charge of the operation.

In any case, while the Mingrelians remained in jail for possible later use, Stalin seems to have shelved the whole matter at least temporarily and, as far as could be seen, Beria remained, however precariously, in favour. Perhaps Stalin, as again a year later, was reluctant to shed the one colleague with whom he could speak in Georgian – a recent Soviet account shows him having more difficulty with his Russian as his end approached. But Khrushchev's guess that he was no longer acting logically, at least in this case, seems plausible.

In the spring of 1952 came what may have been the key event in Stalin's final decision on the Doctors' Plot. His own doctor was V. N. Vinogradov, whom he saw once or twice a year. Vinogradov told him that he must now take a long rest from politics. Stalin at once remembered how, with his collaboration, Lenin had been largely excluded from political activity for reasons of health. He concluded that Vinogradov's advice was a politically motivated attempt to secure his own removal from effective power.

Meanwhile a major case against Jewish writers and others came to court. It was commonly called 'the Crimean Affair', because some members of the Jewish Anti-Fascist Committee had suggested to Stalin after the war that the now-empty Crimea could be settled by Jews. This was now interpreted as an attempt to establish an imperialist war-base in the peninsula. There were in addition the normal accusations of espionage and terrorism. After severe torture had elicited confessions from the defendants, the trial, held in secret in May–June 1952, led to the execution, on 12 August, of all the Soviet Union's leading Yiddish writers, together with the Old Bolshevik Lozovsky and the prominent Moscow doctor Shimeliovich. Stalin is reported as personally signing the order, 'Kill them all except Lena Shtern,' the seventy-year-old physiologist Stalin is said to have still thought capable of life-prolongation research.

5

Meanwhile, in the public sphere, preparations were building up to the Nineteenth Party Congress, the first since 1939. Its tone was one of suffocating suspicion against not only Zionists, but all sorts of other enemies, and against weaklings who were not sufficiently vigilant.

Its other main theme was a concentration of praise and welcome for the last of Stalin's few contributions to theory – *Economic Problems of Socialism*. This is, as is now said in the few recent Soviet publications which have bothered with it, a set of tedious clichés. It argues that 'objective economic laws' cannot be overturned by fiat (but then argues that there is after all a 'basic economic law' of socialism in the 'proportionate development of the economy' which can only be achieved by purposeful planning) ...

The Congress was more interesting on other grounds. Stalin made a short speech, later saying proudly that he was still up to the job. At the plenum of the new Central Committee which followed, he offered his resignation as General Secretary, saying he was too old and tired to hold both that post and chairmanship of the Council of Ministers. This was understood by the Committee members to be insincere, and was rejected in a spate of fulsome appeals to stay on.

He now abolished the Politburo, substituting for it a larger body, the Presidium. This was, as Khrushchev understood it, a manœuvre by which the old leadership could be replaced. Stalin nominated, in addition, an informal 'Bureau of the Presidium' consisting of himself, Malenkov, Beria, Khrushchev, Voroshilov, Kaganovich, Saburov, Pervukhin and Bulganin. Molotov and Mikoyan (though in the Presidium) were omitted from this Bureau. Stalin attacked these two before the plenum as waverers and defeatists. White and shaken, Molotov made a long though dispirited defence, Mikoyan a short one.

Over the ensuing months Molotov and Mikoyan tried to find out when Stalin was having meetings, and turned up as before. 'They were trying to stay close to Stalin because they wanted to save themselves – and not just save their positions in the party and the leadership. They wanted to stay alive,' as Khrushchev put it. Stalin then became angry with Khrushchev and the others who had let the suspects know the schedule, and told them to stop doing this. After that Molotov and Mikoyan gave up. Stalin now let it be known that he suspected them to be spies – Molotov for the Americans, Mikoyan for the British and the Turks (the Mingrelian plotters were supposed to be Turkish agents, so this would link in well). Stalin had expressed some suspicions of Molotov earlier, when the latter had been in America; and Molotov's wife Polina, now in jail as a Jewish agent, actually had a brother in America, Samuel Carp, who had left Russia in 1911 and had become a millionaire – in part through profits from Soviet trade. Mikoyan prepared himself for suicide.

In November 1952 great publicity was given to a gang of Jewish wreckers in Ukrainian industry. But the main public event was the trial in Prague of the Slansky plotters. The vast Zionist conspiracy was traced to a secret American–Israeli agreement by which, in 1947, Ben-Gurion had promised President Truman that in exchange for American support for Israel, the Zionist organizations would undertake espionage and subversion in the socialist countries. Countless foreign Jews were implicated, from Supreme Court Justice Felix Frankfurter to the British Labour Party politician Richard Crossman (not in fact Jewish). Concomitants of the trial included a denunciation of one of the accused by his son; but even more striking as a sign of the success of Stalinist propaganda was the repudiation of Artur London by his French Communist wife, safe in Paris.

One of the crimes alleged against the Slansky conspirators was of

having plotted to use a doctor to kill Stalin's chief Czechoslovak henchman, Klement Gottwald. This last theme was now to receive massive
illustration in the Soviet Union itself. In November, as the Prague
prisoners went to their doom, Stalin ordered the arrests of the leading
Kremlin doctors, and in particular Dr Vinogradov, his own physician,
and Dr Vovsi, former Surgeon General of the Soviet Army, a cousin of
Mikhoels.

Stalin gave the orders on how the investigation should proceed: 'Beat,
beat and beat again' – though in the case of Vinogradov he said that he
knew him well, and putting him in chains should be effective. By early
January confessions had been obtained. Stalin passed them round the
leadership saying, 'You are blind like kittens; what will happen without
me? The country will perish because you do not know how to recognize
enemies.'

The first public announcement appeared on 13 January. The plotters
had murdered Zhdanov, and his brother-in-law Shcherbakov before
him, and had tried to murder several military leaders. 'Most of the
participants', headed by Vovsi, had been agents of Jewish organizations
in the USA serving American intelligence. Vovsi had received instructions through Mikhoels (now for the first time incriminated) and the
already executed Dr Shimeliovich, 'to wipe out the leading cadres of the
USSR'. Other members of the group, headed by Vinogradov, had been
'old agents of British intelligence'.

The atmosphere which now descended on the country was one of
officially sponsored horror and hysteria. A vast and all-pervasive campaign rode a wave of anti-Semitism.

Stalin, in his usual fashion, was to some extent covering himself. As
with the Slansky trial, most of the victims were Jews – but some like
Vinogradov were Gentiles. And Stalin's move to his final aim of making
European Russia *judenrein* was also conceived in devious form. Leading
Jewish Communists were assigned to draft a letter, which by the time
of Stalin's death was already being taken to a number of leading
Jewish figures for their signature. It said that, as loyal Soviet Jews, they
understood the strong feelings against them that the Doctors' Plot had
aroused, and appealed to Stalin to solve the problem by resettling them
in the Far East (where barracks were already being built). The scenario
seems to have been that the doctors would have been tried and hanged
publicly in Red Square in May; a wave of uncontrollable anti-Jewish
feeling would sweep the country; the Jewish appeal to Stalin would be
published; and the Jews would be sent off, like the Chechens and others,

to their new destiny in settlements under MGB control. Fortunately Stalin did not live until the summer.

Polina Molotov was brought to Moscow at about this time. She was now scheduled to be the 'leader' of the Jewish plotters. We can envisage the trial of the doctors being followed by one in which Molotov and Mikoyan would have been the main figures (together with others of not quite equal prominence: for example, Ivan Maisky, the celebrated former ambassador to London, who was arrested on 19 February).

At the time of the announcement of the Doctors' Plot, *Pravda* and *Izvestiya* had noted that the medical murderers had been able to do their nefarious deeds because (in *Pravda*'s words), 'the State Security organs did not uncover in good time the wrecking terrorist organization among the doctors. However, these organs should have been especially vigilant.' On the face of it, this refers particularly to Abakumov (who would certainly have figured in any trial). But Shcherbakov had been murdered when Beria's close colleague Merkulov was head of what was then the NKGB, working under Beria's supervision.

It has been deduced from this that Stalin had once again decided to move against Beria. But if so, there was no overt sign of it. Over January and February, and right up to the last, those who regularly attended Stalin's evening sessions were Beria, Malenkov, Khrushchev and some-times Bulganin – whom Stalin had lately said would be his choice for a successor as Chairman of the Council of Ministers. On 28 February, on the eve of his death, these four were at the Kuntsevo dacha after watching a film in the Kremlin. Dinner had as usual lasted until four or five in the morning. Stalin was 'pretty drunk and in very high spirits', Khrushchev tells us, and showed no signs of being unwell.

This must have been one of the occasional upturns in a general decline. Stalin was no longer getting any medical care at all, merely treating himself with medicines. He used to drink a few drops of iodine in water, or take some pills originally prescribed by Poskrebyshev, who had a little medical training. In his last months Stalin is reported getting occasional treatment from a major of his bodyguard who had once been a veterinary officer. He had, however, given up smoking by late 1952.

This was particularly inadequate as his health deteriorated. He had for some time been heard to say, 'Cursed old age has arrived.' He suffered from rheumatism, from giddy spells, from acid stomach. His teeth had gone and he had high blood pressure.

His circle had grown narrower and narrower. Around the end of 1952 he had dismissed Poskrebyshev, suspected of leaking information. And his chief bodyguard since the 1920s, the oafish Nikolai Vlasik, was also in trouble for different reasons. Stalin's own material demands were modest; his flat, furniture, pictures, clothes were simple and inexpensive. His salary simply accumulated in a drawer. But his dachas and villas and banquets and cars were state property. Stalin had no idea of how much expense this entailed, but he suspected that Vlasik was living royally on much of the allotted funds. He asked for an accounting. When Vlasik presented a very large figure, Beria told Stalin that this was much higher than the sums actually spent to support him. Vlasik was arrested on 16 December and was soon facing charges not merely of Speculation, but also of suspect connections with the Jewish plotters. Officers of lower rank and power, headed by Colonel Khrustalov, took over Stalin's security and general life. Stalin was thus now deprived of his long-term personal doctor (Vinogradov), his personal secretary and his personal guard commander.

6

That Stalin was still capable of any sort of merriment as late as 28 February is remarkable, even though exceptional. Yet it is at any rate clear that he was in reasonably full possession of his faculties almost to the last, however profound his paranoia, and however noticeable his occasional inconsistencies in pursuing a particular point.

But within hours of this last dinner with Beria, Khrushchev, Malenkov and Bulganin, he was dying. His daughter says that his departure from medical advice had gone so far that he had taken a steam bath, contra-indicated for his heart condition. As a result, or perhaps inevitably at some point, he suffered the stroke that was to prove fatal.

His bodyguard heard movement at about midday on 1 March, but became increasingly worried when Stalin failed to appear from his quarters. The lights came on at about 6.30 pm but he still failed to emerge. Finally, at about 10.30 pm, they plucked up courage, broke into the apartment and sent in the deputy commissar of the dacha, Lozgachev. In the smaller living room he found Stalin lying on the carpet by the table. He had not lost consciousness, but was unable to speak. Asked what was wrong he could only make a buzzing sound.

The rest of the guard now entered, and asked him if he wanted to be put on the couch. He gave a faint nod, and they carried him there, while one of them reported to MGB Minister Ignatiev. He referred them to

Beria. Meanwhile Malenkov had also been informed.

Beria and Malenkov arrived at about 3 am on 2 March. When they saw Stalin he appeared to be sleeping quietly, though sometimes snoring. Khrushchev and the others arrived later. Doctors were eventually sent for, arriving at about 8.30 or 9 am. Stalin had now been left untreated for at least ten hours. As his daughter points out, if Poskrebyshev or Vlasik had been present they would have sent for a doctor immediately.

Mikoyan later told the Albanian leader Enver Hoxha that he and others had discussed killing Stalin, but he implied that they were unable to effect this. Beria is often suspected of in some way seeing to it that Stalin was poisoned, but there is no evidence of this at all. What seems a good deal more plausible is the idea that arrangements were made to deny Stalin medical care in the crisis.

He had, it turned out, suffered a burst blood vessel in the brain. Over the next three days he remained on the couch. He was treated with injections, leeches and various medicines, and fed from a spoon. He sometimes seemed to improve. Once, Khrushchev tells us, he pointed up at a reproduction on the wall of a boy and a girl feeding a lamb from a bottle. Khrushchev took this to mean that Stalin saw himself as being in the same position.

Svetlana and Vasily Stalin were brought to the dacha later in the morning of 2 March. Vasily was drunk, and shouted that the doctors had killed or were killing his father. He was eventually sent home.

The vigil went on, with Stalin gradually getting worse. His old comrades waited uncertainly (Beria reportedly looking pleased when Stalin appeared to be dying, but hastening to show devotion when he rallied and opened his eyes).

His daughter describes his end. The haemorrhage had spread through his brain and now affected the breathing centres:

'For the last twelve hours the lack of oxygen became acute. His face and lips blackened as he suffered slow strangulation. The death agony was terrible. He literally choked to death as we watched. At what seemed like the very last moment, he opened his eyes and cast a glance over everyone in the room. It was a terrible glance, insane or perhaps angry, and full of fear of death.'

And then 'he suddenly lifted his left hand as though he were pointing to something up above and bringing down a curse on all. The gesture was incomprehensible and full of menace.'

And so, as his daughter says, on 5 March 1953 'he died a difficult and terrible death' – if not so terrible as many of the millions he had himself procured, or was still planning.

Chapter 15

Stalin Today

It is not within the scope of this book to trace the long-term effects of the life which ended in Kuntsevo on that night in March. They were dreadful and enduring. At Stalin's funeral, the crowds were such that many were crushed to death. Andrei Sakharov describes the scene: 'People roamed the streets, distraught and confused, with funeral music in the background. I too got carried away.' Sakharov tells with shame of how he even wrote in a private letter then that 'I am under the influence of a great man's death. I am thinking of his humanity.' He comments bitterly that though he soon lost this feeling, 'It was years before I fully understood the degree to which deceit, exploitation and outright fraud were inherent in the whole Stalinist system. That shows,' he adds, 'the hypnotic power of mass ideology.' The struggle to cure the political, economic, intellectual and psychological wounds Stalin inflicted on his own people (though not only on his own people) is still being waged in the 1990s.

It started (in a small way) within days of his death when, we are now told, his successor Georgi Malenkov spoke confidentially to a plenum of the Central Committee on 10 March 1953 of the harm done by the 'cult of personality'. The anti-Semitic purge was halted, and the doctors were released – though the actions taken against them in 'gross violation of Soviet law', including 'outright falsification of evidence' were blamed not on Stalin but on the 'despicable adventurer' Ryumin. As far as the public was concerned, over the next year or so Stalin's name was at first only played down a little. But in 1956 Khrushchev, in the famous 'Secret Speech', provided a view of a selection of Stalin's villainies – with some long-indoctrinated Communists going into hysteria or shock as they listened. Yet even Khrushchev granted Stalin good political motives, and a share in creating socialism. And when Khrushchev fell there was a marked reStalinization. In fact, a full rehabilitation of his name was planned in 1969 – and again in 1979 for the hundredth anniversary of his birth. This was only barely averted after strong pressure from leading Soviet intellectuals and foreign Communist leaders.

Meanwhile, the politico-economic system Stalin had created remained in being. It was only in the late 1980s that the Soviet leadership saw that the Stalin-style 'command economy' had ruined the country: and, above all, that its continuance was largely due to self-deception.

Once falsehood, and the absence of freedom of discussion, were seen as ruinous, the whole Stalinist past came gradually under attack until, in the last few years of the decade, there came a campaign of continuous, wholesale and devastating revelation of the truth about Stalinism and about Stalin personally – including not merely fact and argument, but the digging up of mass graves.

Even now there are Stalinists in the Soviet Union, mostly elderly and uneducated, though (as an *Izvestiya* article lately pointed out) these include bureaucrats who care nothing for Stalin, but rally to his memory 'to protect their position' from the threat of democratization.

But the more profound problem lies in eradicating the effects of the Stalin heritage from the minds of men of good will. Such bold champions of glasnost as Lev Razgon and Vitaly Korotich tell the same story. Razgon says, 'The servile terror of Stalin lives in the bones and veins of people who never knew him'; Korotich, 'All my life I had Stalin inside me', though he adds, 'It was a small schoolboy Stalin; those who were politicians, they had big Stalins.' If there is one point that has been insufficiently stressed in this book, if only because it is almost impossible to stress it sufficiently, it is the psychological horrors of mass falsification, more than the physical horrors of mass terror. What was imposed on the population was a disjunction not merely between truth in general and the official interpretation, but between the experienced reality of their own and their country's life and the fantasy world they had mentally to accept. As the Soviet historian Natan Eidelman says, in the Stalin period a significant part of the Soviet population 'was living under a special hypnotic spell'. Exorcism proved immensely difficult and painful.

2

What can we conclude about the personality which had so penetrated the lives and minds of his subjects in Russia and his other realms and territories?

Stalin was in almost every way an outsider. He had no natural allegiance to his family, his home, his nation, his schoolmates. He was neither a Georgian nor a Russian. He was neither a worker nor an intellectual. The milieu in which Lenin and most of the early Bolsheviks of any prominence emerged was that of the Russian intelligentsia. It is true that this intelligentsia was rent by feuds, but they were feuds within a recognized social and intellectual stratum – to which Stalin was only peripherally and patronizingly admitted.

His marital life was an empty front. His social life was an imperfectly maintained pretence, which eventually degenerated into forced jollity with coarse and terrified toadies. And this gloomy and half-hearted simulacrum of good friendship in the long nights of Kremlin suppers seems to have been set up to fulfil, though never successfully, some deep-seated need. As so often with Stalin, we seem to find normal human faculties either lacking or withered to vestigial form.

One of his outstanding characteristics was, in many respects, a profound mediocrity melded with a superhuman will-power. It is as though he had a very ordinary brain, but with some lobes extravagantly over-developed, like the horrible skulls in Dali's early paintings.

It is clear that a profound feeling of insecurity was thickly woven into his personality. This manifested itself in the continuous falsification of his own part in events, right back to the beginning of the century and earlier. But it can also be seen even in fairly minor ways, as with his urge to every variety of external legitimation. His respect for certain Old Bolsheviks' former membership of the tsarist Duma was an obvious example. And we are told, for instance, that he was particularly pleased by the adherence to his cause of Wanda Wasilewska because she was 'the daughter of a well-known pre-war Polish minister'.

His touchiness too was intense, as Robert C. Tucker has ably shown. Even in the 1920s, when the cartoonist Boris Yefimov submitted a friendly caricature to *Pravda*, of a type which Lenin and others had approved of and laughed at when they were the subject, it was returned with a note from Stalin's then-secretary Tovstukha, 'Not approved.' Again, he was at first extremely annoyed when Roosevelt told him that he and Churchill called him 'Uncle Joe', and took some persuading that this did not entail loss of dignity.

Even in small matters, he sought to make an impression. For example, after the war, an admiral had an appointment with him. Stalin called in Poskrebyshev to put a pile of books on linguistics on his desk, and then explained to the sailor that he regretted not being able to get some rare pre-revolutionary works on the subject. A petty example; more often it was a matter of deception by feigned comradely behaviour towards party officials or foreigners who were ostensibly accepted as his allies, but in practice looked on as intended victims.

Many who have written of Stalin have noted his powers as an actor. Adam Ulam speaks of his 'consummate acting talent' and Robert C. Tucker of his 'extraordinary histrionic ability', while George F. Kennan similarly describes him as 'a consummate actor'. But whatever role he was playing, according to one Soviet observer Stalin could sometimes throw himself into it so much that it seemed that he had himself been carried away, and really believed his own deception, at least for a time.

In any case, the borderline between what he believed and what was the best rationalization of a particular action is hard to define. Did he really believe that Bukharin was an agent of Hitler? Presumably, at one level, he did not. But he believed him to be an enemy, and 'objectively' an enemy was in effect an agent of Hitler, whatever the mere details and facts. Such is the way Koestler presents the Stalinist mentality – as an area in which concepts of truth and falsehood in the traditional sense were no longer valid.

3

One image that comes to mind when one thinks of Stalin is Goya's 'Saturn Devouring his Children'. Soon after this had vividly recurred to me, in Moscow a year or two ago, I met a prominent Soviet writer who had just visited the Prado and seen the original. Before I could suggest the parallel, he told me that it had struck him immediately with over-whelming force.

The effect of inhuman horror is indeed much the same. Yet, thinking it over, there are differences. Not just that the huge and ogrish Saturn is eating merely his own children, a limitation not observed by Stalin. But also, Saturn's staring eyes and shaken hair contrast greatly with Stalin's calm and well-groomed public persona. Still, this is not to say that behind that façade there was not a manic and destructive personality of the sort made manifest in the painter's extreme penetration. It is true that sometimes a seething, uncontrollable rage broke through Stalin's usually placid exterior.

The question of whether Stalin was, or became, insane is now being publicly argued by Soviet psychologists. That he was psychologically abnormal is clear enough. If we use the word paranoid of him, not in any clinical sense, but as it is employed in ordinary speech, we will hardly meet objections.

Stalin told his French adulator Barbusse that a healthy distrust was the best basis for collaboration. But this is a mild statement of his unswerving habit of suspecting enemies everywhere – of which we have given so many examples.

Above all, he was by nature cruel. His Soviet biographer Volkogonov 'talked to hundreds of people who knew Stalin personally' and came to the conclusion that 'for this man cruelty was quite simply an inalienable attribute of his being'.

For Stalin's personal inclination to terror and death, it is indeed hardly necessary to do more than look at the record. Seeing enemies all around him, he had one sure cure for their hostility. It is true that his Marxism, in the extreme form it took in his mind, in any case called for the extirpation of supposedly hostile classes like the 'kulaks'. But he went further than this, in personally ordering and signing scores of thousands of death sentences, as often as not of men who had supported him in all his earlier acts of tyranny. And he was aware of, or insisted on, further killings, as when Yezhov was sent to the Ukraine early in 1938 to order 30,000 more executions, the selection of victims being left to the local NKVD. Moreover, he was fully informed of the numbers dying slowly in camps whose lethal characteristics he had personally insisted on worsening in June 1937. And he inflicted not only death, but also torture, giving personal instructions on the beating of innocent prisoners.

Despots who revelled in killing and torture are to be found in various periods of history, and among them Stalin occupies a very high place. But, as his instructions on torture may again remind us, he ruled not only by terror but also by falsification. For the purpose of the torture was to extract false confessions. Nor was this done only in cases where the accused were to be tried in public as great political spectacles, but equally to those shot in secret.

And all this was contained, or concentrated, in an insatiable drive for power. The Soviet sociologist Igor Bestuzhev-Lada says that after 'the catastrophic failures of 1929–33' even Stalin expected to be overthrown, and that the 'logic of his actions' consisted simply of 'a desperate struggle to secure personal power, and then to hold it at any cost ... a wily and merciless struggle using the entire arsenal of cunning and perfidy'.

We have seen how the image of a tiger came to the minds of many: not merely the quintessential beast of prey, the most dangerous killer in the jungle, but also one that lies in wait for its victim with no more than an occasional sign of impatience. A more remarkable, though very different comparison with the animal world was made by Maxim Gorki. When Gorki died, the NKVD took over his private papers. Yagoda is reported cursing at some of Gorki's notes. Among these was a characterization of Stalin. Gorki quoted a comment that a flea, if made thousands of times larger, would be the most dreadful and dangerous of all possible beings. Stalin, he suggested, was just such a being – that is to say a monster insatiable for humanity's blood, yet essentially parasitical.

4

We have been considering Stalin's psychological attitudes. As to the nature of his thought, his intellectual characteristics, Stalin was, in one sense, a product of his times. As his reading at the Tiflis Seminary suggests, he absorbed the ideas which permeated the latter half of the nineteenth century. The amalgam of new science and new economic advance was spiced with another ingredient: revolutionary romanticism. And these strains were all pulled together, for Stalin as for others, by Marxism, as dazzling to such minds as other all-inclusive simplifications had been before it.

In fact at the heart of Stalin's belief-system, with all its scientific pretensions, lay a fantasy which, as Norman Cohn puts it, was 'positively archaic'. Cohn, in his study of medieval chiliastic sects, *The Pursuit of the Millennium*, notes that they too sought 'a state of total community, a society wholly unanimous in its beliefs and wholly free from conflict', claiming 'to be charged with the unique mission of bringing history to its preordained conclusion', and forming for that purpose 'a restlessly dynamic and utterly ruthless group which, obsessed by the apocalyptic fantasy and filled with the conviction of its own infallibility, set itself infinitely above the rest of humanity and recognized no claims save that of its supposed mission'. Their members were, Cohn shows, some of the lower clerisy, including obscure laymen who had somehow acquired a clerical education, plus a few eccentric minor gentry: all in all 'a recognizable social stratum – a frustrated and rather low-grade intelligentsia' who were, even by medieval standards, 'abnormal in their destructiveness and irrationality'.

This 'subterranean world' of 'pathological fantasies', as Cohn puts it in another book, *Warrant for Genocide* (soon to be published in Moscow), always exists in one form or another, and sometimes 'becomes a political power and changes the course of history'.

Stalin was perhaps particularly vulnerable to such a doctrine in its most dogmatic form. His underground reading, his self-education, was not adequately balanced by the education given him by his official instructors. Though he rejected the substance of what the Seminary taught him, he retained all his life the cast of mind of the narrow dogmatics of the place. His style of speech, and evidently of thought too, was catechistic. (It may be because of this half-educated condition that, as Volkogonov says, 'Stalin had a boundless faith in paperwork. If he were shown some document stating that some person was an enemy, he almost always believed it.') For Stalin's way of thinking, even within the narrow confines of his system of beliefs, was extraordinarily constricted. His style of writing has been analysed by Soviet experts, who find a set of assertions, purporting to follow each from the one before, but in fact without logical connection. Conclusion precedes reasoning. As to his particular audience, the party, for many his lack of subtlety in presentation was taken as a sign of a plain man's (or at least a plain Marxist's) knack of grasping essentials. But this merely degraded, or helped to degrade, the party mind to Stalin's level. As Volkogonov puts it, 'His conclusions were invariably categorical. In Gori, where Stalin was born, the rays of the sun fall almost sheer. So it is in his newspaper articles. There are no greys.'

The Zinovievite Peter Zalutsky pointed out in the 1920s that Stalin's analyses were in any case, 'schematic, not analytical'; that his mind was a machine which, however crudely, was applicable to the past and the immediate present, but was never of service to Stalin in anticipating events.

There is thus an intense narrowness about his outlook. But we may perhaps feel that, in a way, the narrowness served to concentrate the force of his will-power.

The Marxism to which he became a convert in the 1890s had as one of its key doctrines the centrality of conflict, with unappeasable enemies who must be destroyed. At the same time it proposed a transcendent aim justifying any sacrifice. This was obviously well-tailored to Stalin's own personality. It was a perhaps inevitable concatenation that an ideology which may itself be regarded as paranoid was incarnated in one of the most purely paranoid leaders in modern history. Marxism in the end empowered Stalin, as 'Leader of the World Proletariat', to wage an implacable struggle against any phenomenon or persons that displeased him, construed as representing the hostile class forces.

But the Marxist, or at least 'socialist', phraseology was also the instrument by which Stalin's dupes, foreign and local, were so easily conditioned to accept his delusional universe. And how easily the spell often worked! C. S. Lewis wrote of 'the stupidity of evil', and if one is to use this phraseology, it clearly could apply in some sense to Stalin. But of his dupes in the West – and in particular when one thinks of the results of their infatuation – one might surely speak in terms of 'the evil of stupidity'.

5

Stalin was confident (at least at first) that he had the key to the future, that his regime was destined to 'catch up to and surpass' the capitalist countries in a party-enforced acceleration of history. In November 1929, he was saying, 'When we have set the USSR on an automobile, and the muzhik on a tractor, let the capitalist gentlemen, who boast so loudly of their "civilization", try to overtake us! We shall then see which countries are to be classified as backward and which as advanced'; and he really appears to have believed it.

Beyond the crudely economic, the delusions of the epoch included, as we have seen, the idea that a 'new man' would emerge, a concept much stressed by Stalin. Did he think of himself as an exemplar, a forerunner embodying the qualities of the new man? At any rate, his socialist order would, on Marxist principle, produce a higher type of human being: moral, responsible, subject to none of the vices imprinted on earlier humanity by capitalism or feudalism. The effects of the 'mode of production' would, indeed, be assisted by a massive effort of re-education. But in so far as a 'new man' emerged he was a denouncer, a terrorist, a conformist, a bureaucrat, an anti-Semite. It was he (as the Soviet writer Lev Ovrutsky puts it) 'who depopulated the Russian countryside,

321

choked our cities with smog, emptied our shops, and filled our souls with apathy'.

We can hardly know whether, and in what way, Stalin's perverse and devious character really nourished anything remotely describable as love of the people. In practice, not much and not often; but if there was somewhere in the obscure declivities of his mind a vestigial remnant of any such feeling, we can surely say with the old poet Griboyedov (who is buried close to Stalin's mother in a little cemetery above Tbilisi): 'Spare us from the worst of evils: a master's anger and a master's love.'

Stalinism was, in part at least, the result of a simple preconception – the nineteenth-century idea that all social and human actions can be calculated, considered and predicted. In the days of Victorian 'scientism' it was believed that, if we had enough data, we could, for example, predict the weather. In fact, it has only recently been understood that even if we had the most accurate knowledge possible of a given atmospheric condition, predictions would break down after four or five days, and be useless after nine or ten. And the complexities of the weather are as nothing compared with the relationships between millions of humans and their productive and distributive interactions. The crux of Marxism was that all the necessary knowledge was available, and that the state and its bureaucracy could use it to reconstruct the social and economic order.

In a narrowly economic sense, the whole Stalin period may be seen as a dogmatic and disastrous attempt to prove, long after failure, that this barracks economy was both socially and productively superior to 'capitalism'. The deceit, and presumably Stalin's self-deceit, went deeper even than that. From 1929, the economic, political and moral situation of the country was worse than it had been in remembered history. There were two ways for a government to cope. They could admit it, and change their policies. Or they could deny it.

In theory, the mass of the peasantry had happily joined collective farms, and were now more productive and prosperous than ever. The truth was that they hated the whole system and were starving while being squeezed out of the bare minimum of food needed to keep the rest of the country alive. In theory, the workers owned the state. In practice, a limited section had been the recruiting ground for the new privileged class, and the proletariat as a whole lived far worse than had their pre-revolutionary predecessors. In theory, enormous enthusiasm for the regime possessed almost the entire population. In practice, a vast – indeed almost incredible – propaganda effort, continuous and total, had, in combination with terror, beaten down disaffection. Huge and regular 'demonstrations', which supposedly showed the vast voluntary mobilization of the 'masses' for the Stalinist order, were compulsory rituals.

6

Churchill's characterization of Stalin as an unnatural man is valid enough. But besides being in this sense unnatural, he had a further striking characteristic – he was unreal.

In 1939 or 1940, Stalin called in his devoted supporter, the writer Alexander Fadeyev, and showed him the two volumes of evidence produced by the NKVD in the case of Mikhail Koltsov, former *Pravda* correspondent in Spain. Koltsov was sentenced to ten years without the right of correspondence in February 1940 and shot next day. The thick accumulation of 'evidence' was entirely faked, and consisted of the confessions of the accused and his accomplices. But Stalin had read the record with care and written his comments in the margins. One of the charges was that Koltsov had been recruited as a French agent by the novelist André Malraux. Stalin expressed his annoyance that French intelligence could rely on the help of French writers, while the NKVD had no such support from Soviet writers. 'Think upon that, Comrade Fadeyev,' he said.

It seems that for Stalin these inventions were more real than the reality. And the enemies who thus confessed had, however reluctantly, confirmed the fantasy, had separately brought useful validation to Stalin's conception of the world. What this, and so many similar incidents, seems to show is that a peculiar disjunction between fact and invention flourished not only in the public sphere, but also in Stalin's own mind.

Stalin's whole career in power may be in fact seen as an attempt first to force the real world to fulfil his fantasy; and then, when this had failed, to impose the belief that the fantasy world had actually been achieved. Pasternak wrote that the 'unexampled cruelty' of the Yezhov terror was due to the fact that collectivization had been a disastrous failure and that this could not be admitted. In a more general sense, the whole of the physical and mental devastation wrought by Stalinism may be seen in terms of the stresses and pressures and distortions produced by the massive grinding of unreality upon the hard materials of fact.

The process is displayed with particular clarity in the treatment of an important fact, or figure – the population of the USSR. In 1934 official speeches and documents told of just over 170 million (170.5 million as reported to the League of Nations). Molotov boasted in January 1935 that 'the gigantic growth of population shows the living forces of Soviet construction', while later in the year Stalin announced that 'the annual increase in population is about three million'. This, and the official predictions of the State Planning Commission as embodied in the Second Five-Year Plan, implied a population of 177–8 million at the beginning of 1937.

A census was taken in January 1937, but the results were suppressed on the grounds that 'a serpent's nest of traitors in the apparatus of Soviet statistics' had 'exerted themselves to diminish the population of the USSR'. Those responsible were, of course, shot.

It was only in 1989–90 that the figure they had arrived at was finally made public: just over 162 million – a deficit of 15 to 16 million!

In January 1939 a new and improved census was taken and on 16 March Stalin was able to announce triumphantly to the Eighteenth Party Congress that the population was now 170 million – later to become official as 170,467,186.

It seems barely credible, but this figure was simply accepted on trust by some Western scholars even in the late 1980s since it was, after all, in an 'official document'. Soviet demographers were even then pointing out reasons for scepticism. First, and most obvious, the execution of their predecessors gave the new census board an extremely strong incentive to inflate the figures. Second, Stalin had announced the total before the census board had made its calculations.

In 1989–90 the leading Soviet statistical and sociological journals made it clear that the figure actually arrived at was 167.3 million, so that some three million 'only existed on paper', and were arbitrarily distributed among areas particularly short of population.

If 167–8 million was the highest even the new census board could come up with, with the best will in the world, it is probably itself exaggerated. Soviet demographers have recently pointed out that, for one thing, at this time the NKVD did not report deaths in custody – and indeed most of the huge number now shot had been sentenced (under another Stalinist deception) to 'ten years without the right of correspondence' and were hence technically still alive.

As an example of Stalin's way with the facts the 1939 'census' is interesting on several grounds. First, there was direct, as well as indirect, falsification. But second, it was not on a very big scale – a few million merely. Stalin settled instead for asserting that the 170 million figure represented an 'unprecedentedly swift growth in the population'. In the USSR there was no one to say to him nay. And abroad, it is very nearly true that for years to come nobody noticed. Thus Stalin had killed millions of people and had now in effect admitted a large part of the damage, but had successfully bluffed his way through. Perhaps he persuaded himself that the 170 million figure was true. Perhaps he found ways to lower the 12–13 million population deficit it implied. But he can hardly have persuaded himself that the result was a demographic triumph. Up until 1937 he may have believed that the slaughter in the countryside was compatible with an upsurge in the general population. But by 1939 he must have known that, in this sphere too, he and his regime were living a lie.

More generally, Stalin invested his whole being in producing illusion or delusion. It was above all this domination by falsehood which kept even the post-Stalin Soviet Union in a state of backwardness, moral corruption, economic falsification and general deterioration until in the past decade the truth became too pressing to be avoided. First the economists, finally some of the political leaders, saw the facts. Self-deception is feasible up to a point – but when your seas start to dry up it becomes intolerable.

The condition of the Soviet Union as it is today is the direct result of Stalin's thought and action. It is perhaps the most striking proof in all history of Burke's analysis:

'Amicable conflict with difficulty obliges us to an intimate acquaintance with our object, and compels us to consider it in all its relations. It will not suffer us to be superficial. It is the want of nerves of understanding for such a task, it is the degenerate fondness for tricking shortcuts and little fallacious facilities, that has in so many parts of the world created governments with arbitrary powers. They have created the late arbitrary monarchy of France. They have created the arbitrary republic of Paris. With them defects in wisdom are to be supplied by the plenitude of force. They get nothing by it ... The difficulties, which they rather had eluded than escaped, meet them again in their course; they multiply and thicken on them; and, in conclusion, the whole of their work becomes feeble, vicious and insecure.'

Or, as a Soviet writer says more generally of Stalin and the Stalinists 'They finally won: they defeated themselves and their people.'

7

A final moral judgement of such a phenomenon as Stalin is perhaps not as simple as it may seem. The Communists of the time, and even Stalin himself, have been excused because of their good intentions – in that they believed, or may have believed, that their actions were morally justifiable in the process of creating an ideal society, with the abolition of income from capital as a virtue transcending all others.

Of course we know, in any case, that unconscious motives may be different from those which a man may think he has. As Gibbon says, 'The conscience may slumber in a mixed and middle state between self-illusion and fraud.' In fact even Stalin may have thought he had a higher justification in the eyes of humanity. Or he may have combined the realization that he enjoyed terror with the notion of a superior justification.

These are obvious points. More refractory is the question which always arises in these cases. If a man is sincerely convinced that what he does is for the best, is he to be absolved of *mens rea*? This has been debated in recent years by Hannah Arendt, Ivor Brown and many others. It presents many difficulties, at least in bare logic.

As Vasily Grossman writes in his *Life and Fate,* the 'sincere' Nazis are able to advance the same plea: 'The sun has been extinguished by the smoke of the gas ovens. And even these crimes, crimes never before seen in the Universe ... have been committed in the name of good.' As we have seen, Grossman, whose own mother died in the gas chamber and who wrote the first accounts of Treblinka, makes the direct comparison between the Hitlerite and the Stalinist terrors.

So suppose Stalin had been right? Suppose the theory that mass murder can lead to utopia had been true? We would have been presented with a version of the old argument that the end justifies the means. But in human history this merely is to say that (in the words of Bryan Magee), 'One set of events close in time ... are referred to as the "means", followed by another more distant set of events which are called the "end". But ... there can be no serious defence for privileges claimed for what is merely the second set of events in an endless series. What is more the first set of events, being closer in time, are more likely to materialize than the second ... Rewards promised by the latter are less sure than sacrifices made for them by the former.' That is, even if the approach sounds plausible at a crude level, it is not logically valid.

In real terms, Milovan Djilas's conclusion stands up: 'All in all,

Stalin was a monster who, while adhering to abstract, absolute and fundamentally utopian ideas, in practice had no criterion but success – and this meant violence, and physical and spiritual extermination.' And as to his unappeasable ideological and political drives, it was said of an earlier revolutionary, Nikolai Speshnev (the original of Dostoevsky's Stavrogin), that his 'devastating radicalism seemed to be only a mask for his own inner desolation. His very face resembled a mask, at once fascinating and repellent.'

In these pages, the character of Stalin has been displayed, rather than dissected. And this summing up, if such it can be called, is not an analysis. It is a broad description of the image of Stalin as it appears to one observer.

In Soviet writing one often comes across references to 'negative' phenomena or 'negative' characters. It would be hard to find a more negative phenomenon, or more negative character, than Stalin. But negative does not mean null. Stalin was the incarnation of an intensely active force, in conflict with humanity and reality, like an only vaguely humanoid troll or demon from some sphere or dimension in which alien physical and moral laws apply, who tries to force the differently ordered Middle Earth to fit his rules. But that is hyperbole. Even if Stalin was one of those in whom the conception of such mythological monstrosities may in earlier times have had their original basis, he was, after all, a human being. He was mortal and he died. After a time his system and his ideas died too.

Stalin represented dogmatism, belief in millennarian theory, at its crudest level. Yet ordinary, coarse and limited though his personality may seem, the last thing that can be said about his career is that we can learn nothing from it, or that it was uninteresting. But it was interesting mainly for the extreme and massive scale of the physical, moral and intellectual destruction it inflicted. If we can now begin to write Stalin into the history of the past, it is in the hope that no one like him will appear again.

Bibliographical Note

There are hundreds of books, and even more articles, in one way or another informative about Stalin, and the student seeking such sources will have no difficulty in searching them out. Here I give only a select bibliography, together with some notes on particular periods or incidents.

There are a number of biographies which in one way or another provide useful contributions to our knowledge, though all but the most recent had no access to the mass of material lately appearing in the Soviet Union. The first serious one was *Stalin: A Critical Survey of Bolshevism* by Boris Souvarine (New York and London, 1939, originally published in Paris, new edition 1977). Souvarine's milieu was that of dissident Communism, and he obtained much useful material from Soviet oppositionists who had had to do with Stalin. If his approach implies certain limitations, the same is of course true of *Stalin: An Appraisal of the Man and his Influence* by Leon Trotsky (New York, 1941), and *Stalin: A Political Biography* by Isaac Deutscher (New York, 1963).

Stalin: The Man and his Era by Adam Ulam (New York, 1973 and 1989) is a weighty and serious work. *Joseph Stalin: Man and Legend* by Ronald Hingley (London, 1974) is lively and penetrating. *The Rise and Fall of Stalin* by Robert Payne (London, 1960) is a 'great ebullient portrait', though out of date or misinformed on some points. *Stalin: Man and Ruler* by Robert H. McNeal (New York, 1988) is a thorough though limited work. *Stalin and the Shaping of the Soviet Union* by Alex de Jonge (New York, 1986) is useful and readable, especially on the international side. The (so far) two volumes *Stalin as Revolutionary 1879–1929* and *Stalin in Power: 1929–1941* by Robert C. Tucker (New York, 1974 and 1990) are outstanding, especially the second.

There are also a number of fairly useless books. First, certain émigré compilations are to one degree or another unreliable or even fictional. *Stalin: The Career of a Fanatic* by Essad Bey (London, 1932) is an uncritical mélange. *My Uncle Joseph Stalin* by 'Budu Svanidze' (New York, 1955), is a complete fabrication – though it took in Isaac Deutscher. A similar book, *Notes for a*

328

Journal by 'Maxim Litvinov' (London, 1955), gives much alleged information about Stalin but is also totally spurious – though it took in E. H. Carr.

On the other side, there are official Soviet biographies or biographical articles printed in Stalin's time. These are, in the main, of little value. It might seem unnecessary to say this, but, just as Stalin would (according to his Soviet biographer Dmitri Volkogonov) believe almost anything if it was in the form of a 'document', there are Western scholars who still prefer officially sponsored products of the period to what they sometimes describe as 'anecdotal' or 'memoir' material.

Of books which are not specifically biographies of Stalin, but which contain much biographical material, mention must be made of Bertram D. Wolfe's classic *Three Who Made a Revolution* (New York, 1955), the other two being Lenin and Trotsky. *Conversations with Stalin* by Milovan Djilas (New York, 1962) is the brilliant record of a few brief but fruitful penetrations of Stalin's behaviour. Naturally, *Twenty Letters to a Friend* (London, 1967) and *Only One Year* (London, 1969) by Svetlana Alliluyeva are also indispensable – together with her later *Kniga dlya Vnuchek* (New York, 1990, reprinted in Moscow in *Oktyabr*). Another book with interesting direct observations of Stalin is *The Rings of Destiny* by Aino Kuusinen, wife of Stalin's Finnish henchman (New York, 1974). Emil Ludwig's *Stalin* (New York, 1942) is useful.

Other works directly relevant to Stalin include, of course, Trotsky's autobiography, *My Life* (New York, 1960). Later memoir material includes, as basic sources, the three volumes *Khrushchev Remembers* (Boston, 1970, 1974 and 1990), in spite of his penchant for self-dramatization. Other memoirs of great use are those of Marshal Zhukov and other military leaders, of Anastas Mikoyan and of other politicians and officials – especially in editions appearing since 1985. Also F. Chuyev's talks with Molotov (*Kommunist Vooruzhennykh Sil*, 1990–1).

There are, of course, hundreds of books on various relevant aspects of Russia and Soviet developments of which we can only list a small selection. On the Leninist background Adam Ulam's *The Bolsheviks* (New York, 1965) and Leonard Schapiro's *The Communist Party of the Soviet Union* (New York, 1960) are among the more useful works. The broader history of the period is excellently portrayed in *The Russian Revolution 1894–1919* by Richard Pipes (New York, 1990). The earlier background of both the tsarist and the revolutionary despotic traditions is best seen in *The Russian Tradition* by Tibor Szamuely (London, 1974). For a view of Russian attitudes in general, Ronald Hingley's *The Russian Mind* (London, 1978) is invaluable. There are many useful memoirs of life under Stalin, e.g. Nadezhda Mandelstam's.

Most of the works so far cited were, however, produced before glasnost, and had no access to the material lately made public for the first time.

Much of the new information is to be found in *Stalin: Triumph and Tragedy*, by Dmitri Volkogonov (Moscow, 1989, and an updated edition, London,

1991) first published in *Oktyabr* in 1988–9. General Volkogonov's more recent contributions to the periodical literature have made a further important contribution (e.g. in *Nedelya,* no. 16, 1990).

The third volume of Khrushchev's memoirs, *Khrushchev Remembers: The Glasnost Tapes,* (Boston, 1990) is another mine of new material. *The Prosecutor and the Prey,* by Arkady Vaksberg (London, 1990), has very useful detail on the purges of the late 1930s, and is also helpful on the postwar period; as are Konstantin Simonov's memoirs, *Glazami Cheloveka Moevo Pokoleniya* (*Znamya,* no. 4, 1988, etc.). *Stalin: The Glasnost Revelations,* by Walter Laqueur (New York, 1990) contains much material published in the USSR in 1986–9. The author prints two useful select lists of his later sources (pp. 317–18) but, as he says, it is now impossible to be exhaustive, and much is still emerging. The new edition of *Let History Judge* by Roy Medvedev (New York, 1988) contains recent material.

Generally speaking the above works cover all, or several, phases of Stalin's career or aspects of his life. For particular periods the following are among the more useful. *Stalin und des Tragödie Georgiens* by Iosif Iremashvili (Berlin, 1932) is the only reasonably direct and independent writing on Stalin's boyhood and youth, though necessarily an incomplete sketch; and (in Trotsky's opinion at least) too highly coloured. Svetlana Alliluyeva's books give the accounts circulating in the Stalin family. Anatoly Rybakov's *Children of the Arbat* (London, 1988) gives an alternative tradition. Though in fictional form, other once-doubted facts in this work can be shown to be veridical (see *Literaturnaya Gazeta,* 18 August 1987; *Literaturnaya Armenia,* no. 2, 1988); and on this particular issue are in accord (for what that is worth) with Stalin's own reported comments. Though a picture different from Iremashvili's emerges, they are not necessarily incompatible.

As stated in our text, there are also a number of reminiscences of Stalin's boyhood published in the USSR in the 1930s by Gori and Tiflis contemporaries of his youth, all adulatory, but some not worthless. They, and all the other material then available, are exhaustively considered in *The Young Stalin* by Edward Ellis Smith (New York, 1967). This is useful for the whole period covered in our first three chapters; its fault lies in the author's determination to prove that Stalin became an Okhrana agent, where he fails to establish the case because the documents are, at best, dubious. For Stalin's years as a revolutionary Anna Alliluyeva's *Vospominaniya* (Moscow, 1946) is also of use, in spite of the limitations we have noted.

The definitive work covering Stalin's role in the Revolution is Robert M. Slusser's *Stalin in October* (Baltimore and London, 1987).

The decade 1918–29 is in the main covered in the normal sources. Payne gives much useful documentation. For Lenin's final period Moshe Lewin's *Lenin's Last Struggle* (London, 1969) remains the outstanding source, though it now needs to be supplemented with the material mentioned in the next section. Boris Bazhanov's very useful, though not always authenticable, account of his time as Stalin's secretary appeared in several recensions, first in German and then in French (*Avec Staline dans le Kremlin,* Paris, 1930) and several decades later in an enlarged, though often less helpful, form. On party disputes in the late 1920s Stephen F. Cohen's *Bukharin* is the clearest short account both in general and as to detail.

The fullest account of the collectivization period remains the present author's *The Harvest of Sorrow* (New York, 1985), and for the Yezhov phase, my *The Great Terror* (new edition New York, 1990) is also reasonably comprehensive – and the new edition contains much new material. Robert C. Tucker's *Stalin in Power: 1929–1941* gives, as noted above, a useful account of the whole period, and in particular the Nazi–Soviet relationship in the 1930s and 1940s. See also *The Incompatible Allies,* by Gustav Hilger (New York, 1956), and *Documents on German Foreign Policy,* series C and D, (Washington, 1959). For the later period see the above plus R. J. Sonntag and J. S. Beddie (eds.), *Nazi–Soviet Relations 1939–1941* (Washington, 1948). For the 1941–5 war, Volkogonov is fullest on the military side. On Soviet–Western relations the obvious memoirs and official documents are well digested in, amongst others, *Between Stalin and Churchill* by Steven M. Miner (Chapel Hill, 1988); *Roosevelt and Stalin* by Robert Nisbet (Washington, 1958), and *Russia's Road to the Cold War* by Vojtech Mastny (New York, 1979).

In the last phase Louis Rappaport's *Stalin's War Against the Jews* (New York, 1990) provides an accumulation of evidence on the anti-Semitic aspect. *The Black Years of Soviet Jewry* by Yehoshua Gilboa (New York, 1971) is fuller but less up-to-date.

On certain particular points or themes see in addition:

CHAPTER 1. Research has very recently appeared in Soviet official journals suggesting that Stalin was in fact born on 6 December 1878, a year and three days before the later official date (see especially *Izvestiya TsK KPSS,* no. 11, 1990); for Soviet rumours about Stalin's paternity see, e.g., *Kazakhstanskaya Pravda,* 10 November 1988; on Mamulov see *Minuvshee,* no. 7, p. 363.

CHAPTER 2. Noe Zhordania's reminiscence of Stalin is in an article by N. Vakar in *Posledniye Novosti* (Paris), 16 December 1936.

CHAPTER 3. Emil Ludwig's account of his conversation with Stalin on expropriations is in his *Leaders of Europe* (London, 1930); Vereshchak's prison memories were printed in *Dni,* 22 & 24 January 1929. Adam Ulam is dismissive of Vereshchak on the insufficient ground that his memoirs (like all memoirs) contain inaccuracies – Ulam is particularly sceptical about the incident of Stalin running, or walking, the gauntlet. Stalin, like most other Bolsheviks, does not at this time seem to have had anything like the sense, later retrospectively attributed to him, of Lenin's infallibility; he even wrote (though not for publication) in a most patronizing manner about Lenin's virtues and faults as a Marxist philosopher as compared with Bogdanov and Plekhanov (see *Ordzhonikidze* by I. Dubinski-Mukhadze, Moscow, 1963, p. 75).

CHAPTER 5. See also a long analysis in *Pravda*, 26 February 1988.

CHAPTER 7. For recent additions to our knowledge see for the Georgian affair *Zarya Vostoka*, 13 August 1988; for leadership issues see *Istoriya SSR*, no. 5, 1988; for Lenin's last days see *Sovietskaya Kultura*, 21 January 1989, *Moskovskie Novosti*, 22 January 1989; excerpts from Fotieva and Ulyanova published in *Izvestiya TsK KPSS*, 1989–90, contain much vital new material.

CHAPTER 8. On the organization of Stalin's office see 'The Origins and Development of Stalin's Chancellery' by Niels Erik Rosenfeldt (*Russian History – Histoire Russe*, no. 9, 1982).

CHAPTER 9. On Frenkel see N. Anstiferov's memoirs in *Zvezda*, no. 4, 1989, and *The Gulag Archipelago* by Alexander Solzhenitsyn, vol. 1. The most recent, and most official, estimate of deaths in the Ukraine alone is c. 4 million (*Izvestiya TsK KPSS*, no. 9, 1990). I had made it c. 5 million: the difference either way is within normal margins of error. For total famine casualties *Vestnik Statistiki*, no. 7, 1990, shows that there were c. 8 million more deaths in the USSR in 1933 than in 1934. The average life expectancy in the USSR is given as 32.8 years in 1932 and 38.1 in 1934, but only 11.6 in 1933, certainly the result of infant death in the famine. On the Ryutin group see especially *Izvestiya TsK KPSS*, no. 8, 1990; *Trud*, 10 April 1990.

CHAPTER 10. On the Nazi–Communist relation see also Josef Skvorecky's essay 'Two Peas in a Pod' in his *Talkin' Moscow Blues*. For Stalin's remark about Hitler's June 1934 purge, see V. Berezhkov (on Mikoyan's authority) in *Nedelya*, 31 July 1989. For the voting at the Seventeenth Congress see *Izvestiya TsK KPSS*, no. 7, 1989. On the 'Kremlin Affair' see *Izvestiya TsK KPSS*, no. 7, 1989. On Kavtaradze see *Literaturnaya Rossiya*, 24 March 1989. For military purge details (including the Landa incident) see, e.g., *Kommunist Vooruzhenikh Sil*, no. 23, 1990. On Krupskaya's last days see *Komsomolets Kirgizii*, 16 May 1990. For the proposal to rename Moscow see *Izvestiya TsK KPSS*, no. 12, 1990. For the numbers of the Soviet soldiery in Spain see *Sovietskaya Voennaya Entsiklopedia*'s article on that country's 'National-Liberation War' (vol. 5, 1978).

CHAPTER 11. For the 'comradely' atmosphere in the Nazi–Soviet meetings in September 1939 see *The Ribbentrop Memoirs* (London, 1954, pp. 131–2). For Stalin's remarks to the Politburo about Nazism in 7 November 1939, see *Izvestiya TsK KPSS*, no. 12, 1989. Among recent Soviet treatments of the Finnish War see *Voprosy Istorii*, no. 5, 1990, and *Avrora*, nos. 2 and 3, 1990. The first Soviet official admissions on Katyn came in 1990; for recent material see *Mezhdunarodnaya Zhizn*, May 1990, which documents the prisoners on

NKVD files in great detail until their disappearance in March–April 1940; *Voprosy Istorii*, no. 7, 1990; *Novaya i Noveyshaya Istoria*, no. 3, 1990; *Novoye Vremya*, no. 52, 1990 (for the photographs). On Beria's report attacking Soviet agents who reported Hitler's plans against the USSR, see Vaksberg, p. 350.

CHAPTER 12. For Mekhlis on new Soviet republics see *Komsomolskaya Pravda*, 23 March 1989. Stalin only seems to have been psychologically incapacitated for two to three days. His appointment book (*Izvestiya TsK KPSS*, no. 6, 1990) shows meetings every day from 21 June to midnight on 28 June after which there is a break, with the information that the next recorded meeting is on 1 July (time not given). On Stalin's personal approval of the execution of 170 political prisoners then in (or recently moved from) Orel jail on 13–18 September 1941, including Khristian Rakovsky, Maria Spiridonova, Dr Dmitri Pletnev and others, see *Izvestiya TsK KPSS*, no. 11, 1990. For the decree on punishing the relatives of Soviet POWs, see *Sovetskoe Gosudarstvo i Pravo*, no. 4, 1990. For the secret decree on evacuating Moscow, see *Izvestiya TsK KPSS*, no. 12, 1990. For the deportation transport figures see *Voprosy Istorii*, no. 7, 1990. For Stalin's role in the war period in general, apart from the obvious historical and memoir sources, see *Politicheskoe Obrazovanie*, no. 9, 1988.

CHAPTER 13. On the Orgburo meeting on *Zvezda*, see *Kommunist*, no. 13, 1990. The first full account of Malenkov's removal from the Secretariat (on 4 May 1946) and the ascendancy of the Zhdanovites was given in *Voprosy Istorii KPSS*, no. 11, 1990; this says that it was associated with a faked case against Aviation Industry Minister Shakhurin, Chief Marshal of Aviation Novikov and others who were jailed in 1946 'not without the cooperation of Vasily Stalin'. For Stalin's views on psychology see *Stalin and the Uses of Psychology*, Rand Working Paper 1955, by Robert C. Tucker. For the secret Soviet Commission on Nuremberg, see Vaksberg, p. 259. On the 12 August 1947 telegram to Tito, see *Rabochii klass i Sovremennyy Mir*, no. 2, 1990. On Zhdanov's 1948 demotion see *Voprosy Istorii KPSS*, no. 7, 1990. On the architectural plans for Moscow see *Moskva*, no. 4, 1990; *Literaturnaya Gazeta*, 29 August 1990; *Nedelya*, no. 47, 1988. On the launching of the Korean War, see (in addition to Khrushchev) *Rodina*, no. 5, 1990. For Polish Communist experiences in the Politburo, see *Them* by Tereza Toranska, New York, 1987. For the 1948–9 purge of 'rootless cosmopolitans' see *Zhurnalist*, no. 6, 1990. A general view of the anti-Semitic campaign, now and later, is to be found in Andrei Sakharov's *Memoirs*, chapter 11.

CHAPTER 14. In September–October 1952 Stalin seems to have been unwell, and Malenkov signed documents for the Secretariat (*Voprosy Istorii KPSS*, no. 11, 1990). On the Doctors' Plot, see especially *Na Rubezhe Dvukh Epokh* by Ya. L. Rapoport (Moscow, 1988). For the accusation that Polina Molotov was the 'underground leader' of the Zionist conspiracy, see *Voprosy Istorii KPSS*, no. 1, 1990. The fullest account of Stalin's death is given by his former MGB guard, A. T. Rybin: later published less usefully in book form, it is best read in *Sotsiologicheskie Issledovanie*, no. 3, 1988. See also A. L. Myasnikov, one of the doctors present, in *Literaturnaya Gazeta*, 1 March 1989; another, N. V. Konovalov, quoted in *Trud*, 3 May 1989; and Fedor Burlatsky, quoting Khrushchev, in *Literaturnaya Gazeta*, 24 February 1988.

CHAPTER 15. On Malenkov's criticism of the cult of personality on 10 March 1953, see *Voprosy Istorii KPSS*, no. 1, 1990. Stalin's conversation with Fadeyev is from Vaksberg, p. 350. For the 1937 and 1939 censuses see *Vestnik Statistiki*, no. 7, 1990; *Rodina*, no. 11, 1989; *Sotsiologicheskie Issledovaniya*, nos. 6, 7 and 8, 1990.

One aspect of Stalin's view of Marxism was strikingly illustrated in a conversation with one of his ideological officials, P. N. Pospelov: 'Marxism is the religion of a class, its symbol of faith' (quoted in *Voprosy Istorii KPSS*, no. 7, 1990, p. 100).

Index